RACETALK

RACETALK

Racism Hiding in Plain Sight

Kristen Myers

ROWMAN & LITTLEFIELD PUBLISHERS, INC.
Lanham • Boulder • New York • Toronto • Oxford

ROWMAN & LITTLEFIELD PUBLISHERS, INC.

Published in the United States of America
by Rowman & Littlefield Publishers, Inc.
A wholly owned subsidiary of The Rowman & Littlefield Publishing Group, Inc.
4501 Forbes Boulevard, Suite 200, Lanham, Maryland 20706
www.rowmanlittlefield.com

PO Box 317
Oxford
OX2 9RU, UK

British Library Cataloguing in Publication Information Available

Library of Congress Cataloging-in-Publication Data

Myers, Kristen A.
 Racetalk : racism hiding in plain sight / Kristen Myers.
   p. cm.
 Includes bibliographical references and index.
 ISBN 0-7425-3533-9 (cloth : alk. paper)—ISBN 0-7425-3534-7 (pbk. : alk. paper)
 1. Racism in language. I. Title. P120.R32M95 2005
 306.44—dc22

                                        2005004853

Printed in the United States of America

∞™ The paper used in this publication meets the minimum requirements of American
National Standard for Information Sciences—Permanence of Paper
for Printed Library Materials, ANSI/NISO Z39.48-1992.

CONTENTS

THE CONSEQUENCES

ACKNOWLEDGMENTS

This project would not have come into being without the help and support of many people. First, I must thank Eduardo Bonilla-Silva and Tyrone Foremen for providing the lightening rod for *Racetalk* with their article, "I'm Not a Racist, But . . ." I appreciate your supporting me at conferences and through informal social networks. You continue to inspire me with your cutting-edge research and unapologetic presentation of findings. You pull no punches and keep finishing on top. You guys rock.

I thank Northern Illinois University's College of Liberal Arts and Sciences for their design and implementation of the Undergraduate Research Apprenticeship Program, through which this project got off the ground. Bill Minor considerately shepherded this project through when the application was accidentally thrown away. He found money to provide food for the focus groups in Phase I—an important enticement to keep the research team involved. Passion Williamson played a major role in Phase I of the project as well, as co-PI and constant muse. Her incisive analysis and tireless antiracism never failed to amaze me.

I thank the sixty-two members of the research team. Although I cannot name you here, you know who you are. I am blowing you kisses right now. Without your hard work, dedication, and reflexivity, this project never would have developed as it has. I owe you!

Like Eduardo and Tyrone, Joe Feagin has been a great mentor. Joe's work has always impacted the way that I think about race. But he has impacted me personally as well. After reading Passion's and my article, Joe casually suggested that I write a book. I honestly had never even considered it until then. His faith in me was a huge shot in the arm. I immediately applied for a sabbatical—thanks to Kay Forest for facilitating my leave—and I went to work on the prospectus and the manuscript. Thanks Joe.

Thank you, Barbara Risman, for being my biggest intellectual cheerleader. Thanks for helping Cindy Anderson and me get our feet wet in writing a prospectus for *Feminist Foundations* and for suggesting Rowman & Littlefield for this book. I spend my career honoring your mentorship.

Thanks to all who have read and commented on drafts of articles and chapters including Don Tomaskovic-Devey, Woody Doane, Eduardo Bonilla-Silva, Joe Feagin, Jammie Price, Jill McCorkel, Ilene Kalish, Amanda Lewis, and all of the unnamed reviewers this project has passed through along the way. Thanks to Jammie, Jill, and Amanda for providing opportunities for me to talk about my work at your home universities and to all of the people who sat through these presentations. Thanks to Alan McClare at Rowman & Littlefield for taking a chance on this book. And thanks to Jason Proetorius at Rowman & Littlefield for tolerating my typos and scatter-brained schedules.

To my friends and colleagues who supported me through draft after draft; who lent me books and articles; who listened patiently while I brainstormed about critical race theory (CRT), Bourdieu, and Giddens; who laughed and grimaced with me over the content of the data—thank you so much for sticking with me. In particular, I am grateful to Jammie Price, Barbara Risman, Carla Goar, Robin Moremen, and Leslie Hossfeld.

Thanks to my students who helped read data and provide insight into what certain terms meant, how to spell the names of pop stars, and to keep me laughing all the way through. Hugs and kisses to Justin Hoy, Reneka Turner, Juan Martinez, Mishel Filisha, Melody Dominguez, Horacio Tristan, Camika Smith, Bob Klasek, Malcolm Newsome, Matthew Johnson, and Jerry Goldstein.

Most importantly, I would never accomplish anything—ever—without my family. Thanks to my parents, Linda Worsham and Richard Myers, who gave me the opportunity to go to graduate school, allowed me to ask the questions that I wanted to know, and tolerated my being obnoxious about the answers. My kind and gentle stepparents, Doug Worsham and Candi Myers, kept my parents sane in spite of my antics, and they loved me no matter what. My mother-in-law, Sandy Miller, treats me like the daughter she never had. She let me ramble on about data, always acting interested, helping me approach old ideas in new ways. I am lucky. I love you all.

My steadfast beloved, Kirk Miller, gave me the everyday boost I needed to keep going. He stepped around my piles of paper, books, and scribbled notes. He encouraged me to buy a new computer when the old one started to wonk out, averting inevitable disaster for the book. Kirk ignored the endless moaning of the soundtrack to *Schindler's List* welling up the stairs from my office. It was the only music I could abide while writing. Weirdly, it became the soundtrack to this book as well. A lesser (saner?) man would have disabled the speakers, or at least damaged the CD. Kirk made every meal (well, I *did* pour bowls of cereal, whip-up cheese and crackers, and a PB&J or two), did all of the laundry, scooped the cat litter, and rearranged his work schedule to accommodate mine. He is a real-life super hero.

My girls, Samantha and Isabel, are super heroes themselves. I began this project when Sam was one. Izi has lived with it her entire life. Both girls were patient when I had to write, sacrificing time with me on the playground, reading books, and playing Polly Pockets. Sam wanted so badly to have her own role in the book. She asked if she could design the cover. She drew and painted several pieces for consideration by the editorial staff at Rowman & Littlefield. We've crossed our fingers that they choose one. It's not every six-year-old who can claim her work has been published. Indeed, most six-year-olds do not spend time imagining ways to visually communicate the ways that racetalk wounds. You girls are my peace and my perspective. I will love you until the moon turns into a ladybug.

❶

HIDING IN PLAIN SIGHT

Racetalk, the Language of Racism

Like desire, language disrupts, refuses to be contained within boundaries.

It speaks itself against our will, in words and thoughts that intrude,
even violate the most private spaces of mind and body.

—bell hooks (1994a: 167)

One evening, while relaxing with his friends at college, Roger (white) participated in this conversation:

> Sam (white) was telling us a story about one time when he was outside working on his car at 11 o'clock at night. A car full of black people stopped and asked for directions. He said, "They scared the shit out of me! I thought they were going to cap my white ass!" We all laughed at his story.

Another college student, Jessica (white), talked to her friends David and Adam (both white) about David's new apartment. Adam asked, "How is it? Is it nice?" David said, "Well it looks like a white person lives there. Not like our [old] house where it looks like a black person would live."

Katie (white) described her job at a major chain restaurant, where she worked as a server:

> We refer to people who we expect not to tip well by certain names. These are "Canadians" (blacks), Puerto Ricans, Mexicans, and of course white trash. It is a philosophy at work that the "—cans" won't tip well, which for the most part is true.

Taylor (white) and her (white) boyfriend Jesse talked about a prank that occurred at a party. Jesse's brother drew a swastika onto their friend's refrigerator. Upset, Taylor asked Jesse if he, too, was prejudiced. He answered "No, I like blacks. I think everyone should have one."

Penelope (black) and her friends went to buy beer at a store owned by Indians. As she and her friends walked out, Penelope said, "Indians are sand-niggas. They ain't nothin' but watered down blacks." Her friend Johnson (black) replied, "Say that in their face and they'll blow yo' ass up!"

Cher (white) was talking to her friends about music. She said, "Erykah Badu said that she would rather be a slave than have a white person buy her record." Brad (white) replied, "That can be arranged."

Ashley (white) and Stef (white) were driving through a parking lot after finishing their shopping at a Super Wal-Mart. When two Mexicans walked out in front of their car, Stef yelled, "Stop! Don't hit those Mexicans: it will take weeks to get the grease off the car."

These remarks were made by college-educated young adults in the context of their everyday routines. The comments were not particularly noteworthy to the people around them—they were simply candid statements made in the safe spaces of private conversations. Why should we take note of these remarks when they were seemingly unproblematic to those who made and overheard them?

As Patricia Hill Collins (1998, xxi) says, "A choice of language transcends mere selection of words—it is inherently a political choice." This book is ultimately about our choices of language and the ways that those choices are political. The words that we choose have the power to shape the opportunities and constraints faced by different groups of people in society at large (Habermas 1984). As bell hooks is quoted above, language violates the private spaces of the mind and body. The power of language transcends individual conversations to shape the ways that we think about others and, eventually, the ways that we act toward them. When we act in concert, we form social structures—like the education system, government, the criminal justice system—that echo and embody the content of our language (Matsuda et al. 1993). Language is political when it is used to empower some groups at the expense of others.

In this study, I examine one particular vein of language—the vocabulary and conceptual frameworks that we use to denigrate different races and ethnicities in our everyday lives. I call this language "racetalk." According to Toni Morrison (1993, 57), racetalk is "the explicit insertion into everyday life of racial signs and symbols that have no meaning other than pressing African Americans to the lowest level of the racial hierarchy." I use "racetalk" more broadly to include any talk that demeans on the basis of race or ethnicity. Why does racetalk matter? Why should you read this book? There are several answers to these questions.

First, analyzing the content and frequency of racetalk is important for understanding the persistence of racial divisions within American society today. The ideas expressed above are not new to us. These ideas invoke old scripts that say African Americans are dangerous. Whites are superior. Latinos are dirty and disposable. People of color avoid paying for the services that they receive. Indians are sinister. Slavery is a trivial—if not nostalgic and amusing—blip on the historical radar screen. While many people may be deeply offended by such sentiments, these old ideas live on in the present through racetalk. By using racetalk, people imbue different racial and ethnic groups with meaning and oppositional statuses, as this study shows. Racetalk delineates boundaries between whiteness, blackness, and brownness. Racetalk is a tool used in policing these boundaries. Most people who cross racial/ethnic boundaries through alliances, friendships, and courtships are sanctioned. Nevertheless some people are able to cross more successfully than others. An analysis of the content of racetalk reveals the process through which people negotiate racial/ethnic meanings and boundaries on a daily basis. In so doing, they often perpetuate old racist ideas. But occasionally they challenge them as well.

Second, the context of racetalk helps to understand how old ideas are disseminated from generation to generation. It is currently punishable to make racialized remarks in public spaces like the workplace, schools, and political offices—if and when the racetalk is reported to an authority figure. Public figures like Trent Lott[1] and Rush Limbaugh[2] have been sanctioned for making comments that are less overtly problematic than the ones cited above. Formal sanctions are geared toward eradicating racism from our society, and such rules are a necessary step toward that end. However, this study shows that people have not expunged racialized thinking from their imaginations—they have simply learned to be more discreet. Formal changes have made the public expression of certain ideas politically incorrect, but their expression endures in the private realm: an unofficial classroom where the old ways can be nurtured, innovated, and passed on with little scrutiny or castigation.

Third, racetalk is contagious. It spreads and evolves from person to person. Debi Van Ausdale and Joe Feagin (2002) show that small children (three to four years old) are capable of expressing racetalk in informed, effective ways. The children innovate racetalk according to the social context, and they learn to hide it when it is sanctioned. Similarly, in my study it is apparent that adults, too, learn from the racetalk of others. Racetalk has a certain allure: it spices up conversations in enjoyable ways; it provides tools for ostensibly analyzing social problems; it is cathartic. A successful racetalker may be admired for her daring wit or incisive social critique. In other words, racetalk is socially valuable in certain settings. It carries "discursive capital" (see Bourdieu 1977) that fledgling racetalkers may seek when they repeat epithets or jokes in future settings. Due to the contagion of racetalk, the data captured here do not represent isolated, unique incidents. Instead, they provide a snapshot of an ongoing, evolving racial dialogue that surrounds and incorporates us all.

Fourth, most everybody uses it. According to this study, racetalk cuts across race, gender, occupation, and age lines. Racetalk is woven into the fabric of the American lexicon. It is an equal opportunity, "normal" activity that seems enjoyable to those who use it. It is everywhere yet nowhere, because people actively hide it. This contradiction makes racetalk eminently relevant and fascinating.

Fifth, racetalk affects everyone. Keeping old racial notions alive means that old structures will remain supported. For example, segregation in housing, schooling, and political districting continues today despite official policies designed to counterbalance it (Bell 1992; Massey and Denton 1993; Matsuda et al. 1993). Segregation is a taproot of poverty in that it cuts off access to important opportunities to improve one's life chances and experiences. Racial profiling among law enforcement continues as well, to the effect that people of color are disproportionately represented in traffic courts and the criminal justice system writ large (Doob 1999). Thus, racetalk is *not* meaningless banter that we should ignore and keep hidden. After compiling and analyzing over six hundred incidents of racetalk, it becomes apparent that racetalk does lasting harm. Racetalk is more than *offensive* talk; it is *injurious* talk (Lawrence 1993). It reinforces racial hierarchies that are antithetical to American tenets of freedom and democracy. Not all racetalk is alike—some may be empowering as well as denigrating. However, by engaging in degrading forms of racetalk, people "do racism" in their everyday lives (West and Zimmerman 1987).

Last, critical sociologists often study social phenomena in the hopes of engendering positive change (Burawoy, Gamson, and Burton 1991). Although much of the data and analysis in this book provides a fatalistic vision of American race relations, I find reason for hope as well.

People avoid talking about race, even in classroom settings geared toward addressing racism (Myers 1998). While this collective silence has multiple explanations, part of people's reluctance to talk may be a fear of misspeaking. They may want to steer clear of situations where they might accidentally make racist remarks. While it would seem easy for people to avoid making racist remarks just by being sensitive and thoughtful (Frye 1992), racist stereotypes are embedded in all of our imaginations—like it or not—due to the prevalence of racism in society. By demystifying and debunking the content of racetalk, we may be able to engage in open, educated, empathetic conversations about race with less fear. People can build bridges across community boundaries. I have found that to be true for the researchers in this project. Perhaps the very act of studying racetalk can facilitate future conversations geared toward dismantling racial oppression. The research process may serve as a means for unlearning and challenging myths about whiteness, blackness, and brownness. It may help to break down interracial/ethnic boundaries, or at least weaken them. It may facilitate the formation of empowering interracial/ethnic allegiances. Thus, although the analysis in this study is sobering, it does not leave us wringing our hands in futility.

WHO CAN USE THIS BOOK?

I have written this book for a broad audience. I write to my sociologist colleagues, upon whose work this project was founded and without whom it would not have been written. I incorporate their analytical insights and concepts in ways that make sense of my own data. I intend for this project to build upon previous works and add to the sociological knowledge base on race and inequality. My professional peers will evaluate this scholarship as to its significance in the field. While I respect my field, I also believe that effective research must have an impact beyond the academy. As such, this book is relevant to nonsociologists as well. People from all walks of life share experiences with the subjects in this study. I have tried to make my analysis of racetalk accessible and meaningful to people who have never read work by scholars such as Anthony Giddens, Jürgen Habermas, Pierre Bourdieu, Derek Bell, Patricia Hill Collins, or Joe Feagin. In speaking to two audiences, I am bound to alienate some. Nevertheless, I attempt to relate to both as best as possible.

A CAVEAT

While I do not claim that you will be forever transformed after reading this book, I do believe that you will be affected by its content. In conducting this research, I have discovered the powerful effects that the data and analysis have on people who consume it. Reading and transcribing the data certainly impacted me. Sometimes the data made me and the research team laugh. But when I read statements like the one quoted at the opening of the chapter, "I like blacks. I think everyone should have one," exasperated gloom began to sink in. The cumulative effect of reading these data was depressing.

I learned new terms, and new ways of using old terms. This knowledge amassed in my computer's data files, but as hooks predicted, it also lodged in a part of my brain where I apparently store easy-to-retrieve information. Racetalk that I had transcribed erupted into my consciousness at unexpected times.

For example, on the way to school one day, my young daughter stumbled on the steps. As I watched her fall, a phrase uttered by a subject from this study popped into my mind: "Bust yo' nigga lip!" Although I always recognized the power of the language used in racetalk, times like these illustrated the ease with which racetalk is uttered. I never gave voice to the data that lurched from the depths. They remained stuck like fish bones in my throat.

This will likely happen to the reader as well. I do not intend for this book to be a glossary of terms for the fledgling racetalker—improve your epithets in twelve short chapters!—but be aware that the material might expand your phraseology in surprising ways. However, I urge the reader to digest the analysis along with the data. Always consider the big picture: the cumulative effect of everyday racetalk serves to reinforce and legitimate segregation, racial profiling, discrimination, and exclusion on a larger structural scale.

The material in this book will likely resonate with everyone who reads it. Racetalk is so much a part of the fabric of our everyday lives that it is hegemonic—we take its existence and persistence for granted, often with only a passing laugh or frown, sometimes both at once. Racetalk hides in plain sight. Part of my job here is to disrupt the hegemony of racetalk: I take mundane interactions, whose significance is hidden by normalcy, and I make them glaringly problematic. I compromise the safety of their hiding places.

Doing so is sure to touch a nerve among readers. Indeed, reading this book promises to be a personal and unique journey for each person. Because racetalk is so pervasive, most everyone can recall at least a handful of incidents where s/he has overheard or spoken racetalk. Some people will be incensed by the cruelty of the comments captured in these pages. When the data are compiled as such, they do undermine one's faith in the colorblind future of America. It is one thing to suspect that your race is being ridiculed; it is quite another to have your suspicions confirmed through documentation. Other people might feel pangs of guilt at having made remarks akin to the ones documented here. Even those who avoid racetalk themselves may be culpable of going along with the talk in the moment. Most of us have at least occasionally left unchallenged—or laughed at—racetalk when it occurs. Still other people may be angered at the critical stance that I take on racetalk, wondering why I am taking it so seriously if it is so ordinary. These readers might ask, "Why don't you just lighten up?"

I am sensitive to the effects that this book will have on readers. I do not intend to make people defensive. I am not attacking the people who use racetalk—that would entail attacking most everyone. This book is not about bad people who do evil things. To attack and condemn the speaker pushes the talk further underground—it does not eliminate it. Rather than closeting racetalkers, I would rather engender a new, albeit difficult, conversation about the content and implications of this talk. This book, then, is about a problematic social practice that is already taken too lightly.

Let me try to be clear on my perspective. I believe that our society would be a much improved place if people no longer engaged in private or public racetalk. It causes damage to those who use it as well as to those who are victimized by it (Lawrence 1993). However, there is a vast gap between my ideal world and the actual society in which we live. Past tactics to eliminate racetalk have failed. As such, I do not advocate rigid censorship as a viable means for erasing racetalk from the landscape of communication. Nor do I subscribe to colorblind language that ignores the presence and values of race in U.S. society. Race is an important, prominent aspect of our lives as Americans, even though many of us wish it were less so. Talking about race—even laughing about race—is not in itself problematic. Talking openly about race can actually help to dispel myths and misinformation (Kivel 1996). Honest, sensitive conversations about race can help to break down interracial/ethnic barriers, as I discuss in later chapters. It is *racetalk*—the ritualistic, persistent degradation of some groups below others—that reinforces racism *writ large*. Singular acts of pernicious racetalk cannot be understood outside the context of the larger culture in which racetalk is rampant and expanding.

So if you begin to feel bruised by the analysis in this book, you should know that you are not alone. You are "normal." But I hope that the analysis in this book encourages you to step back, recognize what aspects of the data are plucking your nerves, and figure out why that bothers you. Our individual experiences are only one aspect of the larger picture. When racetalk is amassed, the themes that emerge from it are much more powerful than harmless fun among friends. The content of racetalk matters for whites, blacks, and browns, and for the future landscape of race relations in society.

CHAPTER OVERVIEW

Before moving on, I will preview the book to come. In chapter 2, I explain the challenges of revealing a social practice that has been so carefully hidden from public scrutiny. In particular, I discuss the research strategies for studying racetalk, as well as some core concepts that help make sense of the entire research endeavor.

In chapter 3, I lay out the theoretical framework for understanding the importance of racetalk. Drawing from the critical school of sociology, as well as dialecticians like Anthony Giddens and Pierre Bourdieu, I frame racism as a complex social process that operates at both the structural and individual levels in society. As a dialectic, racism persists across generations, although the way it is manifested evolves along with the formal rules of society and people's everyday practices. Critical race theory, too, helps analyze the ways that private racetalk contributes to larger structural racism. This chapter examines the social mechanisms through which old racist practices are repackaged and dispensed to a new generation of Americans.

In the next section, I examine the structures that give the racial regime its power. Chapters 4, 5, and 6 examine the three preeminent significations of race in our society as evidenced through racetalk: whiteness, blackness, and brownness. Each category holds a unique place in the American racial hierarchy. They form what Giddens (1984) calls the structure of signification. Although none of these three groups is in actuality a monolithic entity, the racetalk documented in this book invents and reifies such entities.

Because whites are the dominant group, I first examine whiteness in chapter 4. Through racetalk, whiteness is constructed by both whites and other racial and ethnic groups as a privileged and often abused status. Whiteness connotes entitlement and authority, but it is not all-powerful—there are chinks in the white armor that are vigilantly guarded through racetalk. This chapter, like the others, includes the talk of not just whites, but also of African Americans, Latinos, and Asians.

In chapter 5, I examine the ways that racetalk constructs blackness. Jonathan Warren and France Twine (1997) define blackness as the antithesis of whiteness—one has no meaning without the other. If whiteness is elevated to a state of power and grace, then blackness must be devalued and degraded. The racetalk in this book indicates that blackness indeed is a sullied status. This is especially obvious within the racetalk of whites, but it is also evident in the imaginations of browns and blacks through their racetalk.

Chapter 6 looks at the "others"—the browns, the status that is neither black nor white, but sometimes either, depending on the social context. In this study, the browns were Latino/a, Asian, Indian, and Middle Eastern. They occupied a unique standpoint in that they crossed boundaries more easily than blacks or whites. They were neither black nor white in a society that strictly demarcates the two (Rockquemore and Brunsma 2001; Warren and Twine 1997). With many "white characteristics," browns could often pass for white and be treated as insiders[3]—as honorary whites, interlopers. Browns occupied an elevated social status simply by not being black. Browns themselves participated in the denigration of blackness. At the same time, their status was tenuous. In any given situation—most poignantly evidenced by Middle Easterners after 9/11—browns could become outsiders. At the end of the day, browns were still "others"—people who were viciously stereotyped and excluded in the racial hierarchy.

In chapter 7, I move on to examine what Giddens (1984) terms the structure of domination. In particular, chapter 7 examines the ways that boundaries between the categories of white, black, and brown are actively constructed and policed by members of all groups. The categories themselves would have no enduring social power unless people altered their behavior accordingly. Because whiteness occupies the dominant, coveted status—both in the imaginations and in structural realities of whites and other racial and ethnic groups—whites' talk functions to protect that power. There are key patterns in the content of whites' racetalk. Whites fear an impending takeover, and they strive to safely contain people of color by categorizing and dehumanizing them and keeping them under surveillance. Blacks and browns construct and police racial boundaries as well, but they do so for different reasons than do whites. Boundaries for people of color form protective barriers that help to insulate them from white power.

In chapter 8, I examine Giddens's (1984) structure of legitimation. As such, I look at the ways that people justify their talk when challenged—if at all. Much of the data recorded by the research team captures racetalk that was said in an attempt at humor. Some of the talk includes jokes in the traditional sense; other talk is satirical and sarcastic and meant to elicit laughter. Indeed, when people read this data, they often ask, "What's the big deal? Can't you take a joke?" Humor is one method used to legitimize racetalk, even at its most pernicious. Other semantic maneuvers when challenged include attacking the challenger, claiming the authority to judge, changing the subject, and—rarely—apologizing.

After examining the structures of racism, I look at the role of actors in perpetuating the racial regime. In chapter 9, I look at the ways that people strive to communicate across racial and ethnic boundaries—in spite of the risk and social cost for doing so. When bridging boundaries, people sought common ground despite racial/ethnic differences. However, much of the cross-racial talk was actually degradation disguised as bonding. Although this talk took the form of friendly joking, its content reinforced demeaning stereotypes. Rather than true bonding that undermines the structure of domination, this talk served to reinforce racial hierarchies.

Chapter 10 takes a more hopeful look at the possibility for change in the future. In particular, it examines the impact of conducting this research on the research team themselves. Team members reflected about the ways that listening to and recording racetalk among their most intimate circles affected their own ways of thinking about race and racism. For the most part, they argued that the process was transformative—it politicized them in ways they neither anticipated, nor always welcomed. Their new lenses affected their social circles and their own intellectual outlooks in a primarily positive manner. In this chapter, I argue that similar research projects may be useful in raising consciousness about racism (as well as other forms of inequality like sexism and homophobia that get picked up during observation).

In chapter 11, I examine the larger consequences of the racetalk captured in this study. Many people may wonder, so what? Who cares if a handful of people amuse themselves with off-color jokes? This chapter reexamines the dynamics of the dialectic to argue exactly why it matters that people—more than a handful, in fact—incorporate racetalk into their lives so easily and frequently. Racetalk is a form of everyday racial profiling. It shapes behaviors in ways that reproduce segregation in housing, jobs, classrooms, and friendship circles. Segregation reproduces poverty, an unjust criminal justice system, poor education, and unrepresentative governments. Racetalk is everyday Americans "doing racism." It is profoundly important on the structural level as well as the micro level of society.

Chapter 12 concludes by underscoring the argument made by Warren and Twine (1997) that the construction of whiteness in this society only has meaning in juxtaposition to our construction of blackness. My data show that being "black" is continually defined by whites as a corrupting, contaminating factor, even when applied to nonblack minorities and other whites. Thus, although the landscape of structural racism undergoes changes over time, microinteractions keep Jim Crow forms of racist discourse alive. Some have argued that racism is a permanent feature of American society that we must approach cynically yet realistically. In order to interrupt the dialectic of racism, we must challenge everyday practices of racism, like those embodied in racetalk. I offer several strategies for doing so.

NOTES

1. U.S. Senate Republican leader Trent Lott participated in Senator Strom Thurmond's one-hundredth birthday celebration. At that party, Lott said that if Thurmond had been elected president when he ran for office—as a segregationist "Dixiecrat"—in 1948, then "we would not have had all of these problems over the years." While Lott may have simply been trying to compliment the one hundred-year-old senator, his comments also implied that forced racial segregation would be good for the country. As a result of this comment, Lott was removed as Senate Republican leader.

2. As a commentator for the cable sports channel ESPN, Rush Limbaugh said that Philadelphia Eagles quarterback Donovan McNabb was overrated by the media, who just wanted to see a black quarterback succeed. As a result of the criticism surrounding this comment, Limbaugh resigned his post as ESPN commentator. The audience matters, though. Limbaugh routinely makes racially loaded comments on his talk radio show. For example, he told one black caller, "Take that bone out of your nose and call me back" (Delgado and Stefancic 2004, 162). No one officially sanctioned this speech, as it was made within the safe space of the conservative talk radio waves.

3. Not all Latino/as can pass for white, however. Many have darker complexions, and may even be formally categorized as black.

THE FOUNDATIONS OF THIS STUDY

2

REVEALING RACETALK

> We do not separate cross burning from police brutality nor epithets from infant mortality rates. We believe there are systems of culture, privilege, and of power that intertwine in complex ways to tell a sad and continuing story of insider/outsider. We choose to see and to struggle against a world made of burning crosses.
>
> —Mari J. Matsuda and Charles R. Lawrence III (1993, 136)

Like you, I was born and raised in a society imbued with a rich yet taboo language for describing "the other." I grew up in the late 1970s and early 1980s, a middle-class white girl in the South. I heard racetalk on a routine basis. White kids that I knew were fond of quoting lines from popular movies and TV comedy skits, like Steve Martin's "I was born a poor black child," from *The Jerk;* or Eddie Murphy's imitation of Buckwheat: "O-Tay!" We paid homage to the gods of humor, not really concerned about the damage that resulted from such racial mocking. We referred to all Latino/as as "Mexicans." We slanted our eyes in imitation of Chinese (eyes slanted upward) and Japanese (eyes slanted downward). We teased my little sister relentlessly when her black kindergarten teacher taught her to pronounce the letter "R" as "ahra." My siblings and I briefly contemplated naming our black puppy "Nigger," cracking up at the thought of what it would sound like when we called her to dinner. We ended up naming her "Lady"—an interesting juxtaposition. When I was sixteen, my parents decided to decorate our house for Christmas with colored lights rather than the standard white lights. I became angry, yelling, "You are going to make our house look like a nigger house!" They looked disappointed and sad, but they said nothing. They just took the colored lights down and replaced them with white ones.

This harsh, evolving language was a resource for us. We called upon it at will to underscore a point, to get a laugh, and to add texture to an otherwise dull conversation. We kids usually avoided using racetalk around sanctioning adults (see also Van Ausdale and Feagin 2002). We knew that it was unacceptable. But we did not really see what was *wrong* with it. We justified its use as harmless fun. It made us feel cool, and we occasionally glimpsed its power—as when my parents quietly changed the lights on our house. Yet we never saw it as connected to the system of racism. In fact, we considered talk to be completely divorced from practice. For example, we were appalled when our white neighbors would not let our black neighbors swim in their pool. This disconnect between private talk and racist action insulated the two realms from critical inquiry.

With age, the titillation accompanying racetalk wore off, and I learned to see it as harmful and, indeed, shameful. But I did not begin to make the critical connection between racetalk and racism as a system until graduate school. As part of a stratification course, I read William Julius Wilson's *The Declining Significance of Race,* coupled with Joe Feagin's "The Continuing Significance of Race." Wilson argues that, in the modern era, class is more important than race for affecting the life chances of African Americans. According to this argument, if blacks are turned down for jobs, it is because of their class disadvantages rather than racial discrimination. A key to eliminating racism, then, would be for blacks to assimilate into the American middle class. Wilson asserts that race itself is not the problem.

To the contrary, Feagin argues that race continues to negatively impact blacks—even those who are financially successful. Through poignant interview data, Feagin shows that even middle-class blacks—those people who, according to Wilson's argument, should no longer be victimized by racial discrimination—are mistreated by whites on a regular basis. For example, Feagin reports the following incident: a black girl attended a pool party for her white peer's birthday. In the middle of the party, a white boy began screaming "Nigger!" while pointing at the girl. He called the girl a "motherfucker" and said, "get the nigger out of the pool!" The girl was devastated and her parents were incensed, humiliated. Her father demanded to know why his child had been invited to the party when she clearly was not welcome.

Aside from overt harmful acts like the pool party incident, the respondents in Feagin's study reported myriad subtle snubs by whites as well: whites walked across the street when a black pedestrian approached. White cashiers dropped black customers' change on the counter rather than placing it in their hands. Black customers were ignored by white servers at restaurants and other places of business. Feagin's point is that these daily actions are small and, perhaps, dismissible when taken individually. When examined individually, people often wonder whether the behavior was triggered by racial difference or mere colorblind rudeness. However, the incidents have a cumulative psychological effect when experienced regularly over time. They remind middle-class blacks that, even though they have "made it" financially, they are still seen as outsiders by the dominants.

Reading Feagin's piece impacted me personally and professionally. I recognized the ways that I have been subtly infected by a lifetime in the pervasive racism of my environment. Before reading this article, I felt badly about my own racetalk, but I never saw myself as an agent of racist structure. I behaved blithely, assuming all people would know that I was a good person with good intentions. I did not recognize myself as a racialized actor who would be understood through a lens of white privilege and a context of racism (McIntosh 1988/2001). Feagin's work jarred me out of my comfortable bubble of benign racism. Reading the article heightened my sensitivity to my role in the problem. I became reflective about the subtle cues that I may have given to people of color without realizing it. I began to see myself and other whites in a new way, listening to our talk anew, observing our body language. I developed empathy that enabled me to move beyond shame, to look for ways to take action. I developed insight into the ways that individual interactions contribute to the emiseration of countless people by normalizing and justifying structural racism.

This book is a result of my emergent antiracist consciousness. Through this research, I attempt to lay bare the connection between individual talk and structural racism. As Mari Matsuda and Charles Lawrence (1993) are quoted at the opening of this chapter, there is a link between cross burning and police brutality, epithets and infant mortality rates.

RACE, ETHNICITY, AND RACISM: DEFINITION OF KEY CONCEPTS

Before I go any further, I should define some key terms that will be used throughout this book. I conceptualize race and ethnicity through a sociological lens. As such, race and ethnicity are social categories rather than biological ones.

Race

For many decades, social as well as biological scientists presented race as a biologically determined fact. Three distinct racial groups were said to exist:

caucasoids, negroids, and mongoloids (Roberts 1997). Each group was named for the region of the world where it was believed that such people originated: the Caucasus mountains of Southern Russia,[1] Nigeria, and Mongolia, respectively.

Arguing that race is biological has had paradoxical political ramifications. On the one hand, if people with brown skin were essentially human—just differently raced humans than those with pale skin—then it must be morally corrupt to enslave, torture, and murder them (Diamond 1992). However, a biologically based argument also created a slippery slope: if racial differences were genetic, then one could argue that some races of human were inherently superior to others. This line of reasoning has been pursued by many, justifying the devastation of entire societies. The terms "genocide" and "holocaust" were coined to describe such mass murders, often committed in the name of racial purity (see Bergen 2002; Churchill 1998, 2002; Diamond 1992; Loewen 1996; Sherrer 2001). Based on a belief in strict biological distinctions, many societies including our own created laws forbidding the mixing of the races, or "miscegenation," in order to keep the races "pure"—or at least to keep the dominant race pure (Sollors 2000).

Aside from engendering orchestrated "cleansings," the typology of three races was also problematic on a methodological level: the biological categories were not mutually exclusive or exhaustive—violating an analytical requirement for typologies (Berg 2004). How, for example, do you categorize people from Guatemala? From India? From Bali? Where do you put people of mixed race? The answer for generations was that these people were aberrations, interlopers, mulattos, mestizos—impure outsiders (Johnson 2003). Some U.S. states passed laws in order to categorize people of mixed race.[2] The 1890 U.S. Census demarcated degrees of racial diffuseness: a person one-eighth black was called an octoroon, one-fourth black called a quadroon. The 1896 Supreme Court case, *Plessy v. Ferguson,* was initiated by an "octoroon" in an attempt to challenge racial categories. Plessy lost. Laws like those that Plessy opposed were spawned by the notion of a "one drop" rule of race: if you had one drop of "black blood," then you were black.[3] In 1920, the U.S. Census abandoned these categories, recognizing that as many as three-quarters of all American blacks were already of mixed race (Wright 1994). However, the one-drop notion remains alive today. Indeed, as recently as 1986, the U.S. Supreme Court refused to hear a case in which a Louisiana woman appealed to have her race changed from black to white. She had been classified by the state as black because her great-great-great-great-grandmother had been the black mistress of a white plantation owner—the plaintiff herself was no more than one-thirty-second black, yet the state of Louisiana adhered to the one-drop rule (Wright 1994). Of course, there is no such thing as black versus white blood, but people continue to conceptualize race in this way today, as shown in the data in this book. Biology remains an attractive, though inaccurate, explanation for racial differences in society.[4]

Genetic scientists, through the Human Genome Project, now provide evidence that there is no "race" gene (Davies 2001; Hawley and Mori 1999). Race, as we know/see it, is a compilation of genetic traits: skin color, hair color and texture, the shapes of facial features (Marks 2002). We use these traits as mental cues for organizing people into different groups. For example, we see the combination of red hair, pale skin, freckles, and green eyes, and we categorize that person as white.[5] What these categories mean to us is the product of social collaboration. In our society, our meaning system tells us that differences are problematic. Thus, we draw boundaries between the groups—sometimes literally—and we police those boundaries. Therefore, although race clearly is *related* to physical traits, these traits are primarily important to us because we decide that they matter. "One drop" laws (Rockquemore and Brunsma 2001) planted the seeds for this discovery all along: if race were indeed a natural, biological truth, then why would we need to legislate racial categories? They should be naturally apparent to all.[6] Indeed, race need not be any more important to us than the color of one's eyes. But in practice, race is much more important to us than mere difference. As social beings, we construct hierarchies of value and power so that some groups are dominant and others subordinate (Collins 2000).

Ethnicity

Ethnicity, like race, is socially constructed. Ethnicity incorporates race, but expands beyond it to include religion, nationality, heritage, and cultural practices. One racial group may consist of dozens of ethnicities. As with racial groups, some ethnicities are culturally valued while others are devalued. Their value may wax and wane according to the social context. Ethnicity is often symbolic rather than physical, meaning that a person can choose whether or not to reveal or celebrate his/her ethnicity depending on social pressures to do so (Waters 1996). If an ethnicity is contextually valued, it may be openly marked in the form of clothing or other cultural symbols. Religious holidays are examples of ethnically marked contexts. If an ethnicity is devalued in a given context, it may be kept inconspicuous (see Perel 1997 for an extreme example of hiding ethnicity). Some people go so far as to change their names in order to conceal ethnic heritage in the hopes of blending in with the dominants (Zweigenhaft and Domhoff 1999). Like race, then, ethnicity is a social construct and a social practice. However, race is less easily hidden than ethnicity, except among those who can "pass" for another race (see Ginsberg 1996; Sollors 1999; and Wald 2000).

Racism

In conceptualizing racism, I again adhere to a sociological definition that takes power, hierarchical structures, and history into consideration. That is, racism is a systematic means of restricting—if not denying—access to resources and op-portunities to a group of people based on race and/or ethnicity. In a hierarchical system, one group is elevated above all others. This dominant group enjoys dis-proportionate resources and privileges. Although changes occur over time, the institutions in that system are geared toward meeting and protecting the needs of the dominant group at the expense of the other groups (Omi and Winant 1994). Hierarchies are only maintained by exclusion (Parkin 1979): keeping one's place at the top requires the exclusion of rival others who might seek to ex-pel and replace the dominants. Exclusion is accomplished through formal rules, informal practices, and—if need be—the use of force. Exclusion is justified ide-ologically by casting "the others" as dirty, dangerous, undeserving, and perhaps even inhuman (Takaki 1994). When people buy into the ideologies, they often do not consider formally protesting the practices of exclusion. Instead, they see the practices as natural and unavoidable, or "hegemonic" (Gramsci 1932/1971). When ideological control is effective, people do not threaten the status quo, and the dominants maintain their reign (Della Fave 1980).

Throughout history, racial and ethnic hierarchies have been successfully constructed and maintained. American history is no exception. Ronald Takaki (1994) provides a detailed discussion of the development of the United States of America as we know it today, paying particular attention to the relationship between immigration, race/ethnicity, and labor in our capitalist economy. He discusses major racial and ethnic groups as they became part of the paid work-force, including Native Americans; white ethnics like the Irish and Italians; newly freed black slaves; Japanese; Chinese; and the Mexicans who lived in what was once part of Mexico: the states of Texas, Utah, California, New Mex-ico, Nevada, Colorado, and Arizona. With each group, the story is largely the same. Each group came to the United States for various reasons.[7] Sometimes people emigrated because they felt pushed out of their native lands due to war, famine, oppression, or poverty. Others immigrated because they were pulled toward the United States by the hope of jobs and wealth, as well as promises of religious tolerance, vast available lands, and freedom. Still others were brought to the United States by force. As each new group arrived, its members began work on a low rung on the economic ladder: hard labor that paid poorly. Many of the promises made to them turned out to be lies designed to cull a large pool of cheap labor (Takaki 1994).[8]

As Karl Marx (1867) explained, a large pool of cheap labor keeps wages down due to intense competition for even the most menial of jobs. This group

of workers were unlikely to protest work conditions or hours due to their pre-
carious position in the economic system. The workforce was further exploited
by the fact that they lacked a common language, decreasing the likelihood that
they would unite and challenge the owners and managers. Through this system, those who owned the factories and the means of production became extremely wealthy at the expense of the disempowered workforce (for more on
the oppressive mechanisms of capitalism, see Braverman 1976; Burawoy 1982;
Edwards 1980; Gramsci 1932/1975, 1971; Lukacs 1922; and Marx 1867). We
continue to see this pattern of exploitation today with migrant workers (Martinez 2002) and within megachains, like Wal-Mart (Ehrenreich 2002).

Despite their similar experiences, some key differences among the ethnic
groups existed as well. White ethnics like the Irish and Italians were once considered "white niggers"—no more deserving of privilege and respect than
were the indigenous people (Native Americans) or the newly freed slaves
(Takaki 1994). However, the immigrants' white skin allowed them mobility
and access to positions of authority. Irish and Italians eventually held better-
paying positions, such as floor bosses, police officers, and firefighters. As they
assimilated into the power structure, these ethnics became fully "white" rather
than "conditionally white."

Other groups have not been as fortunate. Takaki (1994) explains that
African Americans have been in the United States for as many years as white
immigrants, yet they still do not enjoy the same resources and opportunities as
their white counterparts (see also Doob 1999; Feagin and McKinney 2003;
and Massey and Denton 1993). The first black immigrants arrived in the 1500s
as indentured servants along with whites. Under this system, people came to
the United States on credit. They worked several (four to seven) years to pay
off their debt, and they were eventually free. Thus, the first blacks in the
United States were not slaves but workers on the same plane as many working
whites. Once slavery became enfranchised in the mid-1600s, however, workers were strictly demarcated by race. In many states, blacks had no hope of
ever becoming free, no matter how long or hard they labored. Cultural and legal boundaries were erected that marked blacks as "savages" and whites as civilized. When slavery ended, African Americans entered into the paid labor
force at a gross disadvantage compared to white and even Asian laborers.

As Joe Feagin and Karyn McKinney (2003) argue, African Americans have
been systematically—over the course of centuries—degraded physically and
emotionally. Blacks have been prevented from accumulating knowledge,
wealth, and autonomy. Indeed, they have been characterized as less than human. Under these circumstances, it is extremely difficult to overcome this burden once the policies are officially dropped.[9] To make assimilation more difficult, informal, extralegal obstacles—like lynchings, blockbusting, and

gerrymandering (see Davis 1983; Doob 1993; hooks 1984; Marable 1997; and Sugrue 1996, for examples)—have helped to ensure the continued exclusion of blacks from the white power group. As Jonathan Warren and France Twine (1997) assert, whiteness is a meaningful category only when juxtaposed with blackness, its conceptual opposite. Therefore, blacks must remain a definable, degradable group in order for whites to be insulated and valued. This tension will be evident in the chapters to come.

The key point here is that racist practices, over generations, have become embedded in institutions like the criminal justice system, schools, churches, families, the economy, and the polity (Bonilla-Silva 1997). Racism can be practiced only by those with the means and the hierarchical authority to exclude others. The more powerful group expands and contracts over time—letting some people in while keeping others out (Warren and Twine 1997). Throughout U.S. history, the dominant racial group has been whites. Thus, American racism is a white endeavor (Feagin, Vera, and Batur 2001). Joe Feagin, Hernan Vera, and Pinar Batur (2001, 17) refer to racism in America as "white racism," which they define as "the socially organized set of practices, attitudes and ideas that deny African Americans and other people of color the privileges, dignity, opportunities, freedoms, and rewards that this nation offers to white Americans." I employ their definition in my analysis of racetalk.

Most people of color do not have the structural power or authority to exercise racism (Hacker 2003). The only exceptions to this tenet are the handful of blacks, Asians, and Latinos who have infiltrated the power elite of society. By "power elite," I refer to the less than 1 percent of Americans who are extremely wealthy,[10] primarily white, Christian, and male. The power elite occupy the top leadership in the economy, polity, and military (Mills 2000). The decisions that they make affect all of us. They recruit only like-minded, like-situated members through homosocial reproduction, so as to protect their own interests from outside threats. On the rare occasions when people of color do become members of the power elite, their interests and actions align with their elite counterparts—not with the masses. As Colin Powell—a light-skinned black member of the power elite—said, "I ain't that black" (Zweigenhaft and Domhoff 1999, 112). Powell's physicality, politics, and demeanor work together to facilitate his assimilation into an otherwise exclusive population. In cases similar to Powell's, blacks, Latinos, and Asians in the power elite can exercise racism because they are enmeshed and coopted in the white power structure. Note that this is rare. According to Richard Zweigenhaft and G. William Domhoff (1999), despite the highly visible newcomers to the power elite, it still remains about 90 percent white, Christian, wealthy men. By and large, people of color cannot operate as agents of racism due to their structural disadvantages.

This does not mean that people of color do not harbor ill feelings toward whites, or even toward each other. They do. They may even act on these feelings through hostility and avoidance, as we will see in this study. Feagin et al. (2001, 3) refer to this as "black racism," which includes "judgments made about whites by some black leaders or other commentators of color to the effect that 'no white people can be trusted' or 'the white man is the devil.'" They elaborate that black racism is not the equivalent of white racism. In contrast with white racism, such feelings and actions by nonwhites are not grounded and legitimated by the structure and the culture. Subordinates do not have the power of the military-industrial complex on their side (see also Feagin 2000). Thus, while people of color may be prejudiced, and they may act on that prejudice, their actions are unlikely to result in increased power or status for their group as a whole. Instead, antiwhite behavior among people of color has tended to incur the wrath of the dominants. Insurgencies often eventually result in backlash, through which whites, both informally and through the use of force, remind them of "their place" (see Brown 1992; D'Orso 1996; Ellsworth and Franklin 1992; Gerard 1994; and Shakur 1988 for examples). Even mild resistance among people of color—such as when they point out racist policies—has led to censure and retaliation from dominants, who have argued that being called a racist is the "worst possible epithet" (Delgado and Stefancic 2004, 186).

Of course, not all whites are equally likely to practice racism. Although American society is characterized by a racial hierarchy in which whiteness is the dominant status, it is inaccurate to assert that all whites enjoy equal privilege. Instead, our society is structured by multiple, overlapping hierarchies of class (through capitalism), gender (through patriarchy), sexuality (through heterosexism), age, ability, and on and on. Each hierarchy has dominant and subordinate positions. People occupy statuses of power and disadvantage simultaneously. Patricia Hill Collins (2000) calls this complex interconnection of power and privileges the "matrix of domination." Using this analytical framework underscores the diversity among whiteness: whites are men and women, gay and straight, rich and poor, young and old, abled and disabled, and so on. Obviously, the power elite do not exercise white privilege in the same ways as a white single mother who runs a daycare center out of her home. Power and disadvantage exist concomitantly, thereby obscuring the relations of ruling in society. Incidentally, this mystification helps to protect the power elite from scrutiny, as the less powerful struggle among themselves for crumbs from the master's table (see Fine and Weis 1999).[11]

Despite class and gender differences, however, the dominance of whiteness provides even the poor, single mother more status than afforded her black, Latina, or Asian counterpart. Although whiteness is neither monolithic nor omnipotent, it remains the dominant racial/ethnic status in our hierarchical system. This means that whiteness offers relative advantage even when it is tempered by class, gender, and/or sexuality disadvantage (DuBois 1996). As McIntosh (1988/2001) explains, due to the legacy of white racism in this country, American whites benefit from racism even when they do not overtly practice it or even subscribe to it.

Taken together, the totality of our racialized arrangements forms a *racial regime* that works to perpetuate racism in spite of modern antiracist inroads.[12] Thus, racism is a *system* of exclusion, and it is real in its consequences. People of color experience the ramifications of a racist structure in their everyday lives (Bonilla-Silva 1999; Feagin 1991, 2000). Racism affects people's identities (Omi and Winant 1994), attitudes (Bonilla-Silva and Forman 2000), health (Feagin and McKinney 2003), opportunities (Massey and Denton 1993), and actions (Essed 1991). Racism affects whites as well as people of color. As Paul Kivel (1996, 9) says, "racism affects each and every aspect of our lives, *all the time*, whether people of color are present or not."

Further, as I will elaborate in the next chapter, racism is dialectical. By this, I mean that racism operates at three major social levels: structural, interactional, and ideological. Racism is a hierarchical structure that allows differential opportunities according to race. But in order for this amorphous structure to persist and affect us, real people must buy into and subscribe to its procedures. People act; thus racism operates on an interactional level at which people engage in racist practices—both knowingly and unknowingly. People likely do not view their racist behavior as problematic even if they recognize it. This lack of antiracist-consciousness is explained by the third level of racism: racist ideology, which is a belief system that legitimates racist structure and practice. People are born into or migrate to this society in which racism has existed and mutated over centuries. By becoming members of this society, people "learn the ropes" slowly and without fanfare. Over time, differential treatment of people of color becomes normalized, expected, and de rigueur.

In other words, racism is hegemonic—it is so much a part of the fabric of our past and present lives that it is often invisible or appears to be inevitable (Gramsci 1932/1975, 1971). The hegemony of racism makes it difficult to recognize, discuss, and challenge (Yamato 1988). As Collins (2000, 284) writes:

> To maintain their power, dominant groups create and maintain a popular system of "commonsense" ideas that support their right to rule. In the United States, hegemonic ideologies concerning race, class, gender, sexuality, and nation are often so pervasive that it is difficult to conceptualize alternatives to them.

One of my goals in this book is to disrupt the comfortable, racism-free dream that many have been lulled into believing. I intend to reveal the practice of everyday racism so as to better understand structural racism. The data in this book indicate that racetalk helps to normalize—if not justify—racist attitudes and practices. Racetalk provides insight into the internalization of racist ideology. As Feagin (2000, 69) says,

> An ideology is a set of principles and views that embodies the basic interests of a particular social group. Typically, a broad ideology encompasses expressed attitudes and is constantly reflected in the talk and actions of everyday life. One need not know or accept the entire ideology for it to have an impact on thought or action.

Analyzing racetalk gives insight into racism, which we might use to interrupt its perpetuation as a hierarchical structure.

DOCUMENTING RACISM: METHODOLOGICAL ISSUES

When I decided to study private racetalk, the big question was how to do it. As I mentioned, my personal experience indicates that people carefully hide their racetalk from public scrutiny: it lurks just out of reach. How do you capture something so elusive? Before moving forward, I turned to the literature to explore the pros and cons of various methodologies.

Fortunately, much social science research documents the current state of racist ideology and practice in the United States. Different methods reveal contradictory realities (Kilson and Cottingham 1991). Current social survey data, for example, indicate that most whites are not only tolerant of people of color, but many could be called antiracists (Bobo, Kleugel, and Smith 1997; Bonilla-Silva and Forman 2000). Responding to popular claims of increasing polarization of Americans' views on social issues, Paul DiMaggio, John Evans, and Bethany Bryson (1996) analyze twenty years' worth of General Social Survey and National Election Study data.[13] Among other issues, they examine attitudes toward African Americans, abortion, and sexuality. Their longitudinal analysis indicates increased "liberalism" on every measure. DiMaggio and colleagues conclude that Americans largely agree on ostensibly controversial issues, including race relations. The implication for racial politics is that Americans are becoming less racist (see also Jorgenson and Jorgenson 1992). Yet, even while whites claim to accept people regardless of color, they continue to rate blacks as poor, less intelligent, prone to violence, and less ambitious (Feagin et al. 2001). Surveys point to seemingly incongruent evaluations of people of color by whites.

Eduardo Bonilla-Silva and Tyrone Forman (2000) argue that survey findings are suspect. Using data on white college students from three different regions of the United States, Bonilla-Silva and Forman contrast the results of two methods—surveys and face-to-face interviews—using the same sample of people.[14] In the surveys, white respondents argued that they would welcome multicultural friends, neighbors, and even political representatives, although few actually had any friends of color. The surveys showed that whites opposed official action geared toward leveling the playing field because they see it as already level—color no longer matters in U.S. society. Later, in face-to-face interviews, white interviewers asked the white respondents to elaborate on the attitudes they reported in the survey. Throughout the interviews, whites used myriad "semantic moves" to make racist arguments without sounding like racists themselves. They began their statements with caveats like, "I'm not a racist, but . . .;" or "I don't think this way, but other people might. . . ." They then proceeded to indict affirmative action, blacks' "laziness," and interracial dating. Despite their claims on surveys, then, these whites were not actually colorblind—they used race regularly to explain people's behavior. At the same time, they carefully avoided personal responsibility for such attitudes.

On the whole, qualitative data collection techniques indicate that race and ethnicity still negatively impact daily interactions (Armour 1997; Feagin 1991; Feagin and Sikes 1994). People of color are still followed in stores (St. Jean and Feagin 1998) and on highways (Ramirez 2000), denied equal access to mortgages (Williams 1991), and generally subjected to surveillance by dominants while in the public arena (Collins 1998). Surveys provide a distorted view of Americans' racial acuity that must be interrogated rather than promulgated as the status quo. Far from being obsolete as surveys tend to purport, American racism endures.

There may be several reasons for the disparate findings in race research. First, perhaps the American practice of racism itself is evolving, making it hard to pin down. Racism is thought to emerge from a real or imagined threat to dominants' material standing, through competition for jobs, housing, schools, political representation, and so on (Doob 1999; Takaki 1994). Historically, whites have fought to insulate and protect themselves from outsiders, and the outcome was racist oppression (Bell 1992). Racism persists because the sense of threat persists. However, racism manifests itself differently over time. There is a new form of racism in the United States today that contrasts with the "old," "Jim Crow" racism of the past. Lawrence, Bobo, James Kluegel, and Ryan Smith (1997, 16) describe this as "laissez-faire racism," characterized by "persistent negative stereotyping of African Americans, a tendency to blame blacks themselves for the black-white gap in socioeconomic standing, and resistance to meaningful policy efforts to ameliorate U.S. racist social conditions and institutions."

The post–civil rights climate makes the public expression of racist ideas unacceptable, so their expression becomes more subtle (see Gibson 1998). For example, politicians have been observed to use "coded" language when referring to black people, as with the use of the terms, "welfare queen," "street criminal," or "urban" (Collins 2000). New forms of racism strive to maintain privileged status for the dominants without being openly antagonistic (Bobo et al. 1997). Bonilla-Silva (1999), too, argues that there is a "new racism" in the United States, which destroys the fruits of civil rights while claiming colorblindness. New racism is increasingly covert, unlike the in-your-face nature of old racism. Derrick Bell (1992) discusses the pernicious nature of color-blind racism. No longer do we have signs reading "Colored" and "white." Because these signs have been outlawed, we now operate under the illusion of inclusion: "Indeed, the very absence of visible signs of discrimination creates an atmosphere of racial neutrality and encourages whites to believe that racism is a thing of the past" (6). But Bell argues that there is no race neutrality; it is an illusion as well, which can be used to perpetuate discrimination. He writes:

> This general use of so-called neutral standards to continue exclusionary practices reduces the effectiveness of traditional civil rights laws, while rendering discriminatory actions more oppressive than ever. Racial bias in the pre-*Brown* [*v. Board*] era was stark, open, unalloyed with hypocrisy and blank-faced lies. We blacks, when rejected, knew who our enemies were. They were not us! Today, because bias is masked in unofficial practices and "neutral" standards, we must wrestle with the question whether race or some individual failing has cost us the job, denied us the promotion, or prompted our being rejected as tenants for an apartment. Either conclusion breeds frustration and alienation—and rage we dare not show to others or admit to ourselves. (6)

Colorblind racism allows racism to hide in plain sight. It renders racism invisible even when it is thriving, leaving its victims impotent to critique it.

Second, perhaps the methods used to isolate racism are ill-equipped to deal with such a politically and emotionally charged issue. The research on racist discourse primarily uses survey and interview data, as well as texts and speeches (see Bonilla-Silva and Forman 2000; Doane 1996; Steeh and Schuman 1992). All of these forms of data are *public* talk—ideas knowingly shared with outsiders. This method allows us to see only part of the picture. Even with carefully crafted strategies (as used by Bonilla-Silva and Forman 2000) to reveal the subtext beneath people's colorblind rhetoric, at the end of the day, the face-to-face interviews still involve some posturing. Most people are loath to be called racists (Delgado and Stefancic 2004). To avoid this harsh label, people sensitively sidestep conflict. They "whitewash" their attitudes to preserve their images as nonracist. They refuse ownership of racist ideologies, even when they dispense racist notions themselves.

To illustrate the closeted nature of racetalk, consider this incident recorded by a researcher in this study. Here, Hedwig[15] (white) writes about going out to eat with her friend, Lanie (white):

> The service was really bad. Two black people sitting next to us in a booth got up to leave. I said, "Do you think those people are pissed too and that's why they're leaving?" Lanie said, "Oh, because the service is bad? That's why those. . . . Oh, I stopped myself [from saying niggers]." I said sarcastically, "Oh, I'm so happy I could just cry! I'm so happy that you stopped yourself!" She whispered, "No, they're still niggers. I just didn't want to say it too loud because there are people around."

As will become apparent later in this book, Lanie was an unabashed, self-proclaimed racist. She boasted of her racism even when challenged by Hedwig. Lanie was an atypical subject. Yet, *even she* was careful about what she said and where she said it. If the self-proclaimed racists like Lanie are careful, then how difficult will it be to learn about racetalk among those who consider themselves colorblind?

Another goal of this study, then, is to get beyond the semantic maneuvers to hear what people really think and say when they are in their own comfort zones. This book explores the paradoxical private behavior of people in a society that claims to be colorblind and postracist. I examine what Erving Goffman (1956) calls the "back stage" of social interaction. Using previous research as a solid base, this project goes beyond extant literature in order to examine racist discourse that occurs in private. Bonilla-Silva and Forman show us that people censor and sugarcoat their racial perceptions in public talk. There is often a public outcry when celebrities like John Rocker[16] and Marge Schott[17] casually use racial slurs. But does this outraged public ever use such terms? Is there a racist education occurring behind the scenes? Is there an increased comfort level in private that allows people to speak freely? In such a context, do people give voice to their true minds—ideas that are only glimpsed through Feagin's qualitative and Bonilla-Silva and Forman's dual methodologies?

Further, does the private context in fact conjure up racetalk in ways that would be unlikely to occur in public? Pierre Bourdieu (1977, 26) argues that different settings enable different sorts of communication:

> Communication is possible in practice only when accompanied by a practical spotting of cues which, in enabling speakers to situate others in the hierarchies of age, wealth, power, or culture, guides them unwittingly towards the type of exchange best suited in form and content to the objective situation between the interacting individuals.

Given the importance of the private context, I brainstormed a method that would allow me to do what no other researcher had yet done—to collect data from private conversations.

CHOOSING A METHOD

After analyzing previous research methodologies, I decided that qualitative methods are best geared toward capturing backstage behaviors. There are many benefits to macrolevel, quantitative methodologies: we can see what percentage are poor, finish high school, live in segregated neighborhoods, have health insurance, are victimized by crime. These studies provide us with important statistics. But they do not allow us to understand the daily struggles of going to a job where you are clearly not wanted. They miss nuances such as the stress faced by people of color in a white dominated social world: finding a hairdresser near your home who can/will style your hair; finding positive role models for your children in their schools; hoping that this year the trick-or-treaters will merely collect their Snickers bars and move on to the next house without any cruel pranks. This richness of data can best be achieved through qualitative methods. Qualitative methods help to achieve what Max Weber (1921/1979) called *verstehen*—a deep understanding of the social world around us. If done properly, qualitative methods engender empathy and support for the subjects, and they can help give voice to people who often go unheard (Naples 2003).

Racetalk is a covert social practice. In order to penetrate the barriers that hide racetalk, I recruited and trained a racially/ethnically diverse research team[18] who would act as participant observers, discreetly recording conversations that they heard and/or participated in.[19] The research team collected data as individuals, and each logged data in his/her field notes.[20] They also met routinely in focus groups. Thus, the research team were both data gatherers and data sources. The focus groups allowed me to obtain data from the team themselves about their own racetalk and experiences. Focus groups fostered interaction among the teams. They provided insight into the ways that the team constructed racetalk among themselves. Most of the data in this book come from the team's field notes, but I incorporate focus group data when relevant.

The Researchers

I recruited[21] researchers in three phases over a period of three years.[22] Some phases yielded more researchers and data than others.[23] All researchers signed Informed Consent forms,[24] and they created aliases for themselves. Most of the researchers were undergraduate students majoring in sociology, but there were also students from business, foreign language, general studies, and communications. Most of the team were what Bonilla-Silva and Forman (2000) call "racial progressives," in that they recognized and problematized the racial hierarchy, even though some benefited from it more than others.

Because the research team was diverse, researchers recorded incidents from a broad segment of the community. As already discussed, I see racism as fundamentally about unequal relations of ruling (Smith 1987) that perpetuate a racial hierarchy. However, I also agree with Howard Winant (1999) that subordinates are not utterly powerless—they resist. Thus, I included the racetalk of subordinates in this study to examine the ways that discourse varied according to structural position. Other studies of racetalk deal only with whites (Bobo et al. 1997; Bonilla-Silva and Forman 2000; van Dijk 1993). The inclusion of people of color is an important innovation in this research in that it provides a larger picture of racetalk and its effects.

Thirty-four percent of the researchers participated in Phase 1 of the data collection process. Sixty-four percent of the researchers participated in Phase 2 of the data collection. Phase 3 was the least successful, yielding only five researchers, making 8 percent of the entire team. Taken together, through the three phases of data collection, I recruited sixty-two researchers. Most of the researchers were women (74 percent) and most were white (61 percent) (see table 2.1).

African Americans were overrepresented (22 percent), and the percentage of Latinos (11 percent) was close to the national average. Asians (5 percent) were slightly underrepresented as a percentage of the research team. Overall, this group of researchers was racially/ethnically diverse. They each had access to very different kinds of interactions. Most of their observations took place within diverse work and home settings. Some rode the bus; some went on road trips; some were employed in more than one workplace. Everything that they did while collecting data created opportunities to observe racetalk. Some of the researchers were good friends with each other. There were two sets of roommates among the team, one set of which were romantically involved. Despite their interrelationships, all of the researchers acted as normally as possible while collecting data. They even recorded data on each other's racetalk. Together, they collected 617 incidents of racetalk.

Throughout this book, you will get to know some of the researchers, their friends, and their families quite well. Hedwig, Cher, and Precious, for example, provide extended glimpses into their social networks within their homes and workplaces. Others, like Naomi and Abe, we barely get to know at all. Our familiarity with each researcher is related to the amount of data s/he recorded.

Table 2.1.   Researchers by Race, Sex, and Data Collection Period

Whites (62%)		African Americans (22%)	
Men	Abe (Phase 2)	Men	Ali (Phases 1&2)
	John (Phase 2)		Carter (Phases 1&2)
	Jonathan (Phase 1)		Ralph (Phase 3)
	Kenny (Phase 2)		
	Lars (Phase 2)	Women	Amber (Phase 1)
	Paul (Phase 2)		Anastasia (Phase 2)
	Rocker (Phase 2)		Blueangel (Phase 2)
	Shaggy (Phase 1)		Elizabeth (Phase 1)
	Sigmund (Phase 2)		Honey (Phase 1)
			Janet (Phase 1)
			Passion (Phase 1)
Women	Alice (Phase 2)		Precious (Phase 2)
	Ashley (Phase 2)		Serenity (Phase 2)
	Barbara (Phase 2) +		Sherry (Phase 2) +
	Carmen (Phases 1&2)		Yolanda (Phase 1)
	Carol Ann (Phase 2)		
	Cassandra (Phase 2)	**Latino/as** (11%)	
	Celine (Phase 2)		
	Cher (Phase 1)	Men	Guido (Phase 2)
	Cheyenne (Phase 2)		Yayo (Phase 1)
	Eliza (Phase 3) +		
	Estella (Phase 2)	Women	Cindy (Phase 1)
	Flora (Phase 2) +		Cocoa (Phase 1)
	Gail (Phase 2)		Maggie (Phase 2)
	Harley (Phase 1)		Naomi (Phase 1)
	Hedwig (Phase 2)		Sena (Phase 2)
	Jaime (Phase 2)		
	Jean (Phase 2)	**Asians** (5%)	
	Jessica (Phase 2)		
	Joan (Phase 2)	Men	Monty (Phase 2)
	Katie (Phase 2)		Jay (Phase 3)
	Lavinia (Phase 1)		
	Leigh (Phase 2)		
	Linda (Phase 1)	Women	Adelle (Phase 3)
	Megan (Phases 1&2)		
	Missy (Phase 2)		
	Rachel (Phase 2)		
	Rori (Phase 2)	**Total:**	**63**
	Sophia (Phase 1)		
	Tanya (Phase 3)		
	Taylor (Phase 2) +	% Men:	26%
		% Women:	74%

+ denotes people who were ten or more years older than traditional college students

The length of the field notes ranged from two to thirty pages, with an average of about twelve pages of data. Similarly, the number of incidents recorded by each researcher ranged from two to forty-nine, with an average number of incidents per researcher of ten.

Collecting Data

In orientation sessions, I introduced team members to each other, trained them in data collection, and operationalized racetalk. In so doing, I advised the team that racetalk takes numerous forms, including the following:

- Racetalk can be used to denigrate any person due to color, culture, and/or religion.
- Racetalk may take the form of slurs or epithets.
- Racetalk can be used to celebrate racial and ethnic pride of any group.
- Racetalk can be a way of coding language so as to conceal a racialized subtext or assumptions, such as "welfare mother," "urban," and "ghetto."
- Racetalk may take the form of denying the importance of race, such as "I'm not a racist, but . . .," or "I don't see color when I look at people."

Initially, the research team expressed concern about the possibility of portraying friends and family members as racist. In order to assuage concerns, I told them that "the emphasis is not racist individuals per se but rather on racist practices and their implications" (Tamale 1996, 472). I assured them that *everyone* engages in some form of racetalk. I wanted the research team to record any talk remotely race-based, and to leave the analysis to me. We practiced writing field notes, and I encouraged the team to provide as much contextual information as possible so as to paint a very clear picture of the incident. This helped avoid distortion of the incident in field notes.

Next, I gave the research team a set of data collection guidelines. I advised them that they should do the following:

- Participate in social interactions as naturally as possible, meaning they should make and respond to racial/ethnic comments as they normally would.
- Compile field notes on racetalk for fifteen to twenty minutes a day if possible. Keep field notes unobtrusive and secret. Write about incidents as descriptively as possible to maintain context (Dennis 1993), but create an alias for each person observed for confidentiality.
- Do not incite any racetalk (unless they normally would).
- Make no judgments about themselves and their intimates.

- Avoid exposing other members of the research team when they met outside of focus groups. Secrecy was ultimately important for maintaining a natural setting.
- Log not only incidents of racetalk, but anything they found relevant to the project.

Team members did not strictly follow every guideline. For example, they did not write field notes every day. However, most took the project seriously and followed it through to completion.

Ethics

Although every researcher consented to be a part of this study, I asked them to record private conversations without the informed consent of the subjects themselves. I *only* required these methods of them because the data are not observable without these measures of secrecy. Most people simply do not use racetalk publicly, except by accident (van Dijk 1993). Thus, the participant-as-observer method was necessary. This is similar to research on other deviant activities (see Bulmer 1982; Ronais and Ellis 1989). When the population is hard to reach and/or when the subject matter is highly sensitive—as is racetalk—then covert methods are the only way to get valid data (Miller and Tewksbury 2001). Maintaining a natural setting was of paramount importance.

The project passed through my university's human subjects review board, largely because no one was harmed by the research process. On the contrary, in focus groups, the researchers discussed the positive effects of connecting with people across racial/ethnic lines in the common interest of understanding private racism (which I discuss more in a later chapter). There were two layers of confidentiality: researchers kept confidential those about whom they reported, and they created aliases for themselves.

Coding

In coding the data, I read and reread data, analyzing the content and context of the racetalk. In particular, I used a grounded theory design (Glaser and Strauss 1967).[25] The concepts that I developed from the data are explained through the bulk of this book. One important descriptive code was the race/ethnicity of the racetalker. When I discuss the data in the chapters to come, I always include the race of each person. The race of the person provides information about the context of the talk. For example, if a person declares, "I hate white Hispanics," the race and ethnicity of the speaker matter in analyzing the purpose and effect of the talk. In a hierarchical society such as ours, people speak from different positions of power and authority. Race is one axis in the hierarchy that differentially empowers people (Collins 2000). Thus, I consistently report this information whenever I have it.

I use the racetalkers' language exactly as it was recorded by the researchers in their field notes. I do not edit their grammar or clean up their epithets. As such, the data provide an authentic glimpse into the backstage of racetalk.

My Lens as Researcher

I subscribe to the school of thought that a researcher's race, class, gender, experiences, and values—her positionality (Smith 1987)—affect data collection and analysis (see also McCorkel and Myers 2003). Thus, I lay out my positionality and perspective in this chapter, as they are the lens through which the data were organized and analyzed herein.

Why does a white, middle-class academic from the South wish to study racetalk? I am connected to this project in many ways. I am a white person committed to the tenets and practice of antiracism. That is, racism as a structure must be tackled head-on by those who benefit from its existence—primarily whites like me (see Feagin 2000; Frankenberg 1993; Doane and Bonilla-Silva 2003; and Rassmussen et al. 2001). This book, along with my other research, teaching, and parenting endeavors, is intended to further the antiracist agenda undertaken by many others within and outside of my field.

Despite my political commitment to antiracism, however, writing this book forced me to confront apprehensions that I did not know I had. I analyze the content of talk, yet ironically I have a difficult time talking about the content. Although I advocate open, empirically grounded conversations about race so as to help break down trenchant barriers, such conversations are not easy. Talking about racetalk—a form of degradation—is even thornier. In fact, when people ask me about my book, I sometimes squirm. When I tell people that I study the racial remarks that people make in their private conversations, they tend to want examples. I don't like to provide examples. It is one thing for me to write them down in a scholarly format and another to say them out loud. I have publicly presented data from this project several times. Each time, I felt profoundly uncomfortable giving voice to the ideas and epithets spoken by the subjects in this study. Everyone has heard racetalk. However, it has a different character when spoken by a white associate professor in a formal setting than when it is blurted out in the privacy of a break room at work, around the Thanksgiving dinner table, or at a keg party. In giving voice to my data, I feel like a coconspirator, participating in the very act that I critique. I fear that I might add to its legitimacy.

For example, I guest lectured in a research class at another university. The professor wanted me to talk about my project to exemplify qualitative methods. The class was large and diverse—about sixty-five students of various races and ethnicities. I spoke for about fifteen minutes on method alone, and students quietly took notes. I told them that a key reason for using the method that I do is that the data are hard to capture. Thus, it is illustrative to provide data when justifying the method. When I reached this point in the lecture, I saw two African American women in the middle of the classroom abruptly raise their heads.[26] They both looked at me wide-eyed and discernibly shook their heads, no. Sensing the invective to come, they seemed to be pleading with me to move on, to gloss the data, to spare them the curious glances or outright offensive questions they might receive from their peers.

I was dumbstruck. Here I was, an outsider with no relationship with these students, no trust established. I was a member of the dominant racial group, embarking upon an all-too-dominant act of hurling racist epithets at a captive audience (Lawrence 1993). Even in the context of scientific inquiry, my positionality reflected its veneer of privilege. I did not want to exploit my authority in this site. I had flitted in for an hour and then would be leaving for good. I would not be there to do damage control in the class periods to come. The women's horror was palpable, and I blushed deeply. I quickly scanned my notes and presented some of the gentler racetalk.[27]

Afterward over lunch, the professor asked why I had skimped on the data. I told him what I felt had happened. He told me that a major aspect of the college experience is to be made uncomfortable in the classroom, and that there was no reason to have held back. I agreed with him to an extent: college provides excellent opportunities to be shaken out of one's comfortable, oblivious cocoon in ways that challenge old ways of thinking and open the doors to newer frames of thought. I practice this pedagogy myself. However, these women were not oblivious to the material that I was going to address: based on their positionality, they were most likely all too aware of its meanings and implications. I decided on the spot that I could analyze the import of racetalk without further victimizing them in that setting. My position as a white middle-class academic endowed me with power that—if used too casually—could have a backlash effect and harm the people who are already disproportionately affected by racetalk. It behooved me to take a different tack. Thus, discussing racetalk in formal settings should be undertaken with empathy, patience, and sensitivity on top of a solid scholarly foundation.

When called upon to make an impromptu presentation of racetalk, I hesitate as well, largely out of concern that people will assume that I am attacking them and react defensively (or even aggressively). While I am prepared for that stance at a sociological conference, I am less eager to go there when talking with the plumber or my daughter's teacher. It is difficult to provide the necessary scholarly grounding in a formal setting. It is even more challenging to do so in an informal setting.

There is the possibility that my research topic might affect my own relationships. People actively hide racetalk when they know they might be observed, and I do not want people to alter their behavior around me once they know what I am working on. This is somewhat unavoidable, though. When talking with my close friends, they occasionally stop mid-sentence and ask, "Was that racetalk? Are you going to put it in your book?" Most of my close friends are sociologists, and their racial comments tend to be ironic analyses of structural racism. But, even if they do utter conventional racetalk, I assure them that I do not plan to use any data from my immediate circle.

I omitted my intimate circle of friends and family from this study for three reasons. First, unlike the research team, who collected data for a two-month period, I worked on this project for years. I could not stay "in the field" for such an extended period of time when the field is everyday life. I could not have kept the project confidential, especially after publications started coming out of it. Second—a related issue—my friends and family all knew about the project, which disrupted the natural setting that I was trying to capture. Although most subjects learn to normalize the research process, even when the project is known to them (Berg 2004; Lofland and Lofland 1994), I decided that racetalk was too sensitive to take this risk. Third, the researchers created aliases for themselves and their subjects. Unless I, too, created an alias for myself, my subjects' confidentiality would be jeopardized by their relationship to me—a known entity. This would be unethical. Thus, I decided not to obscure the data collection process by adding myself into the mix.

Despite my hesitance to discuss this project, my fears were largely internal and without validation. I have encountered some people who become argumentative, asserting that racetalk does not really hurt anyone. They say that they are tired of the politically correct movement taking the fun and spontaneity out of life. One white colleague said, "It's not the content of the talk—it's the intent that matters." These conversations have forced me to clearly explain my analysis. This is a good experience, and it improves the project overall. I have listened to people's feedback and tried to incorporate it into my analysis.

MOVING ON

In the next chapter, I describe the theoretical underpinnings of my analysis of racetalk. Using the works of sociologists from the critical school, as well as critical race theory in law, I build a foundation to make sense of the ways that race-talk helps to reproduce the racial regime.

NOTES

1. Incidentally—to underscore the fallacies of this biological argument—the Caucasus mountains are near Mount Ararat, where Noah's ark is said to have landed. Most of the people who reside there are olive skinned rather than fair, and few would be characterized as white under the current U.S. racial regime.

2. Wright (1994) argues that these laws maximized the number of people who qualified as slaves (blacks and Indians), and minimized the number of people eligible for social and economic privilege (whites).

3. The same argument has been made about "Mexican blood" (Feagin 2000).

4. One need only peruse *The Bell Curve* to see this paradigm reified for a contemporary audience. People remain persuaded by Herrnstein and Murray's (1999) argument that blacks have inherently lower intelligence quotients than whites, despite discrediting arguments to the contrary (see Fraser 1995; and Kincheloe et al. 1997).

5. We are not always correct, however. Thus, it is better to allow people to self-identify their race/ethnicity rather than presuming it is based on superficial characteristics. Race and ethnicity are more than physical traits—they include group identification and identity.

6. R. W. Connell (1987) makes the same argument regarding the social construction of gender.

7. Native Americans were obviously here centuries before the colonists arrived, so immigration pressures are not relevant in their analysis.

8. John Steinbeck's *The Grapes of Wrath* exemplifies this well.

9. Native Americans and, to some extent, Latino/as have faced similar circumstances.

10. Wealth refers to one's income, plus assets, minus debt. Wealth in the U.S. system is concentrated in the hands of a few. To be specific, the top 1 percent of U.S. society owns 45.6 percent of the possible wealth. The bottom 80 percent owns 7.8 percent of all possible wealth (Zweigenhaft and Domhoff 1999, 194).

11. Examining corporate crime versus street crime is a good example here. It is much harder to assign blame to and adjudicate corporate criminals than it is to punish street criminals, even though the social and economic cost of corporate crime is more far reaching than is street crime (Timmer and Eitzen 1998). "Suite" criminals are insulated by complex bureaucratic systems and excellent lawyers. The identities of their victims are often hard to decipher. In contrast, street criminals are often disenfranchised individuals whose victims are easy to locate and identify with.

12. Connell (2002) refers to the totality of gender arrangements as the gender regime. I borrow his language here to refer to similar racial arrangements.

13. The General Social Survey—or GSS—is a longitudinal survey operated by the National Opinion Research Center at the University of Chicago. The National Election

Study—or NES—is a time-series study that looks at people's political attitudes and voting behaviors over a long period of time.

14. Surveys may involve a pen-and-paper instrument, a questionnaire, or a phone conversation in which the same questions and response sets are offered to every individual. These are standardized for reliability and generalizability. Face-to-face interviews are more open-ended, structured conversations that allow the respondents to elaborate and provide lengthy examples for pertinent issues.

15. All names used are pseudonyms created by the researchers themselves.

16. Atlanta Braves pitcher John Rocker was suspended after the publication of an interview in which he blatantly stereotyped a variety of New Yorkers (gays, people of color), and for calling a teammate a "fat monkey."

17. As owner of the Cincinnati Reds baseball team, Marge Schott often used racial slurs to refer to her players. She referred to two of her players as her "million-dollar niggers," and she was heard to have used the term "Jap" occasionally. Schott praised Adolf Hitler, saying that he was good at the beginning but then went too far. She was suspended in 1993, and eventually gave up control of the team in 1996. She sold the team in 1999.

18. I refer to the groups of researchers culled through the three phases of data collection as the "research team," even though that is a technically inaccurate term. Instead of being one large team of sixty-two, they actually formed clusters of teams, working together on the same project. However, this project only exists because of the concerted efforts of all of the researchers, even though they did not all know or work with each other. Thus, the term "team" is appropriate.

19. To get this project off of the ground, I took advantage of an opportunity available on my campus. Funds were available for research projects that included substantial collaboration from an undergraduate student. This funding provided a $500 stipend to my then student, Passion Williamson. Passion was one of several students who applied, and I selected her because of her knowledge of race scholarship. As a black woman, Passion also brought another perspective and face to the project. Having a racially diverse research team was necessary, and she helped make that possible. This initial phase of data collection marked Phase 1 of the data reported here in this book (see also Myers and Williamson 2001).

20. In participant observation, a researcher tries to blend in the field so as not to disrupt the natural setting. S/he might take some notes while in the field, if s/he is a known observer or if the notes will be unobtrusive. (In this case, taking notes while in the field was not viable.) After leaving a site, a researcher then writes field notes, which are copious notes describing the setting, the actors, and the content of the interaction. Field notes must be sufficiently detailed so that an outsider can understand the interaction.

21. Recruiting the research team posed interesting methodological questions. On the one hand, I wanted a broad, random representation of researchers to best represent the character and level of racetalk on campus. Ideally, the researchers would be *at least* as diverse as the student body at our large Midwestern public university. In the spring of 2001 when this project began, the racial demographic of our campus was as follows: 12 percent African American, 5 percent Latino/a, 6 percent Asian, 0.2 percent American Indian, 74 percent white, and 1 percent nonresident alien. On the other

hand, I wanted a research team who knew how to recognize and record racetalk in a qualified manner. In this case, random sampling might yield unqualified data collectors. As a compromise, I used a variety of techniques to solicit researchers. I posted fliers around campus, targeting Black Studies, Southeast Asian Studies, and the Center for Latinos, as well as dorms and classrooms. I published advertisements in the campus newspaper. I contacted "qualified" researchers—those who had previously taken research methods and/or race and ethnicity classes. I made announcements in sociology classes dealing with issues of race/ethnicity.

22. After the initial funding of Phase 1 ended, I continued to collect data using the same methodology, but I recruited new team members through four sections of a qualitative research methods course (Phase 2). In Phase 2 of data collection, I structured the racetalk project into the class in order to provide hands-on learning for my students. Focus groups were held as part of class time. Although close to two hundred students participated in this phase of the project, I only used the data of those researchers who gave written permission to do so once the course had ended. I did not reward or coerce them into participating—they simply had to volunteer to have their data included in the formal study, choose an alias, and complete an Informed Consent form. Phases 1 and 2 are not discrete entities, however, because four researchers participated in both phase 1 and Phase 2. Despite differences in recruitment strategies in Phases 1 and 2, the training, operationalization, and execution of the project were the same in both Phases. In Phase 3 of data collection, I intended to recruit researchers from regions of the United States outside the Midwest. Although researchers in Phase 1 and 2 recorded data from subjects both in and out of the Midwest, they mostly recorded what they happened upon in their local region. Phase 3 hypothesized that there might be differences between racetalk in the Midwest and that in the southern and northeastern United States. I planned recruitment trips to Massachusetts and North Carolina. I relied on contacts in universities in each region to give me access to pools of potential researchers.

23. My attempts in North Carolina were unsuccessful. I made one trip and presented a paper on racetalk to a class of sixty sociology students at a small public university. At the end of the period, I asked students to contact me via e-mail if they were interested in becoming part of a research team. The students seemed engaged, asked interesting questions, and I left feeling hopeful. No one contacted me afterward. I planned another trip to the same university to re-recruit and to hold training sessions (with free pizza) on campus. However, hurricane Isabel intervened and I was forced to cancel the trip. I next tried to recruit team members in Massachusetts. At a large public university, I tried to improve my recruitment technique, having fallen flat in North Carolina. Instead of lecturing in one class, I went to eight sociology classes, guest lectured, and gave a presentation to the department's faculty and graduate students. Dozens of students expressed interest in participating in the project. I scheduled a room for the training session, ordered six extralarge pizzas, and went in to start training. No one showed up.

Since that time, I have reflected on what went wrong. Why was I so successful in the Midwest and not in the other regions? One obvious reason is that, in the Midwest, I was able to structure the project into a course. Using a captive audience of students as researchers is always productive. I underscore the fact that most people in the classes did not donate their data to the larger project, and those who did acted purely in the interest of inquiry rather than for any reward. However, using the existing structure of the semester is an obvious asset. Another recruitment strength in the Midwest was the reliability of my physical presence from day to day. The Midwest research team knew where to find me and got to know and trust me over a long period of time. The potential pools in other regions did not have a bond of trust with me, nor a sense that I would be a reliable contact—other than what I promised them in our short encounters. This was a major drawback to Phase 3's strategy. Talking about racetalk is touchy and emotional even among a sustained group of researchers (Myers 1998). It is much more risky for a group of people to come out and talk together about race, if they are unsure that I can shepherd them over the hills and through the valleys of discovery.

I tried to salvage Phase 3 by constructing a Racetalk Project website. I again relied upon my contacts in North Carolina and Massachusetts, but instead of having researchers meet with me and each other face to face, I asked them to send me a private e-mail expressing interest in the project. After the initial e-mail, I would send them the website address—it was not available to the public. After visiting the site, reading the project rationale and guidelines, a researcher would send me back a completed Informed Consent form and begin collecting data on her/his own. The Web method allowed researchers to remain not just confidential but also anonymous, collecting data without anyone else knowing. There would be no focus groups, unfortunately, but at least people outside the Midwest could collect and submit data. This method was also unsuccessful.

24. An Informed Consent form indicates that a person knows s/he is part of a study. S/he knows that her/his identity will be kept confidential, and s/he knows whom to contact if any questions or concerns arise out of the study. The researchers filled out these forms, but their subjects did not. Asking subjects to fill out Informed Consent forms would have likely prohibited data collection at all, given the covert nature of racetalk. However, all subjects have been kept confidential through the use of aliases as well.

25. This method uses three phases of coding: open, axial, and selective. The open coding phase involves examining transcripts and footage for emergent themes, categories, and concepts. In the axial phase, categories are specified more concretely, and the relationships among them are investigated. In the last phase—selective coding—categories and their relationships are systematically mapped in order to develop explanatory concepts and theoretical frameworks (Strauss and Corbin 1990). Some codes are abstract and analytical, while others are simply descriptive. The analytical codes are woven together to form a theory about the dialectical reproduction of racism through racetalk.

26. These women were not the only people of color in the room, but whites were clearly the majority.

27. Even still, several white students asked me why it is OK for blacks to say nigger, but not for whites. The African American women looked at their desks. I offered a long explanation about oppositional identity work (MacLeod 1995; Schwalbe and Mason-Schrock 1996) and the right of a group to define itself. I argued that, due to structural power differentials, "nigger" was a term of oppression when used by whites and a term of resistance when used by blacks.

3

RACETALK AS REPRODUCING RACISM

A Theoretical Toolbox

> The American marketplace of ideas was founded with the idea of the racial inferiority of nonwhites as one of its chief commodities, and ever since the market opened, racism has remained its most active item in trade.
>
> —Charles R. Lawrence III (1993)

In order to understand the power of language, I use a specific theoretical framework. This chapter lays out the theories that are relevant for understanding the importance of racetalk. Drawing from critical scholars, I frame racetalk as a complex social process in which everyday actors reify the historical structure of racism. By investigating the interconnection between structure and action, we can begin to comprehend the social significance of private racetalk.[1]

THE CRITICAL SCHOOL OF SOCIOLOGY

A great deal of the analysis in this book is influenced by the critical school of sociology, originating with the Frankfurt School of sociology in Germany.[2] All sociological theories developed with the intent of criticizing and analyzing the mechanisms of society. However, what is now called "critical theory" coalesced in earnest in Germany in the early 1920s, led by a group of Neo-Marxists who were concerned with what they saw as limitations and inadequacies in Karl Marx's original works.[3]

The critical school thinkers spent much of their careers reexamining and reworking Marx. Influenced by the rise of Nazism and the ruined German economy after World War I, these scholars sought to fill intellectual gaps and elaborate on key concepts so as to make Marxism more relevant and practical. They integrated the critical insights of other sociologists as well, including Max Weber (1921/1979). What emerged was a more nuanced perspective that examined not just the economy, but also the state, ideology, and human agency. Rather than delving deeply into the key figures in the critical school, I will discuss the concepts that most clearly impact my research.

Legitimation

A major contribution by the critical school is the concept of legitimation. Critical scholars argue that oppressive structures persist not just because people are powerless to change them, but because they are seen as *legitimate* in the eyes of the masses. In spite of its oppressive nature, the structure is considered to be legitimate because people see it as unchangeable, a fact of reality that "just is." Georg Lukacs (1922) explained this phenomenon with the concept of "reification." That is, although people created social structures by working together to construct hierarchies, rules, and procedures, they then forget that the structures are human-made. They treat the structures as if they have lives of their own without human agency—they make them real when they are not (see also Bauman 1976; Giddens 1984). A reified structure is likely to be a legitimate structure.

Antonio Gramsci (1932/1975, 1971) was concerned with Marx's structural determinism. Gramsci disagreed with Marx's prediction that workers would form a class consciousness and revolt. Gramsci said that workers "wear their chains willingly"—they go to work even under extremely difficult conditions and for little pay. They do so because (a) they have no viable alternatives and (b) they do not recognize the system as inherently unfair. Gramsci argued that the capitalists were so effective at producing a system that controlled people ideologically as well as physically that workers were unable to question and challenge the economic system that imprisoned them. According to Gramsci, the ruling class controlled the people through the use of hegemony. When a system is hegemonic, it is so pervasive and taken for granted that people are unable to step back, see it for what it is, and challenge it. Thus, the leaders exert control with the tacit assent of the masses.[4] Racism is hegemonic.

DIALECTICS

One of the critical school's major criticisms of Marx was his disproportionate attention to macrolevel structures—like the economy—as the root of social ills and social change. While it is important to focus on rules, hierarchies, and institutions that persist over time,[5] dialectical analysis seeks to integrate the structures of oppression with human agency, theorizing that the two are fundamentally interconnected. Rather than being preoccupied with social order absent actors, dialecticians focus on the social processes through which society is reproduced and/or changed over time.

Dialecticians depart from structuralists in their examination of the role of actors in perpetuating or challenging social order. People are not helplessly constrained by the social structure. Instead, they make choices, innovate, and challenge rules and practices. As Gramsci himself argued, structures would not endure if people did not, to some extent, buy into and work to reproduce them. Thus, ironically, people's actions serve to bolster the very structures that limit their individual freedoms.

Structuration

Anthony Giddens (1984) has clearly been influenced by the dialectical insights of the critical school. In his theory of "structuration," Giddens lays out the ongoing processes in which order is reproduced through people's everyday actions. He discusses both structure and agency at length. Giddens (1984) distinguishes between social structures, social systems, and structuration. *Structures* are at the height of abstraction. Structure is defined as "recursively organized sets of rules and resources, out of time and space—save in its instantiations and coordination as memory traces—and is marked by an 'absence of the subject'" (25). Structures define right and wrong and impose sanctions. *Systems* are less abstract, involving actual humans and their actions: "[Systems] comprise the situated activities of human agents, reproduced across time and space . . . organized as regular social practice" (25). Systems might include the economy, the family, and religion. Structures and systems operate together—they are "recursively implicated" in each other's conceptualization. *Structuration* is the dialectical process through which structures and systems are reproduced.

According to Giddens, there are *three major social structures*. The first structure is "signification," which involves the codes that we use to make sense of the world and to make meanings. Signification impacts the mode of discourse of a society. Mary Romero and Abigail Stewart (1999) call these structures "master narratives," as they are used to make sense of reality. The second structure is "domination." Domination involves the unequal distribution of allocative and authoritative resources in society. Allocative resources include raw materials, land, goods, jobs, and services. Authoritative resources include the ability to speak for oneself, act on one's own behalf, and act in a credible effective manner. The third structure is legitimation, which, as discussed above, allows the overall structure to persist unchallenged. These structures work together so as to constrain us.

Giddens (1984) also discusses *three forms of constraint*: material, structural, and negative sanctions. First, material constraints exist when we do not have the financial or physical means to pursue an action. Financially, for example, some people may not be able to afford to attend college or go on a vacation. Physically, disabled people may not be able to enter a building because there is no handicapped-accessible entrance. Second, structural constraints are defined as "placing limits upon the range of options open to an actor, or plurality of actors, in a given circumstance or type of circumstance" (177). For example, racial segregation in housing and schooling makes it difficult for people in impoverished areas to find decent places to live and work (Massey and Denton 1993). Racial segregation helps to reproduce poverty among minorities, who then have even fewer viable opportunities for improving their lives financially (Doob 1999). Last, negative sanctions punish people who try to act in disregard for other structural constraints. Black people are followed when they shop in expensive stores[6]—marketplaces that truly are accessible only to the very affluent. Assumptions are made that black people cannot be affluent, therefore they cannot legitimately patronize stores that cater to affluent tastes (Anderson 1999).

Taken together, various social factors work together to limit our range of opportunities, despite our dreams and intentions. We tell our children, "You can be anything that you want to be," and they in turn fantasize about being astronauts, doctors, and world leaders. In reality, it is unlikely that most of them will have the resources or opportunities to pursue the kinds of studies and experiences necessary in order to realize these dreams, even if they try their hardest. As Jay MacLeod (1995) showed in his study of white and black teens living in an urban housing project, the structure is a powerful limiting force for poor youths, regardless of their gumption and drive.

However, unlike what pure structuralists would have us believe, our lives are not predetermined by our location in the structure. Dialecticians like Giddens argue that the structure also enables us by providing opportunities for action. Therefore, we are not hopelessly shackled by the structure. We are able to make choices, and we affect each other according to the choices that we make. As Giddens says, "one person's constraint is another's enabling" (176). When we act, we reflexively monitor—as best as we can decipher—the impact that our actions have on our relationships and social standing. Our actions have motives. Our actions have intended consequences. We often attempt to act in ways that benefit our social standing.

Nevertheless, our actions can go awry. We may or may not be able to express our motives. Our best intentions might be confounded. Indeed, many of our actions have unintended, unanticipated consequences as well. Consider this hypothetical example: Sue (white) told a joke about blacks at dinner. She was shocked when her seven-year-old repeated the joke at school. Sue did not intend for her joke to be spread in such a manner, but it happened nonetheless. Sue reminds us that we cannot control all of the ramifications of our actions, even if we try. Giddens mentions the "accordion effect" (or what is also known in chaos theory as the "butterfly effect"), in which a seemingly insignificant action, like the flapping of a butterfly's wings, can set in motion a spiraling series of events that trigger, say, a tsunami across the sea from the butterfly. As Giddens (1984, 11) says,

> The consequences of what actors do, intentionally or unintentionally, are events which would not have happened if that actor had behaved differently, but which are not within the scope of the agent's power to have brought about.

Thus, even though Sue, as a single individual, does not have the power to reproduce a structure by herself, her daughter might repeat the racist joke to a group of African Americans at school. Sue's exercise of racial privilege—an action enabled by the structure—exacerbated the constraints experienced by her daughter's African American peers. As Peter Winch (1970, 105) argues,

> Language games are played by men [sic] who have lives to live—lives involving a wide variety of different interests, which have all kinds of different bearings on each other. Because of this, what a man says or does may make a difference not merely to the performance of the activity upon which he is at present engaged, but to his life and to the lives of other people.

Structuration blends structure with agency—we are constrained, but we can act within the limits of those constraints. Some of us are freer to act than others, and our actions impact others' freedoms.

At the heart of structuration, however, is the fact that we individuals often act in concert. We are not random agents whose actions cancel each other out. Our actions are somewhat ordered and systematic even when we are spontaneous, because our actions stem from our knowledge of and limitations within the structures. Action and order are not separate in Giddens's theory of structuration. In his words, action and order are an interconnected "duality" rather than an unrelated "dualism." How we act is informed by the structure, as it imprints itself on our memory across time and space. Due to the durée of the structures, we tend to act in ways that reinforce the social order. As Giddens (1984, 26) writes, "according to structuration theory, the moment of production of action is also one of reproduction in the contexts of day-to-day enactment of social life." The social world operates as a reflexive feedback loop in which order influences action, and actions tend to reinforce the order—whether intentionally or not.

Positionality

Within social systems, Giddens (1984) argues, individuals occupy different "positions," depending on their relationship to the structures of signification, domination, and legitimacy. Within these structures, some people are systematically more privileged than others. People in different positions or categories have different sets of rules to follow. Drawing on Bruce Biddle (1979) and Erving Goffman (1981), Giddens argues that people's positions affect their identities, access to resources, and range of possible actions. Positionality provides the context for people's actions. As discussed above, due to the interconnectedness of positions, people's actions affect the opportunities of others, both negatively and positively.

Patricia Hill Collins (2000) takes the analysis of positions to a more critical level. Collins argues that there are several systems of oppression operating in American society, including racism, patriarchy, and capitalism. Each system differentially benefits some people over others. For example, capitalism benefits the capitalists, racism benefits whites, and sexism benefits men. But these systems do not operate independently of one another—they intertwine in what Collins calls a "matrix of domination," so that people occupy positions of privilege and disadvantage simultaneously. For example, in a past research project, I studied a volunteer organization founded and operated by a group of wealthy African American and white women. Privilege and disadvantage concomitantly informed the actions of the organization at all times. The women could exercise their class privilege, but doing so might jeopardize their standing in other arenas. Their class privilege was tenuous due to their subordinate status as women and, for some, their race. Thus, the women's actions were always circumspect and tentative (for more, see Myers 2001 and 2003). One's positionality makes action complicated. Exercising one's privilege on one axis of oppression might exacerbate one's subordination on another axis.

Collins's work underscores Giddens's discussion of reflexivity. Giddens argues that people understand the limitations on their actions because they act reflexively. As he explains, "'reflexivity' should be understood not merely as self-consciousness, but as the monitored character of the ongoing flow of social life" (1984, 3). Collins's work suggests that reflexivity involves the careful negotiation of privilege and disadvantage in daily interactions. As such, people benefit from acting in ways that insulate rather than threaten their privilege. Privileges are made possible by one's position in the structure. Therefore, people act rationally when they reinforce structural power differentials, even though such actions help to reify pernicious regimes like racism, patriarchy, and capitalism.

UN/DOING RACISM: AN ANALYTICAL APPLICATION OF DIALECTICS

Candace West and Don Zimmerman (1987) argue that everyday people enact everyday gendered behaviors that in effect reify the structures of sexism and patriarchy. That is, there are innumerable rules and prescriptions we must follow in order to be "good" women and men. These rules maintain the gender regime (Connell 2001). Whenever we follow these rules, we "do gender." We legitimate the rules and the structure through our complicity. We are often unaware that we do gender. We may even like doing it. West and Zimmerman argue that we can choose *not* to do gender in the ways that we do, thereby challenging the gender regime. By defying the hegemonic practices of gender, we can work together to alter gender inequality.

In this book, I make a similar argument about the ways that we do racism in our everyday lives. I intentionally use the term "doing racism" rather than "doing race" to underscore the power dynamics inherent in the racial regime. The emphasis of racial differences in our interactions matters because it bolsters the structure of racism. As with gender, racism consists of structural forces that constrain as well as enable certain categories of people according to the valuation of race/ethnicity at a given historical period. These structural forces continue to have long-lasting material and psychological consequences for all people—particularly for people of color. At the same time, racism is manifested at the micro level in the form of discrimination, prejudice, exclusion, surveillance, and racetalk. When people act in ways that take the structure for granted—when they follow formal rules and informal norms—they help to reinforce the structure of racism so that it continues unchallenged. As a dialectic, racism persists across generations, although the way it is manifested evolves along with the formal rules of society and people's everyday practices.

According to the tenets of the dialectic, structural racism—like gender—can be diminished in a couple of ways. First, people can refuse to do racism, challenging the racist structure. Racism should dissipate once actors fail to subscribe to and follow the old rules. Second, when the rules themselves begin to crumble, then people's practices should change to follow suit. In contemporary U.S. society, we can see current evidence of changes at both levels. Rhetorically, Americans espouse colorblind, antiracist practices, whereby all people should be seen as equal (Bonilla-Silva 2001, 2003). Thus, individuals' racist practices should be abating, and racist structure should be less strident as well. The fact that it is now illegal to discriminate on the basis of race and/or ethnicity should be evidence that racist structure is a thing of the past. According to the tenets of dialectical analysis, we should be seeing the end of racism.

So why does racism continue to exist, as documented by scholars like Joe Feagin, Hernan Vera, Eduardo Bonilla-Silva, Patricia Williams, and many others? There is a social realm previously unexplored where the old prejudices are taught and learned, away from the public eye. That children are learning racism at a surprisingly early age—as young as three years old—has been beautifully documented by Debra Van Ausdale and Feagin (2002). I am interested in revealing the *process* by which these old lessons are (re)learned. By looking behind closed doors and listening to the informal education going on when teachers, politicians, and even sociologists are not paying attention, we glimpse this process in action. We also glimpse ways to undo it.

LANGUAGE AS DIALECTICAL PRACTICE: PIERRE BOURDIEU

Pierre Bourdieu (1977, 1991) focuses on dialogue as the locus at which structural power is reproduced and/or challenged. Bourdieu (1991, 129) argues that "the dialectical process is accomplished . . . in and through the labour of enunciation." As such, Bourdieu's work is crucial for the analysis of racetalk.

Bourdieu's work grows out of a critique of objectivist, positivist science in which scholars seek objective truths and generalizable theories (see, for example, Popper 1965, 1968). Bourdieu argues that we cannot understand social practices without taking into consideration the social context in which they occur. Social interaction is shaped by social structures like class and race. The power dynamics that exist vis-à-vis structures get played out in interpersonal interaction, so that some speakers are more powerful or "authorized" than others. So, for example, we should be able to observe the power dynamics of structural racism evidenced in microinteractions. Bourdieu asserts that power is an inescapable, important aspect of communication that must be examined in its own right (Thompson 1991).[7]

Bourdieu is primarily concerned with discourse—the language used in interactions. He draws heavily on linguistic scholars like Ferdinand de Saussure (1974), Noam Chomsky (1965), and J. L. Austin (1971), in order to understand the relationship between structural inequality and the uses of language. When Bourdieu invokes choices of language, he often means language in the literal sense: French versus Belgian, the familiar form of language versus the formal, slang versus erudite speech. For example, he discusses the power invoked in an interaction when a politician uses the familiar form of speech ("tu" instead of "vous") with a citizen whom s/he has never met. In so doing, the politician reminds the citizen that s/he occupies a position of authority and power that the citizen does not. Despite Bourdieu's concentration on the uses of particular words and phrases, his analysis is relevant to the study of many social phenomena. He incorporates sociological concepts to critique the dialectical power dynamics in language use. Here, I discuss key concepts from Bourdieu that are relevant to the analysis of racetalk.

Habitus

Like Giddens, Bourdieu theorizes that structure and agency work together to reproduce structural inequalities and power dynamics. His use of the Aristotelian concept of the "habitus" provides insight into the ways in which structure and agency operate together. Bourdieu (1977) uses the abstract term "habitus" in many ways. Habitus involves "systems of durable, transposable dispositions . . . which can be 'regulated' and 'regular' without in any way being the product of rules" (72). Bourdieu uses paradoxical language, describing the habitus as "regular improvisations" (78) that tend to reproduce dominant structures: "Each agent, wittingly or unwittingly, willy nilly, is a producer and reproducer of objective meaning" (79). The habitus is orderly, yet impromptu.

The habitus is both subjective and objective. Each person has her/his own experiences, ideas, and worldview, making the habitus subjective and individualized. However, each person will act somewhat predictably because s/he lives in the same structure as millions of others who are affected by the same rituals, laws, and belief systems. This commonality reflects the objective nature of the habitus.

Here, Bourdieu's work overlaps with Gramsci's in that the habitus operates hegemonically: there is a "homogeneity of the habitus" that "causes practices and works to be immediately intelligible and foreseeable, and hence taken for granted" (80). The habitus is a product of history. Like others already discussed, Bourdieu asserts that we are born into an existing world that predates us and will live on after we are gone. The habitus is shaped by that historically trenchant structure. We all learn how to behave and navigate in the structure we are born into. Bourdieu, like others, explicitly incorporates agency: "The past survives in the present and tends to perpetuate itself into the future by making itself present in the practices structured according to its principles" (82). The habitus brings the past into the present in order to make interactions stable and predictable for individual actors. It serves as a "matrix of perceptions, appreciations, and actions" (83). Thus, structures of the past, like racism, are reproduced in the daily interactions of those living in the present. The habitus evolves—de jure racism becomes outlawed—but the old ideas and practices endure as they structure present and even future interactions. The habitus does not determine people's actions, but it does "orient" them to behave in certain ways (Thompson 1991).

The habitus is a loaded imagination, arming individuals with symbols, media, and quasi data from the past that are used to inform everyday life in the present. For example, many whites have been observed to cross the street when a black stranger approaches on the sidewalk. They lock their car doors when waiting at stoplights in black neighborhoods. White women clutch their purses when black strangers engage them in conversation (Feagin 1991, 2000; St. Jean and Feagin 1998). The habitus in these situations predisposes whites to fear blacks. Although black-on-white violence is much more rare than intraracial violence (Eitzen and Baca Zinn 2004), the habitus structures the interaction, often unconsciously. However, even when whites are not aware that they are reacting to blacks as if they are violent, blacks receive that message loud and clear.

Bourdieu's use of the concept "structure" is innovative. Bourdieu incorporates symbolic meanings as structure. Therefore, the ways that we symbolically represent different groups of people both reflect and impact their structural location and opportunities. For example, Marlon Riggs's (1986) film *Ethnic Notions* examines the historical representation of African Americans from slavery to the modern era through art, postcards, product marketing, and films. He shows that during slavery, blacks were depicted as docile, happy, childlike, and nonthreatening. Such images aimed to legitimate slavery by arguing that blacks not only liked being slaves, but they needed the paternalistic care of whites in order to survive. Once slavery ended and blacks entered the paid workforce alongside whites, the images of African Americans radically shifted. Instead of smiling, shuffling, and singing, blacks were shown with sharp teeth and bugged-out eyes, leering at white women and children, caught in barbed wire fences as they devoured whole watermelons. These images were frightening, marking blacks as dangerous threats to white safety. Thus, employers found justification in not hiring black men. Over the years, the pejorative images of blacks have shifted, but elements of the sexualized, brutal, and threatening black lurk around the edges, as we will see in upcoming chapters (see also hooks 1992, 1994b, 1996; St. Jean and Feagin 1998; and Wyatt 1997). In this way, symbolic structure limits blacks' access to resources and opportunities by ideologically justifying their exclusion.

The Doxa

Bourdieu, like others, asserts that a great deal of our social world is taken for granted and uncritically examined—if examined at all. According to Bourdieu, "the doxa" is what we take for granted: "[The doxa] is that which is beyond question and which each agent tacitly accords by the mere fact of acting in accord with social convention" (1977, 169). Within the doxa, people express opinions about the ways that the world works. However, they rarely critique the doxa. Occasionally, people will resist the doxa, through "heterodoxy." They might critique the relations of ruling or question the distribution of resources in society. When heterodoxy risks being seen as legitimate and, hence, revolutionary, the elite invoke a powerful tool to quell or discredit the critique: "orthodoxy." Orthodoxy is the officially sanctioned means to censor threatening critique. It tends to cast heterodoxy as heretical, blasphemous, and dangerous for all—not just for the elites.

Orthodoxy involves more than a dissolution of disruptive conflict within the doxa; it involves the exercise of power and authority. Most people subscribe uncritically to the doxa, thereby enforcing the power and legitimacy of the elites. Heterodoxy allows for challenges on behalf of the "dominated." If effective, these might redistribute power and resources. Such threats must be eliminated in order for the powerful to remain intact. As Bourdieu (1977, 170–71) writes,

> Because any language that can command attention is an "authorized language," invested with the authority of a group, the things it designates are not simply expressed but also authorized and legitimated. This is true not only of establishment language but also of the heretical discourses, which draw their legitimacy and authority from the very groups over which they exert their power and which they literally produce by expressing them: they derive their power from their capacity to objectify unformulated experiences, to make them public—a step on the road to officialization and legitimation.

Indeed, because of the effectiveness of orthodoxy to censor challenges, much heterodoxy is intentionally kept private so as to remain unsanctioned. As such, people tend to self-censor their language so that they express certain ideas only in settings where the ideas would be welcomed.

The Metaphor of Capital/ism

Like Marx and subsequent critical school thinkers, Bourdieu is a vocal critic of capitalism. He sees language as a tool used by the dominants to nurture a false consciousness among the dominated classes.

The Market. Bourdieu theorizes about the language used to legitimate unequal relationships, using the metaphor of the marketplace to make sense of social practices. Bourdieu argues that there is a marketplace of ideas that values some and devalues—even censors—others. At the doxic level, the valuable

ideas are those that benefit the elites, and devalued ideas are those that challenge or resist the elites. However, different markets are more or less receptive to heterodoxy. The speaker uses her/his habitus in order to anticipate
which setting is more amenable to various forms of expression. Even on the
small scale, "heretical" comments might be met with orthodoxy if the market
is not receptive. Thus, speakers must be sensitive and use social cues to decipher which ideas are welcome where. Successful speaking requires a certain
"social competence." As Bourdieu (1991, 82) writes: "The sense of value of
one's own linguistic products is a fundamental dimension of the sense of knowing the place which one occupies in the social space."

   Capital. As in any martketplace, effective communication has its payoffs.
Bourdieu (1991, 77) says, "on the basis of a practical anticipation of the laws
of the market concerned, [speakers], most often unwittingly, and without ex-
pressly seeking to do so, try to maximize the symbolic profit they can obtain." In
keeping with the metaphor, Bourdieu employs the term "capital" to describe
the social currency that is exchanged and accrued through interactions. In
Bourdieu's use of the term, capital can consist of clout, influence, and style.
Bourdieu delineates several forms of capital.

   At its basic level, an effective interaction involves proper "linguistic capital." That is, the speaker must evidence linguistic competence. As discussed
above, Bourdieu is concerned with issues of grammar, dialect, and vocabulary. In this vein, a person might accrue linguistic capital by speaking in "the
King's English" rather than slang when addressing a judge in a courtroom.
However, the concept of linguistic capital has pertinent applications to this
study as well. For example, does one reap more linguistic capital by telling a
Muslim joke or a black joke? Does the exact language used in racetalk affect
the status that is engendered by the talk? Are certain people better at mim-
icking accents than others? Using the right language in the right setting is socially profitable.

   Bourdieu discusses other forms of capital as well. "Cultural capital" demarks
knowledge, skills, and other cultural products. For example, one may accrue
much cultural capital after traveling in Europe, learning to speak four languages fluently, graduating from Julliard, and performing as first chair violin-
ist in major American concert halls. Different contexts value different cultural
accomplishments. For example, in some circles it may be more culturally valuable to have first row seats at a NASCAR race than at a performance of *Oth-
ello*. People might play up certain experiences in contexts where they are valued and underplay them in less sympathetic or envious settings.

   "Symbolic capital" is the "accumulated prestige or honor" accrued due to
one's cultural or economic capital. As with cultural capital, in order for people
to profit from symbolic capital, it must be recognized as valuable by the group.

Celebrity status and respect tends to accompany symbolic capital. Religious figures, political leaders, and entertainment and athletic stars all possess symbolic capital. This capital is related to real authority, power, and influence. People with high symbolic capital possess the authority to impose a particular vision of the world on their followers or subjects.

Bourdieu constructs other forms of capital in addition to these. However, these forms of capital discussed here are the most relevant for understanding the uses of racetalk that I analyze in this book.

Symbolic Violence

Bourdieu believes that, through language, power differentials and unequal structures are legitimated and reproduced. As he writes (1977, 190), "once a system of mechanisms has been constituted capable of objectively ensuring the reproduction of the established order by its own motion, the dominant class have only to let the system they dominate take its own course in order to exercise their domination." Therefore, it is in the best interest of the elites to maintain the unequal status quo. Dialectics are political.

Often, in contentious situations, elites must use overt violence in order to maintain their dominance. However, once a system has become stable and the doxa becomes invisible, the elites need use only symbolic violence in order to reproduce the existing structure. Bourdieu (1977, 196) defines symbolic violence as "the gentle, hidden form that violence takes when overt violence is impossible." Symbolic violence blames the victim, objectifies the dominated, and legitimates the power of the elites. Racetalk is a form of symbolic violence that helps maintain the racist structure and the status quo.

COMMUNICATIVE ACTION: CONTRASTING JÜRGEN HABERMAS

The work of Jürgen Habermas (1984) complements Bourdieu. Like Bourdieu, Habermas argues that interpersonal communication is a means through which individual actors construct and disseminate knowledge—truth or myth, rational or irrational—in ways that affect the social structures. Habermas is concerned with the positive powers of communication, taking a more optimistic view of the power of language than does Bourdieu (who considers Habermas naïve). Habermas envisions a world in which language, when used rationally, can be used to engender positive social change. Rational language can help construct truly equitable communities. Through his theory of communicative action, Habermas sketches a blueprint for making all voices heard, even those who have been traditionally marginalized. Communicative action is defined as such:

> The concept of *communicative action* refers to the interaction of at least two sub-jects capable of speech and action who establish interpersonal relationship (whether by verbal or extraverbal means). The actors seek to reach an under-standing about the action situation and their plans of action in order to coordi-nate their actions by way of agreement. (1984, 86)

In order to make this conversation equitable, each actor must speak as truth-fully and openly as possible so that a fair, honest response can be offered. Communicative action involves rigorous, guileless interplay between actors who are genuinely committed to hearing each other and coming to a new un-derstanding. An actor committed to achieving understanding (*verstehen*) must act in the following manner:

1. S/he must make statements that are true, as far as s/he can be sure.
2. Her/his speech must be normative within the context that is spoken.
3. The speaker must intend exactly what s/he says, rather than being ma-nipulative or trying to "fit in" (99).

In communicative action, power differences between actors are alleviated. This is a major difference between Habermas and Bourdieu, whose central an-alytical focus is the persistence of power differentials that arise in all conver-sations. I side with Bourdieu on this.

Nevertheless, Habermas's concepts overlap with Bourdieu's in many ways. For example, Habermas's concept of the "worldview" is similar to Bourdieu's use of habitus. Habermas explains the importance of worldviews as such:

> Worldviews are constitutive not only for processes of reaching understanding but for social integration and the stabilization of individuals as well. They function in the formation and stabilization of identities, supplying individuals with a core of basic concepts and assumptions that cannot be revised without affecting the iden-tity of the individual and social groups. (64)

The worldview is dialectical in that it frames not only how people think but also how they act: "in the framework of the worldview the members of a lan-guage community come to an understanding on central themes of their per-sonal and social lives" (59). As such, the worldview is not just an individual stance on various issues—it is a socially constructed paradigm for making sense of one's own actions and the actions of others. The worldview, like the habitus, informs future actions.

Habermas conceptualizes a grander scale of ideological understanding, which he calls the "lifeworld." The lifeworld is constructed socially as individuals share their worldviews and build a common perspective of the world as a whole. Similar to Bourdieu's "doxa," the lifeworld is hegemonic—reified to the extent that is unrecognizable as a social construct and, therefore, beyond critique. The lifeworld is reproduced over time because it "stores the interpretive work of preceding generations" (70).

Like Bourdieu, Habermas is concerned with the alignment between individuals' perceptions and the hegemonic ideologies of society as a whole. In his terms, Habermas examines the relationship between the lifeworld and the worldview. Worldviews vary in their centrality to the lifeworld. This affects the ways in which people express their ideas. If a worldview is highly aligned with the lifeworld, then the speaker does not need to spend much time preparing her/his audience to receive her/his message. However, the larger the gap between the lifeworld and the worldview, the more work a speaker must do to make her/his point heard. Misaligned talk is more open to criticism and, according to Habermas, must be presented in a highly rational manner in order for it to be accepted.

CRITICAL RACE THEORY

The last major theoretical framework that has impacted my analysis of racetalk is critical race theory, or CRT. CRT represents the work of a group of progressive legal scholars and activists, including Derrick Bell, Alan Freeman, Patricia Williams, Angela Harris, Richard Delgado, Mari Matsuda, Charles Lawrence, and Kimberle Williams Crenshaw. Grounding their work in the legal debates over U.S. civil liberties, CRT scholars analyze the persistence of racism in our society despite legal inroads over the past century. There are six basic tenets to critical race theory.

First, the theory purports that racism is an ordinary and normal part of U.S. society, rather than rare and exceptional. As far as the experiences of people of color are concerned, racism is business as usual. From a young age, people of color come to expect racism, and they learn to detect and cope with it. In contrast, part of the privilege of the dominant group is not having to manage the negative repercussions of racism on a daily basis. This privilege also makes racism harder for the dominants to recognize and decipher. Thus, the dominant lens is distorted. Racism is ubiquitous.

Second, racism as we know it—"white-over-color ascendancy" (Delgado and Stefancic 2001, 7)—serves many social, psychic, and material purposes that prevent it from being challenged. For example, racism benefits elites financially by ensuring an exploitable workforce and malleable consumer base. Working-class whites are among this exploitable population. Yet, rather than joining with their coworkers of color, working-class whites psychologically identify with elites, due to their common race. CRT scholars call this tenet "interest convergence": less powerful whites see their interests converging with the elites, even though the elites do not actually represent their interests (see also Fine and Weis 1999). Thus, elite and working-class whites both benefit from racism in different ways, making it unlikely for an antiracist movement to take hold within the working class. As the working class is a larger group of people than the elites, this loss of potential allies cripples antiracist action.

Third, like sociologists, CRT scholars see racism as a social construction. That is, people make up the rules about race and they enforce them. These rules are not natural or static. People ignore the similarities among the races and exaggerate the differences for social purposes.

The fourth tenet is called differential racialization. Different minority groups are racialized in different ways at different times, according to the dominants' needs. As the labor market shifts, some minority groups may gain more status over others. Recall from a previous chapter that Ronald Takaki (1994) talks about this process through immigration and labor market requirements, elevating Japanese workers above black workers, for example. However, minority groups may fall out of favor as the context shifts: the U.S. government forced Japanese Americans into interment camps after Pearl Harbor. It put Arab Americans under surveillance after 9/11. Differential racialization underscores the social, fluid, and hierarchical character of racism. Each group has its own ever-developing history in the U.S. racial regime.

Fifth, CRT scholars echo Collins's (2000) argument that privileges and disadvantages intersect and overlap. No one identity is a unified identity due to the intersectionality of positions. That is, there is no singular Jewish experience, or white identity, or Latino/a plight because within each category are multiple intersecting, contradicting statuses. As such, we must avoid making essentialist statements about racial and ethnic groups.[8]

The final tenet asserts that, even though there is no essential nature to race and ethnicity, people of color do speak from a unique perspective. Due to their positionality (Collins 2000), people of color approach social issues from the vantage point of outsider looking in—sometimes included, other times excluded. CRT has led to a "legal storytelling" movement, in which people of color use personal experience to shed light on the law, policy, and shared oppressions. Bell's (1992) *Faces at the Bottom of the Well* is a brilliant example of this strategy for forcing you to think outside of the box about racism, seeking to shatter hegemonic ideologies that help racism to persist.

Critical race theory is a useful paradigm to use alongside critical sociology for analyzing the persistence of racism. CRT scholars' use of state and U.S. Supreme Court decisions helps to illuminate the structural permanence of racism in U.S. society, despite seemingly progressive policy shifts over time. Their work provides the tools to show that racetalk is, in fact, more than mere talk. CRT helps analyze racetalk as dialectical, ultimately affecting the social structure of society.

THEORETICAL RELEVANCE TO THE ANALYSIS OF RACETALK

Because attitudes affect behavior (Feagin 2000), examining private discourse may be the key to understanding the paradox of continued discrimination in a context of colorblindness. Analyses of racist discourse provide a link between people's discriminatory actions and the structure of racial inequality. Teun van Dijk (1993) argues that discourse itself is a "surface structure"—words, gestures, and expressions—that has no meaning without the "underlying structure." In racetalk, the surface structure is only viable due to the larger racist context. The meanings of racetalk are continually contested (Doane 1996; Omi 1999; Winant 1999). Winant (1999, 15) argues that "to represent, interpret or signify race, then, to assign meaning to it, is at least implicitly and often explicitly to locate it in social structural terms." By engaging in everyday racetalk, people help to nurture a racially hostile climate. They also legitimate and reproduce the existing racist structure by taking it for granted (Bonilla-Silva 1999; Bonilla-Silva and Forman 2000; Doane 1996; van Dijk 1993; West and Zimmerman 1987). Racetalk is a dialectical process that has, until now, gone unexamined in a systematic, theoretically grounded manner.

Taken together, this body of scholarship impacts my analysis of racetalk in several ways. Several key concepts will reappear again and again throughout this book as I underscore the importance of racetalk in perpetuating racism.

First, I argue that the main significance of racetalk is that it serves to reproduce the racist order. Racetalk is the interactional locus at which the process of structural reproduction occurs. Clearly, this involves a dialectical analysis. In analyzing the dialectical process, I draw upon Giddens's three structures of signification, domination, and legitimation to explore the different ways that racetalk works to reproduce the racist order writ large. The book is organized so as to give different attention to each structure.

Second, as discussed above, Bourdieu's theories about the power of language are highly relevant to the understanding of racetalk. Bourdieu recognizes that symbolic representations of groups of people exacerbate their structural positions. This dovetails nicely with Giddens's structure of signification. Hence, I combine these analytical frameworks in my dialectical analysis of racetalk.

Third, some people might think that Bourdieu gets a bit carried away with his metaphor of capitalism (see Thomson 1991), but I find it to be an insightful lens. I use a combination of Bourdieu's forms of capital: (a) Racetalk involves cultural capital in that it reflects one's experiences and exposure to various forms of education and cultural repertoires. (b) Racetalk involves symbolic capital as well. Members of a group who have more status might be able to express more pernicious forms of racetalk with few sanctions; likewise, persons with high status might be able to interrupt racetalk without penalty. Prestige and status—or symbolic capital—also accrue from effective racetalk. (c) It involves linguistic capital in that the way one invokes race through talk is a matter of style that may be more or less effective and garner more or less status. The simple choice of "nigga," "nigger," or "ghetto" in making an antiblack comment may make a great difference in whether or not the comment is well-received. I want to capture all of those dynamics in my use of capital. Therefore, I use the term "discursive capital" to incorporate the myriad meanings and influence exchanged through the use of racetalk.

Fourth, the concepts of positionality and intersectionality (Collins 2000; Delgado and Stefancic 2001) are useful for understanding the uses and implications of racetalk. The race of the speaker and that of her/his audience, for example, matter when understanding the ways that the racetalk arose from and worked within a given context. Thus, whenever possible, I discuss the positionality of the speaker in my analysis of the data.

Fifth, Bourdieu's concepts of the habitus, doxa, heterodoxy, and orthodoxy offer insight into the ironies of the ways that racetalk works. In modern society, the doxa—or taken-for-granted ideology on race—is rhetorically antiracist. Using Habermas's framework, this doxa would indicate that racetalk is not salient to the lifeworld. However, Bourdieu's work allows for subversive power dynamics through which individual markets might receive and nurture racetalk. Indeed, extrapolating from the critical school, I argue that proracist talk reinforces the position of the elites in the doxa by shoring up divisions among different racial and ethnic groups. If all racial and ethnic groups were to unite as a class, for example, then the elites would surely be threatened. Thus, racetalk benefits elites by maintaining interracial/interethnic boundaries that allow differential wages, educations, and levels of health care to persist without viable critique (Fine and Weis 1999). We seem to have a false doxa, a façade to mask the continued racist structure underneath. The orthodoxy used to enforce the doxa seems more symbolic than potent. This irony impacts the ways that racetalk is sanctioned, as we shall see.

Last, critical race theory—in particular the work on the First Amendment (Matsuda et al. 1993), but also the legal storytelling (Bell 1992)—illuminates the powerful connection between talk and action. Racetalk is not confined to the interactional level. It justifies racist practice, which reinforces racist structure, which engenders future racetalk.

MOVING ON

In the next three chapters, I use Giddens's conceptualization of a structure of signification to describe and analyze racetalk. In particular, racetalk in these chapters is used to construct symbolic categories of people according to color, each of which is located in the racist structure. These differ from traditional racial categories in that they are socially negotiated signifiers attached to people on their perceived value and status. In these chapters, people construct the significations of whiteness, brownness, and blackness.

NOTES

1. Despite my commitment to writing to readers outside of sociology, this chapter focuses on abstract theories and concepts. It is less accessible than I would like, but the concepts remain central to the following chapters.

2. Although the critical school has been called a failed paradigm (Greisman 1986) and an analytical dead end (Habermas 1984)—even by some of its proponents—I find many of the concepts and analytical frameworks to be useful in understanding racetalk.

3. To make sense of the critical school, it would be useful to provide some background on Marx's major argument about the injustices of capitalism.

In a nutshell, Marx (1867) was concerned about capitalism as he observed it during industrialization. Marx argued that capitalism is an oppressive system in which one class exploits and alienates the others in order to amass great wealth. In particular, capitalism consists of three major economic classes: the capitalists, the proletariat, and the lumpenproletariat. The capitalists are the people who own the means of production: the factories, the transport systems, the capital for investing, and so on. This is a very small group of people who control the purse strings. They do not produce anything themselves, but rely on the labor of others to produce goods and services. The proletariat are the workers. They only thing that the workers own is their labor power, or the ability to work. They sell their labor power for a wage. The lumpenproletariat are also known as the army of the unemployed who serve as a constant threat to the proletariat. Capitalists can say, "Keep working and stop complaining, or we will fire you and hire the unemployed. They will be happy to work for lower wages."

To Marx, this system was inherently oppressive and unfair. Without the workers, the owners would have nothing. Yet owners do not pay the workers an equal share of the value of the products that they produce. Wages are a fraction of the profit value culled by the capitalists once products are sold. Yet workers have no choice—they have no leverage and they are constantly threatened to go along or get along. Marx said that work in a capitalist system was alienating in four ways: it alienated (separated) workers from the product in that they usually could not use what they made at work, unless they purchased it. It alienated workers from the process, because the workers did not get to influence the production techniques or innovate in any way. The workers were alienated from each other because they were rarely permitted much interaction. Collaborative work slowed down the production process, and it also offered opportunities for workers to bond, compare wages, and perhaps unite against the capitalists. And last, capitalism alienated workers from themselves. Industrial labor discouraged free, creative thought among workers. Instead, workers spent their days engaged in repetitive, unskilled tasks that were easily passed on to the next faceless worker. In this way, capitalism separated workers from their "species being"—the creative energy that made them humans rather than animals. To Marx, this was an immoral economic system.

Marx believed that the end of capitalism was inevitable. No system could go on exploiting and emiserating workers without the workers rising up. Marx argued that capitalism contained the seeds of its own destruction. Workers had to work together in order to produce goods. In so doing, they had to notice the gross disparities between the capitalists and themselves. They would grow restless and, eventually, they would join together as a class and throw off the chains of their oppression, demanding an equitable economic system where workers received fair value for their labor power.

4. Herbert Marcuse (1964) expands the notion of hegemony, seeing it as related to modern technology. Technologies like television—and computers today—lull people into a state of unconsciousness. Critical thinking evaporates, and people are more concerned with who will win *Survivor* than how many people have died in Afghanistan and Iraq since 9/11/2001. Of course, it is also much easier to find out who won *Survivor* than it is to find out any comprehensive information about post-9/11 activities abroad. This is due in part to the media monopoly (Bagdikian 2000), working with the power elite to maintain a state of noncritical thinking that insulates those in power from criticism. The television, according to Marcuse, is a brilliant tool to pacify the masses—a technological form of Aldous Huxley's (1998) "soma."

5. A major structuralist theme runs throughout all dialectical theories: history has been imprinted upon the modern world in durable ways. Emile Durkheim (1895/1964)—a "father" of structuralism—argued that social life consists of "social facts," which are norms and values that exist external to and coercive of the members of society. Social facts—like systems of law and kinship—exist before we are born, and they will continue to exist after we die. As such, history endures, even though actors come and go. The structure seems permanent, because we often fail to recognize that it is socially constructed by human beings. In other words, it is reified.

6. Evidence indicates that blacks are followed even in nonaffluent stores (see St. Jean and Feagin 1998, for example). Blackness alone seems to be indicate to many people that a person is likely to disregard the social order.

7. In this way and others, Bourdieu differs from Habermas (1984), who seeks an ideal form of communication in which power dynamics are leveled.

8. Essentialism means that a person's experiences and identity are reduced to a singular, biological essence. Essentialism is rejected by most sociologists as well.

THE STRUCTURES

4

THE STRUCTURE OF SIGNIFICATION

Whiteness

The play of light on dark is the foundational trope of modern culture.

—Charles Lemert (2002, 27)

This chapter is the first of three addressing what Anthony Giddens (1984) calls the structure of signification. Recall from the previous chapter that the structure of signification serves to code the symbols that we use to make sense of the social world. Signification involves the construction of meanings that provide order. They help form the basis of domination as well as the ideological justifications for inequality. Signification defines the habitus of a particular time and place. In this chapter, I examine the signification of whiteness, as negotiated and reified through racetalk. The signification of whiteness matters for our understanding of racism in that the ways that whiteness—the dominant racial status—is defined "will shape intergroup relations, political agendas, and the dynamics of group mobilization" (Doane 2003, 12). As with other structures, signification incorporates our historical memories. Modern significations of whiteness build upon the past conceptualization of it, evolving but maintaining the imprint of time. When examining whiteness, then, it is necessary to first discuss the importance of whiteness in the American experience.

Whiteness as a theoretical construct has been much pondered in sociological scholarship (see Doane and Bonilla-Silva 2003; Fine et al. 1997; Frankenberg 1993; and Rasmussen et al. 2001 for examples). Whiteness has been described by Ashley Doane (2003, 7) as a "hidden identity," due to its dominant status:

> The "hidden" nature of whiteness is grounded in the dynamics of dominant group status. As a sociopolitically and numerically dominant group, whites in the United States have used their political and cultural hegemony to shape the racial order and racial understandings of American society. Historically, white-dominated racial understandings have generally focused upon the characteristics (i.e., "differences") of subordinate groups rather than the nature of whiteness. This emphasis by whites upon the racial "other" has gone hand in hand with the politically constructed role of whiteness as the "unexamined center" of American society. Because whites have historically controlled the major institutions of American society, they have been able to appropriate the social and cultural "mainstream" and make white understandings and practices normative.

In other words, whiteness hides because it is doxic, the hegemonic standard by which everyone else is measured (Bourdieu 1977).

Ruth Frankenberg (2001, 76) cautions us not to dismiss whiteness as the invisible, unmarked norm. Rather, we should examine the ways that it is marked in ongoing ways. She offers eight ways in which whiteness is ever-present in the social world:

1. Whiteness is a location of structural advantage in societies structured in racial dominance.
2. Whiteness is a "standpoint," a location from which to see selves, others, and national and global orders.
3. Whiteness is a site of elaboration of a range of cultural practices and identities, often unmarked and unnamed, or named as national or "normative" rather than specifiably racial.
4. Whiteness is often renamed or displaced within ethnic or class namings.
5. Inclusion within the category "white" is often a matter of contestation, and in different times and places some kinds of whiteness are boundary markers of the category itself.
6. Whiteness as a site of privilege is not absolute but rather crosscut by a range of other axes of relative advantage or subordination; these do not erase or render irrelevant race privilege, but rather inflect or modify it.
7. Whiteness is a product of history, and is a relational category. Like other racial locations, it has no inherent but only socially constructed meanings. As such, whiteness's meanings are complexly layered and variable locally and translocally; also, whiteness's meanings may appear simultaneously malleable and intractable. The relationality and socially con-

structed character of whiteness does not, it must be emphasized, mean that this and other racial locations are unreal in their material and discursive effects.

Frankenberg's eight points indicate the ability of white elites to manipulate the doxa in order to keep whiteness hidden. Like racetalk, whiteness hides in plain sight. As Frankenberg writes, "More shocking than the recognition of whiteness's existence is the idea that it is ever *not* seen" (76). She argues that refusing to see and name whiteness is an act of denial on the part of those who benefit from its existence.

Compounding this denial is the colorblind political rhetoric that (a) racism no longer exists; (b) whites are no longer the oppressors; (c) indeed, whites now are the victims of reverse racism (see also Bonilla-Silva 1999, 2001). In this context, a new orthodoxy has emerged: people who critique racism become accused of being racists themselves. Seeing color and naming white privilege become equated with racism, thereby sanctioning any critical heterodoxy.

Delineating whiteness entails several challenges. First, we must step back from the taken-for-granted order and approach whiteness with new, critical eyes: I was blind, but now I see. Seeing is difficult, as Jonathan Warren and France Twine (1997) argue, because the definition of whiteness remains elusive. Whiteness is fluid rather than fixed in nature. As Doane (2003, 10) also states, "historically, 'whiteness' has exhibited tremendous flexibility in redefining itself and group boundaries in order to maintain a dominant position" (see also Doane 1997). For example, when white immigrants came to the United States they were not automatically accepted into the protective fold of whiteness. As discussed in a previous chapter, the Irish were even called "white niggers" when they competed with other "real" whites for jobs (Takaki 1994). Italians were seen as whites, but still experienced significant mistreatment due to their devalued ethnicity (Guglielmo 2003). Before 9/11, many Middle Easterners were accepted as honorary whites.

Second, when we recognize and name whiteness as a tool of the powerful, we must be prepared to deal with racist orthodoxy that is used to sanction the inquirer. Shifts in the habitus have had powerful effects on the average person's perception of racial dynamics in the United States in recent years. For example, changing demographics have been a cause for alarm among whites, who see themselves as soon to be outnumbered. My university students continue to believe this whites-as-minority rhetoric, and they openly challenge me when I assure them that 75.14 percent of the U.S. population is indeed still white (according to the 2000 census). Even after I take them to the census website, they contend that the numbers must be inaccurate. Chip Gallagher

(2003, 383) argues the there are two major reasons why whites miscount people of color:

> (1) They believe that their social status is diminished when they share space with racial groups they perceive as being socially stigmatized and (2) the lack of physical or social contact creates the impression that these groups are larger and constitute a potential threat to white privilege.

Whites readily buy into the perception that they are being crowded out, leading to what I have called "white fright." White fright engenders and legitimates the shoring up of racial boundaries (see Myers 2003). Howard Winant (1997) argues that, within this context, whites feel confused and displaced, despite their continued dominance—a state that he refers to as "white racial dualism."

Warren and Twine (1997) point out that the fluidity of whiteness helps to protect whites from becoming the numerical minority. Dominance has its perks—one of which is the power to (re)define oneself and the boundaries to one's own group (Collins 2000; hooks 1994). If whites' numbers ever get too low, then they can change the definition of whiteness to let others in. There is nothing inherently "real" about whiteness—it is merely a statistical category. The U.S. government has begun to make whiteness an option for some groups of people. For example, in the 2000 U.S. Census, 47.89 percent of Latinos self-identified as whites. As Warren and Twine argue, when whiteness is an option, many people will choose it even if their choice is not welcomed by the dominant group. Indeed, as will become apparent in later chapters, merely claiming membership to a group does not necessarily translate into the accumulation of privileges associated with that group.

But not everyone is even given the option to self-identify as white. A major element of the power of whiteness is its ability to exclude others from its privileges. As Frankenberg (2001, 75) argues, whites "have through history named themselves in order to say, 'I am not the other.'" Michelle Fine (1997, 58) argues that "whiteness is actually *coproduced* with other colors, usually alongside blackness, in symbiotic relation" (emphasis in original). More pointedly, Warren and Twine (1997) assert that whiteness is always defined *in opposition to blackness*. The valorization of some other groups is flexible. Again, some people may be considered more or less "white" over time, and allowed into the ranks of whiteness by the dominants in an attempt to shore up the percentage of whites and thereby reinforce their supremacy. However, most blacks will continue to be excluded from the ranks of whiteness. Even black/white biracial people tend to be categorized as black (Hunter 2002a; Rockquemore and Brunsma 2001).

ANOTHER CAVEAT

This discussion of the flexibility of whiteness may imply—incorrectly—that whiteness is "arbitrary and whimsical" (Duster 2001, 115), and therefore not the powerful force that I argue it to be. Thus, I provide another caveat: whiteness is flexible in order to maintain its dominance. It is not so flexible as to become meaningless in any immediate future period of time. As Troy Duster (2001) asserts, whiteness is a structurally legitimated and enabled tool of the powerful that endures over time. As with tax laws, flexibility indicates loopholes to be used to benefit the powerful. Such loopholes do not operate in ways that will revolutionize the racial regime for the good of the whole.

Whiteness is a fortress designed to seal off privileges for some over others. White fright keeps out intruders. In this book, I look at how everyday people construct whiteness—both from within its fortress and from outside the gates. The walls are rebuilt every day by individual actors, even though most people are unconscious of their artisanship. The consequences of that process become apparent as this book progresses. By exposing the hegemony of whiteness as a structure of signification, this chapter contributes to the overall body of whiteness studies, whose goal is to help "to 'destabilize' white identity—to expose, examine, and challenge it" (Anderson 2003, 25). Margaret Anderson (2003) asserts that most literature on whiteness ignores the "mechanisms" and "sites" of racial domination and subordination. This chapter helps to fill the gaps in the literature by examining the ways that whiteness is signified through racetalk, both by whites and by people of color. In their racetalk, whites construct an archetype or trope of whiteness that is at once self-aggrandizing and—occasionally—self-deprecating When whiteness is addressed by people of color, they too see whiteness as distinct from other categories. Sometimes they see whiteness as a desirable status, but most often they are highly critical of whiteness and its social implications.

THE CONTRADICTORY TROPE OF WHITENESS

Through racetalk, subjects in this study—whites and people of color—addressed and negotiated meanings of whiteness. The overall picture of whiteness was contradictory. To be white was to be a boring, uncoordinated, overindulgent hedonist. Whiteness connoted sloth, filth, and disrespect. Yet, simultaneously, whiteness was a status to be respected and protected; whiteness embodied power as well as flagrant abuses thereof.

As Frankenberg's and Doane's work might have predicted, whites in this study seemed to have difficulty identifying the importance of whiteness. For example, Missy (white) recorded this incident:

> I was at my Mexican friend's house and her husband, Jesus [who is also Mexican], was talking about a guy at work. He said, "This white guy at my work . . ." I said, "Why does he have to be white?" He said, "Well, he is white." I said, "Why can't you just say, some guy at work." Jesus said, "Because it makes a difference."

To Jesus, the man's whiteness affected the context of his story and helped to make sense of the encounter that he planned to describe. For him, whiteness was more than a demographic descriptor—he used it as an analytic, explanatory factor. Missy, who avowed colorblindness, took offense to his problematizing whiteness. She bristled at whites being singled out, and she denied its significance. As Peggy McIntosh (1988) tells us, this is a prime example of white privilege—the ability to deny the significance of whiteness. However, Jesus held his ground and assured Missy that whiteness is always relevant.

In general, there were several competing significations of whiteness delineated within the racetalk in this study. I will discuss the various meanings associated with whiteness, ranging from benign to threatening.

The Soullessness of Whiteness

In much of the racetalk in this study, whiteness was seen as devoid of character. Whiteness meant blandness. Bland food, as Missy (white) documented:

> One of my black friends is married to a white girl. I told my roommate that he was complaining about how sick he was of his wife's cooking because all she cooked was baked chicken. My roommate said, "He shouldn't have married her because she doesn't know how to cook soul food."

Bland clothes, as indicated in this incident recorded by Serenity (black):

> Jade (black) was getting ready to go out shopping with her girlfriend, Talia (black). She couldn't decide what shoes to wear. She searched her whole closet and then her roommate's closet, but she couldn't find the perfect pair. "Talia, put on those white girl shoes." Jade said, "What are white girl shoes?" Talia said, "Those plain white ones in your closet."

And—most frequently—bland culture, as Rori (white) documented:

> I asked my boyfriend if he thought he was a good dancer. He said, "I like to think I'm a good dancer." I asked why. He said, "Because I'm white."

Rori's boyfriend used the stereotype that whites cannot dance in order to make fun of himself. Later, Rori was able to observe her boyfriend dancing at a wedding reception: "Jason (white) and his friends commented on each other's dancing abilities, and my boyfriend called his, 'white boy dancing.'" Rori's boyfriend used whiteness to excuse his poor moves—as a white man he should not be expected to be very good at dancing.

In a similar vein, white music was thought to be bland and soulless. Here, Roger (white) recorded an incident that occurred while his white roommate was watching a TV commercial: "It was making fun of that 1980s song "Karma Chameleon" by having a bunch of different people sing different parts of it. My roommate said, 'That is the whitest song ever!'" White, here, implied uncool or embarrassing. Blueangel (black) also recorded an incident in which "white" music was lampooned. Blueangel went to the taping of a *Jenny Jones* show, and they were waiting for the taping to begin:

> They played music in the studio, so people began to dance. At one point, the audience producer, a white male, started picking people to come on the stage audience. He picked all black audience members. At one point, they started playing a song called "Dooky Booty," and more black audience members ran onto the stage. When the song was over, the producer said to the whites in the audience, "You might not know what just happened, and you might feel a little uncomfortable. That's OK, because we are white and it's not for us to know." Then he said, "Let's put on some music more for us." Then country music came on. Everyone started to laugh.

Country music—music associated with whites, even though many whites may not be fans—was seen as unenjoyable if not laughable in contrast with the interesting, energetic beats of music associated with blacks. The producer was joking, but his humor indicated that whites cannot relate to nonwhite forms of entertainment. Whiteness is cultural vacuity.

In a final example, this incident recorded by Serenity (black) again showed the conceptualization of white singing and dancing as a reason for ridicule:

> [I was] sitting in the lounge in the dorm doing my homework, a group of [black] people were having fun watching television, so I decided to join them. They were going through the channels and stopped a country video and started laughing loudly. Someone said it looked like a broke down N'Sync video. Someone else said, "Why don't those people just stick to line dancing?"

Whites were the butt of the joke. The stereotype of whites as clumsy, uncoordinated dancers was an old one, but it lived on in contemporary racetalk.

Other racetalk indicated that the white party scene in general was problematic. Rachel (white) recorded this incident:

> I was sitting in one of my classes waiting for the teacher to arrive when some black students behind me were talking about a new club opening in town. One girl said, "It's just gonna be some gay ass white folk."

Consider as well this incident recorded by Maggie (Latina) at a party:

> Mayra (Latina) walked in, visibly upset. I said "What's up, Where are you coming from?" Mayra said, "From some party." I asked, "How was it? Was it fun?" Mayra said, "Hell no. It was a bunk ass white party." Everyone sitting around Mayra shh-hed her, pointing to the whites in the room. Mayra said, "oops." Marco (Latino) said, "It's cool. Now they know how it feels to be us all the time. The minority." (laughing)

In both incidents, people of color openly—in front of whites—expressed their disdain for the white party scene. They did not explain why, but their distaste may have been related to the bland music and dancing associated with whites and white parties. This talk is also a form of resistance: it points out the paradox of a white-dominated culture that has no soul of its own.

On a related note, there was a recurring conceptualization of whiteness among people of color: whites as binge drinkers. Take these two examples from Precious's (black) field notes: "The weekend of homecoming, my friend, Sam (black), called and left me a voice message saying, 'Let's go tailgating like the white people.'" Sam sincerely did want to go tailgating, but the way that he invited Precious indicated, in a playful manner, "This is not something we usually do—it's what the whites do." Later, Precious recorded a similar incident: "David (black) and I were getting drunk and he said, 'I feel like the white people on Thursday night.'" David referred to the practice among many white students on campus to go out drinking on Thursday nights. While both blacks and Latinos in this study drank alcohol, their racetalk associated overindulgence with whites.

Whiteness meant wimpiness. For example, Roger (white) overheard two muscular black guys lifting weights at the gym:

> One guy was spotting the other and he was saying, "Come on, lift! Even a scrawny white boy could do that!" His lifting partner struggled to lift 220 pounds, and I was doing 160.

The insult of weak whiteness was used to goad this man into lifting more weight. This comment was effective in part because it appealed to his masculinity—do not be a wimpy white guy—as well as to the racial association of

weakness with whiteness. Race and other hierarchies are, of course, interconnected (Collins 2000). The comment also put Roger's own strength into perspective.

Whiteness was used by people of color to indicate general disapproval. For
example, Precious (black) overheard a black guy ask to borrow a book from a
black girl. She did not have the book that he asked for. Disappointed, he said,
"Look at you wit' your white ass."

Overall then, whiteness at its most benign level signified being out of touch
with cultural trends and being too self-indulgent (as with binge drinking) to
notice. The subtext in all of this racetalk was that whiteness was removed from
the rest of the social world. Indeed, as the producer on the *Jenny Jones* show
implied, whites may not even be able to successfully communicate with people outside of their race. This notion was echoed by the white director of a
graduate program whom Elizabeth (black) met with:

> We talked about the program and he asked me questions. Then he said, "I'm
> looking for students who are willing to question me, let me know when I'm be-
> ing too white." What in the world is being too white? He says that he's trying to
> attract more minorities.

The graduate director implied that, because of his whiteness, he might inadvertently offend or exclude minorities because he could not relate to them
very easily. Perhaps he had been accused of being whitecentric before, and he
was trying to be more inclusive. However, he did not clarify this to Elizabeth,
and she was not in a position to interrogate him. She left the meeting with the
message that this man saw his whiteness as a potential cultural handicap for
connecting with people of color. If nothing else, it was a ready excuse for any
politically incorrect foibles that he might commit.

Filling the Void: From Admiration to the Cooptation of Color

Above, racetalk signified whiteness as a cultural void, but it also revealed
ways that whites themselves borrowed the cultural stylings of other groups in
order to help fill that void. Through their admiration and cooptation of styles,
foods, and behaviors associated with people of color, whites sought to recast
whiteness as colorful, tasteful, and exciting.

Admiration.   Whites in this study occasionally admired other racial and
ethnic groups for their "colorful" ways of life. For example, Cher's (white)
white friend said, "I had a friend that was half white and half black. He grew
his hair out and it was awesome." The texture and color of this biracial person's
hair was unusual and interesting to Cher's friend—so much so that she remarked

upon it to Cher. Similarly, Jaime (white) recorded this incident in her field notes:

> I was telling a friend about my weekend riding along with the police. I said, "I got to go with two Mexican police officers and we got to go on translator calls and I got to hear Spanish. It was so cool!"

Jaime did not take note of the fact that members of the police force were being used to translate Spanish, rather than being used—as with English-speaking officers—to enforce laws. Instead, she saw the officers' work as a form of entertainment. Jaime described her second police ride-along to another friend:

> We stopped at a Mexican grocery store, and in front they sold corn on the cob. The police officer told me it was very good and he was gonna get one. I said I would try it too. We did, and it had parmesan cheese and chili on it. It was awesome! My friend said, "Leave it to a Mexican to show you the good food!."

Here, the Mexican officer's skills were expanded to include the ability to locate new and delicious foods. Jaime clearly enjoyed her experience with the officers. However, rather than remarking on the ways that the Mexican officers transcended racial boundaries through their police work, she focused on the expansion of her own cultural horizons that was made possible by her association with people of color.

Both Cher's and Jaime's field notes indicated that some whites were intrigued by other cultures. Other whites went a step further, seeing the presence of people of color as a resource for improving the white experience. Rori (white) recorded this incident:

> At work I asked Ron (white) whether he had any black people on his floor because I didn't. He said that he didn't either. We thought it was kind of weird that we weren't very heterogeneous. I said that I would like to have more black people on the floor to add a little much-needed diversity.

The implication here was that whites would benefit from experiencing diversity. This is probably true. However, Rori did not want black people around because she wanted to get to know them. Instead, she saw them as a way to provide a service for sheltered whites. Megan's (white) friend Andrew (white) made the same point:

> Sammie and her boyfriend, Andrew (both white), were putting together a basketball league and they asked my boyfriend, Ali, and his friend Charlie (both black) to play. I was at Sammie's and she was talking about it with her boyfriend, Andrew, telling him how excited she was that Ali and Charlie were playing. An-

drew said that he was too, because they would bring some "ghettoness" to the game and make it more interesting.

Again, Ali and Charlie were not welcomed to the team because they were good friends and talented players. They were stereotyped as "ghetto"—a racially laden term that associates blacks with street crime and poverty. Despite the underlying racism in this connection, Andrew apparently saw some entertainment value in the idea of "ghetto" blacks playing with bland whites. Charlie and Ali could "keep the game real."

In their admiration, then, many whites in this study "othered" the people around them as exotic, entertaining commodities. They did not truly see people of color as potential friends and colleagues, moving beyond a racial boundary. Instead, blacks and Latinos provided a much-needed splash of color to the landscape and a spice to the palette. Once whiteness was affected by color and spice, it seemed to evolve from a void into a vortex, drawing the cultural commodities of others toward itself for its own uses.

Cooptation In the racetalk in this study, whiteness was signified as coopting the culture of others. Many whites did not just admire from afar, but took for themselves the cultural signifiers of people of color. This was not a new phenomenon. Throughout colonial history, white imperialists entered into foreign lands only to abscond with newly discovered products, taken home to enhance the white way of life. Commodities like tea, salt, sugar, tools, jewelry, gold, fruits, and vegetables as well as skills like language, farming, and food preparation and storage were adopted, borrowed, and stolen by white colonists (Loewen 1996). American and British museums and zoos are filled with religious artifacts, architectural and artistic treasures, and rare animals taken from their homelands in the interest of enriching the dominants' culture.

Today, whites continue to coopt and commodify the culture of other racial and ethnic groups through their everyday behavior. As Gallagher (forthcoming A) discusses, whites wear FUBU—a name that means "For Us By Us," specifically demarcating blacks as the targeted consumers. Whites wear do-rags, and they cornrow their hair. They sport tattoos with Chinese and Native American symbols. Gallagher argues that these are the cultural spoils of colorblind ideologies. In other words, whites who adopt the color-coded cultural practices of others also attempt to claim, "I don't see color. I can identify with any culture that I want to without feeling guilty or stigmatized."

Why does this cooptation matter? Why isn't it the sincere erasure of racial/ethnic boundaries? Author bell hooks (1994a, 171) discusses the crossover appeal of rap music to white audiences in her explanation of a key problem with cooptation:

> In contemporary black popular culture, rap music has become one of the spaces where black vernacular speech is used in a manner that invites dominant

mainstream culture to listen—to hear—and, to some extent, be transformed. However, one of the risks of this attempt at cultural translation is that it will trivialize black vernacular speech. When young white kids imitate this speech in ways that suggest it is the speech of those who are stupid or who are only interested in entertaining or being funny, then the subversive power of this speech is undermined.

Cooptation is not sincere admiration of cultural expression. On the contrary, it involves the objectification and consumption of the context-specific meanings of others. This is done without permission or reflection, and without the goal of ultimately uniting with "the other." Greg Tate (2003) argues that white people have coopted "everything but the burden" from African Americans. Indeed, rather than alleviating the burden of racism, cooptation constructs caricatures that reify it.

In my study, many whites coopted the language typically associated with blacks. For example, Jaime (white) recorded this incident:

> I called my friend and when she answered I said, "Yo homie. What's up?" She just said, "Not much," because she's used to it.

Jonathan (white) and his white friends routinely greeted each other with, "What's up, my nigga?" The use of the term "ghetto" among whites was rampant in the racetalk. Whites adopted what they considered to be catchy phrases from African Americans' lexicon. But then they used them unreflexively, ignoring their historical roots and cultural ramifications. Indeed, whites in this study were confused when they were sanctioned for using such language, which I will discuss more in future chapters.

Gallagher (forthcoming A) argues that whites go beyond borrowing the vernacular to coopt the traditional cultural practices of other races and ethnicities. When this occurred in the field notes, racetalk among people of color emerged. For example, Precious (black) overheard a conversation between a black man and woman on the bus:

> The guy said, "I work with this white guy who has earrings that stretched his earlobes about two inches." The girl started talking about how piercing the earlobes in this fashion is a tradition in some African cultures. Then she said, "You should tell him, 'You're not in Africa, white boy.'"

Imagine a Christian wearing a yarmulke just because it matched his outfit. It is hard to conceive of this happening due to the overtly religious symbolism attached to the yarmulke. Yet white people are increasingly seen reflecting the cultural practices of Africans, such as piercing and wearing dashikis and pooka beads. The woman on the bus invoked the comment often made to blacks by whites: "Go back to Africa."[1] But the woman on the bus turned this comment around—pointing to the ironies inherent in the white man's behavior. Blacks were enslaved for hundreds of years, kept in a bestial state, utterly dehumanized and devalued except for their labor power. Yet in contemporary society—when so many whites deny the relevance of slavery for understanding American wealth, segregation, and politics—white people now romanticize and coopt African cultural signifiers. Another incident drove this irony home more clearly. In this example, Elizabeth (black) walked with a friend by a tanning booth center: "I laughed and I stated, 'They a trip. Don't like black people, but always frying their skin trying to look like us!'"

Shades of Whiteness

As already stated, there is tremendous diversity among all racial groups—including whites. Not all whites are equally powerful or equally positioned to take advantage of racial privilege. The racetalk in this study indicated that whites themselves recognized a hierarchy of whiteness, and their racetalk sorted whites into categories of varying status.

Ethnic Whiteness.   Racetalk, primarily among whites, ranked members of white ethnic groups lower than whites who were more Anglo. The signification of ethnic groups in the racetalk was not new or surprising. Poles were cast as idiots. For example, Precious (black) recorded this incident: "I overheard my friend's coach say, 'I'm just a stupid Polack from Minnesota, what do I know?'" Here is a similar incident recorded by Megan (white/Greek):

> I was at a classmate's house doing homework when her roommate came home. She told my friend a story about how this guy in her class did something so stupid and made no sense to her. She tried to make sense of it by saying, "I think he's Polish."

People from Mediterranean countries were stereotyped as greasy and hairy. Roger (white) captured several such incidents in his field notes. For example, in this incident, Roger was eating dinner with white friends from his floor. One said, "Look at that guy back there! He totally looks like a stereotypical Italian." Roger looked and said, "Shit, you're right! He's got the slicked back hair, the black leather coat, and even the gold necklace with the bull horns. That's crazy!" They then moved to another topic. In another incident, Roger and a couple of white friends were watching a television show in which a man had to remove his shirt. Jake, Roger's white roommate, declared, "Jesus, look at that guy! There's hair on his back! He looks like a Greek!" Another friend replied: "He sure is hairy." These stereotypes are commodified and reified in the media through programs such as *The Sopranos* and films like *My Big Fat Greek*

Wedding, making them readily available even to non-Greeks and non-Italians. In another example, Jaime (white) wrote this:

> I was going on my ride-along with the police and as we left the station, my [white] guy yelled to another cop who was hanging out: "Hey dago bastard, how ya do-ing?" The other guy replied, "How's that half dago ass of yours doing?"

There is a difference when members of an ethnic group make fun of their own stereotypes or use ethnic slurs among themselves. Jews, Greeks, and Poles often tease each other about their ethnic peculiarities. However, when a nonmember of the group uses the stereotype in order to differentiate and rank the ethnic group as less valuable, the nonmember is exercising the power of signification.

Most prevalent in the racetalk was the continued signification of Jewish people as stingy—and the term "Jew" was applied to anyone who was being careful with money, even if that person was not Jewish. For example, Estella (white) recorded this incident:

> I was talking on the phone to my friend Marie (white), and I asked her when Mary and Josie (both white) were getting home from Washington, D.C. Marie said, "I don't know. Probably tonight. You know what a Jew Josie is with her money. She hates spending it on stupid shit, so I am sure she will drag Mary back home soon."

Taylor (white) recorded this similar incident she observed while wandering into the furniture aisle at Wal-Mart. There, two white guys were looking at book cases:

> Guy A: Which one are you getting?
> Guy B pointed to the one that he picked.
> Guy A: Why not get this one? It's a lot nicer.
> Guy B: It is too expensive for me right now.
> Guy A: What do you mean it's too much? You hate to spend any money. You're tighter than a Jew.
> Guy B (laughing): Fuck off.

Both Marie and "Guy A" used the term "Jew" as an ethnic slur used to indict the conservative use of money of their peers. In this era, when Americans spend beyond their means on a regular basis, being frugal should be respected as disciplined. However, these racetalkers seemed to have been infected by consumerism as well as racism, and they used them in tandem in order to en-courage spending. Karl Marx might see this as evidence of the success of cap-italists in using racial and ethnic differences to perpetuate their own accumu-lation of wealth.

The denigration of Jews was revealed through the use of a new term, "Jew-bag." For example, in this incident, Rori (white) talked to her friend Ariel (white) about lousy boyfriends:

> I told her about my ex-boyfriend from high school and the nickname his friends had given him. I started out by saying how wrong it was to call him this, but they called him a Jewbag because he was so cheap. I said that he was very, very cheap, but that didn't justify them calling him that.

Rori flinched at the harshness of the term, even though she repeated it to Ariel. Jewbag seemed to go beyond a mere reference to ethnic identity by de-humanizing Jews. Indeed, it conjured up the term, "douche bag," a clearly crude epithet.

In the racetalk in this study, the negative repercussions of anti-Jewish stereotyping seemed more pernicious than the stereotyping of white Euro-peans. As we have seen throughout history, there is much sympathy for anti-Semitism. There was evidence in the racetalk in this study that anti-Semitism lived on. Roger's roommate Jake was especially anti-Semitic, finding the most nonsensical opportunities to make anti-Jewish comments. For example, Roger and Jake were watching a news segment about an investigation into corrupt banking practices. Jake said, "The Jews are probably taking [the money]." Roger noted that Jake laughed for a long time at his comment. When Jake learned that the movie *Traffic* was directed by a Jew, he said, "Fuck seeing that!" Jake heard the commercial: "Beef: It's what's for dinner." And he said, "Jews: It's what's for dinner." Although Jake was just one person, and he was clearly preoccupied with his dislike of Jews, we can look to history to find ev-idence that his sentiments were not outlandish or unique.

Even though people in this study delineated different shades of whiteness, in which ethnic whites were not as worthy, they did provide some exceptions to the rule. For example, at Thanksgiving, Cher's (white) aunt said this: "No dago is ever going to sit at our table. They don't eat traditional holiday food." Cher's cousin's husband, John, had been adopted by an Italian family. Cher's aunt made an exception for him, saying, "It's ok that John's here—he's not a real dago [because he was adopted]."

White Trash.   Another trend in the nuanced signification of whiteness was the distinction between a suburban-style, economically secure whiteness and what the racetalkers saw as rural and/or poor versions of whiteness. The racetalk contained disdain for poor white people in general. Roger (white) and his friends were particularly preoccupied with poverty among whites. In one incident, Roger called Marcy (white), his girlfriend, "white trash" because her family lived in a trailer park in Florida. On another occasion, he and Marcy were eating at KFC. He said, "We are white trash for eating this chicken."

Roger jokingly told Marcy to throw away a dead plant. He said, "Throw this damn thing away. Are we living in a trailer or what?!" While driving to a Mc-Donald's with friends in Indiana, Roger's friend commented that he would hate to live in rural Indiana: "There's nothing but ghetto homes, hicks and white trash. It would be terrible." Everyone in the car agreed that "It would definitely suck."

Here, the racetalkers invoked the term "ghetto" to indicate their disdain for white poverty. "Ghetto" is a term with a long racialized history. It was originally used to refer to the places where Jews were forced to live before being shipped to concentration camps during World War II. Later, it was used to condemn the quality of life in American housing projects during the 1960s. Although it was applied to housing projects in order to shame the government into improving the caliber of housing and maintenance, people quickly adopted the term as a code word for the projects. Over time, "ghetto" came to embody the ills of the projects. "Ghetto" eventually became associated with black people themselves, even though whites have always lived in housing projects across America. As shown through the racetalk in this study, "ghetto" was used frequently by whites to signify any object, place, or behavior as problematic. Although people applied "ghetto" to whites' behaviors as well as blacks', the term retained its racialized patina. Whites who were condemned as ghetto were declared contaminated by blackness, as I will discuss more fully in the following chapter.

Whites who did not live up to the American Dream of economic security, as well as the conspicuous consumption glorified in suburbia today, were signified as less white, less gleamingly valued than the elite standard. Class intersects with racial privilege (Collins 2000), leveling the privileges of some over others (Lipset 1981). Taken together, the racetalk in this study indicated an effort among people to nuance the signification of whiteness. Not all whites were equally valued. Some became contaminated for various reasons.

Reverse Discrimination

Although whiteness is theorized as "hidden" or "invisible," there are some times when whiteness is patently obvious—such as when a person is the only white in the room. Due to whites' demographic numerical majority, many whites will never experience being the only white person in a social setting—except by accident or by choice. Whites did not comment on the occasions when they were in the numerical majority. However, when they were in the minority, it was noteworthy to the whites who experienced it.[2] For example, Jaime (white) went to a class and told her boyfriend (white) about it:

I said it was very interesting being the minority since I had never felt what it was like before, at least racially. There were about two other white people, the rest were black, or Kenyan, or African. It was a cool experience.

Similarly, Katie (white) recorded this incident:

My roommate Tim is Mexican and he belongs to a fraternity that is predominantly Latino. He says they accept all races, which is true. But he states that the one guy, John, is the only white guy in a brown house.

Some whites approached this situation as an interesting opportunity to take the role of the other—to see what it feels like to be "the only." The people cited above seemed to have positive feelings about their experiences. However, some were uncomfortable in situations where their whiteness marked them as unwelcome outsiders. For example, Sophia (white) reported an incident that occurred when she was standing in line at the bank on campus:

There was a girl passing out little fliers. She was black. The five people in front of me happened to be black. The girl handed the fliers to each other people in front of me. She was making small talk with them and everything. She came up to us and was about to turn away. I made eye contact with her. Then, reluctantly, she handed me one of the fliers and then just walked away. The flier was for a deejay party that was going on that weekend. It was weird.

Weeks later, Sophia had a similar encounter: two "black guys" were handing out fliers to other black students. This time, making eye contact did not work. Sophia was befuddled about being "left out" just because of her whiteness.

The racetalk in this study indicated that whites were sensitive about the ways that they were treated in relation to people of color. Harley's (white) friends debated why there was a black choir and not a white choir on campus. Cher's (white) friends fought about why there was a black caucus. Joan (white) recorded this incident:

I was watching TV with Belle (white) and Margie (white), and a McDonalds story came on the news. It was about Hollywood McDonalds, where they decorated the restaurant with famous stars. Most of the people being honored there were black. Belle said, "I think it's great that they are including (pause) African Americans, but they are discriminating against us [whites]. They should call it 'black Hollywood' or something."

Hollywood, then, should be the celebration of whiteness, not blackness. Blacks should get their own.

Such discussions portrayed blacks as insurgents attempting to amass special privileges that might unjustly usurp white resources. Indeed, whiteness—despite its drawbacks—was signified as the sole group deserving of advancement and reward. By this logic, advancement by people of color could not be meritocratic, since they were not worthy (not white). Such progress could only result from special treatment or "reverse discrimination." This argument was explained clearly by Blueangel's (black) friend, Andy (white):

> I was talking to my friend, Andy, about racism. I said that only white people can be racist. He said that racism is the acquisition of power by denying power to others. On a grand scale, white people are racist. But that does not mean that minorities can't be racist against whites. Andy said, for example, "You know that I can play ball pretty well. When I go to the gym, I'm usually the only white guy to play. Everyone else is black. Since the majority group is black, they have the power over me because I am the minority. They would not choose me [to play]—not because of my skills, but because I was white. That was an act of racism because they had the power and they denied me any right to obtain that power."

Andy echoed the arguments made by many whites—that reverse discrimination occurs when blacks deny whites access to whatever whites feel entitled to do. For example, some whites expressed dismay that they could not say whatever they wanted to say. Gail (white) recorded this:

> I heard two African American guys talking in the hall. One said to the other, "Come here, nigger." This comment angered me because if I had said that, I would have been called a racist.

Gail was angry that she could not say "nigger" without repercussions. She felt that her freedom has been limited. In another example, a white man in Rori's class made an argument during a discussion of prejudice:

> He said that people today were too sensitive about politically correct terms. He thought that we should know by now what is and is not meant to hurt a person's feelings. This comment received a lot of sighs and one girl commented that she felt the opposite.

This man seemed to be saying, please assume that I mean well. On what basis should people of color make that assumption? Historically, there has been little evidence that whites as a group are trustworthy. This man worried that he was not being given the benefit of the doubt. He complained about having to work harder to make sure he was communicating effectively, which he seemed to consider an avoidable waste of time. He noted that his privileges had been limited as well: he could not speak as he wanted to without being expected to clarify his meanings. He seemed wistful for an ideal, colorblind society, where—ironically—his white privileges would be fully restored.

Many whites were on guard for a double standard for whites versus non-whites. Of course, nonwhites have been aware of this double standard for generations because it has worked in favor of the whites rather than the nonwhites (Golden 2003). However, in the current doxa in which advancements by people of color are suspect, whites were quick to assume that the needs and desires of people of color were unfairly given precedence above their own. They assumed "reverse discrimination." For example, Harley (white) reported this about her coworker on the student police patrol:

> Jerry (white) told me at work that he is sick of "them," save a few exceptions, saying that we owe them. He said he doesn't like that he can get hurt and it's okay, but he can't hurt one of them without all hell breaking loose. He is upset with people who expect overcompensation for something that is done and over with. His last statement was, "Let it go!"

Harley herself echoed these ideas in her field notes:

> I find a lot of black people I've met overcompensate in areas, and often put their suffering above others. I feel my anger rise when they say things like my ancestors oppressed theirs when it is completely untrue, simply because I am white. Many times I have felt discriminated against because I am white, like I owe them for the stupidity of whites in the past.

Indeed, it is a mighty burden to shoulder the legacy of white racism in this nation. Most whites would rather shrug off this responsibility as oversensitivity on the part of people of color who have failed to move on. Other whites expressed concern that they were not being taken seriously regarding racially charged historical events. For example, Katie (White) wrote:

> I have noticed that whenever I express my feelings about racism, I am told that I am ignorant because I never went through it. However, these college kids never went through slavery or civil rights movements either, and I feel that makes them prejudiced, as well.

Most of the time, such comments were kept among whites themselves. Occasionally, however, whites challenged people of color as to the fairness of their actions. For example, Serenity (black) recorded this incident:

> I was at work at the hotel desk. A white couple checked out. The total for their room was $60. They were still at the front desk putting their paper work away when a black couple came to check out. Their bill was $45. They paid their bill

and left, and the white couple were still there. The woman asked me, "Why was their bill cheaper?" She asked this in a rude way, implying that I gave them a better rate because they were black. I told them that their lower rate wasn't because of their skin color, it was because they were senior citizens. They just gave me a funny look and walked away.

The white couple merely "implied" that race was a factor in the discrepancy in the bills. Serenity inferred their meaning, based on her knowledge of racetalk and her past experiences as a black woman working in a white-owned and -managed business. We do not know if she was correct in her assumption, but her response seemed to satisfy the couple's curiosity.

Whiteness embodies privilege and entitlement, and with that comes exclusivity. What good are privileges if everyone can have them? As such, much of the white racetalk bemoaned the loss of whites' privileges in a time in which whites must share with others. Now that whites have been forced—sometimes through penalty of law—to take seriously the claims of discrimination by people of color, whites are no longer free to say and act however they please without facing consequences. As a result, many whites were highly sensitive to any loss of entitlements that they felt they still deserved.

White Supremacy: White as Right

At the most pernicious end of the spectrum of whiteness was the signification of white supremacy. White supremacy represented a version of whiteness that uncritically glorified the natural dominance of whiteness over other racial/ethnic groups. White supremacy took many forms: whiteness was equated with rightness, serving as the standard for the good life. It lurked in the standards used to measure "appropriate" behavior. For example, after cleaning up his room, Roger's (white) roommate, Jake (white), stood back and said, "There. Now it looks like a white person lives here." Similarly, Jessica (white) recorded a conversation between white friends Adam and David. David moved into a new apartment and Adam asked, "How is it, is it nice?" David said, "Well it looks like a white person lives there. Not like our house where it looks like a black person would live."

The use of "white as right" appeared in many different contexts. Barbara's (white) white friend "was describing her job, and she said, 'I am working like a white woman,' describing how hard she was working." When Roger almost rear-ended a car, his girlfriend said, "Jesus! Drive like you're white!" Catching the implied comparison, Roger took the bait and replied: "Bitch! I ain't white. Now shut yo' damn mouth!" Eliza (white) returned a plate she had borrowed from her neighbor (white). The neighbor, pleased to have the plate back, responded, "That was mighty white of you." Sena (Latina) recorded this incident:

I was at a bar with my [white] friend Anna who told me that one day she thought about and she admired me. She said that she admired me because I can date all race types and she can't. She said that the only people good enough for her to date are white.

Whiteness as goodness is not a new signification. Paul Kivel (1996) provides a list of concepts associated with whiteness throughout history, including pure, clean, civilized, honest, holy, and righteous. Contemporary whiteness maintains this luster even today. For example, Carmen observed a white teacher interacting with white preschoolers in a Sunday school class:

One of the group's activities was to discuss what sin means. The teacher used two sheets of paper: one was black and the other was white. She held up the black piece of paper and said that this was sin. Then she held up the white sheet and said something to the effect that this was goodness.

It is likely that these children did not catch their teacher's exact meaning—how does paper translate into salvation or damnation? However, Debra Van Ausdale and Joe Feagin (2002) illustrate the ways that white supremacy does sink into the imaginations of children—white and nonwhite—at a very young age (three to five years old), through various stimuli. Most of the white supremacist lessons that children learn are probably more subtle than this Sunday school teacher's curriculum. Still, as these ideas accumulate, they effectively communicate to whites that they are more valuable, more deserving than other races and ethnicities. At the same time, they teach children of color that they are less valuable and less deserving than their white counterparts.

In the data in this study, the supremacy of whiteness was celebrated in subtle and overt ways. Rocker (white), for example, wrote,

I saw a white dude with a shaved head with a lot of skinhead tattoos. He had one on his forehead that read, "SKINS." I thought about it and he has a lot of balls to wear that.

Rocker admired the bravery of this man to display his skinhead identity so publicly and permanently through a facial tattoo. Rocker's sentiment was powerfully prowhite. However, his views were not commonly expressed, even in the privately spoken conversations that are captured in these data.

Instead, more subtle celebrations of whiteness were the norm. An interesting example is the following. Flora (white) went to a high school football game in her town:

> Since it was the last home game and senior night, most of the town was there. Out of approximately 350 people that attended, only 1 person was black. There was a German exchange student attending the high school. I noticed that during the warm-up before the game, the players had their last names written on the back of their warm-up clothes. The German student had "German" written on his instead of his name. The fans wanted Harold (his name) to dance with the cheerleaders during the half-time show. The fans loved it. They were screaming, stomping their feet, whistling and clapping. The coach let Harold in the game in the last 10 minutes, and the fans screamed, whistled, stomped their feet and clapped in support until the game was over.

These people created a white mascot. There was nothing noteworthy about Harold except that he was from Germany. He was at once devalued for his ethnicity—they simply called him "German" rather than by his name—and literally celebrated for his whiteness. They raised him up for the glorification of the spectators.

White supremacy impacted people of color in this study. As Elizabeth (black) recorded in her field notes, her black friend was struck by an observation as they drove up Michigan Avenue in Chicago: "White people have everything." While this is not categorically true—indeed it is a gross overgeneralization—Elizabeth's friend experienced relative deprivation, and she was taken aback by the displays of white wealth that glittered along the "magnificent mile." Her comment indicated that she felt excluded from the possibility of sharing the spoils.

Taken together, whiteness was signified in a contradictory manner. It was seen as culturally bland and embarrassing. Yet, it was a blank slate ready to be painted with the cultural practices of others. The power of whiteness was underscored by the ability of whites to coopt and commodify the cultures of others with impunity. Indeed, much of the racetalk was geared toward the insulation of white privileges.

WHITE FOLKS ARE CRAZY LIKE THAT: THE DISSENTING OPINION

Despite the overall positive significations of whiteness, not everyone in this study was a fan. Indeed, the racetalk contained some heterodoxy, indicating a critique of whiteness among people of color, as well as among whites.

Heterodoxy among People of Color

People of color often critiqued the signification of whiteness in their race-talk. Some of the critique was minor. For example, Rachel recorded this minor complaint about whites: "I have a friend who is a DJ and who is Mexican. He always talks about my white friends who have multiple tattoos, and he calls them 'stupid hillbillies.'" Rachel's friend took issue with the tattooing trend among white college students today, but his heterodoxy was not very threatening. Indeed, he invoked a term used by many whites themselves. "Hillbillies" was the white version of "ghetto," referring to the white poverty in Appalachia. While whites may not have found the term flattering, it was not terribly offensive, either. Other racetalk, however, was more cutting. Serenity (black) recorded this incident:

> It was a stormy morning, and I caught the bus to class. I was one of the first ones on the bus. As we stopped at each stop, more and more people piled onto the bus. We came to the last stop, and ten drenched people got on. They were soaked from head to toe from the pouring rain outside. I was sitting next to this black girl and her friend was sitting directly behind her. They were holding a conversation across the seats. One of them said, "White people smell like dog when they are wet." All of a sudden, everyone that was white on the bus looked at them with a scowl. I felt bad because I was sitting next to them and I didn't want anyone to think I felt that way.

Whiteness stinks: a common complaint that has been documented elsewhere (see Russell and Wilson 1997, for example). The racetalk recorded by Serenity was rather public. The intent apparently was to embarrass the whites on the bus, reminding them that they were not entirely superior after all.

The counterhegemonic racetalk captured in this study pointed out the chinks in the white fortress. In the racetalk, white people were thought to be capable of all sorts of irrational acts. This sentiment ran counter to the notion of "white as right." Here is an excerpt from Precious's (black) field notes:

> Penelope (black), Johnson (black) and I were watching an action movie. There were scenes where a white man was torturing another man. Penelope said, "White folks are crazy like that."

In another example, Elizabeth (black) wrote about a seventy-degree day in February in our usually frigid Midwestern town. She was people-watching on the bus:

> This Black boy was walking down the road with no shirt and some sandals, and the Black girl sitting next to me said, "He look like a fool. He must think he white

walking outside like it's summer time." And she said, "You know they can't wait until it gets warm to bust out the summer gear."

Precious's (black) roommate Penelope (black) argued that whites drink too much alcohol:

> Penelope told me that she was in class and they [classmates] were talking about getting drunk. A white girl stood up and exposed her shoulder to show the bruises she got. She was so drunk at a bar that she was piggy-back riding someone, and fell off.

Penelope was shocked that this girl was so proud of bruises. She was even more shocked that the girl did not seem to regret having drunk so much. To the contrary, she treated her bruises like battle scars, to be admired rather than pitied.

In all of these incidents, strange, irrational behavior was attributed to race, to whiteness. Such behavior was not explained away according to individuals' idiosyncrasies. Instead, it was associated with an entire race of seemingly unpredictable, unwise people. Among some racetalkers, whiteness was useful for profiling what kinds of people would commit the most outlandish acts. Blueangel (black) worked as a residence assistant. She recorded this bizarre incident:

> Someone took a crap in the men's shower stall [in my dorm], and I was asking people if they knew or heard of anyone talking about doing that. Two black residents said that it could not have been a black person because we know better. They went on to say that it had to be a white person because they are the only people who find shit like that to be funny, and they're nasty enough to do it. I told them that I agreed that it had to be a white person.

Many whites might be surprised to learn that they were profiled to be such uncouth pranksters. Indeed, as we will see in the next chapter, many whites might have assumed that the perpetrator was black, based on the same habitus.

Whiteness was associated with filth by people of color, as in this incident recorded by Precious (black):

> Penelope (black) and I went to visit Sharrell (black), a close family friend. We took a different route to the house and didn't notice that we were knocking on the wrong door. We saw people moving around in the house, but no one answered the door. After a few minutes, we decided to call our friend on the phone to let her know we were there. We found out we were at the wrong house. When we got to the right house, Sharrell said, "My neighbors are white and they are dirty. I don't know how you could've mistaken my house for theirs! Mine would never be that dirty."

Whites were thought to be demonic, according to Sena's (Latina) field notes: "I was sitting with my friends Mia and Rhonda (both black) when they started talking about how white people are always out to screw blacks. They also went on to say that white people are devils." For many people of color, the cumulative effect of living with the racial regime led to anger. Amber (black) described this interaction with her grandfather:

> Today I was discussing with my family about dating out of your race. My grandfather told me that if I was to marry a white man he would spit on the invitation and disown me.

Occasionally, anger led to action, as in this incident recorded by Anastasia (black):

> I went to the mall with my friend Valarie (black). Valarie said that she and her grandmother were shopping and a white worker got an attitude with her grandmother. Her grandmother said that she hates white people. Valarie said, "They walk around as though we're supposed to move out of their way. I don't move out of their way." I said that was especially true at school. I asked her if she remembered the Martin Lawrence comedy special where he was imitating white people. Especially the part when [whites] are walking, they say, "Move out the way, Darky!" She told me about an incident where she was walking and a white person walked right in front of her and proceeded to walk slowly in front of her. She kept on walking on the heels of his shoes until he decided to walk faster. She said, "I bet he won't do that again!"

Valarie and Anastasia showed an accurate awareness of the way that many whites view blacks, as will be evident in the next chapter. According to the racetalk in this study, many whites indeed expected black people to defer, to move out of the way. Valarie resisted and retaliated. While her actions may have reified the negative image of blackness in the minds of some whites, Valarie stood up for herself.

Taken together, the heterodoxy among people of color signified whiteness as irrational and morally questionable—if not entirely morally corrupt. This is not to say that all people of color saw all whites in this manner. People of color might consider each person on a case-by-case basis. They might also make exceptions, as was evidenced in this incident recorded by Cheyenne (white):

> I was at a bar with my friend Tee (black). Tee came up to me, and she was aggravated about some guy who kept hitting on her. She said, "Man. White boys are some stupid motherfuckers." I said, "Hey—I'm white!" She said, "Yeah, but you're not white to me, you're different."

Although Cheyenne was neither amused nor flattered, Tee sincerely contended that she saw Cheyenne as an exception to the otherwise problematic category of whiteness.

Heterodoxy among Whites

Occasionally, whites were able to step back from white orthodoxy and offer counterhegemonic insight about the dialectics of white supremacy. Sometimes heteordoxic racetalk emerged when a white person witnessed the mistreatment of a person of color. For example, Hedwig (white) talked to Molly (white) about a coworker's behavior that she found troubling:

> I said, "I feel bad because Belinda (white teenager) is so obnoxious to Chuck (black adult). He's always telling me how she says stuff to him like, 'Hey Chuck, isn't it scary living in the ghetto! Word, Homie! Yo yo yo!' That shit pisses me off. She may be young, but she is just so ignorant." Molly said, "Now see, that kind of stuff makes me so mad that people can be that ignorant. Chuck is really just such a nice guy." I said, "Yeah, I agree. I think that he gets a lot of respect from people who work here. That's good for him, too, because he told me that, at first, no one would respect him because he's the only black guy that works here." Molly said, "Yeah. Everyone respects him a lot. He's smart, you know? He knows how to conform to the white rules." I asked her what she meant by "white rules." She said, "Well, you know. It's sad but there are a set of white rules. Chuck just knows how to act white. Who knows, maybe he acts differently when he's with his friends at home. But he knows that he has to act a certain way around here because he's the only black guy." I said, "Yeah. I see what you're saying."

Hedwig expressed empathy with Chuck, recognizing the demeaning racialization of him at work. Molly's responses skirted the line between critique and reification of racism. On the one hand, she asserted that Chuck "acted white." As such, the implication may be that Chuck had (a) betrayed his race in order to succeed at work and (b) was more likeable because he acted "white" rather than "black." If he "acted black," for instance, would he be less sympathetic when singled out by Belinda's racetalk? At the same time, Molly seemed dismayed at the existence of "white rules" that would prohibit a range of human expression. This complex incident indicates the potential for witnessing derogatory racetalk to undermine the hegemony of white privilege. Similarly, Megan (white) recorded this incident:

> Charlie (black) and I went to the gas station to buy packs of cigarettes. When I bought mine, the guy behind the counter put my cigarettes and my change in my hands. He thanked me. When Charlie bought his, the guy put his change and his cigarettes on the counter and didn't thank him.

This is exactly the kind of incident recorded by Feagin (1991) through interviews with middle-class African Americans. Many white people might not notice the subtle mistreatment. However, Megan noticed things other whites might not because she spent a lot of time in the black community—her boyfriend was black and she read a lot of antiracist material. When she witnessed small acts of prejudice, they fueled her antiracist lens. Jaime (white) recorded another incident:

> Michael (my white boyfriend) said that there was a guy, Lonnie (white), at work that he couldn't stand. Lonnie was talking about politics at lunch and he said, "I can't stand those minority groups. They're always crying about this and that trying to get preferential treatment laws for their own selves." Michael said that he didn't say anything to Lonnie, but that he didn't want to hang out with him and his wife any more. I told him that I understood.

Michael was so offended by Lonnie's comments that he curtailed their relationship. Perhaps in the future he will be emboldened to interrupt the racetalk itself.

Some of the heterodoxic critique of whiteness was more scathing, focusing on the structural elements of white supremacy. For example, Megan (white) recorded this incident:

> Reba (white/Assyrian) and I were talking about the different race classifications that are on various surveys that we fill out. She told me that even though she is Assyrian, which most people would check as "white, non-Hispanic," she can't check white because she hates white people. When she hears "white," she thinks of the ignorant, KKK, racist people and she doesn't want to be classified with them.

Of course, Reba was treated as white according to social practice, which means that she reaped the benefits of whiteness even if she did not celebrate white supremacy. Also, by checking "other," Reba confounded the measurement tools used by the federal government to bring attention to racial and ethnic inequities in the United States. Therefore, this act of rebellion may not be the most effective way to buck the system. However, Reba's discussion with Megan indicated a critical analysis of the category "white" for perpetuating racism *writ large*.

Much counterhegemonic racetalk was engendered during the recent war with the Taliban in Afghanistan. Estella (white) recorded this incident:

> Sharon and I were talking about the war in Afghanistan and the entire prejudice stuff going on in the world. She told me a story of a man who worked at a store in Dallas who was shot forty times just because he was from Afghanistan. She said, "Hate crime is what is going to do the damage. I hate that shit. Now there are children and a wife out there without a husband or a father." I said, "I know what you mean."

Rori (white) talked with her boyfriend, Jason (white):

> We discussed the events in Afghanistan and how scared he was of war occurring.
> He said the other countries in the Middle East were scared that the United States
> would start to become hostile to them as well because of religion, location, and
> involvement with Bin Laden [prophetic]. He said the countries in the Middle
> East don't like Americans. I replied that I could understand that, considering
> how we treat their customs.

She had a similar conversation with a friend in her dorm:

> I talked to Cori (white) on my floor about the bombs in Afghanistan. We agreed
> that we should be critical of anything happening now, looking at events as if we
> were reading them from a textbook in the future. She and I agreed that America
> is a country that feels its ways are correct and fails to recognize the ways of other
> countries and religions, as in Afghanistan. We both felt sorry for the victims of the
> bombings in that country because, like the people in the United States, they
> should be assumed innocent until proven guilty.

In the months immediately following 9/11, pro-U.S. orthodoxy was strong. Any
criticism of U.S. foreign policy was silenced with swift, angry response. When
people persevered and asked hard questions about the war, they often became
strongly empathetic with Afghanis as well as American soldiers.

This section indicates that some whites, as well as people of color, launched
heterodoxy against white supremacy. These racetalkers did not accept white
orthodoxy uncritically. They risked rejection by friends and family in their pur-
suit of an alternative perspective on race and racism. As members of the dominant group, their critique may have been convincing in that (a) they were insiders and therefore qualified to speak about their own positionality; and (b)
whiteness connoted authority, which might have given their remarks more discursive capital. Regardless, their racetalk indicated the potential for undermining the hegemony of whiteness as signified in this study.

CONCLUSION

Far from being devoid of color as the term connotes in conventional wisdom,
whiteness provided a patina rich with conflicting meanings—at once repug-
nant and magnificent. Those meanings were alive in each social setting
whether the actors involved acknowledged them or not. Peggy McIntosh
(1988) said this years ago when she described whiteness as an ever-present, often invisible knapsack of privileges that one carries everywhere. This study

shows that the contents of the knapsack of whiteness are complex. The data in this chapter indicate that—even if all of the privileges culled by whiteness were underplayed and/or even denied by those who benefited from them—*whiteness itself was not invisible,* neither to whites nor to people of color. As Frankenberg (2001) predicted, whiteness was ever-present and ever-negotiated through people's racetalk.

Within the racetalk, some forms of whiteness were more valuable than others. White ethnicities and poor whites had less status than nonmarginalized whites. These data indicate that there are multiple forms of whiteness and that there is a ranking system within whiteness, even though whiteness is the dominant status. R. W. Connell (1987, 2001) makes a similar argument about another dominant status: masculinity. Connell asserts that there are multiple masculinities, some of which are valued while others are devalued. The ultimate form of masculinity is called "hegemonic masculinity." It is the ideal standard by which all men are judged, even though most men will not successfully attain the status of hegemonic masculinity. It is used to exclude both women and devalued men from status and power. Whiteness seems to be signified in a similar manner. There is an ultimate form of whiteness—white as right—that is the standard by which other whitenesses are evaluated. Even if most whites are not white supremacists, the "white as right" standard denigrates less valued whites as well as people of color.

Doane (2003, 5) argues that we are currently undergoing a "crisis of whiteness: the continuing challenge to white supremacy and normative whiteness in social institutions and in American culture, and the withering away of white ethnic identities." Bourdieu might conceptualize this crisis as effective heterodoxy wearing down the power of the racist doxa. As in any conflict, the powerful can be expected to strike back, to invoke racist orthodoxy in order to maintain dominance. In the data in this book, we can see the interplay between heterodoxy and orthodoxy.

After examining the data in this chapter, however, we should ask ourselves, Is whiteness in crisis as Doane suggests? Or is any critique of the dominants considered so threatening as to invoke emotional language to quell it? Terms like "crisis" and "attack" imply that the dominance of whiteness is soon to be destroyed, putting whites on the defensive. Based on the content of racetalk on whiteness, we can see evidence of this defensiveness among whites. Yet, the critique of whiteness in the racetalk was not threatening at all. Whiteness incorporated dorkiness, drunkenness, abuses of power, and incompetence. This commentary was unflattering, but it was not an overwhelming heterodoxy.

However, the very existence of a critique of whiteness indicated that the hegemony of dominance had been breached. The commentary revealed a recognition that whiteness was visible, rather than hidden. Perhaps whiteness was not such a formidable foe after all. As we shall see later in this book, the perception among whites that they were under siege—despite their overreaction to mild critique—seeped into whites' consciousness in ways that continued to pit whites against other races/ethnicities.

NOTES

1. Indeed, a white man actually said this to a black woman in this study, as we shall see.

2. By the same token, people of color regularly experience being "the only" or one of the only minorities in a setting, whether they choose to do so or not.

5

THE STRUCTURE OF SIGNIFICATION

Blackness

This is the oppressor's language yet I need it to talk to you.

—Adrienne Rich (1974)

Reflecting on Adrienne Rich's words, I know that it is not the English language that hurts me, but what the oppressors do with it, how they shape it to become a territory that limits and defines, how they make it a weapon that can shame, humiliate, colonize.

—bell hooks (1994a, 168)

In *Teaching to Transgress*, bell hooks (1994a) discusses the paradoxes inherent when African Americans use the oppressor's language. She speculates that Africans who were brought to America as slaves feared the unknown language of their captors, but that they also saw it as a necessary tool to acquire in order to create community and resistance. The result was a fractured English that formed a counterlanguage—a source of empowerment in the face of severe adversity. She asserts (1994a, 170) that "using English in a way that ruptured standard usage and meaning, so that white folks could often not understand black speech, made English into more than the oppressor's language."

While hooks points out the empowering nature of resistance through language, in the end, this resistance was turned against people, used as evidence of "otherness." In this chapter, I examine the ways that language—both that of the oppressor as well the resistance—signified blackness as a structure that enabled and reproduced racial dominance. Racetalk in this study reified and innovated the blackness of our historic imaginations.[1]

THE BLACKNESSES OF OUR HISTORIC IMAGININGS

Throughout American history, the prevailing images of blackness have been largely negative. Slavery informs the habitus, providing the historical context of the negotiated meanings of blackness in American history, in which black people had to fight just to be seen as human beings. As a former slave, Sojourner Truth, demanded at the second annual convention of women's rights in Akron, Ohio, in 1852, "Ain't I a Woman?" (see hooks 1981). Conceptualized as property, animals, and perpetual children, African Americans have engaged in a steep, uphill battle in merely claiming a right to humanity. Marlon Riggs's (1986) film *Ethnic Notions* depicts the power of these controlling images brilliantly. The images have differed for black women and men.

Black women have been cast as mammies, matriarchs, welfare queens, black ladies, and hot mamas. These are often contradictory images, but they have in common a debasing, mythic quality that degraded black women and girls as a group. The signification of black women as such feeds into other structures of oppression. As Patricia Hill Collins (2000) argues in her analysis of these images, they serve to justify black women's oppression in America. Collins discusses each image in turn.

The mammy embodies the faithful, obedient servant, willing to sacrifice her own family, autonomy, and well-being in order to improve the lives of her white masters or employers. Examples of the mammy can be found in films like *Gone With the Wind* and *The Color Purple*.[2] She is supposedly well-loved by her white family, yet she is denied the same freedoms that her "family" enjoys. Mary Romero's (2002) interview data with domestic servants underscore this irony. The mammy may have authority in the house—she runs the kitchen, tends the children, maintains the order of the home. However, she is still a servant and she must "know her place" at all times. This image continues to affect black professionals today, who are expected to defer to white coworkers as well as employers, and they are expected to perform emotion-work (Hochschild 1985) without complaint.

When white people encounter the image of the mammy, bell hooks (1992) argues, they often find it appealing even though they do not recognize its roots. As an example, she relays an incident in which she and some white colleagues went to a restaurant for dessert. The first thing that they noticed in the dessert case were "a row of gigantic chocolate breasts complete with nipples—

huge edible tits" (61). Her colleagues burst into laughter, finding the whole concept charming and delicious. She problematizes their reaction:

> They do not see this representation of chocolate breasts as a sign of displaced longing for a racist past when the bodies of black women were commodity, available to anyone white who could pay the price. I look at these dark breasts and think about the representation of black female bodies in popular culture. (61–62)

The mammy persists even when we do not recognize her.

Another pervasive image of black women is the matriarch. She represents the black single mother who is held responsible for every problem within the black community including poverty and crime. She is seen as emasculating or even castrating to black men, thereby corrupting the strength of the traditional male-dominated family. In contrasting the mammy and the matriarch, Collins (2000, 75) writes, "just as the mammy represents the 'good' black mother, the matriarch symbolizes the 'bad' black mother." She is a failed mammy. In contemporary society, this image is used to sanction all black women as overly aggressive and unfeminine. The image also has negative implications for black people in general:

> Assuming that black poverty in the United States is passed on intergenerationally via the values that parents teach their children, dominant ideology suggests that black children lack the attention and care lavished on white, middle-class children. This alleged cultural deficiency seriously retards black children's achievement. Such a view diverts attention from political and economic inequalities that increasingly characterize global capitalism. . . . In this context, portraying African-American women as matriarchs allows white men and women to blame black women for their children's failures in school and with the law, as well as black children's subsequent poverty. (Collins 2000, 76)

The heart of this image reveals Americans' rejection—if not demonization—of black women as powerful.

Collins discusses the image of the welfare mother, or welfare queen. This is an image constructed as a backlash to black women's access to state entitlements that were previously unavailable to them. Although most government aid goes to subsidize programs that benefit middle class-to-wealthy Americans (Eitzen and Baca Zinn 2004), disproportionate attention is paid to welfare as a form of unfair, unearned advantage. Black women become the scapegoat for what is portrayed as a misuse of "hard-working, deserving" Americans' money. The stereotype depicts black women as having more and more babies in order to live off of the system at taxpayers' expense.

Collins ties the contemporary welfare mother image to the use of black women as breeders during slavery, which allowed white people to control black women's fertility and reproduction. Attempts to do so continued into the post–World War II era, when poor black women were often sterilized against their will. This image resembles the matriarch in that the welfare mother is a bad mother. However, they differ in that the welfare mother is not aggressive at all; indeed, she is lazy. Collins (2000, 79) argues,

> The welfare mother has no male authority figure to assist her. Typically portrayed as an unwed mother, she violates one cardinal tenet of white, male-dominated ideology: she is a woman alone.

This image provides a subtext to the legislation proposed in 2004 by President George W. Bush, which called for heterosexual marriages among welfare recipients.[3]

A related image discussed by Collins is the black lady. The black lady represents women who stay in school, pursue careers, and postpone starting families. This image comes out of the literature on the Black Club Movement (see Giddings 1996; and Shaw 1996), in which upwardly mobile black women sought respectability in society. Collins argues that, even though this image seems empowering, it, too, can be used to control black women. These women are seen as failing because they often do not marry. As she writes,

> This image seems to be yet another version of the modern mammy, namely the black professional who works twice as hard as everyone else. The image of the black lady also resembles the matriarchy thesis—black ladies have jobs that are so all-consuming that they have no time for men or have forgotten how to treat them. (81)

This image affects the ways that black men view professional black women: they might see black women as taking their jobs away from them, and they might see them as undesirable partners due to their association with emasculating independence. Collins (2000, 81) concludes that "when taken together, the welfare queen and the black lady constitute class-specific versions of a matriarchy thesis whose fundamental purpose is to discredit black women's full exercise of citizenship rights."

The last image discussed by Collins (2000) is the hot mama, jezebel, or whore. This image is a sexually wanton, perpetually available woman. She is both a sex object and an amoral agent in a society that says that women should be sexually passive. This image is the "nexus" of all other images: "Because efforts to control black women's sexuality lie at the heart of black women's oppression, historical jezebels and contemporary 'hoochies' represent a deviant black female sexuality" (81). It has been used to justify sexual assault by white men against black women for generations. Collins laments that this image has been adopted by black culture as well as white—as you can observe in music and literature. She "can't get enough," she is a "freak," and she is "masculinized" because her sexual appetite is more like a man's than a woman's (83; see also Collins 2004).

Many of these images were constructed generations ago, but their impact lingers. As Collins (2000, 69–70) argues,

> Even when the initial conditions that foster controlling images disappear, such images prove remarkably tenacious because they not only subjugate U.S. black women but are key in maintaining intersecting oppressions. . . . African-American women's status as outsiders becomes the point from which other groups define their normality.

Here, she echoes a major insight from Jonathan Warren and France Twine (1997): in order for other groups' privileges to have meaning and value, they require a foil. Black women's (and men's) denigration defines and protects the status of other racial and ethnic groups. Collins argues that these images are perpetuated by many social institutions, including schools, churches, and families, to the continuing detriment of black people.

The images of black men are degrading as well. Michele Wallace (1994) discusses major stereotypes of black masculinity, including the Tom, the Coon, and the Buck. Toms derive from Harriet Beecher Stowe's main character in *Uncle Tom's Cabin*. The image symbolizes passive, gentle, hard-working black men who were devoted to whites. They are the male counterpart to the mammy. In contemporary society, black men who succeed in jobs that have been traditionally reserved for whites are often dismissed as Toms.

Coons were happy-go-lucky buffoons, always dancing and clowning like children. This image was used during Reconstruction by whites to justify revoking privileges and positions of authority from newly freed blacks. Powerful whites at the time argued that blacks were too childlike and wild to properly run things, and that they would destroy the work accomplished by generations of "civilized" whites (Loewen 1996). Today, this image remains powerful: African American men are seen as too immature to settle down to raise families and keep jobs (see Anderson 1999). They cannot be trusted in demanding workplaces, and their white colleagues often assume that black men are only able to get such jobs through affirmative action rather than merit (Gallagher, forthcoming B).

The Buck was given notoriety in the film *Birth of a Nation*, a silent picture that featured a white man in blackface stalking a helpless white virgin. The virgin was so desperate to escape the predatory buck that she jumped from a cliff rather than submitting to him. His image was hypersexual and animalistic, striking fear into the hearts of white women and men. The buck image was used to justify lynchings of black men who were accused of threatening the purity of white women. Emmitt Till, for example, was brutally lynched after making the fatal error of whistling at a white woman (Davis 1983). The image of the black Buck remains alive and well.

Wallace (1994) also describes a fourth image, which she calls "black macho." This is a form of masculinity that glorifies patriarchal male dominance, often though violence. Violence and aggression are seen as the major resources available to men who have been denied access to more legitimate forms of masculine expression. These include owning property, working in professions whose earnings are enough to provide for families, and being able to protect women and children from want and harm. Although many poor white men have also been unable to attain legitimate masculinity (see Fine and Weis 1999), black men's inability to access it was institutionalized. Due to the legacy of slavery, black men were often denied access to jobs; employers preferred to hire black women, who were less expensive and deemed less threatening (Giddings 1996). Black men were often unable to earn a "family wage," making it difficult to measure up to the white middle-class standard of masculinity. Thus, in order to be seen as "real men," black men's masculinity became reflected in their bodies—the only resource to which they had equal access. Wallace's black macho is also a highly sexual image—always expecting sex, often coercing it from others. Wallace argues that this image was fundamentally embedded in the Black Power movement, which she asserts contributed to the movement's limitations.[4] Indeed, the shadow of Eldridge Cleaver looms within the black macho image.

There is much debate about the salience of these images within the black community. For example, hooks (1992) argues that black men and women have been outraged at the images of black masculinity over time, and they have resisted them. However, the images—embedded in the habitus—have sunk into their consciousnesses as well. Collins (2000) asserts that, when black men and women internalize such images of black men, heterosexual relationships and families are harmed (see also Walker 1983). It is clear that many white people have bought into the images wholesale. As mentioned above, pejorative images of black men justify discriminatory education, housing, and hiring practices, and they legitimate if not encourage violence against African Americans as a group.

Writer Brent Staples (1986) poignantly describes his realization at age twenty-two that his black male body communicated information to white strangers that he did not intend. White people saw him walking alone on the streets at night and they were afraid: they crossed the street to avoid him; walked faster if he was behind them; locked their doors if he walked past them at a streetlight. One night, he entered a jewelry store to browse, and the white salesperson went to the back room and reemerged with a large Doberman Pinscher on a leash. She refused to answer his questions and glared at him until he left. On another occasion, Staples went to work late at night to finish a project. He was chased to his office by the security guard, who assumed he did not belong there. Luckily, Staples's boss was also at work to vouch for his right to be there.

Staples concludes by offering a strategy that he uses to set white pedestrians at ease as he passes them by: he whistles Vivaldi and Beethoven tunes. Whites seem to relax when they recognize the classical, "white" music coming from this otherwise sinister character. Staples said that sometimes they laugh or even whistle along with him. Ironically—even though Staples has done nothing to intentionally make whites ill at ease—Staples interpreted it to be his responsibility to help whites relax, to assure them that he is not a villain. His race and gender embody the images of the Coon, the Buck, the black macho—white constructs forced upon black men in order to control them. Why is it *his problem* to allay their invalid fears, products of their own imaginations—what Charles Lemert (2002) calls "dark thoughts"? Most likely Staples acts in self-interest: if whites' fear of him escalates rather than abates, he might very well pay the price for their fear. He or someone who looks like him. The habitus is real in its effects even though it is a social construct.

In my study, racetalkers signified blackness in ways that built upon the foundation produced throughout American history to the present. Much of their talk reproduced or recast old images in a new and garish light. Racetalk among African Americans themselves both resisted and embraced these pejorative images of blackness.

OLD TROPES REMADE

The racetalk in this study modernized old images: from matriarch and Coon to freeloader and reprobate; from black macho to gangster; from Buck and hot mama to player and dirty ass bitch; from mammy and Tom to sellout. I discuss each in turn, but first I discuss the language used in the reconstruction of old tropes.

An Evolving Vocabulary

Within the racetalk, the vocabulary for invoking blackness was broad. Old slurs were used, including brother/sister, spook, coon, nigger/nigga, colored, and "those people." Other terms were morphed and updated. "Niglet" referred to anyone/anything Black. For example, a white male pointed at Cher's black cat and remarked, "Look at the little niglet." Its most common use was in reference to children. African Americans were still associated with monkeys, as illustrated in Roger's field notes:

> We were watching a chimpanzee on TV, and Sam said, "Shit! Look at that monkey!" So we all did and the chimp was running around and did a back flip and climbed a tree. Sam said, "How'd they get that Black guy to do that?" We all laughed.

This was an age-old form of degradation that lived on in today's racetalk.

To mask racial coding, people innovated. One person used "Bubblins" (shortened from "Bubblin' Brown Sugar") to refer to African Americans, and Baby Bubblins to refer to black children. The term "Canadians" was used by whites to refer secretly to African Americans. An inner-city teacher explained that she and her peers used it to refer to their black students; a police officer reported that he and his colleagues used it when talking about blacks over the radio. Several restaurant workers reported using "Bostons" or "Canadians" to refer to black customers—one server went to the kitchen as soon as black customers entered the restaurant (before they were even seated), and announced: "We're going to need some lemonade and chicken wings for the Canadians." Estella (white) recorded an incident in which white novices learned how to use the term:

Alyssa, Nicole, Somer, and Martie were all sitting at the table after work. They were talking about how much money they made. Alyssa said that her boyfriend, Tony, worked at a new upscale restaurant in town. Martie asked her if cheapasses came into his restaurant, bought tons of food, and left shitty tips. Alyssa said no. Tony made $200 there last night. Martie asked if he has ever bitched about the job at all. Alyssa said no. Tony said that even the Canadians leave good tips and are not Jewbags. Somer started laughing and asked, "Why do you call them Canadians?" Alyssa said, "Just an undercover word." Nicole said that her friends use that word all of the time. Tony calls them "Bostons." Nicole said, "I am going to use that word now because I think it's funny."

Katie (white) used the term "Canadians" herself, which she defended in her field notes:

> [At the restaurant where I work,] we refer to people who we expect not to tip well by certain names. These are Canadians (blacks), Puerto Ricans, Mexicans, and of course white trash. It is a philosophy at work that the "—cans" won't tip well, which for the most part is true.

Despite Katie's argument, however, the use of the coded language represented more than economic resistance among oppressed service workers. Instead, it revealed disdain for an entire group of people, as captured in this incident in Estella's (white) field notes:

> I was working Friday night and Alyssa (white) came up to me and Mark (white) and said, "Look at Matt (our white manager)." I asked what he was doing. She said, "He is talking to the Canadians." "About what?," I asked. Alyssa said, "They think that the computer charged them a higher gratuity than 15 percent. What dumb people who bitch about dumb things." Mark talked about his own table of Canadians too: "Canadians are always cheapasses, you know that. I waited on the same two for two weeks in a row, and the first time they bitched about the food and got it for free. Tonight they are bitching again but Matt said forget it because this is the third or fourth time they have come in and tried to get free food." Alyssa said, "What assholes."

"Canadians" was a term that freed whites to degrade African Americans without fear of being overheard and sanctioned. It had a covert cache that made it appealing in various contexts.

Most people did not employ an undercover code in their degradation of blackness, relying on more common slurs instead. Monty's (Asian) friends used "ghetto" to refer to something old or bad. For example, when microwaving popcorn, he said, "This might take a while. I have the most ghetto ass microwave in the world." Indeed, if people found any object remarkable, they often derisively associated it with blackness. For example, Carmen's white roommate informed her that her headphones made her look "like a nigger." Later, the same woman proclaimed that her new shoes made her look like she had "nigger feet."

Body parts were racialized as well. For instance, Carmen's white friends bantered: "Audrey began to rip on her roommate about how big her butt was. She called her butt a ghetto butt; her butt might rip through her pants." Flora (white) required knee surgery, and she had two options: surgically stretch her own ligament to fit the kneecap, or receive a donated ligament. She asked her white friend Tony for advice. When Tony had knee surgery, he chose the donated ligament. The ligament failed, as he explained: "The first donor ligament came from a lazy Black man. Blacks are so lazy, even their body parts are lazy. Their parts don't want to work either."

Even smells were racially coded. When Sophia's family's van was stolen, a white police officer found it abandoned and returned it to them, saying, "You could tell it was one of them. You could because of the way it smelled." Then he gestured to his hair on his head. He mumbled something under his breath about Afro-Sheen. In another incident, Maggie (Latina) talked to Maria (Latina) about their roommates' annoying habits. Maria said, "I don't want to room with Frida (Latina) again next semester. I don't know what to do." Maggie answered:

> Well it's on you. If you think you got it bad and are willing to take some chances, then go for it. Unless you have someone in mind. I don't think you have it bad now. You are both Hispanic and have a lot of the same habits. She's clean and doesn't stink.

Maria replied, "I'm not a racist and I don't want to sound like one, because I'm not. But I don't want to get stuck with a black girl." Maggie introduced the issue of cleanliness: she's clean and doesn't stink. Intuitively Maria equivocated poor hygiene with blackness. This exchange speaks to the effectiveness of the racist habitus. Monty (Asian) recorded another incident:

> One of my roommate's girlfriends spends an excessive amount of time in our house. I asked her, "Don't you have your own place to stay?" I smiled and said it in a joking manner. She looked at me and said, "I live in the dorms, and my floor smells terrible. I live on a floor with all black people and you know they have that smell. Why couldn't I live on a clean floor?" I thought this girl was sweet and innocent. I never figured her to be a racist. I asked, "You're kidding right?" She responded, "Yeah, right."

Blackness stinks. Here, Monty showed that even "sweet and innocent" people have been affected by the pejorative trope of blackness.

As with questionable hygiene, anything done poorly could become a signifier of blackness. Taylor (white) recorded this incident:

> I was visiting my (white) neighbors one evening when their little girl started crying because her ankle strap on her sandal broke. Her dad said for her to bring him the sandal, and he told his wife to get him some black electrical tape so he could nigger rig it.

"Nigger-rig" referred to a slipshod method of fixing something. It included cutting corners and sloppy craftsmanship. The term conjured up the coon again—a worker who had no pride in his work, but who just wanted to get done as quickly as possible. Katie (white) reported a similar incident from the restaurant where she worked:

> I was in the back and Sean (white) was having a cigarette and I asked for a drag off of his while I was back there. He said yes. While I was smoking he said, "Sorry, I nigger-lip my cigarettes." I was so shocked that he said that that I coughed up smoke, and he realized that he had said that in front of Don, the only black cook at our restaurant.

"Nigger-lipping" referred to the unsavory practice of wetting the end of a cigarette while smoking. Because black people were stereotyped as having big lips, this practice became associated with blackness, further underscoring its unpleasantness. Here, Katie was surprised not by Sean's use of the term, but by his indiscreet language. Overall, by racially degrading objects, bodies, and practices, racetalkers articulated the message that blackness was an undesirable status. This was exacerbated by the modernization of old racialized tropes.

Freeloaders and Reprobates: Modernized Coons and Matriarchs

In the literature, the images of the coon and the matriarch overlap in many ways: they are shiftless, lazy, and undeserving. They deplete resources that they did not earn. Yet the coon is benign while the matriarch is aggressive. In the data, blackness was signified in such a way that blended the worst of the coon and the matriarch. This modern version depicted freeloading reprobates: humorous, loud, raucous, and uncivilized. They usurp the resources of the more deserving. They are consummate welfare bandits. In this section, I provide evidence of this modern image and analyze its implications for the signification of blackness.

Funny and Entertaining.   Historically, the coon image was always good for laughs among dominants. Early twentieth-century cartoons and caricatures evidence the entertainment value of the coon (Riggs 1986). Similarly, racetalk in this study occasionally indicated that people considered the actions of African Americans to be funny and entertaining, worthy of consumption. For example, Cindy (Latina) and her roommate Maggie (Latina) discussed an upcoming episode of the television show *Politically Incorrect*. When Cindy learned that the show would primarily feature African Americans, she said, "Ah shit—it's going to be funny tonight. It's all black people." To Cindy, watching black people promised to be an entertaining event.

Many television programs capitalize on this perspective, constructing racial caricatures to lampoon certain behaviors. These racial caricatures come to define behavior that only "those people" do. For example, Sophia (white) entered her dorm room to find her white roommate watching *Ricki Lake*. Typical of sensationalized talk shows, the audience was "going crazy." Sophia reported:

> I asked what the heck was going on. My roommate said, "Someone must have dropped some chicken on the floor." She said it because most of the people on the screen were black.

Programs like *Ricki Lake* and *Jerry Springer* intentionally caricature people of color, perpetuating amusing stereotypes for profit. Everyday people pick up on the discursive capital associated with the caricatures and use them as well. Sophia wrote about her brother:

> He does these "impressions" of what he calls "brothers." He was telling about one of his friends and he mentioned something about a black guy. He started moving his hands around, flashing what he thinks to be gang signals, and talking crap. Then he went on to tell his story. I asked him why he felt the need to do that. He replied, "That was how the guy was."

Like the coon of old, this image of African Americans signified blackness as comical rather than genuine. Blackness is immaturity, childishness.

Lazy and Shifty.   Modern blackness, like the coon and matriarch, signified laziness and a shifty manipulation of the system. In the racetalk in this study, blacks were seen as trying to get something for nothing. For example, Taylor (white) recorded this incident:

> Jesse (white) said, "I am not a racist, it is just that every black person I have interacted with is the same." I asked him, "What do you mean, the same?" He said, "They are all lazy slackers who don't want to work. They are uneducated and ignorant." I said, "People who are racist are ignorant."

Jesse's comments were not rare. Similarly, Roger's (white) roommate, Jake (white), responded to a bit on the television channel Comedy Central. The bit featured an advertisement for a pogo stick that began with, "Are you too lazy to get up? If so, buy a pogo stick." Jake said, "Are you too lazy to get up? You might have Black man syndrome." Guido (Latino) reported, "My brother-in-law and I were talking about teaching in the inner-city public schools. He said, 'niggers are lazy,' and basically that is the reason that students suck in the public schools." This racetalk blamed black people for their socioeconomic shortcomings as compared to the white standard. In so doing, racetalkers ignored the historic context in which whites actively oppressed blacks for their own economic gain (Wilson 1990, 1997).

Sometimes African Americans themselves made comments joking on what they saw as a lack of concern among fellow blacks for deadlines. As Blueangel (black) recorded,

> I was late meeting a couple of friends for lunch. My excuse was that I was on Black People Time. If they wanted me to be on time, they should have told me to meet them at 11:45, so I'd be there by the time they really wanted me to be there, which was 12:00.

Although joking and showing camaraderie with her friends, Blueangel played upon a coonlike stereotype in doing so: blacks are lazy and unconcerned about time. Therefore, they cannot be counted upon. This is a damaging stereotype used to legitimate discriminatory hiring practices, for example.

Related to laziness was shiftiness: trying not to get caught. The mantra embedded in this image was this: play hard, avoid hard work, and deny responsibility for your actions. Monty's (Asian) friend Mary (white) talked about an incident involving the bowl that she used to smoke marijuana. She shared it with people at Monty's house and it broke. Mary explained:

> This black guy—I'm not saying that in a racist way—just to describe him. Anyway, he asked to use my bowl. I didn't feel like smoking so I let him use it. He was totally ghetto but I couldn't say no. I have a problem with saying that you know. He gave it back to me later and it was in the case so I didn't bother to look at it right away. Later when I wanted to smoke I took it out of its case. It was broken. I confronted him and he totally denied it. He was completely shady.

Although Mary assured Monty and his friends that she was not referring to the man's race in a "racist way," her underlying subtext indicated that his race was a key explanatory factor of his behavior. Mary's assumptions were laced with racial profiling as well: she assumed that he broke it in part due to his "ghettoness," his blackness. She did not see him break it; indeed, she was at a party with many other people. But she seemed to require no further research to establish her conclusion. Blackness is shadiness.

Ignorant.   The coon and the matriarch are uneducated and unskilled. They are unable to take care of themselves without the help of the dominants, in the forms of slavery and welfare. Much of the racetalk in this study echoed this image of African Americans as uneducated and ignorant. For example, Jessica's (white) white friend Sarah condemned the African Americans standing in front of a classroom building: "You know how they stand in one group and they don't move. The only words you hear in each of the circles of conversation is 'mother fucker'—it's like those are the only words they know." Similarly, Roger's (white) white friends talked about the bad service at McDonald's, saying that if you want to get what you order, "you have to speak Ebonics." Whites made the following assumptions about people who did not conforms to white standards of speech: (a) They did so because they did not know any other way of communicating, and (b) such language was an underlying indicator of ignorance. As such, whites did not have to make an effort to communicate with blacks, as evidenced in this incident recorded by Jean (white) as she walked with white friends between classes:

> Our previous class had a lively discussion. My friend asked, "You know that one black guy in our class?" (there was only one). I said that I did. She said, "Well

when he talks, it drives me nuts. I can't understand what he is saying half of the time." I didn't respond and we continued to our next class.

Jean did not elaborate on the characteristics of the black man's speech. She implied that he talked "black," signified as incomprehensibility. The man's speech led Jean's friend to dismiss him as annoying and, perhaps, irrelevant.

Another piece of evidence tying blackness with ignorance was recorded in Carter's (black) field notes. He and Antonio (Latino) worked on a project together. Their task was to administer a survey to students that involved reading a court case and answering a series of questions. On average, it took most students between forty-five and sixty minutes to complete it. Carter noticed that one black male finished after only thirty minutes. He brought this up with Antonio:

> I said, "So I had a guy that finished in thirty minutes. I wonder if he read the entire thing." Antonio said, "Wow! Well, did you look at the questions to see that he filled them all in?" I said, "Yeah, everything is there." Antonio said, "Well, I saw the guy leave early. I don't think he read it all through. He didn't look like he'd be able to read that fast."

Carter, a black man himself, was struck by Antonio's implication—the student was black, therefore he probably could not read very fast. Perhaps Antonio was reacting to some other information. Maybe the guy was looking around the room rather than at his paper, for example. But Carter did not observe any other information that might explain Antonio's assumption—it seemed like race was the key explanatory factor.

The assumption that blacks are unable to learn as well as other racial groups was prevalent within the racetalk. Elizabeth (black), who came from the inner city herself, recorded this incident:

> Today in my education class my teacher was discussing teaching in the inner city. He said many teachers retire early or quit because of *those* students. He stated that *they* have social and emotional problems. [emphasis his]

According to the signification of blackness in the racetalk, blacks either could not or would not learn, thereby putting undue stress on the system. Education was signified in the habitus as a white endeavor sullied by blackness.

Rude and Obnoxious.   The coon and the matriarch diverged in their demeanor: the coon was docile while the matriarch was aggressive and overbearing. The difference in demeanor, however, is largely due to the political contexts in which they emerged. The coon was an image born of slavery, and it was designed to legitimate slavery: blacks were docile, silly, and ignorant;

hence, they depended on whites for their well-being. The matriarch image was a product of the backlash on welfare programs, and she, too, is used to justify that political stance. She is loud, obnoxious, disrespectful, and ungrateful for all that she is given. She is an uppity black woman with an attitude.

As with the other modernized images above, this image of loud, inappropriate blackness was applied to both men and women in the racetalk in this study. For example, Leigh's (white) white roommate was watching TV and she said, "I'm not racist at all, but have you noticed that black people around here are rude? Or is it just me?" Here, Leigh's roommate used what Eduardo Bonilla-Silva and Tyrone Forman (2000) call a semantic maneuver to deny the racism of the comment before making it. The remark itself reinvested the old matriarch image with new life. Although Leigh's roommate did not think of herself as a racist, this racist connection of blackness with rudeness seemed well entrenched.

Katie (white) was much more pointed in her signification of blackness as rudeness and aggression:

I was taking a nap in a classroom building between classes and I noticed that there was a car accident outside. Of course everyone looked, but the only people who felt the need to make a very loud comment about it were black. Two of the men actually went outside to ask the people what happened. There were a total of seven black men and two women and zero white people. One guy actually said, "Damn. That is some nasty ass shit. Ripped the fucking door off!"

Katie was bothered by being awakened in this manner, especially by what she saw as typical black behavior. She continued on her rant in her field notes:

While I was watching [the car accident], I also noticed that many of the cars [driven by black people] had very loud stereos. They feel they need to show off their quality sound systems. I thought maybe it was to prove their flow of money, power, and prestige. Most of the music had a lot of loud bass.

Black people intruded upon her quietude, and she unleashed her wrath by indicting blackness in general.

Katie was not the only person to signify blackness as loudness. Leigh (white) recorded this incident:

Patty (white), Jill (white), and I were studying in the common area of the dorm. There was a group of African Americans making a lot of noise. I was annoyed already because my roommate kept making noises while doing her homework. That's why I went to the Commons in the first place. I did what I usually do and said, "Shut up!" really loud. Jill commented that black people always make a lot of noise.

John (white) overheard a similar comment among two white women while walking through the hallway on campus. One said to the other: "I'm not racist, but damn black people are so loud!" Again, white racetalkers seemed to know that their comments conjured up old images, even as they denied it.

Usurping Resources.   According to the imagery, both the coon and the matriarch live off of the charity of the dominants: either the benevolent slaveholder or the benevolent welfare state. The racetalk in this study associated blackness with this image as well. Indeed, racetalk interrogated any use of resources—both public and private resources—by African Americans. In every case, their use of space and resources was deemed unfair, unearned, and abused. For example, Abe's (white) white friend Mike noticed black people standing in hallways in campus and said, "It seems like all these [black] people do is stand around and get in our way." Similarly, Sena's (Latina) white roommate observed this: "All Black people congregate all over the buildings [on campus]. They stand in front of all the doors. They are so ghetto."

Here, blacks were thought to be usurping space—literally—in the crowded hallways. This indicated their sense of entitlement, which Sena's roommate tied to blackness in her use of the term "ghetto."

Jaime's (white) white friend Carrie was an RA in a dorm. She commented to Jaime that all of the students who park illegally outside of the building came from a community college. They were also all black. Carrie said, "I don't mean to be like that but in this case it's true." Carrie argued that the data speak for themselves: black people just are that way, and it is not racist to point it out.

Deference—or lack thereof—emerged as a theme in the racetalk on resources. It seemed that if only blacks would be deferent and grateful to whites for sharing "their" space, then whites might not condemn them so. This was exemplified by this excerpt from Hedwig (white) who went to the gym with her friend Marsha (white).

Marsha showed the indoor tennis courts to me, since I had never seen them. The tennis courts abut the basketball courts, and both were encircled by a track: Marsha tells me, "They just spent tons of money fixing up the indoor track, but I don't like to run here any more. All of the black people always come to watch their friends play basketball. They just stand around in the middle of the track. They don't even move off to one side. When you walk past them, they reek of weed. I mean reek of it. They just stand around and you have to run around them. They don't even move." "That's shitty," I said.

The implication: blacks are freeloading drug users who have abused the privilege of sharing white space. In another incident, Jessica's (white) white friend attacked African Americans for such an infraction:

I hate how they cross the street with their nose in the air like they own everything. They don't even say thank you when you stop. Do they think we won't hit them?

Similarly, Rocker's (white) white friend said, "Blacks don't look anywhere when they cross the street." In the racetalk, blackness was constructed as false entitlement, and white subjects tensed when people of color did not openly defer to them in public (a.k.a. white) spaces.

At the same time, racetalk interrogated the ways that blacks used their own private resources. For instance, whites turned a critical eye to the ways that people of color spent money. Kenny's (white) white friends wondered how black people can afford "such nice cars." Rocker (white) recorded the following rant in his field notes:

Dude, I hate all these fucking niggers. They drive these nice cars, wear nice clothes. They have their fucking bass on so loud you can't even hear anything else. How do they afford it? Well, they don't pay for school, because they're poor. So they get free tuition, and when they sell their drugs, they buy this shit.

Similarly, Gail (white) reported this:

I overheard two white guys talking about how much they had to work to get what they have. One guy said to the other: "These Black people don't even work and they have cell phones and designer clothes." The other guy said, "Yeah man, I work so much just to pay my bills and these people just go and spend money like it's water." I had to agree that I had seen more Black people with cell phones than whites, but I don't think that we should be so judgmental about it just because they are Black.

Carmen's (white) field notes also captured financial surveillance:

My [white] roommate was telling us about when she used to work at the grocery store, and behind the store were what she described to be housing projects. She said that all of the black people spent money on useless items like Nike shoes for very young children, instead of spending it on reasonable things like food and shelter.

White subjects spoke as fiscal experts, openly evaluating African Americans' material consumption. The assumption inherent in all of this racetalk was that blacks were not capable of earning honest livings and, therefore, any gains that they made had to be unfair and unearned. As Blueangel (black) observed, this assumption may have real consequences for people who are actually poor and struggling:

At my staff meeting, I proposed a community service program that we could do as a building. The program was a toy drive sponsored by the Walter Peyton

Foundation, which benefited children in DCFS. Marie (white) commented that [the toys] just go to the inner city children. I said that it would also go toward DCFS in a suburb, and she was much more relieved. Now she was interested and willing to contribute. The only reaction to her comment came from the black staff members, who understood exactly what she was hinting at. We all gave each other disapproving stares.

Marie wanted to reserve charity for suburban people. Blueangel surmised that Marie favored the suburbs for racial reasons: she would rather help whites—who deserved help—than blacks—who did not deserve it.

Overall, this modernized image of the coon/matriarch was signified as a loud, ignorant, irresponsible freeloader who takes up too much space and resources. This new image resembles the old ones. The key points of contention in the racetalk about this image seemed to be the "unfair" use of resources and the lack of deference shown to whites. The subtext of white supremacy conjured a contemporary Jim Crow (C. Johnson 1943).

Gangsters: Black Macho Modernized

Black macho was signified as a violent, domineering, controlling, somewhat frightening black man who used force to get what he wanted and needed. Although many have argued that Wallace (1994) unfairly simplified Black Panthers by associating them with black macho, the image has had a powerful effect on the ways that black men continue to be seen by dominants. In the racetalk in this study, black men were repeatedly linked with violence and crime. For example, Rori (white) saw a large crowd of black students hanging around outside of her dorm:

> I said to Jerry (white), "One of the black fraternities must be having a party." He said, "I sure don't see any whites or Hispanics around." We then saw about 10–15 police cars and I said, "Something must be up." Jerry said, "Gangsters to the left."

In Rori's town, ten to fifteen police cars was probably the entire police squad. I am unsure whether this was an accurate figure or the result of her perception that a lot of lights were flashing and a lot of police officers were walking around. Nevertheless, even the lower end of the range—ten—would constitute a major reaction to a gathering on campus.[5]

When blacks gathered en masse, racetalkers assumed that violence was inevitable. But individual blacks were presumed to be criminals as well. For example, Roger (white) was watching television with white friends Joe and Sue:

> They showed a clip of an African American man running with a football in a practice session. Sue asked, "How do they run so fast?" Her boyfriend, Joe, said,

"Straight out of Africa and into our sports." I said, "I'm sure I can run faster than a lot of black people." Joe said, "Yeah, but how many times have you run from the cops?" He laughed and Sue hit him. I laughed and said, "Maybe five or six times."

Roger attempted to disrupt this racetalk associating blacks with athletic prowess. But in doing so, he inadvertently invoked the blacks-as-gangster image in its stead. When this new image emerged, Roger again tried to challenge it by saying he—a white guy—had been chased by the police before too. He was joking rather than offering a serious critique, and so the image remained: blacks run fast because they get lots of practice running away from the police.

What kinds of crime were associated with blackness in the racetalk? Property crime was a black endeavor, according to the subjects in this study. Estella (white) recorded this incident that characterized blacks as thieves:

Josie (white), Mary (white), and I were sitting at Josie's kitchen table. Josie began talking about the *Ricki Lake Show* and how there were some "niggers" [on the show] saying that they steal all of the time for their children. Josie said that they did not care that they stole from others because it was how they supported themselves. She said that this is why the economy is so fucked up. I said, "Please don't say the N word—you know how much I hate that." Mary agreed. Josie said, "You know there is a difference between niggers and black people. Just like there is a huge difference between white people and white trash." Mary and I both agreed.

In this incident, the women took issue with the use of a racial slur, but not with the underlying analysis of blacks as criminals. They did offer an alternative explanation: niggers steal while blacks do not. This comment—which was uncontested—introduced a class analysis in which poor blacks are the people who steal. While these women attempted to provide a nuanced portrayal of race and class, it fell short. Josie's comment seemed to be an attempt to deflect responsibility for her use of a racial slur. In the end, the image of blacks as criminals remained intact.

Maggie (Latina) recorded a similar incident in which her roommate Cindy (Latina) was on the phone with her boyfriend, trying to convince him to fly to New Orleans rather than drive:

You shouldn't drive down there, babe. You just finished hookin' up your car again with the rims, the TVs and the system. It's dangerous down there. Shit, that's the dirty South. The niggers don't give a shit down there. They're ruthless. They don't give a fuck.

After Cindy hung up, she spoke to Maggie: "Man, girl, I'm so relieved. I don't think my man is going to New Orleans any more. I'm glad. It gets crazy down there, the dirty South." Cindy associated the South with blackness and rampant, unfettered criminality. Precious (black) recorded this incident:

> Penelope (black), Monica (black), and I pulled up to the convenient store and through the window we could see a black man behind the counter, working the register. He was speaking with a white man, also behind the counter, who appeared to be a supervisor due to the difference in his uniform. Penelope said, "You know his ass is stealing up some shit." I said, "Who?" and she said, "The black man." I said, "The one behind the counter?" and she said, "Hell yeah! You know he is."

Based on an observation of race alone, Penelope inferred that the white man was reprimanding the black man—and she assumed that the black man was actually in the wrong. She did not infer that they were talking about politics, sports, or women. This incident underscores the power of the black macho image even in the imaginations of African Americans.

Blackness was also associated with random violence—especially violent encounters involving a black aggressor and a white victim. In this incident, Jaime was on the phone with her mother:

> I told her of an incident that happened in my dorm. There were two guys that were roommates. Friday night, one roommate got on top of the other one and was choking him, trying to kill him. The victim got away and ran to his RA and told her what went on. He had to go to the hospital and they didn't even arrest the guy that choked him. The perpetrator had seven days to live here before he can be kicked out. I was outraged by this. My mom asked, "Were both black, or one of them?" I said that one was black—the perpetrator—who is on probation. She said, "Just think of how lucky you are to be with [your white roommate] Carrie. They could have put you with a black person and you don't know what could happen. [A black roommate] could have been on probation." I said, "I don't think so. I'm sure that doesn't happen too often."

Despite Jaime's attempt to alter the path that this conversation was taking, her mother insisted that one act of black-on-white aggression predicted legions of incidents to come. Blackness signified unbridled criminal impulses. Roger (white) recorded a similar incident:

> Sam (white) was telling us a story about one time when he was outside working on his car at 11 o'clock at night when a car full of black people stopped and asked for directions. He said, "They scared the shit out of me! I thought they were going to cap my white ass!" We all laughed at his story.

In another incident, Rocker's (white) white friend Sean fell down and got banged up. Rocker said, "We thought black people jumped him." Sean considered himself a skinhead. Sean might be more likely to get into a fight with black people than Sam, who was merely providing directions. However, the context did not seem to affect the content of the racetalk. The core signification was this: blacks are dangerous, ticking bombs likely to explode at any time.

In many of these scenarios, whites were portrayed as innocent while blacks were portrayed as unprovoked, unrestrained, and just giving in to their violent nature. Occasionally, however, the field notes indicated that whites were not at all blameless in creating or escalating conflict. Indeed, we all might expect blacks to express outrage given the circumstances. For example, Roger (white) told a white friend about a stunt he liked to pull "to get a rise out of people driving." He stood on the curb and pretended that he was going to cross the street just as a car sped by. He fake-stepped out into the street, causing cars to honk and/or swerve. He thought that this was a funny game. He told her:

> This one time I almost got my ass kicked because I had done my little stunt as this big old Cadillac drive by, with its bass blasting. This car, full of black people, slammed on its brakes and began to back up to try to "get me." So I got the hell out of there, because I didn't want to be harmed in any way, shape, or form.

In his field notes, Roger critiqued himself for coding his racetalk. He noted that he played on whites' fears of black men in order to make his point. He did not, however, acknowledge that the people whom he tricked had reason to be angry at him for jeopardizing their safety for his own fun.

Occasionally, black men were granted exceptional status to the gangster trope. Hedwig (white) recorded this incident:

> I was at a party one night and I had a discussion with a white guy whom I just met. He told me about a black man that he worked with who had just gotten shot and murdered at a 7–11 that weekend. He said, "It sucks man! It really does! He was a brother. He was the coolest black guy. He was, like, white, ya know? See, there are black people, there's brothers, and then there's niggers. He was a brother. The guys that shot him were niggers. Those stupid fucking niggers!"

So "brothers," or cool black men, were "like whites." Therefore they were not subject to the gangster/black macho stigma. It is unclear how one earned the privilege of being a brother versus being a nigger. It was equally unclear whether or not that privilege was fluid, and under what circumstances the privilege could be revoked. Nevertheless, the ability of African Americans to acquire this status seemed to be in the hands of whites, who seemed to assume "nigger" until proven otherwise.

The gangster image, which is often celebrated and glamorized in contemporary music and film, is just a high-gloss version of the black macho. Within some circles, the gangster may represent an empowering image that is meant to embrace whites' fear of blacks, subvert the dominant culture, and use the image against the dominants: "You think we're bad? You don't know the half of it." When a group reclaims a pejorative stereotype of themselves and manipulates it into an empowering symbol, this is called "oppositional identity work" (see MacLeod 1995; Schwalbe and Mason-Schrock 1996). This process is a form of resistance among oppressed peoples.

Yet, oppositional identity work can have unintended consequences for the people who seek empowerment. The dominant group looks on in interest as subordinates rework previously pejorative images. Eventually, the dominants coopt these morphed images for their own purposes. When dominants use the new images and symbols in their own discourse, they strip them of subversive power. They acquire them in order to put the subordinates back in their place. Thus, in this study, when whites used the gangster image in their discourse, it was not to celebrate black empowerment. Instead, the gangster image was used to profile blacks as criminals and to legitimate their continued disenfranchisement from the status quo.

Thugs and Dirty Ass Bitches: Modernized Bucks and Hot Mamas

The Buck and the hot mama were cut from the same cloth: they had insatiable, even predatory sexual appetites. They were not capable of self-control. They were base and animalistic. Both images were used in regard to miscengenation, or the intermixing of the races. However, they were used in a gendered manner. The Buck was a threat to the purity of white women. Thus, black men must keep their distance from white women. Conversely, because the hot mamas always wanted sex—indeed they begged for it—it was not white men's fault for raping them. According to this image, black women deserved to be raped, and they probably even enjoyed it.

Within the racetalk in this study, there was evidence of the hypersexualization of black men. The predatory Buck image thrived. However, no data in this study depicted black women as hot mamas. Instead, white women who had sex with black men embodied the hot mama—they were filthy, base, contaminated. I discuss these images as they emerged from the data.

The old stereotype about black men having exceptionally large penises was documented in the data. Megan (white) recorded this incident:

> I was at the gynecologist, and he was finishing up our appointment and telling me what to do and what to avoid doing. He told me that sex may be painful for a while, "especially since your boyfriend is black." He realized that what he said did not come out right, so he then tried to clarify by saying how, statistically, black men have larger penises than other men and so on and so forth.

Here, the old adage was propagated by a member of the medical profession, who even cited statistics to underscore his point. This doctor embodied authority on multiple levels, giving disproportionate weight to his racetalk. Though Megan was appalled by his racism, other patients may have interpreted such advice as learned and credible.

Miscegenators.   The data indicate that black men were still thought to be fixated on white women. Hedwig (white) recorded this conversation with Marsha (white) as they walked to a bar:

> We passed by a black guy walking in the opposite direction. Marsha said, "I don't know what it is but they [black people] always hit on me. This one night, I was at a bar with some people and they were making fun of me because I was being thugged all night." I asked her what "thugged" means. "Oh, that's when a black guy hits on you. This guy was just following me around all night and he wouldn't leave me alone. I just don't know why they always hit on me."

The signification: black men were drawn helplessly to white women. Both blacks and whites maintained this image. For example, Elizabeth (black) recorded this incident:

> While in the student center, me and a couple of friends were discussing this white girl who had a baby by a black boy, and my friend stated, "She's just trying to be black, taking our men. I can't stand them." Then another girl said that only white trash date black guys and that white girls are easy, that's why black guys date them.

Similarly, Precious (black) recorded this incident:

> Sherice (black) made a comment about how her brother had sex with a white girl and the girl thinks she may be pregnant. She said, "Why is he fuckin' them nasty ass dirty white bitches anyway? They're jealous and they always think you wanna fuck they nigga. Plus, I wouldn't want to mess with him after he slept with their dirty asses anyway!"

In both of these incidents, the traditional hot mama image was inverted: white women craved sex with black men. They seemed to beg for it. They were nasty, trashy, dirty. White women were sexually irresponsible. Therefore, black men could not help themselves but take advantage of what white women offered. The cost of giving in was to become contaminated by the white woman's filth. Worse, he might become permanently entangled with her due to an unplanned pregnancy.

Unlike the Buck—who cannot help raping unwilling white women—these black men courted white women. They formed meaningful relationships with them. Such relationships evoked anger from black women, who felt betrayed. As Precious recorded in her field notes:

> Penelope (black), Monica (black) and I were driving down the street. Monica looked over and told us that there was a couple in the next car to us, arguing. We looked over and we saw a black man, with veins bulging out of his forehead, arguing with what appeared to be his white girlfriend. Monica said, "Look at that. Her stupid ass is just gonna take that shit from that nigga. White girls are dumb as hell. They act like they're scared of their niggas. Have you ever noticed when you do see a nigga with a white girl, they those fat, ugly white girls. Probably just so they can get their dicks sucked." Penelope said, "It's all about control." We continued to drive alongside the couple and Penelope said, "He should just beat her ass. Yeah, hit her!" As she looked, she made cheering motions and gestures to the couple in the car.

This incident was complex. Monica connected with the white woman along gender lines, wondering why she took abuse from this man. Why didn't she fight back? The matriarch would fight back. Perhaps the woman's devalued status—fat, ugly—made her a prime target. If so, maybe she considered herself lucky to have a man at all, even if he was abusive. This conversation evolved quickly from a sort of gendered empathy to a reification of old racial images. Penelope invoked the black macho/buck: beat her, hit her—put her in her place.

Despite their initial empathy, these black women saw white women as usurping what was "theirs": black men. Elizabeth (black) documented an illustrative incident. She and her sister were talking about black basketball players and entertainers. Elizabeth said, "They all get money and want to date a white girl. Like a sister ain't good enough." Literature shows that the pool of eligible black men is waning, due to death and incarceration (Anderson 1999; Franklin 2001). Here, black women made the same kinds of arguments about scarce resources as put forth by whites in previous sections: you are taking what is rightfully mine, according to the racial regime—a regime that you helped establish! The major difference, however, was that these black women did not benefit from institutionalized racism in the ways that whites—even anti-racist whites—did (McIntosh 1988/2001; Kivel 1996). Structural power disparities took the muscle out of this racetalk among women of color.

In the black racetalk, then, black men became contaminated by dirty white women. White racetalk indicated similar assessments, but with a different spin on the matter. According to the white racetalk, when black men dated white women, blackness debased the white women. For example, Megan (white) recorded this incident:

> I was watching *A Wedding Story* with Sammie (white). The groom was a black ex-NFL football player, and the bride was a white elementary school teacher.

Sammie blurted out, "Why do all the dirty professional athletes, who probably have fucked over 100 girls, always end up marrying a white girl?"

Sammie was careful—she knew that Megan dated a black man. She coded her statement in terms of athletes, not blacks. But in the end, she invoked race when she indicted the pollution of a white girl. Taylor's (white) white boyfriend also implied that black men pollute white women:

> When my boyfriend, Jesse, and I first started dating, we got to know each other and talked about our pasts. Jesse asked me in a nonchalant way, "You haven't dated a black guy, have you?" I said, "Not yet." He asked if I ever would go out with a black guy and I said, "Sure, why not? I dated a Mexican and Filipino before." He said, "Mexicans are ok." But he apparently didn't think that blacks were ok.

Flora's (white) white husband was less coy:

> I told my husband about a friend who had a date with a black man. I said that the date was a success and she ended up sleeping with the guy. I was happy for her because she had come out of a bad relationship and had been depressed for a while. My husband said, "Why didn't you tell her that she had fucked a nigger?"

Racetalk revealed skepticism that genuine, positive black/white relationships could exist. They were cast as prurient, unnatural, corrupt. Such relationships damaged either black men or white women, depending on the positionality of the racetalker.

Predators.   The major implication of the Buck image was that white women were unsafe from predatory black men. This theme emerged repeatedly in the data. For example, Jean (white) recorded this incident:

> I was talking with Daniel (white) about whether I should head back to school on Sunday night or wait and get up in the morning to go back. I said that I didn't like going back to an empty apartment. My roommate wouldn't be there until after midnight. Daniel asked if I was afraid that a big, black man was going to come and get me. I said that he wasn't funny and that I was going back on Sunday night.

Daniel was kidding, invoking the stereotype to make fun of Jean's fears. However, others were serious. For example, Celine (white) was at a party and her white friend Casey walked in:

> The first thing that came out of Casey's mouth when she walked in was, "There sure are a lot of black people next door." Then after her shock of all the black people congregating by Fred's apartment, she said, "I'm not prejudiced or anything." She didn't want any of us to think that she meant that she didn't like blacks—just

that there was a rather large amount of them outside. She later commented that she was hesitant to leave. I think she was scared in a way.

These black people were neighbors of their friends. As such, they likely had much in common socially and economically. Thus, Casey's fear that she would be victimized by the black people next door made sense only in a society that demonizes black men as rapists. Similarly, Estella (white) reported this incident:

> I asked Mary (white) how she got home from tailgating after homecoming. She said she and Bruce (white) started walking and then hitched the rest of the way home. She started laughing. "With whom?" I asked. She said, "With this ghetto black guy. I mean he was very ghetto." I asked, "And you got in the car with him?" She said, "Well, I figured that since I was with a guy I would be OK. But seriously, listen to this. He was wearing a bandana and had on black gloves with the fingers cut out." We both started laughing.

Here, this man was nice enough to help out Mary and Bruce—who were too drunk to drive, thereby living up to a characteristic of whiteness discussed in the last chapter. Yet, even though he got them home safely, Mary and Estella degraded him as a thug whom Mary ought to have feared rather than trusted.

The image of black man as frightening predator was so pervasive that people often expressed surprise when it did not hold true. Megan recorded this incident:

> Sammie (white) and I were at her apartment and her (white) friend Kim came over. Like me, Kim is also dating a black guy. We were all talking about our boyfriends, since we are all in relationships that have lasted longer than two years. Sammie looked at us and said, "I love your boyfriends. They are so different from the rest of them. They're so cool." Kim and I looked at each other because we both didn't know if we should think that we were thinking. Kim then confronted Sammie and asked her what she meant by that. Sammie said that it must be hard being white and dating a black guy. She said, at least our boyfriends were not thugs, and were nice, even-tempered guys.

Similarly, Jean (white) recorded this incident:

> Rose (white) told me something that happened at her apartment. She was looking out her window as she was getting ready to go to work. All of a sudden three black guys were walking toward her building. One of them entered and the other two stayed outside. They stood right by her car, and they were looking in at her stuff. Rose was upset because she needed to go to work, but she didn't want to go outside with those two black men standing right beside her car. She finally

went out and said, "Excuse me," when she walked by them. One of them said, "Pardon me, ma'am." She told me that she couldn't believe how polite he was. She seemed surprised at his manners and that he wasn't, in fact, scary.

Rose used language like "all of a sudden" to indicate her level of fear of these men. She was so paralyzed by her imagination of what these men would do to her that she almost did not leave her apartment at all. Thus, her relief was even greater when the men disproved the stereotype.

The Buck image has been transformed in an era where interracial dating is legal and more common. However, the old value judgments associated with interracial mixing remained largely the same. There were no data on black women dating white men. If so, the traditional hot mama image might have emerged. Instead, white women were the contemporary hot mamas, or dirty ass bitches, who deserved what they got. These data did not bode well for the ability of interracial couples to assimilate in either black or white cultures.

Servants and Traitors: Uncle Tom and Mammy Today

The images of the Uncle Tom and the mammy invoked both pity and disdain. They were pitiful because they were forced to sacrifice their own families and freedoms in the service of whites. They were disdained for their alignment with whites against their fellow blacks. The Tom and the mammy helped the dominants to pit the favored against the disenfranchised, keeping black people divided and oppressed within the racial regime. In this study, these images lived on. For example, Jaime (white) observed this interaction:

> I was with Roy (black) in the cafeteria where he works. One of his supervisors came by and Roy said to her, "You need to do something about that black girl serving pizza. She has an attitude and is very rude." The supervisor said she would look into it. Roy didn't need to mention the girl's race because she was the only person serving pizza.

In this incident, Roy underscored the problems with the Tom in several ways. Roy exercised his authority over this woman, invoking race in the process. He used her race to explain the need to sanction her at all: black people are uppity. She needed to be reminded of her place. Because Roy was black too, his comments carried extra weight (Bell 1992), adding legitimacy to his racialized evaluation. By marking this black woman as rude, Roy set himself apart as exceptional, entitled. He implied that blacks have two stations in this regime: (1) serving demurely, or (2) if exceptional, acting as agents of the racist regime. Both are useful yet reviled by the dominants. The latter are marked as traitors by the subordinates.

Serving Up. In the data, the notion that blacks exist to serve whites re-mained. For example, Taylor (white) visited with her ninety-two-year-old grandmother over lunch in her retirement facility:

> As we left lunch, my grandmother told me how those colored girls [on the dietary staff] were so nice to her, getting her coffee and anything she needed. I asked her, "Do you like a lot of the staff here?" She said, yes. The nurse came to see her once a day in the morning, and the housekeeper, a colored girl, came once a week. She told me what a good worker she was and finished by saying, "They are good workers, those colored folks."

This comment was not surprising given the racetalker's age. She lived during the heyday of Jim Crow, which likely left a lasting mark. Yet, younger people, too, expressed the idea that blacks made good workers, even trivializing the power of slavery altogether. Cher recorded this conversation between herself and Buddy (white):

> I said, "Erykah Badu said she would rather be a slave than have a white person buy her record." Buddy said, "That can be arranged. My grandpa said he wants to make my cousin's ex-husband a slave. He's black and his son is mulatto."

Taylor recorded a similar example in reaction to a racial incident:

> I went with my boyfriend Jesse (white, 35, divorced) to a NASCAR party at a friend's house to watch the race. There were approximately 25 people present. Most were single white guys between twenty-five to forty years old. A large num-ber of them worked together in an industrial trade. It is a tradition that the guests go to the garage and sign the refrigerator that holds the keg. Usually, people sign their name, the date and a funny or cute little message. The notes remain there from party to party. At this party, someone drew a swastika and wrote KKK. The next day, our host Jay tried to cover the writing the best he could. He told me on the phone that he was really angry about the comments. He said, "I have many black friends and they come over frequently for parties and 'guy nights.' I don't want them to see that on the refrigerator and think that I support those views."

Disturbed, she talked about the incident to her boyfriend:

> I told Jesse what had happened, saying "It is hard to believe that someone I know could actually write that and feel that way about others." Jesse said that he knew that it was his brother who wrote that, and he apologized on his behalf. I asked, "What are your feelings? Are you prejudiced as well?" He said, "No, I like blacks. I think everyone should have one." My face must have shown my disapproval be-cause he quickly said that he was just joking.

In both of these incidents, slavery was treated casually. It was romanticized as a desirable social arrangement. As discussed above, most of the historical images of blackness have denigrated blacks as incompetent and unworthy.

Selling Out.   Due to the divisive legacy of the Tom and the mammy, blacks who defied controlling images that justified their repression—those who stepped out of their designated location in the racial regime—were critiqued by their peers as being overly white-identified, as selling out to whiteness. For example, Amber (black) reported being followed in a store by a clerk. The clerk asked Amber repeatedly if she needed help. Finally, Amber confronted the woman, asking why she was following her: "She told me that there was suspicion that I was stealing and made me empty my bags. I didn't steal anything, and the bad part about it was that [the clerk] was black." Amber was less concerned about being falsely accused of stealing. That had happened before. She was disappointed that a black clerk had been coopted by the white structure. Similarly, Precious (black) noted: "A black female acquaintance of mine got fired. She said, 'I know who got me fired: a black bitch.'" When blacks acted on the behalf of the white system, insult compounded injury. In another example, Janet (black) talked with her friend James (black). She remarked to him that he always had new shoes and wore Eddie Bauer clothes. She asked him why he never wore any jewelry. He said he was not a "jewelry person," explaining that he cannot wear jewelry to work. Janet relayed the conversation:

> I said, "Not even a chain?" and James said, "You never see white men wearing jewelry." I said, "Why do you compare your attire to the 'working white man?' You don't have to be like them."

Janet was concerned, and she wrote this in her field notes: "He thought to be professional you had to look plain and dress like the 'white worker.'" She did not want James to sell out in order to succeed. Amber, Precious's friend, and Janet worried that blacks might lose their own identity by conforming to the white status quo.

The Tom/mammy image remained powerful and controlling. In the hands of the dominants, this image was used to argue that the only reasonable work for competent blacks was servitude to whites. This argument limits all African Americans to poorly paying jobs, if not prison. Yet, if blacks exceeded their bounds and excelled in the white world—the context in which all African Americans must compete—then they sold out, showed disloyalty to other blacks. Success among black people is a very difficult staircase to climb—they are damned if they try and equally damned for not trying. Still, many would argue that the payoff in terms of economic security is worth the social sting.

Taken together, these data indicated that old tropes of blackness remain alive today, with a new veneer for a new millennium. The habitus persists. Although some tropes have cultivated a measure of value among African Americans—through oppositional identity work—all of the images have negative uses and implications for African Americans when invoked by the dominants. Thus, in the next section, I discuss the ripple effects of these pejorative, degrading—yet enduring—images of blackness.

INVISIBILITY

The paradox of the mark of blackness was that it rendered people at once glaringly obvious and yet invisible. Janet (black) illustrated invisibility well in her field notes. In one incident, she went to a department on campus to find out about a class. The white secretary wouldn't look at her at all. She said, "I found it really hilarious." The next day, she got onto an elevator with the same secretary:

> Man you should have seen her. She dropped her head so far down that I thought she was going to hit her head on the concrete. I laughed not because it was funny but because she was so stupid and ignorant. That's a damn shame, but she will get over it.

In another incident, Janet went to a high school where she was to student teach. When introduced to the white teacher with whom she would be working, Janet's ethnographic instincts kicked in:

> I stuck my hand out to give him a shake. The hand-shake was so flimsy. He barely shook my hand. Didn't even touch it. He looked at me but the hand-shake was horrible. Throughout the day, he really didn't converse with me at all. I'd ask him questions and he'd give me real quick answers. When we left, he said, "Bye, nice meeting you." But it seemed so fake. Maybe I was tripping, but who really knows?

Janet was left to wonder if her race was a factor in the cold encounter, or if the teacher was just socially inept. Past experience and the collective experiences of others told her it was racism. But there was no "proof." Janet left an important career opportunity feeling empty and confused.

African Americans in this study tuned into cues and subtext in order to gauge the safety of various social settings, what bell hooks (1995) calls an "ethnographic gaze." She asserts that because blacks live in both the margins and center of society, they are able to see whites from a special vantage point.

During slavery and Jim Crow, blacks were privy to white conversations as they served them their meals or tended their children. They observed whites without being noticed. The ethnographic gaze provided insight into the oppressor that could be used as a protective shield in times of open hostility. It helped make the oppressor more predictable and less dangerous. It prepared them for being singled out, and it also prepared them for being erased. For example, Carter's (black) dad lightheartedly complained as they watched a collegiate basketball game: "It's all white boys. Where are all the brothers at?" Precious (black) recorded several such observations:

> David (black) and I were watching the movie, *X-men*. It came to a scene with about fifty police and FBI agents with their guns drawn. David asked, "Do you notice how none of them cops are black?" By the time he finished his sentence, they showed an entire line-up of the law enforcement team and there was not one black officer. I said, "um hm."

Sometimes white people noticed this tendency in films as well, as noted by Rori's (white) mother:

> My mom was telling me about the black version of the movie, *Leprechaun*, in which the bad guy wins and all of the black people die. She said, "Black people have it hard. They can't even win in their own movies."

In another incident, Precious and Penelope (black) went to a bar in a suburban [white] area:

> We were meeting her white friend, Thomas, to have a few drinks. When the waitress came to our table, she requested our IDs. After she inspected them, she asked us what we wanted to drink. We ordered and it took her a while to come back to the table with the drinks. We were looking for her at one point and she was in the corner talking to some man. When she did come back, Penelope tasted her drink and was mad because the drink lacked potency. Penelope said, "I hate this fucking bar. I feel violated. Our waitress ain't been to check on us. My drink is all juice. Doesn't she know that you get your best tips when your customers are drunk?" She ordered a shot and the waitress slammed her change down on the table. We left shortly afterwards.

Precious and Penelope felt unwanted, and they acquiesced by leaving. In another incident, Precious observed the invisibility of a random black man in a public place:

> I was standing in the check out line at the gas station. There were several white men standing in front of and behind me. A black man made his purchases and

proceeded out the door. He walked past the white man and said, to no one in particular, "How ya doin'?" No one responded or acknowledged the man.

In the margin of her field notes, Precious penciled "outcast." Although blackness marked African Americans for intense scrutiny, it also marked them as unimportant and invisible.

EXCEPTIONS

Derrick Bell (1992) argues that "Modern discrimination is not practiced indiscriminately" (6). Whites support some blacks like athletes and entertainers, but reject most others. They pick and choose whom to accept and whom to reject. There's a pattern to "these seemingly arbitrary racial actions" (7). When whites benefit in some way (or it is at least cost-free), they make an exception. Therefore, "selections and rejections reflect preference as much as prejudice" (7)—it is indeed rational. In the racetalk, whites made exceptions for some blacks—they discriminated discriminately. A major exception to the trope of blackness could be made if the person "acted white." Cher (white) provided an example of this in her field notes:

> I was going to a family member's house for Christmas dinner. I was forewarned of the guests coming. All of the normal people: close family and friends. Then I was informed that an uncle of mine was bringing a friend—a black friend—with his black 5 year old daughter. A family member said that it figured he'd be a single father and black. Then another informed me, "They are good black people, not like the rest. They act white."

On the one hand "it figured" the man would be black if he was a single father—he's irresponsible and good for nothing. At the same time, he was partially absolved of blackness by "acting white." In another example, Celine (white) was riding home from class with white friends Candice and Ahna. Ahna was talking about her boyfriend Jimmy's black friend. After she was done, she added that he was Jimmy's roommate. Celine said, "I was shocked":

> "Jimmy has a black roommate? That's cool." Ahna said, "Yes he's black. But he acts white." We all laughed and Candice said, "What do you mean?" Ahna said, "He acts white," and she smiled and laughed. I don't know what it was such a shock for me to know that Jimmy had a black roommate. I think it's just because it is so rare for everyone I know. But then it somehow seemed to make sense that he acted white, like it didn't count any more that he was black.

Here, Celine's shock that Jimmy shared his home with a black person was ameliorated by the roommate's exceptional status: "He acts white."[6]

"Acting white" may have been intended as a compliment among whites; it was not necessarily celebrated among African Americans, as in this conversation recorded by Blueangel (black):

> My friend Tanaya (black) and I were talking about a male co-worker, who is black but acts white. From the clothes he wears to women he dates—he's an all around wannabe. I found a song about black men like him and I was tempted to play it for him at the staff meeting. Tanaya said how sad it is that he is like that when he has so much potential.

As discussed in the chapter on blackness, African Americans might interpret exceptional status as a sign of selling out to the white establishment (see also Collins 1998).

The most common way to become decontaminated and be granted exceptional status was if a person was deemed attractive. For example, Maggie's (Latina) friend Tonia (Latina) pointed out two "morenitos" (dark-skinned people) who walked by. Tonia said, "One of them is cute, you know, for a black guy." Similarly, Taylor (white) recorded this:

> One night at work on break, I was sitting with two other white girls who were looking at a magazine. One saw a photo of Denzel Washington. She said, "He sure is hot, for a black guy." The other girl agreed with her.

Carol Ann (white) wrote, "I was watching television with my [white] roommate, and she said, 'He is hot for being black.'" When whites admired blacks, they often qualified their attraction by pointing out that they did not usually admire blacks as a rule—this black was exceptional. Thus, they were not ready to admire blacks as a group. Bell (1992) argues that being granted exception status is not necessarily a boon. When some blacks are seen as excelling, their success does not trickle down to blacks as a group. Their success is evidence of the rareness of black excellence—a fluke. Black leaders are put onto pedestals, and quickly dethroned at the slightest mistake. Bell writes, "You may be committed to black people but, believe me, you have to work very hard to do as much *good* for black people as you do harm simply by being good at whatever you do for a living!" (26).

Taken together, blackness was overwhelmingly negative most of the time. Some black people could limit the impact of their black mark by acting white. They could become exceptional blacks. But that status had to be granted to them by the more powerful white group.

RESISTANCE

Despite the pejorative signification of blackness and its negative consequences for African Americans, racetalk among blacks indicated a critique of the structure of blackness and an analysis of racial dominance. Blacks' ethnographic gaze allowed them to resist the structural forces that caricatured, vilified, and dismissed them.

Striving for an Authentic Identity

As already mentioned, African Americans took note of discrepancies in treatment between whites and themselves, and they were critical of differential treatment. For example, Elizabeth (black) overheard African American women talking in a department store:

> While in the store a black lady referred to these two little white kids as out of control. She said that if they were black they would not dare act up. But then she said if they were black, the store clerk would have complained by now.

Much racetalk among blacks involved distancing themselves from whites, as in this conversation about hair among Anastasia's friends (all black). Anastasia wore her hair natural:

> Dinah said, "It is interesting how when black people get to college they want to find their identity by wearing their hair nappy." She looked at me when she said this. I told her that I was 18 when I got my first perm and I always had afro puffs when I was in high school. I still have my identity as being black. We got to talking about why blacks want to wear their hair natural. Shayna said, "Blacks don't want to get permed no more because it makes them look as though they are trying to be white." April said, "Having a perm is part of my culture and I'm tired of getting burned with I get my hair pressed."

Anastasia felt as if Dinah was judging her for not perming her hair, and she and Shayna defended natural hair as being nonwhite, oppositional to the dominant status. This is an old conversation, beginning when Madame C. J. Walker invented hair straightener for black women (Giddings 1996). The critique then, as it is now, was that black women feel pressured to wear their hair long and straight like white women in order to be attractive. Anastasia and Shayna resisted that model of beauty. Sigmund (white) recorded another incident in which an African American distanced herself from whiteness:

> A white professor talked about how most serial killers are white people—not black, not Latino. In response, a black female student said, "It's like white peo-

ple's parents get divorced and their whole world comes to a stop. Black people are used to their parents getting divorced. They like, 'oh well.'"

This student asserted that blacks were more adaptive to hardship and hence less volatile.

Overidentification with whites was a recurring issue for Precious, who was so light skinned as to often be assumed to be biracial and "too white." Precious (black) recorded this conversation: "A black guy at Wal-Mart asked me where I was from. I told him the name of the suburb, and he commented, 'So you grew up around honkies all you life?'" Precious's light skin instantly associated her with white people to those who encountered her. Yet, at the same time, she was not accepted as white by the dominants.

"Just Like a Nigga": Oppositional Identity Work

Recall that oppositional identity work is a strategy used by marginalized groups to reinvest their identity with value. In doing so, they seize upon an aspect of their identity that has been systematically devalued by the dominants, and they reclaim it. They invert the power dynamic, diminishing its pejorative impact. The refurbished identity becomes a source of unity and celebration. In the racetalk, the term "nigger" or "nigga" had been reclaimed by some African Americans as a term of solidarity. In using "nigger" among themselves, blacks provided lighthearted critiques of blackness that enhanced their sense of in-group identity. For example, Precious (black) wrote: "I heard a black man and woman talking, and the woman said, 'You's a sorry ass nigga.'"

A recurring phrase used in this racetalk was "just like a nigga . . ." For example, Precious (black) wrote:

Penelope, Johnson, and I were watching a movie in which some (black) criminals were helping a couple and after they gained their trust, they ended up robbing them. Johnson said, "Just like some niggaz to help you then rob you."

Here is another incident recorded by Precious:

A group of my friends and I were just sitting around talking. There was a bi-racial (black and white) toddler, about two years old, playing in our presence. It was quiet for about ten seconds, and we heard a fart. Of course, everyone was saying, "Ugggh" and "Gross!" The toddler laughed and ran out of the room. I said, "Just like a nigga, he's gonna fart and leave the room."

Even though the child was biracial, his blackness trumped his whiteness: the term "nigga" was used to explain the social inappropriateness displayed by the child. Yet it was concomitantly used to bond as blacks. Similarly, Megan (white) wrote:

> I was watching the baseball game with my boyfriend, Ali, and his friend, Charlie, who are both black. It was the game where Mark McGuire hit the record breaking homerun. As the ball sailed into the crowd, it bounced back onto the field. The outfielder playing for the other team, who was black, took the ball and instead of giving it back to Mark McGuire, he put it in his pocket—it could be sold for an enormous amount of money. We all couldn't believe what he just did. Charlie yelled, "Just like a nigga—always looking to make a few extra bucks."

"Nigga" was used as a term of camaraderie, even as it reified the image of blacks as petty thieves. Other racetalkers used tempered language to convey the same sentiment, as in these incidents recorded by Precious:

> David (black) and I were driving around the residence hall area and saw a bus flying around the corner without slowing down. Upon noticing that the bus driver was black, I said, "Just like black people to be flyin' 'round the corners." David said, "Black people are going to fly in whatever we drive."

On another occasion, Precious wrote:

> I was at David's house, and his roommate, Chuck (black), was listening to some unfamiliar [white] music. David apologized for not agreeing with Chuck's taste and made a hip hop request. Chuck said, "Don't trip. You're black. You just wanna hear some real nigga gangsta shit, I know." He proceeded to change the music selection.

In yet another incident, Precious and David went to a black friend's house:

> When we entered, the room was about 100 degrees, but Pam had her fan blowing directly on her while she sat at the kitchen table. I said, "That is just like a black muthafucka to have the heat all the way up and the fan going at the same time." Pam said, "I don't care. I don't have to pay for it. Shit, I'm gonna use up all their heat I can." David said, "No, that is just ghetto."

These incidents bring us back to the pejorative images discussed at the beginning of the chapter. Chuck invoked the gangster image. Pam expressed the exact perception that whites have of "ghetto" matriarchs—wasting resources that they do not have to pay for. Precious and David were joking with their friends, but their humor had a critical edge to it as well.

Like other oppositional identity work (see MacLeod 1995; and Schwalbe and Mason-Schrock 1996), saying "just like a nigga" has its downside. By reclaiming a status that is culturally loaded in a negative way—something that has been historically used to devalue a particular group, as "nigger" has been—a group risks participating in their own ritualistic degradation. Indeed, as evidenced in this study, the pervasive use of "nigger" among African Americans has been misunderstood by many whites, who see it as a term divorced from racial content. As Barbara (white) wrote,

> I work part time at Wal-Mart. Infrequently, I will hear the word "nigger" when groups of black youths talk between themselves. I am not always sure whether this is good or bad.

Cheyenne (white) recorded a similar incident:

> My friend Anita called me on the phone and said, "What's up nigga?" Well she is black and I was taken aback by [her comment] because she had never said anything like that to me before. I responded by saying, "Not much, honky!" We went on to talk about other stuff.

Many whites were confused by what they saw as an inconsistent use of "nigger" (see also Kennedy 2003). Some whites misconstrued its use, thinking that they had equal access to the term. As already shown, whites claim entitlement to many cultural practices that do not directly pertain to them. Many whites used "nigger" themselves without reflexive awareness or concern of its historical roots and discursive power, treating it as an equal opportunity term. When this happens, the negative signification of blackness is reinforced.

CONCLUSION

These data provide insight into the ways that racetalk is used to signify the structure of blackness. Whites were disturbed when blacks congregated together in public, when they displayed self-confidence or pride, when they seemed to usurp resources. These data allow us to see the ways that blackness is constructed as threatening. Blackness is undeserving of resources and self-confidence. In the racetalk, blackness was painted in a way that resembled Elijah Anderson's (1999) description of the "hyper-ghetto." In this rendering, African Americans are drug dealers who spend their ill-gotten money on nice clothes and cars. They walk about with hostile attitudes, designed to keep potential attackers at bay. They are uncivil and dangerous. Although few racetalkers in this study have likely spent any time in a hyper-ghetto, their perception of blackness as "ghetto" has been successfully fabricated by media generalizations. Individuals' talk helps reify this distorted image. Thus, whites get worried or angry when they see black people in white spaces, taking their presence as evidence that the ghetto is seeping into their own communities. Other ethnic groups are suspect as well, but few elicit the same level of hostility as African Americans. These findings are consistent with Warren and Twine's (1997) argument that whiteness only has meaning in opposition to blackness.

Based on the racetalk in this study, it seems that whites were wistful for the days of Jim Crow. Gone were the glory days when blacks in public spaces kept their eyes down and tried to pass unnoticed. In the olden days, blacks knew their place as inferiors and deferred to superior whites, as dictated by an extensive racial etiquette.[7] As Charles Johnson (1943, 123) wrote in the Jim Crow era, "Generally speaking, there is no problem in casual public contacts if the Negroes do not make themselves conspicuous by their aggressive behavior." Modern racetalk tried to make sense of unapologetic, "aggressive" African Americans by implicitly juxtaposing the (bad) present with the (good) past. The habitus persisted.

NOTES

1. Recall from pervious chapters that the signification of whiteness is fundamentally linked to the signification of blackness. As I have already mentioned, Warren and Twine (1997) contend that whiteness only has meaning in juxtaposition with blackness. Indeed, in writing this book, it was difficult to decide when to discuss whiteness and when to discuss blackness. So much of their meanings are constructed in opposition to one another that it is impossible to completely separate the two. Although they are different systems of meaning—one constructed out of privilege and the other from enslavement—it behooves me to include one when analyzing the other.

2. Although *Gone With the Wind* glorifies the image while *The Color Purple* offers a critique.

3. This legislation was proposed in response to increased support for gay marriage.

4. Wallace has been much criticized over the years for being too harsh on black men.

5. I talked to a colleague of mine who studies policing and often has his students ride along with officers in this community. He said that on a typical night, the department has twelve cars in circulation. On nights when more activity is expected—like Homecoming—it might have up to fifteen cars. He said it is not unusual for four cars to respond to a traffic stop, so it would not surprise him if ten cars responded in the scenario described by Rori.

6. Interestingly, Richard Zweigenhaft and G. William Domhoff (1999) quote Colin Powell as making the exact same comment about himself in explaining why he blends in so well with his white peers in the military and the government.

7. This etiquette was far-reaching, delineating how "Negroes" should share sidewalks and highways, how to speak to whites, when to remove your hat, and how to act around white women (see C. Johnson 1943). The punishments for violating the etiquette were, of course, severe.

6

THE STRUCTURE OF SIGNIFICATION

Brownness

This is her home this thin edge of barbwire.

—Gloria Anzaldua (1999, 35)

As implied in Anzaldua's poetry above, brown people must walk a thin, contentious, painful racial line. Brown people are neither black nor white in a society that strictly delineates the two (Hacker 2003). Brownness incorporates refugees, nonwhite immigrants, biracial people, and disenfranchised indigenous people. They are *mestizaje*, interlopers.

Brownness as a structure of signification (Giddens 1984) differs from blackness and whiteness in a couple of ways. First, it is not tied to one specific racial/ethnic group. Instead, brownness incorporates Asians, Latino/as, Middle Easterners, Native Americans, and any "other" group that falls outside of the dualistic racial structure of the United States. Of course, blackness and whiteness are not firmly tied to a particular group either. As alluded to in the previous chapter, blackness is not just about African Americans—other groups can become "contaminated" by blackness. Likewise, whiteness can be an honorary status among people of color who transcend the signification of their positions. These people become "whites in waiting" (Hacker 2003). However, unlike brownness, the effects of blackness and whiteness have a disproportionate effect on African Americans and whites, respectively. A second difference in this structure is that brownness is more fluid. Its signification varies across contexts more than blackness and whiteness do.

Due to their complexity, the roots of brownness are less clear-cut than the other structures of signification. In the United States, we continue to have a dualistic, bifurcated measure of race that emphasizes a black/white divide (Hunter 2002b). As Yen Le Espiritu (1997, 108) writes,

> Societies tend to organize themselves around sets of mutually exclusive binaries: white or black, man or woman, professional or laborer, citizen or alien. In the United States, this binary construction of difference—of privileging and empowering the first term and disempowering the second—structures and maintains race, gender, and class privilege and power.

Although not everyone is either black or white, our preoccupation with the binary allows us to lump everyone else together as "other."

Cutting-edge scholarship argues that the black/white binary is giving way to a new racial regime. Specifically, Eduardo Bonilla-Silva et al. (2003) and Tyrone Forman, Carla Goar, and Amanda Lewis (2002) have explored what they call the Latin Americanization thesis. They argue that the United States is evolving from a two-tiered racial system of black versus white to a three-tiered system like that in Latin America. The three tiers are these: (1) white, (2) honorary white, and (3) collective black. "Honorary white" represents a racially mobile group that is able to escape the degraded signification of blackness to appropriate some white capital.

Using survey data from a racially diverse, nationally representative sample, Forman et al. (2002) delineate which racial and ethnic groups fall into which tier. They focus on the racialization of Cubans, Puerto Ricans, Mexican Americans, blacks, and whites. Relevant factors include skin color (see also Hunter 2002a), perception of discrimination, and the degree to which a group identifies with whites versus blacks. They find much diversity among Latinos in terms of complexion and politics, but there are still some key issues—like immigration—that unite Latinos purposefully. Nevertheless, Forman and colleagues' data indicate the fluidity of racialization in this new racial regime. I, too, find a fluidity of racialization within the signification of brownness. I see a bleeding over of whiteness into blackness and vice versa, affecting the identities, experiences, and life chances of those who fall in between. I conceptualize honorary whiteness as a tenuous, temporary status granted to browns according to context.

Unlike Forman et al. (2002), most of my data do not allow for a fine-tuned analysis of self-reported ethnic identities. Instead, my data illustrate the simplistic ways that everyday people impose racial meanings upon others, with or without their cooperation. Indeed, most racetalkers do not discern variation within an ethnic group. All Asians are Chinese. All Latinos are Mexican. All Middle Easterners are Muslim. It would be methodologically and analytically easier for me to divide the composite ethnicities into their respective categories, and then to explore the signification of each. However, doing so would not accurately represent the racetalk.

Thus, although racetalk does not articulate the reality of American ethnicities, it does reflect the coarse cataloging system that many people use to make sense of difference. This chunky, inaccurate system has consequences for real people: the ability to claim racial identity, to act autonomously, and to think critically are all affected by the signification of brownness through racetalk. As such, despite cutting-edge insights, I treat brownness as "other"—as non-white/nonblack.

In conceptualizing brownness this way, I collapse myriad racial and ethnic categories into one. I do not do this unreflexively. I recognize the cultural insensitivity inherent in approaching these cultures as if they are entirely alike. Indeed, within the categories of Latina/o, Asian, Native American, and Middle Eastern, there are vast differences in language, religion, and cultural practices. I collapse these different cultures into brownness because that is how the racetalk packages them. Rather than focusing solely on differences between ethnic groups, I compare and contrast these groups' experiences as browns.

OUTSIDERS WITHIN

A major point of similarity among the "others" is that they do not fit into the prevailing major categories in society. In discussing the place of Asians in the binary discussed above, Espiritu (1997, 109) argues that they are a third group who have been

> marginalized to the periphery of U.S. race relations or reinscribed within the black-white dyad as "near-blacks" (as in "cheap and exploitable labor"), or "near-whites" (as in "model minority"). But importantly, Asian Americans have also been constructed to be neither black nor white—and therein lies the source of their oppression. As members of both the "nonwhite other" and an intermediate group between black and white, Asian Americans have received some special opportunities but have also faced unique disabilities (see also Okhiro 1994).

As critical race theorists would tell us (Delgado and Stefancic 2001; Matsuda et al. 1993), the various groups subsumed under brownness have had different experiences than Asians.[1] However, they have all faced this tension in one form or another. For instance, the myth of the model minority is tied only to Asians,[2] but Middle Easterners and Latino/as experience similar episodes of conditional whiteness, depending on the historic context (see Anzaldua 1999;

Moraga 1995; and Takaki 1994). Due to shifting statuses, brownness is signified as both ally and enemy—to both blacks and whites. Brownness involves the dizzy experience of being caught in the middle of a racial polemic, in which brown people both benefit and suffer from the blurry boundaries. Browns are what Patricia Hill Collins (2000) calls "outsiders within"—people who no longer belong to any one group. W. E. B. Du Bois (1996) would have called them a group with "double consciousness" in what Michelle Fine and Lois Weis (1998, 97) refer to as a "bifurcated racial tapestry."

La Facultad

Another commonality within brownness is that its members—as outsiders within—have become sensitized to oppression. Anzaldua (1999, 60) refers to this sensitivity as *la facultad*, or "the capacity to see in surface phenomena the meaning of deeper realities, to see the deep structure below the surface." This is similar to hooks's (1995) description of an "ethnographic gaze." Anzaldua argues that *la facultad* is an organic outcome of feeling psychologically and/or physically unsafe in the world. It comes from being scrutinized, attacked, marginalized:

> When we're up against the wall, when we have all sorts of oppressions coming at us, we are forced to develop this faculty so that we'll know when the next person is going to slap us or lock us away. . . . Pain makes us acutely anxious to avoid more of it, so we hone that radar. It's a kind of survival tactic that people, caught between the worlds, unknowingly cultivate. It is latent in all of us. (60–61)

Mari Matsuda (1993, 21) writes about the ways that her parents first awakened her sensitivity to racism:

> As a young child I was told never to let anyone call me a J_p [sic]. My parents, normally peaceable and indulgent folk, told me this in the tone reserved for dead-serious warnings. Don't accept rides from strangers. Don't play with matches. Don't let anyone call you that name. In their tone they transmitted a message of danger, that the word was dangerous to me, tied to violence.

Matsuda (1993, 22) took her parents' warnings to heart, learning to recognize the connections between race and violence on her own:

> Just as I grew up to learn the facts about the unspoken danger my parents saw in the stranger in the car, I learned how they connected the violence of California lynch mobs and Hiroshima atom bombs to racist slurs against Japanese Americans.

La Facultad is armor against every word that wounds (Matsuda et al. 1993).

INVISIBILITY

Like blackness, brownness is ironic. Brown people are seen as outsiders, as un-invited intruders. Yet, they are dismissed, overlooked, erased. Indeed, there is much pressure by the dominants for browns to assimilate as much as possible into whiteness. Browns are urged to blend in, to cast off their particular cul-tures, and not to call attention to themselves. There are negative outcomes of assimilation. Generation gaps are created between first and second generation immigrants, and the children may no longer be able to relate to their parents and vice versa (Xiong and Tatum 1999).[3] Many cultures have been lost to this process over the years, as Anzaldua (1999, 108) argues: "The dominant white culture is killing us slowly with its ignorance." She reacts to this phenomenon, asserting,

> I am visible—see this Indian face—yet I am invisible. I both blind them with my beak nose and am their blind spot. But I exist, we exist. They'd like to think I have melted in the pot. But I haven't. We haven't. (108)

NAMING ONESELF: THE POWER OF LANGUAGE

Another issue embedded in the structure of brownness is the right to name oneself and to use one's own language. This struggle is not unique to brown-ness, as I discussed in the previous chapter. However, because language is such a large part of the "otherness" inherent in brownness, it has a particu-lar role in the disempowerment of its members (Shultz et al. 1999). Anzal-dua (1999, 75) remembered being caught speaking Spanish at recess, for which she received three sharp smacks on her knuckles with a ruler. She writes,

> I remember being sent to the corner of the classroom for "talking back" to the Anglo teacher when all I was trying to tell her was how to pronounce my name. "If you want to be American, speak 'American.' If you don't like it, go back to Mexico where you belong."

"Speaking American" involves more than just speaking English. It involves as-similating to the dominant culture. Anzaldua (1999, 81) goes on to emphasize the linkages between language and identity:

> So if you really want to hurt me, talk badly about my language. Ethnic identity is twin skin to linguistic identity—I am my language. Until I can take pride in my language, I cannot take pride in myself.

Anzaldua (1999, 81) writes of reclaiming her identity, of naming herself:

> I will no longer be made to feel ashamed of existing. I will have my voice: Indian,
> Spanish, white. I will have my serpent's tongue—my woman's voice, my sexual
> voice, my poet's voice. I will overcome the tradition of silence.

Cherrie Moraga (1995, 215), too, demonstrates the power in self-identification:

> I call myself a Chicana writer. Not a Mexican-American writer, not a Hispanic
> writer, not a half-breed writer. To be a Chicana is not merely to name one's
> racial/cultural identity, but also to name a politic that refuses assimilation into the
> U.S. mainstream. It acknowledges our *mestizaje*—Indian, Spanish and *africano*.

When the dominants define "others," they often do so in demeaning ways.
The term "Sioux," for example, was used by whites to refer to the Lakota tribe
of Native Americans. While "sioux" is a Lakota term, it means "snakes" (T. Wilson 1994). Similarly, the term "Eskimo" means "dirty raw-fish eater." Not surprisingly, then, the "Eskimos" prefer to be called "Inuit," which means "the
people" (Loewen 2000). Empowerment involves the ability to define oneself
rather than being defined/degraded by the dominants. Language is a tool for
oppression and resistance.

COUNTERSTANCE: CONTRADICTION AND AMBIGUITY

As a result of marginalization, brownness incorporates a counterstance to
dominant culture and structure. Anzaldua (1999, 100) defines the counterstance as such:

> The counterstance refutes the dominant culture's views and beliefs, and, for this,
> it is proudly defiant. All reaction is limited by, and dependent on, what it is re-
> acting against. Because the counterstance stems from a problem with authority—
> outer as well as inner—it's a step towards liberation from cultural domination.
> But it's not a way of life.

At some point, even those with a counterstance have to ally themselves with
one side or another. This is an ongoing tension that underlies brownness. As
Anzaldua (1999, 101) elaborates, "These numerous possibilities leave *la mestiza* floundering in unchartered seas. . . . The new *mestiza* copes by developing a tolerance for contradictions, a tolerance for ambiguity."

Taken together, brownness is a fluid, ambiguous structure that is at odds
with both whiteness and blackness. Indeed, it is a buffer zone between the

two, and therefore caught in the middle. Brownness is sometimes valued and other times devalued. It involves political struggles for power. The racetalk in this study further fleshed out the ambiguous, contradictory nature of brownness and its effects on real people.

SHIFTING STATUS: BROWNNESS IN MYRIAD CONTEXTS

In the racetalk, brownness was signified in ways that both resonated with and elaborated upon the concepts laid out in the literature. The data show that the signification of brownness changed as the context changed. For example, during this period of study, the World Trade Center and the Pentagon were attacked by Al Qaeda terrorists. As such, Middle Easterners—who had previously been ignored in racetalk except for the occasional random slur—became systematically problematized in people's conversations. As critical race theorists assert (Delgado and Stefancic 2001), the positionality of brownness shifted according to the social and political expectations of each setting.

Othering: The Dominants' Definitions of Brownness

As with blackness, subjects used an expanding vocabulary in their construction of a brown group. Old slurs were used, including spic, Chink, Gook, dog eater, rag head, towel head (both of which enjoyed a post-9/11 renaissance), dot head/dot, Dago, sand nigger, dune coon, and "those people." Other terms were morphed and updated. Ranchero, beaner, and brazer suggested Latinos, especially Mexicans. Hispanic children were called "spiclets." "Chiefing" was slang for smoking marijuana. East Indians were referred to as "gandhis" and "quickies," in reference to Quickie Marts. Colombians were associated with drug dealers. "Panface" referenced Asians. Racetalkers used this language to construct complicated, pejorative images of brownness.

Caricatures. In the racetalk, brown cultures were distorted, caricatured, and decontextualized from their histories. For instance, Missy (white) wrote this: "My roommate's black boyfriend always says that I'm 80 percent Mexican because I put hot sauce on everything that I eat, I cook Mexican food, and I like to go salsa/meringue dancing." Precious's (black) friend Penelope (black) said:

> The Chinese and Japanese muthafuckas be on they P's and Q's. I bet it's because they are one day ahead of us. That's why they are so advanced.

Carol Ann (white) observed this: "My (white) friend was doing an impression of a guy who works at the 7–11. He said, 'I am Habbib and I want a slurpy.'"

Carol Ann's white roommate said, as they drove along, "Oh my gosh—you almost hit a Habbib." Carol Ann also recorded this incident:

> I was at Teri's house, and she was blow drying her hair with a bag on her head, because she had just dyed it. She said, "I look like a freakin' Arab with this bag on my head like this."

Blueangel had a pimple on her forehead: "A few people have called me 'Indian dot' over the past few weeks because of the bump on my head." These caricatures are so pervasive in our culture as to be cartoonish: turban-wearing men selling Slurpies; quiet, obedient Asians; Mexicans dancing and eating spicy foods. Racetalkers called upon them with the ease that comes from living in a culture infused with such images.

Behaviors became associated with certain ethnic groups as a result of caricatures. For example, Harley (white) reported this conversation with her father: "We saw an SUV with low rider type tires. I giggled because it looked funny, and my dad said, 'Mexicans,' in a tsk-tsk manner." Carmen and her friend called a slow-moving car driven by Latinos a "Mexi-mobile," concluding, "the reason it was going so slow is because they are so poor, and they cannot get insurance." Driving "Mexican style" meant packing a car full of people—even if all of the passengers were white.

Caricatures trivialized the historical and contemporary suffering of various ethnic groups. For example, Roger's (white) roommate Jake (white) woke up in the middle of the night to find Roger doing homework and said, "You're still doing homework? You're working like a Mexican." Jake trivialized the hard work of immigrants who try to provide for their entire families. This sentiment was reiterated in another incident recorded by Roger, who complained to a friend (white) about the late spring:

> I said how I was sick of the cold weather and the fact that my shoes were all muddy from cutting through the grass. My friend said, "Don't worry. Soon it will be warm and the Mexicans can whip all of the grass back into shape." We both snickered and changed the subject.

In yet another incident, Roger went to his (white) girlfriend's apartment after working out:

> Tina said, "You look like a wetback!" I looked at my back which was covered in sweat, and said, "Yeah, did you want me to mow your lawn or what?" She said, no. Then I ran and gave her a hug and she screamed.

Tina could have just said that Roger looked gross. Instead, she underscored her revulsion by associating him with a devalued ethnic group. Roger played along and helped to devalue the group. Other groups were demeaned in this acontextual manner as well. Carmen's (white) friend planned to go camping. Carmen reported: "Jenn (white) had to go to get her gear from the recreation center. When she came back, she said she felt like a Vietnamese refugee with all the stuff on her bike." Here, Jenn made light of the need for thousands of Vietnamese to flee their homes due to war and poverty. Similarly, Jean (white) pointed out an Asian neighbor to her friends who are visiting her: "I demonstrated how she walks across the floor above us in baby steps. All of my friends laughed and Ree (white) said that she took baby steps because she was a chink. Everyone laughed." These women joked about the debilitating practice of foot-binding among girls in China. Such unreflexive comments accentuated the racial and ethnic privileges of the speakers.

That's How They Are: Generalizing from Caricatures. Once race-talkers caricatured members of a group, it was easy to generalize their "observations" to the entire group. Missy's (white) white roommate asserted that most Mexican men were perverts. In another incident, Missy was in Spanish class:

> We were talking about how the men in Mexico think that American women are easy because their only impression of us is what they see in the movies. A girl (half white, half Mexican) said, "All Mexican men are macho."

Taylor (white) found more evidence of Mexican men's problems:

> I was visiting with my friend. She was telling me about some of her Mexican neighbors, who are apparently here illegally. She referred to them as "damn spics," and "beaners." She told me that the man beat his wife and then said, "But that's how the Mexican men are." I said, "Not all Mexicans beat their wives." She said, "They are so jealous and controlling. They think they can do whatever they want to their families."

Singular observations were recorded, perhaps misunderstood, and used to understand an entire group. This process reflected a sense of cultural entitlement on the part of the racetalkers.

Pollutants.   As a part of the process of othering, the browns as a group were signified as pollutants: dirty and disgusting. Like blackness, brownness stinks. Naomi (Latina) recorded this incident:

> A group of Indian students were hanging around outside of the campus library. Naomi overheard a group of whites reacting to the Indians as they passed them: A white girl covered her mouth and said, "Whatever they wear as perfume smells horrible while they think it smells great."

Kenny (white) recorded a more blatant assessment: "Indians smell like shit." Abe's (white) friend (white) wondered, "Do Dot-Heads ever shower?" Precious (black) recorded this:

> Johnson, Penelope, Vikki, and I (all black) were sitting around the kitchen table just having small talk. Penelope started talking about how at school that day she was in the computer lab and could not get anything accomplished. She said, "Those stankin' ass Indians. They were talking all loud and shit. It was a gang of 'em in a big group in the computer lab." Vikki asked her, "Did they really stink, Penelope, or are you just saying that?" Penelope laughed and raised her voice, "Hell yeah, they asses stank! I could smell the curry seeping out of their skin. 'Cuz you know they don't use regular soap. They bathe in, cook, and eat this stuff called curry."

Monty (Asian) lived in a multicultural fraternity house with many international students. He recorded this incident:

> After a Saturday morning feast in the house, an American roommate (white) came home to see the kitchen in a total disaster. I walked down a few minutes later to see him cleaning up the dishes and the mess all around. He said, "Those fuckin' foreigners never clean up their shit. I mean, look at this. This is grease from the George Foreman grill. They used a real plate to catch the grease instead of cleaning out the dish that is supposed to catch it. And this kitchen smells like ass. What did those disgusting foreigners cook?"

So browns stunk because of the food they ate, their bathing habits, and their perfume—they were culturally different from the norm and therefore attacked. As a result they repelled many of the whites and blacks around them, as Precious (black) observed:

> Penelope (black) and I were fixing sandwiches. I chose an orange colored cheese and Penelope said, "You're going to use that kind of cheese? Do you even like that kind?" I said, "Yeah, I like this kind of cheese. What's wrong with this cheese." Penelope said, "It's Mexican cheese." Johnson (black) was sitting near and he said, "No, it's not. It's Colby Jack cheese, with your ignorant ass."

Because Penelope associated the cheese with a degraded brown group, she was repelled by it. More pointedly, the repellent applied to members of the brown group as well, as recorded by Rori (white), whose mother was married to a Mexican. Her mother often said, "I love Jose, but other Mexicans are dirty." While Rori's mother was able to make an exception, Jessica's (white) friend Sarah (white) could not:

> Sarah (white) said, "I was dating a Mexican guy, but I thought he was Italian. Then, when it came up, he said he was Mexican and I said, 'Wow, I don't go there. I just don't.'"

This man was seen as a viable date until Sarah learned that he was not white. Then, he became polluted.

Troublemakers.   As with other devalued groups, brownness signified troublemaking. Browns were people who damaged the homes and workplaces of more valuable people (whites). They were conceptualized as out of control, as in this incident recorded by Cher (white). Her friend Seth (white) said,

> Those fuckin' spics are always causing trouble. My dad just hired a guy. He is so fucking stupid he can't even speak English. Also, my dad drives these carts around the warehouse going about 60 mph. This bastard goes like 15 mph. He's a fucking spic idiot and they hired him! Dumb ass.

Seth was persuaded that Latinos are "always causing trouble" by an authority figure—his father—and he passed along this assessment of browns in an un- critical manner. Brownness was signified—like blackness—as criminality. Ash- ley (white) recorded this incident:

> It was Labor Day so a few friends and I had a cookout at a local park. My little sister, who is 15 years old, had a few of her friends at the park also. My friends and I were playing volleyball, which was quite a distance from the pavilion where our food was. A few of us were getting hungry, so we asked my little sister's friends if there was any more food left. One of the boys answered, "Probably not because I just saw a few beaners over by the food. They probably ate it all."

Brownness embodied a threat to dominants. For example, Flora (white) talked with her father-in-law about his daughter's choices for lunch at work:

> She could either take a paid hour and eat in the lunchroom or take an unpaid hour and eat outside the premises. I said that if I were her, I would eat in the lunchroom because it's cheaper and she gets paid for it. He told me, "Well, there are mostly Mexicans in the company. One day, she went into the lunchroom and felt uncomfortable because she was the only white person in the room." I said there was nothing wrong with that; they would not bother her because they would mind their own business like everybody else. He said that he knew this be- cause he worked with Mexicans in the factory where he worked. He said, "I can handle them."

Flora's father-in-law implied that the brown men were menacing to this white woman. As such, these men resembled black bucks, voracious sexual predators of white virginity. These Latinos had never given any cause for this white woman to fear them. She found them suspicious because of their pejorative signification, which was exacerbated by the fact that they outnumbered the whites. They were seen as a danger that needed to be "handled."

The ultimate group of troublemakers within brownness were Middle East-erners, at least after 9/11. Hedwig (white) and Matt (white) had this conversation about September 11th shortly after it occurred:

> Matt: It's pretty cool driving around and seeing all those cars with big American flags flapping around. It's like all those Mexicans with their little Mexican flags on their cars (he gave a sarcastic laugh).
>
> Hedwig: What's the matter with that? That's their heritage just like the American flags represent ours.
>
> Matt: Anyway, I've been giving a lot of Arabs I see dirty looks (laughs).
>
> Hedwig: Why would you do that? They're not all terrorists.
>
> Matt: The other day, I think I saw two terrorists driving down the highway. They were driving a car with no license plates. It just had a rental sticker on it. These two guys were wearing big black turbans on their heads.
>
> Hedwig interrupted: Wait a minute. I don't think that terrorists wear turbans. They want to blend in. They're not the big bearded turban headed ones. That would draw too much attention, which is not what they want.
>
> Matt: I don't know. I think they're terrorists. Anyway, you can't trust anyone.
>
> Hedwig: Yeah, that's right. You can't trust anyone no matter what their race.
>
> Matt: No—you can trust Americans.
>
> Hedwig: How do you know there's not some crazy white man who's pissed off at us and thinks that the Taliban is cool? You can't trust them either. You know, like Charles Manson?
>
> Matt: Nah. Charles Manson wasn't a terrorist. He was just a murderer.

This conversation occurred during a period of intense jingoism, when any dissent was silenced as un-American. Nevertheless, Hedwig was brave and stood her ground. Due to the devastating acts of a few, Middle Easterners in general became signified as troublemakers. This was more than mere rhetoric. Estella's (white) friend Louise (white) was convinced that she would be harmed by Middle Easterners in the months following 9/11. Estella and her friend Sharon (white) discussed Louise's fear. Sharon said:

> Louise is so weird. She won't go to the gas station off of 26 any more because the man who runs it is Arabian. I was going to get a pack of cigarettes from the gas station and Louise said not to buy them there. I told her she could walk to get her cigarettes because I was buying them there.

Blueangel (black) recorded a similar incident about her coworker Al (Asian):

> Al just got back from California, and he wanted to share with the office his flying experience (post 9/11). He made a comment, which everyone took as a joke but me. He kept repeating his stupid joke over and over again. Every time someone new came into the office, he told this joke—or maybe it wasn't a joke. This is what

Al said: "If you see a guy on a carpet kneeling and sweating (he then put his hands together as if praying and started bobbing his head), you don't get on a plane. Also, if I see three or more Middle Eastern guys going on a plane, I will be on standby." He then went on to say, "I don't want to racial profile, but you know." Everyone started laughing.

Everyone laughed except for Blueangel. In her focus group, Blueangel questioned the "united we stand" rhetoric that prevailed in the post-9/11 period. She said,

> We're not united now, and we weren't before 9/11. Black people are not part of the "we." As soon as we're done hating Middle-Easterners, we'll go back to hating black people.

Blueangel recognized and critiqued the malleable signification of brownness as compared to the intractable signification of blackness in modern America.

Offensive Language: Speaking American

As discussed above, a major element of brownness is the use of language that differs from that of the dominants. As such, racetalkers interrogated the ways that browns spoke—their accents as well as their language—underscoring their outsider positions. For example, Leigh (white) was studying in the Commons with Patty (white):

> Patty went to get something to drink. It was nice and quiet, then this group of three people came and took a table about three away from ours. The girl in the group, her voice was irritating me because she was so loud and squeaky. When Patty came back, I told her that the girls' voice was irritating me. When Patty heard her talk, she looked at me with a look saying that I was right. Then she looked at the girl, looked back at me, and said, "Orientals have the most annoying voices."

Jaime (white) wrote:

> I was in the car with Michael (white) and we passed a big huge white car with the music playing really loud and bass thumping. It was full to capacity. Michael joked that people in the car were probably those with English as a second language. We looked and it was a car full of Mexicans.

Accents were commonly mimicked. For example, Lavinia (white) and her white roommate wondered who changed their burnt-out light bulb. The roommate speculated, "One of the [Latina] housekeepers probably said, 'Light bulb is no working.'"

The critique of accents and the use of languages other than English went beyond mere ridicule, invoking real anger among racetalkers. For example, Jonathan's (white) white friend criticized his Asian professor: "Goddamn gooks. Can't speak our language, I can't understand what the hell they're saying." Hedwig's (white) friend Matt (white) talked about work:

> Matt said, "I swear there are so many Mexican people that work around here. None of 'em speak even a word of English. No green card, no nothing. And they're making good money. It pisses me off." I asked, "Now how do you know they don't have green cards or anything?" He said, "I just know, okay? I've talked to enough of them to know. That's how they all are."

Interestingly, Matt claimed to have "talked to them" even though they spoke no English and he spoke no Spanish. He likely overplayed the situation to make his point stronger. Ashley (white) recorded a similar sentiment:

> My (white) neighbor was talking about his new job at a grocery store. He told me about a man who came in and couldn't speak English. All he could speak was Spanish. My neighbor made the comment: "If they can't speak our language, they should go back to their own country." I insisted on telling him that Mexicans came to this country to better themselves, not necessarily meaning that they had to learn our language.

Jaime (white) found a racetalker who expressed this idea more plainly:

> I was at a friend's house and his dad (white) was talking about the maintenance guys that were Mexican. He said, "Those banditos should all learn English if they want to work in America."

Sigmund (white) and his white coworker had this more gentle conversation:

> Sigmund: Have you ever noticed with Spanish-speaking customers that they always come in groups of three?
> Ned: Three or four.
> Sigmund: And only one of them knows English? All speak Spanish but only one can translate the English?
> Ned: Nothing against their people, but that's just how they are.
> Sigmund: I don't have anything against them.
> Ned: Well, me either, but if you're going to come to this country you should learn how to speak the language.

Apparently these racetalkers believed the credo mentioned by Anzaldua above: "When in America, speak American."

The underlying analysis in this racetalk seems to be that people who do not speak fluent, flawless English are less intelligent than white Americans. As Seth (white) said of the Latino whom his father hired: "He is so fucking stupid he can't even speak English. . . . Dumb ass!" This notion was prevalent. It was also myopic. Most Americans speak only one language—English—(Gonzalez and Melis 2000; Schmidt 2000), and they do not speak it very well on average. Yet, rather than recognizing and appreciating the skills and intellect that it takes to learn multiple languages, these racetalkers categorically dismissed those who had not yet mastered English. Language was used as a proxy for deservedness. The conclusion: browns who fail to speak fluent English should not work in American jobs, use American child or health care, or reside in American neighborhoods. American immigration policies have long reflected these sentiments (Takaki 1994).

Interlopers: Outsiders Within

Due to their intermediate status as nonwhite/nonblack, the browns in this study crossed racial and ethnic boundaries in ways that other groups could not. None of them had very dark skin, but they all had ethnic identities. They fit into some white settings and were cast out of others. Thus, the browns experienced being "insiders" as well as being "outsiders," sometimes simultaneously.

Becoming a White Insider.   Being a white insider meant being seen as not-so-brown. These people might be allowed to join a white group, to bond with a white family, to access white resources and white racetalk. In other words, browns could become "honorary whites" (Bonilla-Silva et al. 2003; Forman et al. 2002) or "whites in waiting" (Hacker 2003). Browns had to prove themselves before being admitted to the white club, however, as evidenced in Sena's (Latina) data:

> When I received my letter from my future roommate (white) freshman year, she gave me her phone number to call her. We met, and because I was Hispanic, she acted strange. She later told me that she assumed because I was Hispanic that was going to be "ghetto" and "a bitch" and we wouldn't get along.

Eventually, Sena proved herself to be worthy as an honorary white. In another example recorded by Jaime (white), we can see a white racetalker weighing whether or not a Latino was acceptable as a white consort. Her friend Carrie (white) spent a weekend in downtown Chicago where she lost her driver's license. A man found it and returned it to her. Carrie described him like this:

> His name is Ricardo. He is half white, half Mexican. He wore clean clothes, was clean cut, and his clothes and car were expensive. So you would think drug dealer, but he said he was in sports management. So that is money. His clothes were kind of hip-hoppy but very clean and not ghetto. He is also very hot!

Carrie had a positive interaction with Ricardo in spite of his brownness. He was "hot," clean, and affluent as juxtaposed to the prevailing trope of brownness: dirty, greasy, dangerous. Based on her comments, Ricardo had one foot through the door of honorary whiteness. Jaime recorded a similar incident with Carrie:

> Carrie put on a shirt and exclaimed, "This shirt is so ghetto! I look so ghetto!" She put on the shirt anyway because it was a gift from a soccer player who was cute: "He's a short little Mexican guy who is so cute!"

The warm fuzzy associations with the giver of the shirt outweighed the ghettoness of it—a sign that its giver had been accepted as an honorary insider.

As "honorary whites," browns witnessed whites' backstage behavior. Honorary whites were privy to antiblack racetalk. For example, Coco (Latina) was engaged to a white man. She had cross-cutting experiences regularly. In this example, Coco and her fiancé went to see Betty (white), who was making Coco's wedding dress:

> Betty was showing us pictures of her dress and wedding. She was telling us who came to her wedding. "This is my brother and his nigger bitch girlfriend." I was so shocked and so was my fiancé. I don't think I'll be needing her help any more.

Betty clearly assumed that Coco would be open to her racetalk because of her engagement to a white man. She was wrong. When browns entered whitehood, they were honored by being set apart from blacks, who were viewed as despicable and/or dangerous. As such, browns occupied an elevated social status.

Tenuous Inclusion.   At the same time, this status was tenuous. In any given situation, Latina/os' white privileges could be revoked, and they could again become outsiders. Naomi (Latina) experienced this sudden shift in terrain while on a retreat with the foreign language program. This incident occurred in the dining hall:

> We all have to place silverware in its proper place after we are done eating so the person who washes dishes does not have such a complicated job. My friends who

are white took their dirty silverware after eating and placed them correctly and were not being watched by the food director. Once I got up to put my plate and silverware in its proper place, the director stared at every movement I made and gave me a "fake" smile. When I left, I looked back. She grabbed my silverware and plate and began putting them back again. I knew I had placed them in the correct manner. The director of the foreign language retreat saw what had happened and said, "Don't worry. She shouldn't be working here in the first place. She's kind of racist."

Naomi's status shifted without warning: she was made to feel like an outsider by a random white woman mere minutes after being included as an insider among her white friends. Naomi's degrading experience echoed those of her black peers, except that she had instant confirmation from a white authority that she was reading the situation correctly. In another example, Leigh (white) wrote:

A group of my girlfriends and I were at a bar. Erica (white) is an engineering major. These two Hispanic guy friends of hers came over and said hi. As they talked, Colleen (white) asked me how Erica knew them. I told her that they are engineering majors too. She looked at them again and turned to me and said, "Those two . . . really?" She had the look and tone as if she were shocked by the fact that two Hispanic men had that major.

These Latinos had become insiders by proving their intellectual merits as engineers. Engineering is a challenging field. Yet, the legitimacy of their status was questioned due to the pejorative signification of brownness. Colleen seemed to wonder, How could brown men have achieved the proper qualifications?

Had these men been of another brown ethnicity—such as Indian or Pakistani—Colleen might have simply assumed that they were qualified to be insiders. For example, Celine (white) recorded this incident that associated certain browns with the discipline of psychology:

Candice (white), Ahna (white) and I were walking out of the psychology building after class. We started talking about what was going on with the new war [in Afghanistan]. Candice said, "We should be safe in the psychology building because it's full of 'em." I said, "My boyfriend feels the same way about his home town because there are so many of them there too. He says they wouldn't kill their own kind."

Some browns belonged in certain white spaces due to their intellectual prowess. However, these people were still marked as treacherous outsiders. Thus, there were gradations of acceptance within brownness, and even their hard-won insider status was fragile.

People often pretended to accept browns to their face, but made it clear that they still saw them as outsiders when talking among themselves. For example, Taylor (white) observed this racetalk at the nursing home where she worked:

> The nurse's assistant came in looking for a housekeeper because one of the resident's bathrooms was out of paper towels. The housekeeper working that unit that day was Hispanic. He asked me, "Did spic-and-span already go home?" I knew who he meant, but I asked, "Do you mean Juanita?" He said yes, and I told him that I didn't know, but he should refer to her by her name.

The aide was friendly to Juanita when they were both at work, but he degraded her—using the term "spic"—when she was not around. In another example, Rachel (white) wrote:

> Pat (white) was telling me about how proud he was to be able to go and get his little four year old sister off the bus every day. I said, "Pat, what's your sister's name again? She is so cute." He said, "Olivia. She's a little Mexican girl." I said, "Pat, your mom is white. Oh yeah, your step-dad's Mexican, right?" He said, "Yeah, she's just a little Mexican."

Even though Pat clearly loved his half sister, he used a double entendre to mark her as an outsider: she's just a little Mexican. In a similar incident, Megan (white) and her friend talked about interracial adoption in a condescending manner:

> I was at Wal-mart with my friend Juana (black). We saw a white man and woman and their Asian daughter. Among ourselves, we commended them for (probably) adopting the girl. We thought that was very honorable. Juana went on and on about how cute the little girl was. She said that her friend Mark's parents had adopted a little Asian girl and she was just as cute: "Well, she looks like that little girl. You know how all Asian kids look alike."

Juana—a black woman—jokingly invoked a comment that is often used to stereotype blacks. However, she and Megan pointed out that even when whites do an "honorable" thing by adopting a brown child, the child remained an outsider despite her newfound white privileges.

Many of the browns in this study were integrated into supportive white social networks. Yet, they had the dizzy experience of being caught in the middle of a racial polemic. They both benefited and suffered from the blurry boundaries (see Fine and Weis 1999). They were outsiders within—people who no longer belonged to any one group. Due to structural conflicts, their lives were riddled with contradictions that they constantly negotiated.

At Home on the Barbwire: Walking the Thin Line

The signification of the structure of brownness enforced an ideal-type person. Many browns found this type appealing even as it was demeaning. In order to fit the type, browns had to conform to a standard of behavior and appearance.

Not Brown Enough.   Life on the barbwire was contradictory and painful for many. Those who did not "measure up" were told that they were not being true to their culture. Among the browns, Latina/os experienced this most often. For example, Coco (Latina) ran into a man who taught a Salsa class on campus:

> He asked me, "You don't hang out with any Latinos on campus, do you?" I think he was insinuating that I was less than a Latina for that. I get that from a lot of people. They always say, "I didn't even know you were Hispanic. You don't act like it," or "You don't look like one."

According to Gloria Yamato (1988), judging a person's racial/ethnic authenticity is called self-righteous racism. Yet Latino/as actively judged one another according to an ideal type. Perhaps because of their ability to span boundaries, the tensions among Latino/as were exacerbated: how can I cross boundaries and still be true to myself?

Too Brown.   At the same time, browns recognized the diversity among themselves, and they sought to distance themselves from overt stereotypes of brownness. Flora's (white) husband (white) relayed an incident that he observed between two Puerto Ricans at work, one of whom was his boss, and the other a chief engineer. His boss did not speak English fluently. He, his boss, and the engineer had a conference call. During the call, the engineer called the boss a "dumb spic," and told him to stop speaking "Spanglish." Flora's husband was shocked and the boss was embarrassed. The engineer seemed offended by the boss's flawed English. He implied that it reflected badly on Puerto Ricans in general.

Yayo (Latino) worked at a Mexican restaurant with many other Latino/as. Not all of them spoke Spanish. Expectations of bilingualism caused tensions on many occasions. In one, "a group of four Spaniard men" harassed a server, telling her "to quit acting white and to speak Spanish to them." On yet another occasion, Yayo became angry and he wrote this in his field notes:

> I had to help a customer because one of the bartenders doesn't speak Spanish. It pisses me off that they don't speak Spanish. To save time and work, all of our staff should be bilingual or at least be able to take an order in Spanish. Why should I have to do their work?

Sena (Latina) recorded a similar intraracial critique:

> I was at my friend Maria's house and her neighbors are Mexicans. When they came out, although she's Mexican [too], she made the statement that they are all a bunch of wetbacks, *mojados*.

Coco (Latina) talked about her roommate's concern with complexion:

> My (Latina) roommate is sometimes mistaken for someone of Indian heritage. She has dark skin and has facial features very similar to those of Indians. Someone thought she was Indian, and she said, "I am not a dot-head!"

This woman used a slur to distance herself from a "dark," devalued group. Similarly Maggie's (Latina) friend Luis (Latino) asked her, "Have you seen Saul's baby girl?" She said, "No, not yet. How does she look?" Luis replied, "She is so pretty man. She has green eyes and is real white. Not like my nephew. When he was born, he looked all dark and red." The baby looked whiter and therefore prettier (see Hunter 2002a). In these instances, people of color argued that certain significations of brownness—like dark skin—were bad. Indeed, this problem should be remedied if possible. This form of racetalk lowers people's self-esteem, and it helps reify racist constructions of "the other."

People who were seen as too attached to their devalued culture were contaminated by that culture. Maggie (Latina) recorded this incident at a political science panel discussion on the Middle East:

> My friend Nina was sitting next to me mumbling sarcastic and joking remarks to me like, "Man those rag heads; sand niggas." I asked her, "Aren't you Arabian?" She said, "Yeah, but I look Hispanic, so I'm not a rag head or sand nigga." I said, "Yeah you are."

Nina did not want to be rejected for her culture in the post-9/11 hate frenzy. Her devalued status was a rather recent sociohistorical product, directly related to current events. According to these racetalkers, the browns whom they observed were too ethnic, embarrassing to the rest of the brown group for one reason or another. Their private racetalk sanctioned their overt enactment of stereotyped ethnicity and served to distance the talkers from that signification of brownness: I may be brown, but I am not like *that*.

Contradictions.   Living on barbwire meant that the system for evaluating brownness involved complex and contradictory identity politics. People may be admired and degraded at the same time, as illustrated in this conversation between Latina/os Maggie and Marco. They sat in the student center and observed two black women studying what appeared to be nursing texts. Some Latino friends of theirs, Dan and Mitch, were sitting two tables down:

Maggie: It seems that a large majority of African American girls here on campus are nursing majors.

Marco: Hmmm. They don't do well though. I mean some might graduate, but they struggle just like Hispanics in engineering, you know. It's like me wanting to major in physics. I'm a Bio major.

Maggie: Isn't Dan an engineering major? How difficult.

Marco: Yeah, dorky Dan and his brother Mitch are both engineering majors. We'll see how that plays out.

Maggie: (laughing) Why do you call him "dorky Dan?"

Marco: They both are. They look straight up ranchero/beaner/brazer. They look as if they came up here and parked their horses right in front of the library and tied them up to a tree (laughing).

Maggie: They are both in that co-ed Hispanic fraternity. I don't understand why people join.

Marco: (laughing) Bogus! Because it gives them cohesiveness, a feeling of belonging. You know, they feel tight, like a family. It's better than joining a gang. White people just want to party and get drunk. And black folks just want to be cool.

Here, Marco reproduced the notion that challenging school work should be reserved for whites, who are more qualified. He caricatured them harshly. Yet, at the same time, Marco seemed to admire them as well as the black nursing students. Maggie had a similar conversation with him at a colloquium at which sociologist and race scholar Eduardo Bonilla-Silva spoke:

Marco: You came for the extra credit huh? That's igg [ignorant].

Maggie: No, not just for that. I want to hear what he has to say. Why did you come? Oh yeah, I forgot. You love to hear about how you are constantly being discriminated against and feel sorry for yourself.

Marco: You too, nigga. We both Mexican.

Maggie: Yeah, but I don't feel sorry for myself and that isn't all I think about. I perhaps get more discriminated against than you. Did you forget that I'm a girl within our culture? You beaner males are dicks. I'm tryin' to do something about it—not just bitch.

Marco: Me too. Anyways, I came because he's Latino. I think he's Rican, but still that's not bad. He is an Hispanic with a Ph.D. That's cool. That shit motivates me.

After Bonilla-Silva walked up to the podium, Maggie and Marco saw that he was a black Puerto Rican:

Marco: No doubt he's Rican. Dark as hell.

Maggie: He is your color, so shhh.

Mexican Americans in this study used a play on words to devalue Puerto Ricans. "Rican" is code for its homonym, "reekin,'" through which they othered this non-Mexican ethnic group. Bonilla-Silva was at once denigrated as "Ri-can" while celebrated as a "Latino with a Ph.D."

Taken together, looking at life on the barbwire showed the ways that browns themselves bought into and helped reproduce racial/ethnic hierarchies. In so doing, they "did racism." There was a double-edged sharpness to barbwire: on the one hand, this position helped insulate and protect subordinates. On the other hand, reifying otherness helped to perpetuate structural inequality by taking the racial regime for granted.

Counterstance

As Anzaldua argued, the intermediate status of brownness generated a counterstance, through which group members used racetalk to assert their identity and autonomy. For example, Gail (white) overheard a group of Indi-ans joking about how much they have improved American society:

> I heard an Indian guy and an Indian girl talking about how if Indian people hadn't come to America, Americans wouldn't have any doctors, computer programmers, or engineers. My boyfriend is Indian, but sometimes I think they hype their cul-ture too much. I know that they think all Americans do is worry about partying and stuff while they're in high school and college. I feel this stereotype is not true for all Americans, though.

These Indian students asserted their superiority to whiteness. They under-scored the irony of their outsider status in U.S. society: they hate us but they need us. They can't live without us.

Browns occasionally saw whites as their enemies. For example, Yayo (Latino) and a friend joked about white people: "My friend said, 'They'll come to the bar-rio for food, but floor it out of here when they're done!' She and I are totally against gentrification." Yayo and his brother argued about how to fill out their family's census form. Yayo declared that they were not white after his brother had marked that they were. They ended up requesting a second form to correct the "error." Unlike most Latino/as, who choose "white" when given the option (War-ren and Twine 1997), Yayo criticized the power relations built into the "choice." He refused to be coopted by whites for their own gains. In a focus group, Yayo explained his concerns: choosing "white" would (a) undermine Chicana/os' dis-tinct ethnic heritage, and (b) excuse dominants for centuries of imperialism. As-sociating with whites could mean selling out to a culture that devalued and mis-constructed them, as illustrated in this incident recorded by Sena (Latina):

> I was in class and my teacher tried to say that all Mexican women are dominated by their men. I was offended, being half Mexican, because my family is not like that.

She then went on to say, "They clean people's houses and watch other people's kids, because they have no education or experience outside the home." I was so mad. This woman made the assumption the *all* women of Mexican descent are uneducated.

Sena was incensed at this generalization—one made in the voice of professorial authority to a blended group of whites, browns, and blacks. Sena used her field notes to voice her anger. She did not contradict the professor, however.

Overall, I found a stronger counterstance in the data among African Americans than among browns. Why was there not more opposition in the racetalk among browns? Perhaps because of the cross-cutting allegiances of brownness to the dominant and subordinate groups. Browns were honorary whites, even though that status was fragile. Though disenfranchised, browns were not considered black, a completely devalued status. Nevertheless, browns often identified with the oppression spawned by the signification of blackness. Perhaps being caught in the middle obscures power relations and makes a counterstance less realizable.

CONCLUSION: *LA FACULTAD* IN PRACTICE

In sum, the people associated with brownness—despite the myriad cultural differences subsumed under this social category—had a great deal in common with each other. In this study, they occupied a unique standpoint in that they crossed boundaries more easily than did blacks or whites. With many "white characteristics," some browns could often pass for white and be treated as insiders.[4] Nevertheless, this insider status was often temporary and situational. They were interlopers. At the end of the day, browns were still "others"—people who were viciously stereotyped and excluded in the racial regime.

The racetalk in this study indicates that the dual status of brownness affected people's senses of self and their public behavior. Naomi was hurt when the white woman reorganized her silverware. Yayo balked at identifying with whites. Nina avoided being scapegoated as a terrorist due to her Middle Eastern background. In public, browns kept a watchful eye, regardless of which group they occupied at the moment. Brownness involved pressures of crossing over racial/ethnic boundaries. Due to structural conflicts, their lives were riddled with contradictions that they constantly negotiated.

LOOKING FORWARD: FROM SIGNIFICATION TO DOMINATION

Thus far, I have argued that there are three structures of signification (Giddens 1984) within the overarching system of racism: whiteness, blackness, and brownness. As discussed in these chapters, the racetalk in this study constructed systems of meaning used to code and understand the behaviors of different racial and ethnic groups. Consistent with Toni Morrison's (1993) original definition of racetalk, it was largely used to degrade "others." According to Fine and Weis (1998), dominants create an "other" with "unpleasant personal characteristics," upon whom they project the causes of—and deny personal responsibility for—their problems. The construction of an other demarcates whiteness as the standard by which everyone else must be measured (Fine and Weis 1998; Frankenburg 1993). Racetalk signified blackness and brownness as devalued statuses that served to bolster the status of whiteness while keeping the other groups divided and disempowered.

In the next chapter, I move on to examine the structure of domination, whereby the coded meanings discussed so far are put into action. In particular, the significations of blackness and brownness—constructed in opposition to whiteness—become tools of the dominants to maintain racism *writ large*.

NOTES

1. Indeed, disparities exist within the category Asian: Japanese Americans were interred during World War II, Chinese immigrants suffered under the U.S. Chinese Exclusion Act, and so on (Takaki 1994).

2. The myth of the model minority emerged after World War II, and was more recently popularized by Ronald Reagan, who held Asian Americans up as a comparison to other racial/ethnic groups. The argument is this: look how well Asians have done in the United States in schools and the economy. The rest of you should try to emulate them. The key problems with this "myth" are these: many Asians live in areas with high costs of living (like San Francisco or New York) that inflate their economic status. Many Asians work in low-wage, low-opportunity jobs, and they are more likely to work year-round than other racial/ethnic groups. They also often experience downward mobility when they come to the United States when their foreign credentials are discounted, and they are forced to take manual labor jobs rather than professional occupations for which they were trained (Woo 1989—see also Wu 2003; Xiong and Tatum 1999).

3. Asian writers poignantly illustrate this generation gap through their fiction. For examples, see Chin (1991), Choi (2003), Okada (1978), and Tan (1990, 1992, 1996).

4. Not all browns can pass for white, however. Many have darker complexions, and may even be formally categorized as black, as in the example of [Eduardo] Bonilla-Silva above.

7

THE STRUCTURE OF DOMINATION

Surveillance and the Policing of Boundaries

Although hate speech appears to come from nowhere, it is actually everywhere.

—Patricia Hill Collins (1998, 83)

In this chapter, I move on to the *structure of domination*. According to Anthony Giddens (1984), this structure concerns the unequal distribution of resources and opportunities. In this study, racetalk was used to construct and police racial and ethnic boundaries so that some had greater access to resources,
autonomy, and authority. In this manner, racetalk was a tool for reinforcing
racist domination.

In this chapter more than in the previous ones, whiteness comes to the forefront as the vehicle for maintaining racial hierarchies. As will become clear as
this chapter evolves, domination involves the explicit exercise of power—
power that is disproportionately allocated to whites. As previously discussed,
brownness and particularly blackness are signified in opposition to whiteness.
Indeed, it is this oppositional tension that insulates whiteness as the dominant
status. Domination occurs when the more privileged group capitalizes on its
power. As Ashley Doane (2003, 7–8) says, "whiteness is defined through
boundaries and exclusion, by being 'not of color.'"

SURVEILLANCE

The racetalk analyzed in this study up to this point constructed whites as a superior group, whose interests were threatened by the very presence of people
of color. As a result, they used racetalk to establish boundaries—both figura-
tive and literal—among the different groups.[1] Boundaries exist to keep some
people in and others out. Once people have constructed and recognized
boundaries, they may easily problematize the comings and goings across those
boundaries. Patricia Hill Collins (1998) asserts that people of color are under
surveillance when they are in the white-controlled public sphere. Seen as un-
invited intruders, people of color are interrogated officially by the police and
store security guards. They are unofficially interrogated as well, through racetalk. According to Giddens's (1984, 127) definition, "Surveillance . . . connects
two related phenomena: the collation of information used to co-
ordinate social activities of subordinates, and the direct supervision of the conduct of those subordinates." In this study, racetalkers—particularly the
dominants—collated information about the status of subordinates. They then
used this information to supervise their activities and assess the legitimacy of
such actions.

Naming the Boundaries

In the post–Jim Crow era, many racial boundaries in public spaces are fig-
urative rather than literal, although literal boundaries remain. Racial boundaries would not maintain their power if people did not recognize them for
what they are. Racetalkers made invisible boundaries visible by naming them.
   Places.   In this study, racetalkers perceived a boundary between themselves and certain places of business. For example, Roger (white) went shopping with his girlfriend, Trina (white):

> We passed a store called "The Playground" which sold dark jeans, boots, hats, and
> various shirts with Looney Tunes characters and FUBU emblems on them. I
> asked Trina if she wanted to go in there, and she said, "No it looks too ethnic." At
> first I didn't know what she meant, but as I looked inside the store I did: about
> ten or so people were in there, all African American. So I said ok and we moved
> on.

Roger reflected on their behavior later in his field notes:

> The people, the clothes, the name of the store all created a very racial overtone
> (to me) that whites were not truly welcome. I didn't feel as if I would be wel-
> comed in there, like I wouldn't blend in or be accepted.

Whites took their presence in social spaces for granted. Because they were members of the dominant group, they often came and went from various places without pause or reflection (Anderson 1999). Thus, Roger was taken aback by his perception of a "racial overtone" that discouraged him from entering the store. Because most public spaces are white spaces, this experience was rare.

Conversely, people of color often wondered whether they were welcome or not in predominantly white spaces. This sentiment was captured in Elizabeth's (black) field notes. She and Jasmine (black) pulled into the parking lot of a restaurant: "Jasmine stated that she didn't want to eat there because there were too many white people." So they left. In both incidents, people chose not to cross the boundary. In so doing, they "did racism," reifying racial boundaries. In considering whether or not to cross the line, positionality came into play. The consequences would be different for Elizabeth and Jasmine than for Roger and Trina. Traditionally, people of color—especially blacks—have been in harm's way when they entered the white domain (see Fields 1985). Their caution, therefore, had a different dynamic to it than Roger's, who simply felt "unwelcomed."

There was evidence in the racetalk that whites deliberately constructed boundaries in order to limit crossover by people of color, intentionally making them feel unwelcome. For example, Megan (white) recorded this incident at a club:

> Reba went up to the waitress and asked if they would be playing any sort of different music. The waitress told her, "Hip hop? No. We don't play that here. We have a certain crowd that we want here and that's why we play only this type of music (progressive)."

Megan inferred that the establishment chose music that would not appeal to people of color. As we will see below, Megan was right.

In American society, there are actual lines that divide places according to race and ethnicity. Walls are built to keep some people out and others in. Property lines and neighborhood borders are used to justify segregation (Fine and Weis 1999; Sugrue 1996). National borders are established and policed in order to serve the same purpose (Martinez 2002; Takaki 1994). In the racetalk, all of these boundaries were illuminated and justified. For example, while driving through a largely Hispanic suburb of Chicago, Cher's (white) friend Dale (white) pointed out the wall separating the houses and the road. Dale lived near the wall:

> Dale: You know, that wall does jack to keep the spics out.
> Cher: They put up a wall to keep out the Mexicans?
> Dale: Yeah—look at it as we drive down it later.

Later in the evening, Dale referred to the wall again:

> See all the crappy houses they wall in are on the east side and my house is on the
> west. But it doesn't keep them out. We got those beaners hopping the fence right
> into our back yard. Especially when the cops are chasing them.

Dale not only noted the wall, he argued that it was useful—it kept his family
from having to look at the Latinos' "crappy houses." If you buy his argument,
who would not want to keep such degenerates out of their yards?

Author bell hooks (1984) discusses the railroad tracks from her childhood
that served the purpose of dividing whites from blacks. It is likely that many
towns across the United States have comparable boundaries. Indeed, around
Chicago, Illinois, entire towns are associated with particular ethnic groups.
Chicago is highly racially diverse, but it is one of the most segregated cities in
the United States (Massey and Denton 1993). Subjects who lived in or around
Chicago easily associated different races/ethnicities with towns, as illustrated
in this conversation between Mexican Americans Maggie and Marco:

> Marco: I was trying to get my flirt on with your girl Vanessa today at work.
> Maggie: Oh yeah? She's cool as hell.
> Marco: Where is she from anyway?
> Maggie: I think she told me that she lived around Humboldt Park.
> Marco: Illlll—she's Rican? Just joking.
> Maggie: She's half Puerto Rican, half Colombian.
> Marco: Half Rican, half drug dealer, huh? Hahaha I'm just joking.

Katie (white) recorded a similar incident:

> Alyson (white) told me a story that she told a couple guys. She told them that
> Belvedere is full of dirty Mexicans and the only reason that the town is still
> around is because they sell drugs. She said that people pay the cops off so that
> they don't go to jail. These guys told her that she was being racist (even though
> the information was true). As they drove past a mobile home complex in Loves
> Park, one of the guys asked if all the dirty Mexicans live there.

Not only did Alyson denigrate Mexicans, she and her friends included a class
analysis—trailer parks—into their boundary marking.

Racetalkers looked to geopolitical borders as well. The U.S.-Mexico border
was a hot topic in boundary marking, as in this conversation recorded by Cher
(white):

> Bill (white): I have a plan.
> Zach (white): Huh?

Bill: My dad was bitchin' about this dumb ass spic at his work. So I have a plan.
We [whites] should move to Mexico because all the Mexicans moved here.
Zach: I want to go to Cancun.
Bill: I thought we already took that from Mexico.
Zach: No, it's still Mexican.

Similarly, Celine (white) recorded this incident:

Bill, Rob, Sarah (all white) and I were at my kitchen table talking about where
we wanted to go for spring break. I asked if this one place in Mexico was dirty,
because I had heard it was. Billy said, "It depends. If you walk two blocks past
your hotel, you'll run right into tons of Mexicans with their dingos." Rob said,
"I thought only Australians had dingos." Bill said, "No, the Mexicans have 'em
too."

Here, Celine's friends were willing to cross the border to vacation in Mexico,
a tropical paradise. However, they wanted to ensure that they would not encounter any "real" Mexicans, people who might taint their vacation. In this racetalk, the resources of Mexico were valued, but Mexicans themselves were devalued. These subjects constructed borders within borders. In both incidents,
it is clear that racetalkers lack accurate information regarding geography and
history. They reify their misinformation through their racetalk, conferring
upon them false entitlement.

Tasks.   Within workplaces, tasks were divided according to race/ethnicity,
as recorded in this incident by Serenity (black):

I work at a hotel that holds lots of special functions. Sasha (white) is the manager
of special functions, and she oversees the group of people working the events. On
Saturday night, there was a wedding reception and a retirement party. The wedding guests were all white, and the guests at the retirement party were all black.
The events were underway, and the retirement party guests were asking for a lot
of things such as napkins, silverware, etc. Sasha sent her black workers to that
event saying, "Those are not my kind of people. My black workers can handle
them better than the white ones."

Sasha said, "my black workers," implying ownership of their efforts. Indeed,
she had the power to segregate them. Sasha also implied that the black party
was too challenging for various racialized reasons—they were too demanding—
and for that reason, members of their "own group" would relate better. She
reified racial boundaries when she acted on her assumptions.

Segregating workers by race is not a new practice, but in many cases it is
now illegal. For example, one cannot discriminate in hiring. Nevertheless, it

still occurs. In this incident, Megan (white) caught her employer in a racially discriminatory practice:

> I am quitting my job, so my boss (white) put an ad in the paper for someone to replace me. When I walked into work today, she looked at me and said, "How come the only people who are applying for jobs are black females between the ages of twenty-one and twenty-five? I think I'm going to pull the old applications from when you applied and mix things up a bit."

Although a racialized division of labor does not have a physical presence as does a wall or a river, it too literally divides people from one another. Such divisions have been used to justify differential pay and career opportunities (Padavic and Reskin 2002). Racetalkers reified this boundary.

Collating Information

After naming boundaries, racetalkers observed action around and across them. White people tallied boundary crossing, they compiled their data, and shared it among themselves. Kenny's (white) friend (white) noted, "Too many Asians is bad—same for blacks. Someone must ship them in." On another occasion, Kenny and his white friends were watching hockey. One guy said, "At least there aren't so many black people in hockey." Sophia (white) watched television with her father (white): "He made some comment about all the 'black shows' on television. He thinks there are too many." Sigmund's (white) girlfriend (white) said, "Nothing against Black people, but it's like they have to have something of everything, you know." Sigmund replied, "Like BET: [Blacks say,] 'we have to have our own TV station.'" Whites counted the number of others in their white spaces.[2] This seemed to provide a barometer of how secure whites felt as a group. In this conversation between white friends Paul and Robert, who sat outside a suburban mall, we see the barometer in action:

> Robert: I refuse to shop here if we are outnumbered by guads.[3] [Hispanics] (laughs)
> Paul: (laughs) Well while we are waiting, let's see how many drive by (they tallied the number of Hispanics driving by for the next fifteen minutes).
> Paul: Another guad.
> Robert: They were Asian.
> Paul: It's all the same (both laugh).
> Robert: Well, I guess we will be ok here—so far we outnumber them.

Robert and Paul were not merely joking about the proportion of whites to nonwhites. They actually spent a quarter of an hour compiling information before deciding to enter the mall. The implication was that their shopping experience would be marred by too many "others."

In collating the proportions of races and ethnicities, whites in this study perceived that people of color were "gaining on" them. They ignored the vast white privileges structured into American institutions. The perception that whites were being overrun and possibly surpassed stemmed in part from the sense that whites were losing their jobs to "them." Flora's (white) sister-in-law (white) complained about Mexicans at her work:

> She told me that she believed that people should be hired based on qualifications and not on color. I agreed with her. She said that when she worked with Mexicans at the factory, she found it unfair that they did not have to pay taxes because they were not residents of the United States. She said all they did was receive wages and save it so they could go back to Mexico. She said she didn't care about Mexicans who lived here permanently and paid taxes. She thought it was unfair that these other Mexicans took jobs away from other people who needed employment to pay their mortgage and chase the American dream. I told her that I knew a person who was in the Army with me. This person was Mexican and was married. He did not have to pay for housing and utilities. His wife babysat for cash because she did not work. She did not pay taxes, but he did. They saved their money so they could support their family in Mexico. She replied that this story did not surprise her.

These "Mexicans" were seen as unfairly usurping white resources. Even though at least one of them was a member of the U.S. Armed Forces, his patriotism did not absolve him of his Mexicanness.

Cheyenne's (white) cousin, John (white), worried about losing housing to "them." John called her to tell her that he was going to have to move. He lived in an apartment in the upper part of a house:

> He said the people downstairs are going to buy the house and kick him out from upstairs so they could move their relatives in up there. He mentioned that the people downstairs are Mexican and I said, "So?" He said, "Man, the Mexicans are taking over everywhere." I told him that I don't talk bad about Mexicans. After all my kids are half Mexican. He said, "Well yeah, but look at their dads—need I say more?"

The pejorative tropes of blackness and brownness impacted whites' perception of them as they collated information on boundary crossing. Flora's sister-in-law and Cheyenne's cousin both invoked the lazy, good-for-nothing images of people of color to justify concern over their presence.

In explaining the roots of surveillance, Michelle Fine and Lois Weis (1998) argue that whites—especially poor and working-class white men—feel an increasing sense of loss due to recent structural changes. Many whites have experienced shrinking wages, the demise of all-white neighborhoods, and the decline of the male role as head of the household. Fine and Weis's white respondents explain their "package of loss" by blaming minority insurgence, rather than critiquing the changing social structures. The racetalk cited above indicates such a mind-set among some people. I call this mind-set "white fright" (Myers 2003).

Supervising Conduct

Once whites began to collate information, white fright kicked in. Whites perceived a threat to their possessions, neighborhoods, safety, jobs, and their overall way of life (Fine and Weis 1999; Warren and Twine 1997). As discussed above, whites in this study were hyperaware of the boundaries of their "own" spaces. As such, they felt entitled to supervise the behaviors of people of color if they crossed boundaries.

We're Watching.   As implied by the term "surveillance," a major component of supervising people's conduct was to literally do just that—to follow them around and supervise what they did. Joan (white) recorded this incident:

> I was at work [in retail] and my boss came up to us and told us to watch the guy in the yellow coat. When he came up to the register, I saw that he was black. But there was no reason that he should have been followed.

Joan was somewhat naïve in this instance. Her boss wanted the man followed simply because he was black and, according to racial profiling, likely to commit theft. Many of the black researchers on the team reported being followed in stores while white customers were left unmolested. In one focus group, Passion (black) and Carter (black) ruefully laughed about the fact that they both carefully controlled their own bodies when they went into stores. They always made sure that their hands were out in the open, never in their pockets. Blackness itself made them suspicious, so they monitored their own movements through the same eyes as the store clerks.

This sense of being watched due to race was great among subjects of color in this study as well. Precious (black) recorded this: "Penelope (black) was pulled over by the police. When Johnson (black) asked why she had been pulled over, Penelope answered, 'Because I'm black.'" This experience was so common among African Americans that they often shared such experiential data with one another. An incident from Precious's (black) field notes illustrates this practice:

> An older, close relative of mine, Sherice (black), told me about how the police in her neighborhood were so bored that all they had to do for fun was pull over

black people and harass them. She gave me examples of how she got pulled over twice in one week but did not receive any ticket or citations, just warnings. In the first incident, she described being pulled over. When she stopped the car, she proceeded to get out. The officer shouted, "Get back in the car!" and he pulled out his gun. When he approached the car, he told her that he thought she might have a gun, and that is the reason he pulled his gun out. He ran through a list of violations with her car, ranging from having no rear view mirror to not having the license plate attached properly to the front bumper. In the second incident, she was given a verbal warning for not turning on her signal within 100 feet of a controlled traffic device. She concluded with the comment, "I'm black and they have nothing else better to do."

In the first incident, the officer pulled out his gun when Sherice got out of the car. On what grounds? Apparently, her most dangerous infraction was having no rearview mirror. As Sherice suspected, the officer probably drew his weapon due to her blackness. Profiling Sherice as a menace to society, he thought that his explanation was adequate: she might have a gun. The second incident underscores the discretion of the police. Sherice did not signal until the last minute as she approached the intersection—something that most drivers can recall doing over the years. Yet how many drivers are stopped for this infraction? How many of them are white? Asian? Latino/a? Poor? Old? Sherice was left to ponder these data, speculating that she had been singled out due to blackness.

Sherice exemplified hooks's (1995) "ethnographic gaze," and what Gloria Anzaldua (1999) calls *la facultad*: an ever-humming radar that listens for and detects racial hostility. The subjects in this study used their heightened perceptions to collect and analyze data. They shared their results. In so doing, they created a bond, reminding each other to be on guard at all times.[4]

Perceiving that they were being watched, African Americans in this study were indeed on guard, anticipating and analyzing the subtext of every encounter with whites. Elizabeth (black) wrote:

> Today I sat in class and found myself analyzing everything the professor said and how he said it. I feel as a black female I am always looking for people to treat me different. I have in the past noticed how professors tend to show favoritism among white and male students. Though I have gotten upset about these things in the past, I never acted on them or questioned my professors.

She noticed that one of her white professors awakened a sleeping black student in class, banging on the desk and announcing, "No one sleeps in this class." The same professor ignored a sleeping white student on more than one occasion. Elizabeth felt that this professor told her she was wrong every time she answered a question. Then he restated her ideas in different words. During

Elizabeth's end-of-the-semester oral presentation, she felt that the professor was "grilling" her with difficult, hostile questions. In contrast, he asked amiable questions of her white and Latina/o peers. Elizabeth confronted the professor a couple of times in private, putting her grade at risk. He made light of her concerns, saying that she was oversensitive.

So how should African American students navigate through these muddy waters? Elizabeth looked for outside evidence that professors treated her differently. Bolstering Elizabeth's fears, another white professor confirmed that she was under surveillance in his class: once when she and a black peer were late to class, he approached them saying, "I thought you guys weren't going to show, and you know you are hard to miss." Elizabeth analyzed this incident in her field notes:

> Now this comment would seem natural; but by me and my friend being the only blacks in the class, it hit me another way: I have to make sure I'm in class, knowing that if I miss, it won't go unnoticed as it would for my white peers.

In yet another class, Elizabeth was singled out:

> Today in class my professor asked me, "Why do black people call each other nigga but don't like it when it comes from a white person?" I proudly stated that I am just one person and I do not represent the black race nor do I speak for them. He looked so stupid.

Elizabeth negotiated racial boundaries regularly throughout this project, and it caused her great anxiety. She exemplified the ways that the signification of blackness can leave many feeling exposed and unprotected.

Although some black people grew accustomed to surveillance, others became incensed. They balked at being singled out, being assumed to be in the wrong, as in this incident recorded by Gail (white):

> I was at work on campus, and an African American girl came in. She was upset because she takes the bus to work and thought that the bus driver was prejudiced against blacks. She said that every time she went to get on the bus, the woman asked to see her college ID. But when a white person or any other ethnicity got on, the woman did not ask for their IDs. She made a telephone call to the bus company and they said they would talk to the bus driver about it.

Two weeks later, the same woman came in to complain:

> The same girl came in today and said the same thing happened to her again. She called the bus company again and they said they had already written up the bus

THE STRUCTURE OF DOMINATION

driver for discrimination, but they would have someone anonymously ride the bus to see if she was still doing it.

In this woman's experience, even formal complaints did not deter whites from supervising people of color. Were these people being oversensitive? Were they being watched? According to the racetalk data, they were indeed.

Know Your Place. Racetalkers' supervision of people of color suggested that they should know their place as subordinates in the racial hierarchy. For example, Carol Ann (white) observed this incident:

> I was in class and two white girls in front of me commented that a black girl in the class is so stupid. She just needs to be quiet like the rest of them.

So blacks should shut up and not be heard. Amber (black) was chastised for not knowing her place in the racial regime. This incident occurred as she walked to class:

> Me and my friends were walking down the hall at school when a white boy bumped into one of my friends. She stopped and asked him to say, "Excuse me!" But he didn't say anything back, so we walked on. Well the next period, the same guy bumped into me and I said, "Excuse me." But his reply was "It's about time the niggers start respecting us!" I wrote an incident report on him.

Blacks should demur, shuffle along, and avoid complaining about injustice, as in this incident recorded by Maggie (Latina):

> My roommate Cindy (Latina) yelled at the TV as we watched Politically Incorrect. She said, "Blacks should leave all that slave bullshit in the past. They are always bringing up old shit. Get over it." Then she saw a commercial with Jennifer Lopez in it: "First J-Lo wanted to keep it real and married a fine ass Cuban. Then she was with Puffy trying to be all ghetto and now I hear she's dating a white guy. I bet she starts acting white."

Cindy, a Latina, argued that people of color—both blacks and Latinas—should know their place and not try to change their status in any way. A minority member herself, Cindy seemed to buy into the racial structure—indeed, she reinforced it.

Go Back Where You Belong. Racetalkers argued that people of color did not belong in white spaces at all. They should leave "white society"—which was broadly interpreted to be anything from a particular neighborhood to the entire United States—and go back "where they belong." Amber (black) was walking down the hallway in school, and a white guy said to her: "April Fool's day is over; go back to your country." In another example, Celine (white) recorded this incident:

> Candice (white) and I were walking across the street to go to class. All of a sudden a black guy in his car came zooming out, almost running us over. Candice yelled out, "This isn't the ghetto. Go back where you belong."

In another incident, Cher's roommate (white) reacted to the Elian Gonzales news story:

> I don't understand Elian. They should send him back to Cuba. We don't need anymore Mexicans. We let him in, they'll think they can all sneak in.

Again, Cher's friends had a weak grasp of geography and politics—equating Cuba and Mexico, not knowing where Cancun is—but they understood the us-them scenario surrounding the border itself: keep them out; keep us safe. We are superior and entitled to take what we want from them.

Similarly, Hedwig (white) observed an interaction among strangers while at a restaurant with her friend Lanie (white). This occurred shortly after 9/11:

> We were standing by the door waiting to pay, and there were these three white men lined up at a bar near the door. One of them was talking to the waitress, who was Indian. He asked her if she was Indian or Arab. The girl had her back turned so I don't know what she said. He asked, "So are you here on a work program?" The girl shook her head no. Then he asked if she was an American citizen and she nodded. Then he asked, "Can you say the American pledge of allegiance? Repeat after me: I am an American citizen. I love America. . . ." She said, "I did all of that a long time ago," and she walked away. As we were leaving, I commented to Lanie about how rude that guy was to the waitress. Lanie said, "I'm glad that he was making fun of her. She was such a bitch. Plus, she's a dumb Indian/Arab. She needs to go back to her own country. They all do."

The entitlement of whiteness expressed in these two incidents was flagrant, underscoring the equivocation of "public" spaces with "white" spaces.

After the 9/11 attacks on New York and Washington, D.C., the borders between the United States and all other nations became visible in a new way. Whites became fearful of ambiguous browns. People who were not clearly Latino or Asian were seen as threatening, swarthy. Tensions were high. As discussed in the previous chapter, brown people's status shifted literally overnight, so that many were detained for questioning and even prohibited from flying, simply because of their skin color or ethnic markings. The racetalk revealed this shift in status as well. For example, Hedwig (white) wrote,

I was talking to Don and Marie (both white) at dinner after 9/11. Don said, "You know, we should take all of those Middle Easterners and send them back to their country. Get those bastards out of here." I said, "Don, for half of those people, this is their country." Marie said, "Yeah, but most of those terrorists were here legally and look what that got us."

There was much evidence in the data that Don and Marie's sentiment was a popular one, as in this incident recorded by Missy (white):

I was on the bus on the way home. This one bus driver never stops the bus for late people once he has started to take off. There was a guy who wanted to get on the bus who looked like he was possibly Middle Eastern. The bus driver wouldn't let him on. A white guy on the bus said, "Yeah, the bus driver knows better than to let *that* guy on!"

Many browns and blacks are immigrants—some of whom have not yet become naturalized citizens of the United States. To argue that they be segregated or removed from this country was and is a realistic threat. Indeed, immigration policies have been amended many times throughout history to stem the flow of certain groups (Takaki 1994).[5] The USA Patriot Act legalized the surveillance and detainment of suspicious others, without legal review (Clarke 2004). In this context, surveillance racetalk becomes more legitimate.

Thus, the racist habitus signified blacks and browns as literal outsiders. Race-talkers reacted viscerally to tangible markers of outsiderness—color, language, and nationality—urging that some people should be expunged for the good of the whole. This racetalk underscored and even reified the literal boundaries separating whites from polluted others.

Surveillance occurred when whites felt infiltrated by "others"—when they sensed that people of color had crossed a racial boundary without permission. It also occurred when other people of color—like Cindy (Latina)—felt that the racial hierarchy had been unjustly breached. A striking aspect of the race-talk was that, according to these data, most any action by people of color—going to work, driving, crossing the street—could be interpreted as crossing a boundary. Thus, through surveillance, the social world in general was constructed to be a white world, whereby the very presence of nonwhites was treated as a breached border.

Policing

Much of the surveillance racetalk was rhetorical. It was private racetalk that reified and legitimated boundaries, but most of it was not shared directly with its targets. In order for the boundaries among the groups to serve any useful purpose—in order for them to reinforce white dominance—the boundaries had to be policed. Fine and Weis (1998) argue that dominants police their borders both literally and figuratively in order to "reclaim their waning dominance." They literally police them though neighborhood clubs, and they figuratively police them through what I call racetalk. In the racetalk in this study, policing was largely done through the invocation of racist orthodoxy. People used racetalk to sanction others for breaching boundaries. This talk was action. The underlying message was that "birds of a feather must flock together," or pay the consequences. Policing orthodoxy took various forms.

Birds of a Feather

The old adage "birds of a feather flock together" provided the subtext for much of the policing racetalk. In other words, people were sanctioned for spending time with those outside of their race/ethnicity. Roger (white) recorded this incident:

> I was talking to a friend on the phone and mentioned that I had seen a speech on racism, and afterward I had gone to the Black Studies Center. I said, "I went there and was hanging out with a couple of friends." He interrupted and said, "And black people?" laughing as he said it. I responded, "Yeah, some black people. My sociology teachers were there too."

Roger's friend considered the categories "friends" and "blacks" to be mutually exclusive. His comments reminded Roger of the inappropriateness of going into a "black space."

When people actually became *friends* with members of another race/ethnicity, they were sanctioned through racetalk. For example, Guido's (Latino) fraternity brother, Burt (white), called over to him, "Your little black boy called." He was referring to Guido's friend Claudio, who was Puerto Rican/Mexican. Burt then called Claudio a "nigger." Even though Claudio was not black, Burt used blackness to sanction Guido's friendship with him. Using "nigger" to denigrate anyone or anything was a common tactic in the racetalk.

When people *dated* across racial lines, racist orthodoxy emerged to remind them that they were violating age-old taboos. Estella (white) recorded an incident in which interracial flirtation was sanctioned:

> Last night at work (in the restaurant), I was rolling silverware and my friend, Harry (black) was talking to me. We always joke around and flirt, nothing big. We were sitting talking and he grabbed my hand. Then our friend Tony started singing, "Jungle Fever." It was funny. We all laughed.

Even though Tony made them laugh, he effectively highlighted the fact that Estella and Harry were crossing a racial boundary. Rachel (white) recorded a similar incident:

> I met a guy in his late twenties, Daniel (black), at a bar one night. This bar had about twenty local white people in it, mostly guys I know. Daniel and I started talking and we realized that we had gone to the same high school. He was a senior when I was a freshman. He asked about certain people in my class and he knew Alvin, a black guy whom I dated through seventh and eighth grade. He said, "So was Alvin your first black boyfriend?" Joe (white), a guy in his mid-twenties, overheard us and came up to me and gave me a long look. Then he said, "You had a black boyfriend? Damn. They say once you go black you never go back." Daniel didn't say a word. He looked at Joe and then at me. I told Joe, "Get the hell out of here." Joe walked away laughing.

Joe policed interracial boundaries by invoking the Buck image. Daniel's nonplussed reaction may have been a technique for telling Joe that his comments were unwelcome. Or he might have sensed a potential danger. There was good reason for caution: history is filled with profound consequences for black men who have crossed the color line in dating relationships. Rachel, who knew Joe, excused his behavior as a joke.

Birds-of-a-feather orthodoxy also came from strangers, as observed by Megan (white) in this incident:

> My white friend Neal came to visit from back home. We went to a dorm to see Dana, a black girl he used to date in high school. When we got to the dorm, we called her from downstairs to meet us. There were a lot of people in the common room, most of them black. As soon as Dana came down, she began to hug Neal and I heard all sorts of comments: "Look at that white boy, trying to be with a sister." "She should know better than to mess with a white boy. What's wrong with a brother?" Neal and Dana either ignored it or didn't hear because they didn't even acknowledge the comments.

Due to their history together, Neal and Dana were probably used to hearing such comments. This racetalk reminded them that things had not changed much.

The mere *prospect* of dating across racial lines often evoked direct confrontation, as in this incident documented by Sena (Latina): "My sister came over to my grandparents' house with her son. When my grandfather saw her, he asked my mother if my sister was still with the 'Negrito' [black boy]." Carol Ann's (white) grandfather said basically the same thing: "My grandpa asked me if I was dating anybody. Then right away he told me, 'I hope it isn't anybody with shoe polish on their face!'" This comment may be dismissed by some as a generational fluke—perhaps older men fear miscegenation. However, I found the same pattern among younger people. For example, Taylor (white) broke up with her white boyfriend, Jesse, and began dating a black man, DeWayne. She and DeWayne went to a restaurant where they ran into Jesse and his friend Martin (Asian):

> I went over to introduce DeWayne to Martin. As we walked away, I heard Jesse remark, "She sure lowered her standards with this one." Martin said, "Stay out of this. You two broke up." Jesse implied that I have lowered my standards, which must be a color issue since DeWayne was a college graduate with a good job. He didn't smoke and he was nicely dressed—unlike Jesse.

Recall that Jesse once quipped that he liked black people—"everyone should have one." His comment here, therefore, was not surprising. However, Taylor's neighbor made a comment that conveyed the same message:

> He said, "What in the hell you doin' going out with a coon?" I said, "He's black. What do you care?" He said that he didn't mean anything by it, it was just a comment, and so maybe he used the wrong word. He didn't mean to offend me.

Hedwig's (white) interest in black men was sanctioned by her friend Lanie (white), a self-avowed white supremacist:

> We were playing darts [at a bar] and Lanie made the comment, "God there are a lot of niggers here tonight. Where do all of these niggers come from? We're in Wisconsin." I said, "Why do you have to say dicky things like that?" The subject was dropped. A little later, we walked over to another area of the bar (near the dance floor) and I told her I felt like dancing. She said, "No thanks. Look. The only people dancing are niggers." We went to the bar near the dance floor and there was a black man there. I smiled at him and he said hi. Lanie said she wanted a beer but that bar only had hard liquor, so I told the guy that we had to go back to the other room [in the bar]. He asked me to come back so I said that I would. I went with Lanie to get her beer. We got there and she sat down at a table. I told her that I wanted to go back to talk to that guy. She said, "I don't want to go over there and talk to those niggers. I'm gonna sit here and finish my drink and I'm leaving without you if you're not back by the time my beer is gone." I asked her what her problem was and she said, "I'll tell you later. You know why." I got angry and said, "You wouldn't be acting this way if the guy was white. You would come with me and you'd probably even want them to go back to your cottage or something." She said, "Damn right. But they're not white; they're niggers. And I don't want niggers at my house."

Angry, Hedwig left Lanie alone to talk to the man:

> I asked him if he wants to play a game of arcade basketball. We played a game
> and then I told him I had to leave. He gave me his number and I gave him mine.
> Lanie and I left. In the car, she said, "I can't believe you gave your number to a
> nigger." I asked her why she was so ignorant, and I pointed out that one of her
> favorite teachers at her school is a black man. "Oh yeah, I love Tom. He's a really
> cool nigger. I'll be friends with them but I would never date them. I love them as
> friends, but they're fucking niggers. I'm not going to have a half and half kid.
> That's what they want. They want half and half kids. That's why they're always try-
> ing to get white girls. Niggers hate white people and they want to wipe out the
> white race because they're pissed off about slavery. I won't have a half white kid."

Lanie expressed her deep revulsion for black men in order to persuade Hedwig to avoid them in the future. She used fear tactics: blacks want half-and-
half children. They want "to wipe out the white race." She tried to pierce Hedwig's antiracist armor. Lanie used hard-core policing techniques, but her
efforts were largely unsuccessful. Hedwig continued to pursue black men as
dating interests.

Other friends tried to curb Hedwig's interest in black men as well. In this
incident, Hedwig talked to white friends Don and Marie about Chuck (black),
whom she liked:

> Marie said, "You don't want a relationship right now anyway. You guys are just
> friends. You just hang out." I said, "Yeah, but that doesn't mean that things
> couldn't work out later." Marie said, "Maybe, but it would be very hard to have a
> black relationship like that." I said, "Would it bother you if I dated him?" Almost
> defensively, she said, "No. But lots of people don't like that.'"

Marie explained that people would harass her for dating a black man. Marie
said, "It would just be very hard." Hedwig said, "I guess, but that would be
their problem. It sucks that people are like that." Marie said, "It does, but
that's how it is." Marie argued that it was in her own best interest—due to
other people's racism—to avoid an interracial relationship. She distanced herself from her own racism by framing her argument in this way.

Taylor's (white) white girlfriend made a similar argument to deter her relationship with DeWayne:

> I told my girlfriend that I was going on a date with someone new. She met De-
> Wayne later that week and said, "Why didn't you tell me that he was black?" I
> said, "I don't know. Does it matter?" She said, "No, but be careful. You know
> what they say about white girls that go out with black guys." Another girlfriend
> joined us at our table, so the conversation was dropped.

The subtext in this racist orthodoxy was that white women would be polluted by their association with blackness. Indeed, as I show in the next section, pollution was a major theme in the policing orthodoxy.

Pollution

Due to the continued signification of blackness and brownness as contaminated, many things that became associated with these structures came to be seen through the veneer of these tropes. That is, the trope had a polluting effect on all that was associated with it. In the racetalk in this study, that was particularly true for blackness. Racetalkers linked "otherness" to people, animals, activities, and objects in order to degrade them. Once nonwhites were fully degraded, it was easy to come to see them as a source of contamination. Racetalk indicated that people believed that the contaminating effect of "otherness" was contagious, and they avoided being associated with it. In order to degrade any object, person, or practice, racetalkers associated it with blackness or brownness. These tropes seemed to be a code or a shorthand for their disdain and therefore useful in policing racial/ethnic boundaries.

Contamination. A degraded object, body, or practice became contaminated and shunned. This affected white people's perceptions of and interactions with people of color. It altered white people's behaviors. And it affected self-perceptions among people of color.

Flora (white) reported an incident where she and some white friends carpooled their kids to Hooters for a birthday party. Flora's husband (white) put on a rap CD. Todd said, "Shut off the fucking nigger music!" Flora asked him if he disliked black people. Todd replied, "Yes, they are a bunch of niggers!" He asked his son to pass him the CD case. He looked at it and said, "Yep, he looks like a nigger to me." This family was more concerned about the contaminating effect of the black CD on the children than they were about the racist language that they used in front of them. Todd's refusal to listen to the music coupled with his invective taught the kids in the car a powerful lesson in racism: steer clear of blacks.

In this study, racetalkers invoked pejorative tropes any time they wanted to underscore their contempt or to sanction someone's actions. This rhetorical strategy was effective. For example, Jessica quarreled with her friend Adam (white):

> I made a suggestion to him. He didn't agree with me, and after hearing my suggestion, he said, "That is black." I asked him what he meant by that and he said, "It's not important. Don't worry about it."

Although Jessica was unsure of what Adam meant, Rocker was more clear:

> We sat around on Saturday night, and sometimes we called each other niggers be-
> cause something stupid would happen. I guess we sometimes refer stupidity to
> Black people. For example, we were playing a card game called circle of death. I
> did something wrong, and my friend asked me, "Why are you such a Black person?"

Guido's (Latino) white roommate acted similarly: "Throughout the day, Skippy
used the word 'nigger' to refer to anything that was negatively happening to
him, even if it was something humorous." In another part of his field notes,
Guido reported, "Skippy called me 'nigger' several times today because I beat
him at Dr. Mario, a Nintendo game." Maggie (Latina) almost fell up the stairs,
and Marco (Latino) said: "Slip and bust yo' nigga lip!" Here, Marco used
blackness to sanction her clumsiness. Maggie was going to work out with her
friend Maria (Latina). She put all of her long curly hair up inside her winter
hat. Maria said, "You look like you are going to go robbing and looting! You
aren't black." Jean (white) wrote:

> I was writing a paper on a racism scale that I developed for a class. I needed to
> come up with a name for this scale so I could refer to it in the paper. I yelled to
> Daniel (my boyfriend—who was reading a magazine), "What do you think I
> should name my racism scale?" He yelled back, "Call it a nigger rater."

Daniel trivialized Jean's intellectual and antiracist intentions. In so doing, he
devalued her endeavors, sanctioned her for caring about racism, and reaf-
firmed the racial regime.

People used a plethora of codes to demark blackness as contamination. For
example, Monty (Asian) wrote this:

> A term often used in my [fraternity] house is "kaffir." The word comes from my
> South African roommate. Its real meaning is "nigger," but it is used differently
> every time. Most of the time, it replaces the word "idiot," or "fucker." For exam-
> ple, one roommate walks into a room and spills a glass of OJ on the carpet. An-
> other roommate in the room says, "You stupid kaffir—what were you thinking?"
> This is usually followed by a laugh or a smile.

Among Monty's friends, being called a kaffir was a joke, a gentle ribbing to out
someone's faults. However, it became a true epithet when hurled at strangers:

> A friend was driving to practice one afternoon when a car abruptly stopped in
> front of us. Then the driver started backing up, not noticing that we were behind
> her. A roommate in the back yelled, "fucking kaffir driver!" A Hispanic woman
> was driving the car that caused us so much trouble.

The term "ghetto" was used frequently not just to denigrate objects and practices, but also in order to police people's behaviors. For example, Missy (white) told her white friend Charity that their Jamaican friend, Geoff, didn't want to go to a club with them because it cost $20 to get in. Charity said, "jokingly," "He's so ghetto! Did you tell him they accept food stamps?" Missy tried to shame Geoff into going out with her. She threatened to contaminate him with (American) blackness if he did not comply.

Although a lot of these comments were made in jest, they communicated to their audience that being associated with blackness was a bad thing, something to be avoided. If one were to become associated with blackness, the logic followed that they would become devalued as well. Contamination is not, in fact, a joke. It is a form of what Collins (1998) and critical race theorists refer to as hate speech. At its heart, it indicates a profound revulsion at all things associated with people of color. Belief in other-as-contamination formed the basis of a powerful argument for maintaining social boundaries. Indeed, if the structures of signification of blackness and brownness involve contamination, there may be implications for policies on racial segregation. In the data, workplaces were seen as contaminated, as illustrated by this excerpt from Cher's (white) field notes:

> My friend Joey's father (white) said, "I used to work in a job for minimum wage in a grain plant. All these black people started taking the jobs. Since then, the plant has gone to shit."

Thus, we should not hire black people. Public spaces were contaminated by otherness, as evidenced in Carol Ann's (white) data:

> At a bar with a bunch of white friends, one of them asked if it would be OK to go to another bar. She explained that it was not as classy any more because black people go there now.

Cher's (white) white friend said:

> I hate fuckin' niggers. They're always in my club. No one dances better than me. Why do they try to disrespect me and my club? Why can't they just stay in their projects and not bother me?

Thus, we should have policies that limit black people's participation in white spaces.

Integrated housing was contaminated. Carmen's (white) father observed a new family that moved into their neighborhood:

> First my dad said something about the African American man and how he looked like a big hairy gorilla. Then he made a comment about the family of "dot heads"

that were walking up the driveway to their house. Then a car came with two men in it and he said, "First we have niggers, then dots, and now gay men—what else?"

Cher's (white) white friend reported, "The Mexicans in my town are like flies on horse shit. There are 70 to one house. That's the only way they can live." Carmen's (white) white roommate voiced concerns about people of color in their dorm:

> My roommate and I frequently have our door open. One time when an Indian passed by she said, "Why does he always look in here?" She doesn't have a problem normally when other people pass by.

In a similar incident, Hedwig (white) and her friend Marsha (white) walked to a bar one night:

> We walked past some apartment buildings and she said, "It would be shorter if we cut through those apartments, but that's like the ghetto. It's scary to walk in there." I asked what she meant by ghetto. She said, "Oh all the black people live there. All the moms with their babies. It sucks too because those are nice apartments. I wanted to live there, but then it turned into the ghetto."

Marsha invoked many images of blackness in justifying the contaminating effect of blackness, which ruined otherwise good housing. She changed her behavior as a result of the contamination: "I wanted to live there, but it turned into a ghetto." Thus, this rhetorical denigration translated into action. This perception was popular: Carmen and Rocker (both white) independently observed that one of the dorms on campus housed a disproportionate number of African American students. Consequently, white students referred to this dorm as a "project" or a "ghetto." Black people contaminated living space. Harley (white) wrote,

> My dad and I were driving around, looking for dinner, when he asked, "Are there more blacks than whites?" He then told me that when I travel, that's how I can tell if it's a bad neighborhood.

The message: stay away from black neighborhoods. Which must mean that she should stay away from black people. A parent's admonition might have the power to alter one's behavior. The practical implications of this racetalk is that we should segregate neighborhoods.

School standards were damaged by the presence of people of color. For example, Jonathan's (white) friends compared their majors:

> Brad (white) said there were many Indians in his major, while Chris (white) commented that his major had a lot of blacks. Brad then commented that "They're trying to take back the night."

Chris and Brad clearly found their majors to be contaminated. Carol Ann (white) wrote this: "Marilyn (white) said that she would not register for a certain class because it had 'a lot of stupid Mexicans in it.'" Marilyn changed her course schedule to avoid "stupid Mexicans." Lavinia's (white) friend, a white English major, argued that British and Jamaican accents have definite linguistic structure, but "the American Southern accent and Ebonics both destroy grammar patterns written in English." Thus, we should keep blacks out of white schools, preserve valued linguistic structures, and let people of color learn from each other in their own "language."

Although the strategy of contamination was most commonly used among whites, even some black people employed it. In this incident, Blueangel (black) was talking to her friend Monica (black) about their white hall leader and her white boyfriend:

> Monica said how the hall leader's boyfriend is always on the floor, which is all female. She said that she is sick of seeing that Negro's face every damn morning.

Monica did not like this man being on her hall, and she underscored her contempt by associating him with blackness, even though he was white. Cheyenne (white) recorded a similar incident:

> My friend Tanya, who is black, came over to visit me with her son, who is half Mexican. Her son was telling her that some black kids were being mean to him on the bus that day. Tanya got upset and said to her son, "What do you mean 'black kids?' You are black too! Where do you get this stuff from?"

Tanya's son thought blackness alone explained the children's bad behavior, even though his own mother was black. Thus, these data indicate that African Americans have been affected by this rhetoric as have whites, Latinos, and Asians.

The ideological origins of this association are clear. "White" and "black" have long correlated with good and evil (Kivel 1996). In contrast with the positive concepts associated with whiteness, highly negative concepts are associated with blackness, such as dirty, uncivilized, savage, evil, and ugly. Some racetalkers constructed gradients of evil regarding blacks. At Barbara's (white) church potluck, a white woman stated, "Jesse Jackson is an example of a black nigger," supposedly distinguishing him from typical, benign blacks. Derrick Bell (1992) has argued that Jackson went from being black to being a nigger when he became an antiracist activist: a troublemaker who made whites uncomfortable. Similarly, Guido's (Latino) white friend asserted to their black friend that "niggers are lower class Blacks that commit crimes."

Whites' concerns about "impending invasions" underscored their sense of absolute racial entitlement. Indignant, angry, and/or violent, whites actively resisted sharing "white space," a.k.a. any space, with people of color.

One indicator of the power of American racist structure and culture is that people of color—like whites—also tend to disdain darker skin. They internalize racism and learn to hate themselves (Brown 1992; hooks 1995; Hunter 2002a; M. Wilson et al. 1993). Members of the research team who were black or brown reported evidence of internalized racism in their field notes. For example, Amber (black) wrote, "Today my cousin Michelle said I was too black to be related to her and I should marry a white guy." Michelle advised Amber to lighten the gene pool by mixing with whites. Similarly, Cheyenne (white) went to her friend DeAnn's (biracial) house because they were going out together. DeAnn was doing her hair in the bathroom mirror:

> She asked me, "How does my hair look?" She was styling it differently than normal. It looked nice and I told her so. She said, "Joel says it looks like a black girl." Joel is her husband. He is Mexican. DeAnn is biracial, black and white. I said to her, "Well you are black." She looked at me with shock, her eyes widened and she said, "Don't say that, no don't ever say that!" I said, "Why not? It's the truth, and besides you should be proud of who you are."

Precious (black) recorded this incident:

> I was sitting around reminiscing about high school with Penelope and Monica. Monica talked about how weird this one black boy looked, and it turned out he was in some of her classes. She admitted that when she first discovered he was in her advanced classes, she thought it was a mistake, especially since she was used to being the only black in her accelerated classes while growing up.

Being the "only one" led Monica to infer a message about blacks: blacks don't belong in these classes. There must be some mistake. She was surprised when she realized that she had internalized this message. Anastasia (black) recorded this incident:

> I was talking to my friend Danny (Asian). Lately, he has been a little isolated and depressed. He said that he doesn't want to be Asian. He feels as though he should be white because he seems more like a white person. Also, he said that he just doesn't like himself.

Danny internalized a racial hierarchy that glorified whites, and, thus saw himself as degraded. These examples indicate that even people of color internalized damaging messages of contamination.

This talk was pointed. It was meant to alter action and identity. As such, it was more pernicious than merely rhetorical, private racetalk.

Contagion. If a group is contaminated, it makes sense that some people might fear that their vileness is contagious. Can the damning residues of blackness and brownness rub off on people associated with them? Wielding the threat of contamination in order to sanction people's behaviors only worked because of the possibility of contagion. Racetalk indicated that people feared catching the devaluing nature of color. Under certain circumstances, nonblack people could be seen as black. Indeed, some whites who associated frequently and identified with blacks came to be called "black" themselves. As Celine (white) recorded:

> Lindsay (white) told me about this cute guy that is in one of her classes. After she described him, she added, "But he's black." I asked, "What?" and she said, "Well he isn't actually black, but he dresses, talks like, and hangs out with all black people." I said, "Oh, I know a girl like that. She grew up in a mostly bi-racial community." Although Lindsay thought that this guy was really attractive, she acted as though she wouldn't consider dating him because he acted black.

Jaime (white) recorded this incident:

> Carrie (white) and I were talking to Jason about a guy that Jason and Carrie know. He said, "He is white but he looks black. He wears FUBU shirts and baggy pants and always has a huge cross necklace on."

Rori's (white) friend Mike (white) called whites who cross racial boundaries "wiggers:"

> Mike told us that he and his brother made up a "spectrum of wiggerhood for you know . . ., white people who . . ." He let people figure out that he was talking about whites who act black. He said that the spectrum went from Anglo to Wigger.

Wigger was not a flattering term. Its root was "nigger." "Wigger" was used to impart the negativity of blackness onto whites who betrayed their whiteness. Carol Ann (white) recorded a similar incident:

> My roommate (white) and I were watching TV. A Pink video came on and his response was, "She is cool, but acts way too ghetto."

Pink is a white artist who performs music that appeals to both whites and blacks. Perhaps she had crossed racial boundaries too many times for Carol Ann's roommate, thereby becoming infected by blackness. Whites, therefore, could be black-by-proxy if they overidentified with blacks. Such whites are often called "race traitors" (Feagin 2000). Here, they were simply defined by otherness. Thus, the polluting effects discussed above were indeed contagious. Once infected, even the privileges of whiteness could be undermined.

People of color were associated with negative characteristics to the point of becoming polluted. Their pollution was used to sanction interracial interactions. Sometimes the pollution was contagious—as in the case of "wiggers"—and in other cases it was suspended, as for the "hot" black guys discussed above. Overwhelmingly, blackness and brownness themselves became reified as tools for policing boundaries and enforcing segregation.

Aggression

White racetalkers expressed resentment and anger at having to share with the "other." As a result, they sometimes acted aggressively and even threatened to use force in order to remove the offending people from "their" spaces. For example, Rocker (white) relayed an incident incited by the need to share a scarce resource: parking spaces.

> Me and Cat (white) were waiting for a parking spot and this black guy with ski glasses walked out [to the parking lot]. He walked to a car, then across the parking lot. I said, "You fucking crack head—go rob a store." I was pissed because I was going to be late for class and he made it look like he was going to a car but he didn't. I hate these fucks. They make it look like they're the best when they're not.

This black man was minding his own business. He must have been shocked by Rocker's unprovoked assault, but he did not react. Similarly, Sophia's (white) white friend balked at the inconvenience of slowing down his car:

> There was this Black guy walking by the sidewalk, crossing the street. The guy I was with yelled, "Come on you fucking nigger!" I was all, "Hey watch it!" to my friend. The guy crossing the street couldn't hear because the windows were rolled up (thank god!). But I was really pissed. I asked him why he would say that. He came back with "They have been pissing me off lately."

These two incidents not only reveal the racial anger the some whites felt toward blacks; they also provide a glimpse into the randomness of racial epithets and verbal assaults on people of color. Anything could set whites off. Jessica (white) recorded this conversation:

> After visiting my grandma in the hospital, I was telling my [white] friends a story about two men who came into the hospital after being shot. Adam asked, "What were they?" I asked what he meant. He said, "They were niggers, right? Figures, that is just population control."

Adam reified the gangsta image, showing his disdain for black men. He seemed to relish their injuries: "That's just population control."

Most disturbing in the data were the violent overtones in much of the whites' policing. As Cher's (white) friend said, "My dad wants to take a gun to all the Mexicans around here." Jonathan's (white) field notes were laced with images of lynching. He reported this conversation between coworkers.

Dave (white): I have a new enemy here.
Chris (white): Who's that?
Dave: That nigger from down the hall.
Chris: Why?
Dave: He acts like he runs the place. Tells me what I should be doing.
Chris: I don't like him either.
Dave: I'm going to get a rope. (He said this sarcastically.)

Here was another conversation among the same group:

Chris: Why is that Black guy standing by that tree?
Dave: He's waiting to be hung in it.
Chris: (laughs) Oh man . . . we can get some rope.
Dave: (laughs) String him up!

For several generations, lynching was a pervasive means of quelling black independence (Dray 2003). It is not a joke, yet it was casually invoked by Chris and Dave, revealing their contempt.

Megan (white) showed that, under certain circumstances, nonwhites could threaten force as well. Here, her friend Charlie (black) was going to travel just after 9/11:

Charlie was getting ready to go home on the Greyhound bus, and I asked him if he's at all a little scared because of everything that has been happening. He said, "I will beat the shit out of any turban wearing dot-head that even looks at me funny."

Charlie threatened to use force at the slightest provocation. Cher's (white) roommate, Tara (white), said: "My dad wants to take a gun to all the Mexicans around here. They make $120 a week so they can all live together." Cher (white) recorded a similar incident from a night out with a group of family members. They went to a bar on St. Patrick's Day and everyone was drunk:

Casey: That fuckin' spic was looking at me. I'm gonna go beat his ass.
Cher: Relax. What is going on?
Casey: Cher—get out of here.

Casey's dad: Where's he at?
Casey's uncle: Over by the bar. I'll smash his face in.
Bouncer: Come on you guys, relax. Let's go over here.
Casey's uncle: No—I wanna fuck that spic up!
Cher: Relax. He's not bothering anyone.
Casey's uncle: No, we come here all of the time. There's no reason for this disrespect.

This incident was a family affair, incited by a sense of violation. They interpreted the mere presence of nonwhites as a sign of disrespect, revealing an entrenched feeling of entitlement.

In other incidents, people of color were forcibly removed from white spaces, as in this example recorded by Megan (white). Recall from above that Megan went to a bar that only played progressive music so as to attract a certain crowd. This incident occurred there that night:

Reba (white) and I went to the new club in town. As soon as we walked in, we knew that the atmosphere was not what we liked, and neither was the music. A few minutes after us, in walked four black guys with four non-black girls. The guys were the only black people in the club that I saw. Reba and I were trying to make the best of the club, since we figured we'd paid to get in, so we might as well get our money's worth of it. So we danced. The black guys and their girls were all dancing right next to us. Out of nowhere, I noticed the head of security go up to another security guy and tell him that he wanted them (the black guys) out of there. He was pointing and gesturing toward them. As far as I know, they had not done anything at all. The [lower ranked] security guy kept saying, "You can't do this. . . ." The security head got on his radio and called for backup. He told the black guys that they had to leave. The guys hit the roof. At first they tried to keep their cool to find out what they did wrong and why they wanted them out of there. But they were given no legitimate reason. Eventually, the security guys forcibly removed them from the club.

Ashley (white) recorded a similar incident:

I went home for the weekend. When I visited my parents, my mother told me about a car that broke down behind their house. The person walked through their field to get to the nearest gas station. The person was black, and when my stepfather saw him, he kicked the black man off of our land and said he should never come back again.

Racetalkers freely threatened race-based violence in order to convey their feelings. As Mari Matsuda (1993) argued, epithets and violence are two sides of the same coin.

Threatening force was problematic, as it primed the pump to act on the threat. In this study, there were several incidents when people actually took their threats to fruition. The use of force took various forms. Most often the force played out as verbal assault with promises of violence. For example, Rachel (white) recorded this observation:

> Outside a bar one night, a group of white guys were yelling back and forth into the faces of three Hispanic-looking guys. Apparently, Aaron (white) left his phone in the bar when he went outside to get a girl's phone number. While gone, one of the three Hispanics had stolen his phone. The girl whom Aaron was talking to was one of their girlfriends. Aaron figured they took his phone as they were leaving. He followed them out, then went back inside to get some of his friends to come out and back him up. About five of his drunk, white friends came out, and there was a serious confrontation. Tom was the first to get in the Hispanics' faces: "Bring it on you motherfucking spics! What the fuck are you going to do? You come down here and want to fuck with us, you fucking Mexicans!" The yelling persisted from both sides, and escalated to more serious threats of violence. People outside broke up the fight before punches were thrown, but not before one Hispanic threatened to get a gun. On his way to his truck, he yelled, "I'll shoot you, you fucking skinny ass hillbilly. What the fuck are you gonna do?" Tom replied, "I'll stab you, you fucking spic!" and pulled out a switch blade. The fight was officially broken up then.

Aaron crossed a racial boundary by soliciting a phone number from a Latina. Conflict erupted to sanction the border crossing, and it escalated into race-based violence.

Surveillance of boundaries was not merely harmless curiosity of difference, nor was it empty threats about maintaining said boundaries. Instead, surveillance could lead to conflict, force, and the reification of racial divisions that exist to reproduce racism *writ large*.

BOUNDARY MAINTENANCE AS RESISTANCE

As alluded to above, people in this study not only engaged in interracial/ethnic boundary policing, but they also policed each other within racial/ethnic boundaries. While some of this talk indicated that people of color had internalized racism, turning it inward on themselves, other intraracial policing took the form of group insulation. That is, people of color also worked to preserve the boundaries, shoring up the fortress from within in order to protect themselves from outside assault. As shown in the last section, racial assault could come out of nowhere. People of color had to construct coping mechanisms.

Thus, some racetalk worked to resist the detrimental effects of pollution and degradation.

At some level, the perpetuation of racial inequality depends on internal boundary maintenance. Candace West and Don Zimmerman (1987) make this argument about gender inequality: society is organized unequally according to gender, so that male privilege is institutionalized through gendered rules and organizations. However, men *and women* must follow these rules in order for gender inequality to continue. They must police each other and themselves. Similarly, people of color *as well as whites* must buy into the racist order to some extent so that white privilege endures.

At its historical inception, racial/ethnic segregation was designed to limit interaction between whites and "others" so that inequality could be more easily maintained (Collins 1998). Douglas Massey and Nancy Denton (1993) argue that segregation is the leading cause of poverty and crime among African Americans in the United States. Segregation helps to ensure the economic isolation of "others." Despite these negative aspects, however, segregated communities have historically provided loci for oppressed groups to form protective enclaves of resistance (Collins 1998). Ironically, interracial boundaries, established to degrade and control people of color, may be valued by those same people as demarcating places of refuge from whites (occasionally referred to by subjects in this study as "white devils"). Consequently, people of color may actively maintain these boundaries to keep the devil at bay. For example, Amber (black) wrote:

> Today as I was leaving church with my white friend, I overheard a couple of ladies say, "I don't know why she brought that white girl to this church. She should've left her at home!"

Black churches have always served the purpose of building community and providing an antiracist activist base (Giddings 1996). Amber violated the black/white boundary by bringing her friend to church, even though she thought the friend would be welcomed. She was informally punished for her violation.

Some white researchers uncovered similar advice. For example, John (white) was a youth mentor. In a meeting at work, a counselor (white) referenced one of the youth (black): "He thinks all white people are against him. His mom taught him that." Jaime (white) made a similar observation:

> I was working at a school for kids who are wards of the state for various reasons. There were a bunch of kids playing tag, and there was a 7 year old black girl just sitting there. Her staff member asked her why she wasn't playing. She said, "I

don't want to play with that white boy." The staff person talked to her right away
and told her it's OK to play with the white boy.

Whites who encountered resistance of this kind were surprised, and they
urged the black children that they should not draw a boundary between whites
and blacks. However, as discussed above, whites drew such boundaries all of
the time. These black children were likely acting in ways designed to insulate
themselves from potential racial degradation. They may even have drawn the
boundary as a result of a degrading incident. Nevertheless, they were resisting, which whites found curious.

People of color occasionally drew a boundary when they felt they were being patronized by whites. For example, Rori (white) classified this incident as
racetalk in her field notes, even though it did not overtly employ racial terms.
Instead, a racial message—boundaries as resistance—lurked within the subtext of the interaction:

> Jason (white) and I were going up to my dorm room, and I told the black
> woman behind the desk that I needed to check him in. She asked me if I was
> leaving the building any more tonight. I told her, no, but I still needed to
> check him in. She then got very upset with me and said that she knows the
> rules, she works behind the desk. "Don't tell me how to do my job." I said that
> it was OK. Another black woman came up to the desk and they talked for a
> minute, and then she asked me my room number. She started to check in my
> boyfriend. She continually talked to the other woman, mocking whatever I
> said, such as my room number, because she apparently could not hear me (I
> have a soft voice). After that whole process, I said to Jason, "Well, she certainly
> had an attitude." Jason said that he has encountered girls like that before. He
> told me about his theater class where the girls in his groups goof off the entire
> period and when someone suggests that they get started working, the girls get
> very upset and say that they're insulted and don't want to do work. Jason said,
> "God forbid someone wants to get some work done."

Rori—a resident assistant—coached this black woman on how to do her job.
Rori might have seen her actions as part of her job. The black woman, on the
other hand, seemed to see Rori's comments as the exercise of white privilege.
Jason dismissed "girls like that" by invoking the matriarch image—lazy black
woman with a bad attitude—thereby explaining it away.

Among themselves, people of color delineated racial boundaries as well. For
example, Blueangel (black) watched a movie, *Down to Earth*, with her friend
E'Maya (black), in which Chris Rock played a black man who was stuck in a
white man's body. In one scene, he was at a hot dog stand, and he started
singing a DMX song:

During the course of the song, he said, "Nigga," a few times. He eventually got decked by this black guy who overheard him singing. I asked E'Maya, "If a white person were singing the lyrics to a song that said Nigga in it, would you be pissed?" She said, "No, but they would get hurt saying words like that around certain boys who don't play with that shit. They should know their place."

Here, E'Maya invoked the very language used by whites to contain people of color: they should "know their place." However, she did not mean that whites should show deference, be silent, and move about without calling attention to themselves, which was the implication when whites used the phrase. Instead, E'Maya meant that whites should recognize the power differentials among whites and blacks. They should appreciate that they are not insiders to black culture. "Nigger" is a term that has been used to systematically degrade people for centuries. Whites should, therefore, show some respect and not use it. Blueangel (black) recorded another related incident:

I was telling my friend Tanaya (black) how this white girl was calling her suburban neighborhood the ghetto. I said, "I'd rather live in that ghetto than the ones around my house." Tanaya said, "White people should be banned from using that word because they don't even know what it means, and they stupid. How can someone have a ghetto book bag, booty, and whatever else they consider ghetto? That's why I stopped saying certain words around white people because they start using it and don't know what it means. They think they sound cute. They need to find the definition of a word before they get slapped saying something they should not."

Tanaya hit the nail on the head: racetalk carries power and those who use it must recognize the power that they wield. This intraracial racetalk and others like it allowed people of color to debrief after racial assaults. It helped prepare them for future assault. In talking like this, they drew boundaries between themselves and whites. However, they did so as a means of resistance.

CONCLUSION

At its heart, boundaries were marked and maintained because racetalkers were concerned with territorial rights. Ultimately, racetalk served as policing orthodoxy that reinforced the structure of domination, helping to reproduce white supremacy. As Bell (1992) writes, "By focusing on a distinct, subordinate 'other,' whites include themselves in the dominant circle—an arena in which they hold almost no real power, but only their privileged identity" (8).

These data indicate that the presence of people of color in public arenas elicited angry racetalk geared toward putting "them" back in their place: out of the public eye, away from "white" resources. Through surveillance, whites amassed anecdotal data to support their hypotheses that "those people are taking over" (Fine and Weis 1998; Warren and Twine 1997). Racetalk among people of color indicated both complicity and resistance. Boundary maintenance may aid what Collins (1998, 17) calls a "politics of containment" geared toward limiting if not reversing the expanding rights of subordinates. At the very least, it reifies segregation, a lynchpin in maintaining racial inequality (Massey and Denton 1993).

LOOKING FORWARD:
FROM DOMINATION TO LEGITIMATION

In the next chapter, I examine the last of Giddens's (1984) three structures: the structure of legitimation. As I will show, this structure works in concert with the other two in order to maintain the hegemony of racism. Indeed, the structure of legitimation helps to make the entire system invisible if not acceptable in the worldviews of everyday people.

NOTES

1. Much of the work in boundary construction has already been accomplished by the structures of signification, simply through the coding of difference and the establishment of hierarchies of value. According to Giddens, the overlap among the structures should not be a cause for concern. Instead, the fact that they intersect is evidence that the different structures work together, always impacting each other in order to maintain the status quo.

2. However, they tended not to count the number of whites in any given setting. Had they done that, they would have seen that whites were the overwhelming majority in most settings.

3. Shortened from Guadalajara.

4. Patricia Turner (1993) talks about the role of rumor among African Americans, which serves a similar purpose.

5 This is not to argue that blacks have an easier go at it than browns. Rather than being deported, blacks must worry about being imprisoned and segregated in housing, education, and work. I am merely arguing that being literally cast out of the United States is a realistic possibility for browns as compared to blacks, who have a greater—albeit tempered—claim to citizenship.

8

THE STRUCTURE OF LEGITIMATION

Accounting for Racetalk

My words fly up, my thoughts remain below: Words without thought never to heaven go.

—William Shakespeare (Hamlet 3.3)

We have finally arrived at Anthony Giddens's (1984) third structure: the structure of legitimation. This structure is important indeed. In order for the structures of signification and domination to persist, everyday people must buy into the practices that they engender, at least to some extent. If people were fundamentally concerned by the social processes fostered in this society, they would rise up to challenge and dismantle them. But, as Antonio Gramsci (1932/1975; 1971) said, people wear their chains willingly. We do not protest on a regular basis. Candace West and Don Zimmerman (1987) argue that people tend to act in ways that reproduce the structures. Why? Because the structures are hegemonic, taken for granted. We agree with them, if not overtly then tacitly through our compliance. As Pierre Bourdieu (1977) argued, the power of the orthodoxy is strong in maintaining the legitimacy of power relations—even when those power relations are inherently oppressive.

Here I ask, Was the racetalk seen by its participants as the expression of legitimate ideas? Much of it, as we have seen, was flagrant racism in which old tropes were reified and reincarnated. How *could* these ideas be legitimate? The United States is a society that purports to be colorblind (Bonilla-Silva 2001, 2003) and postracist (Collins 1998), in which we no longer see race, let alone judge people on the basis of it. Indeed, such overtly racist talk is supposed to be formally sanctioned when uttered in certain contexts, like the workplace. However, as we see here, racetalk goes on in workplaces, schools, families, restaurants, and myriad other public spaces. It is everywhere. If racism is defunct as purported by public rhetoric, then why is all of this talk occurring? If no one is racist any more, then how do these old ideas and expressions thrive? As Eduardo Bonilla-Silva (2003) argues, we seem to be perpetuating racism without any racists. In other work, Bonilla-Silva (1999) argues that the public face of racism is very different from its covert, private face. The element of privacy in a conversation seems to grant talkers permission to express ideas that they tactically avoid in public talk (see Bonilla-Silva and Forman 2000).

In this chapter, I examine the extent to which the racetalk in this study was accepted as legitimate. Under what circumstances was it challenged? How were the challenges received, when and if they occurred? If the doxa (Bourdieu 1977) in U.S. society is genuinely antiracist as purported, then we should expect to find that racetalk is challenged with sanctioning orthodoxy, geared toward correcting or silencing racetalk as heterodoxic. If the racetalk disrupts an agreed-upon, legitimate antiracist ideology, then its audience should seek to quash it.

Marvin Scott and Stanford Lyman (1968), drawing on Erving Goffman (1956), provide a framework for analyzing responses to controversial talk, such as racetalk. They explore the statements that people make in order to make sense of their "unanticipated or untoward behavior" (46). These statements, or "accounts," are requested by members of a shocked or disturbed audience. Using a complex typology, Scott and Lyman argue that people either try to *excuse* or *justify* their remarks when challenged. With an excuse, the speaker admits that the talk was wrong or inappropriate, but denies full responsibility for it. In justifying, a speaker owns responsibility for the talk, but denies wrongdoing. Providing—and accepting—an account of the problematic talk helps to restabilize a potentially explosive conversation.

In analyzing the structure of legitimation, I examine incidents where shocked listeners demanded accounts. Surely in today's colorblind society people would openly take offense to such remarks. The short answer: not really. When the data are examined in their entirety, surprisingly few accounts were called for at all. In incidents where accounts were requested, I examine the various strategies for responding. I find that the response strategies were somewhat more complex than the two possibilities offered by Scott and Lyman.

ACCOUNTS: CHALLENGES AND EXPLANATIONS

I combed the data for incidents in which a participant in a racetalk conversation initiated a challenge to the content and implications of the talk. A challenge might occur if participants in the racetalk were offended by its content and/or if they thought that the racetalk unfairly characterized a group or individual. When people did challenge racetalk, they received several types of response. I discuss each category of response below, including the two discussed by Scott and Lyman.

All in all, there were very few accounts requested at all: approximately forty incidents out of the over six hundred incidents recorded in this study involved a request for an account. I analyze the paucity of challenges below.

Avoidance

When challenged, a racetalker might try to avoid conflict altogether by rerouting the entire conversation onto "safer" (less controversial) ground. Cheyenne (white) recorded the following incident:

> I was at work (at a convenience store) when Viv, a regular customer, came in. Usually she'll hang around and chat for a while. I mentioned that I used to live in Elgin [a suburb of Chicago]. She said, "Well isn't Elgin mostly Mexican?" I said, "So?" Viv scrunched up her face and said, "Eww!" So then I said, "Hey—my kids are half Mexican so be quiet." She said, "Well, they're not *all* bad." I was kind of pissed off and then I told her, "You know, there are plenty of fucked up white people. You ever hear the term 'white trash?'" Viv then totally changed the subject.

Viv assumed, based on their common whiteness, that her comment was innocuous. She unwittingly treaded upon Cheyenne's family, and she quickly tried to qualify it: "They're not *all* bad." However, Viv miscalculated more than Cheyenne's ethnic allegiance. Cheyenne was an ardent defender of people of color. In the end, Viv changed the subject rather than try to repair the damage directly.

Excuses

As Scott and Lyman (1968) explained, excuses are used when a speaker admits that the talk was wrong, but denies responsibility for uttering it. The most common way that a racetalker used an excuse was to claim that s/he was "just joking." This response qualified as an excuse because it simultaneously recognized that the talk was "wrong" or "uncool," and it deflected responsibility from the speaker by denying intent. Consider this example recorded by Rocker (white):

> My friend Chad (white) and I were on the computer scanning photos. We went on-line to send the photos. Chad said, "I saw your password." I said, "Don't use

it to get online and then get me kicked off, like you did before." Laughing, Chad recalled what he had done in a chat room the last time he found out my password: "My name is Rocker, and I hate niggers. I love Hitler. All niggers die." It was bad, but he meant it as a joke.

Chad made racist comments in a chat room while using Rocker's name, which even Rocker—a skinhead wannabe—admitted was "bad." But Rocker excused him from this behavior because "he meant it as a joke."

There were several examples of this type of excuse when racetalk was challenged. For example, Jean (white) wrote:

> I was shopping with Marsha and Rose (both white). I was tired because I had taken a test, driven an hour home, and then driven another hour to go shopping. We were turning onto the interstate to head back home after a couple of hours of shopping and dinner. This purple, iridescent-looking van was two lanes over from us. Marsha started to laugh and said that it looked like a vehicle that should have a little Mexican guy in it. I replied "That was stupid. How would you know if a Mexican was driving the vehicle?" She laughed and said she was just kidding.

Note that in this incident, Jean made it clear that she would not have challenged Marsha at all had she not been tired. Yet she did, and Marsha deflected responsibility from the talk with an excuse. Although excuses *acknowledged* that the talk was problematic, they did not *apologize* for the content of the talk at all. Instead, this problematic talk hung in the air. Similarly, Rachel (white) recorded this incident:

> I was at my history class early and sat outside of the room reading for class before it started. Mike (white), a guy in his late thirties, walked by where I was sitting. He said jokingly, "Aren't those damn injuns frustrating? It is so hard to keep 'em all straight." I looked at him with a disapproving eye, and he said, "Oh, I'm just kidding. This reading is very dense, though, isn't it?"

Mike and Rachel were not friends, just classmates of the same race. She only needed to give him a "disapproving eye" in order for him to recognize the challenge. Like Marsha, Mike responded by deflecting responsibility for the talk, but did not apologize for the *content* of the talk itself. Their excuses showed that they knew that the talk was the wrong choice for the particular setting, but not that the talk was wrong in and of itself.

The commonality here, then, was that challenged racetalkers merely sought to avoid responsibility for the talk. They did not "take back" the content of the racetalk. As such, the pejorative implications of the talk lingered on like a bad aftertaste. Why does it matter that, if challenged, talkers did not defuse the content of the talk? It matters because the talk reified old, demeaning tropes of subordinates in the racial hierarchy. To illustrate, consider the following jokes that were recorded as part of data collection. Paul (white) recorded this joke:

> Three contractors are working on a sky scraper—one is Chinese, one Italian, one Polish. They are sitting on the top of the building when the lunch whistle blows. They pull out their packed lunches. The Chinese guy says, "If my wife gave me rice again, I'm jumping off this building." He opens his lunch box and finds rice. He then jumps off the building. The Italian guy says, "If my wife gave me spaghetti, I'm going to join him." It is spaghetti, so he jumps. The Polish guy says to himself, "if this is Polish sausage, I'm gonna jump too." He opens his lunch box, sees the sausage, and jumps. At their funeral, the wife of the Chinese guy is crying saying, "I thought he like rice!" The Italian guy's wife is crying too, saying, "I thought he liked spaghetti!" The Polish guy's wife is laughing as she says, "That Polack packed his own lunch!"

Paul recorded this joke as well: "Mexicans are like cue balls—the harder you hit them, the more English you get out of them." Eliza's (white) son told this joke: "How many Jews can fit into a [compact car]? Two in the seats and six million in the ashtray." Jokes were powerful racetalk because they were meant to be shared—that is the very purpose of a joke. People might scorn the joke when it was told; but if they left the content of the talk undisputed, then casual participants in the racetalk might have uncritically recycled the talk in a new, less contentious context.

Some people recognized the power of jokes and tried to interrupt them when possible. Jokes passed on by e-mail provided an excellent opportunity to stop the spread of racist material. For example, Sophia (white) wrote:

> Every day I get a ton of e-mail forwards. They are usually tasteless jokes and today I received one that hit a chord. It went on about an Irishman and Italian man, and a "Chinaman." The punch line said something about the Chinaman and his big line was, "supplies!" It was a crack on the pronunciation of the word, surprise. This "joke" bothered me because I hosted three exchange students last semester. One of them was a guy from Japan. During one of our many conversations about the cultural differences we all had, the Japanese exchange student explained that they don't have any "ls" or the sound of them in their language. This is why it is so difficult for many Asians (particularly Japanese) to pronounce the sound. Knowing what a great command of language this student had, as well as his great personality, I had a lot of respect for him because he worked hard to get into the program and he was really doing well in it. I can barely learn Spanish! And here was this kid in a foreign country, speaking the language better than many of the people born here. I didn't forward the "joke."

In the end, "just joking" was an excuse used to perpetuate old racist ideas without being personally responsible for spreading them. Jaime's (white) boyfriend Michael (white) used his jokes to support inadequate schools for people of color:

> Michael jokes with me because I am concerned about Hispanic kids being discriminated against in schools in Chicago. He jokes that our money could be spent on better things than teaching those people to speak English.

Michael joked that Latinos were a drain on the system. His jokes resembled the angry border-marking talk in previous chapters. Does the content differ if the talker is smiling rather than scowling? The information may be easier to receive when said with a smile, but the information is the same.

Jokes can be used in public spaces to remind people of color that they are outsiders, as in this incident recorded by Megan (white):

> I took my boyfriend, Ali (black), to the hospital because he sprained his ankle jumping for the basketball in a game. While we were waiting for the doctor, the nurse came in to check on him. She asked him what happened, and he told her. She said, "I thought it was white men who couldn't jump?" She tried to make a joke, but it sounded like a stereotype. We didn't laugh.

By not laughing, Megan and Ali let the nurse know that her joke was neither funny nor appropriate.

People use jokes in all sorts of settings to communicate meanings in a socially acceptable form, as in this incident that Sophia (white) observed at work:

> I work weekends with this small company. It is a real tight company. Everyone there knows each other pretty well. At lunch time we all eat around the same table at the same time. There are always jokes of people of different races, especially black people. Everyone who works there is white. The joke that I remember from today was: "How do you start all black jokes?. . ." Then the guy telling it looked to his left and then his right. I think that it was supposed to mean that you look around for black people who might be offended by your racist joke. I really didn't get it. All eight of the people at the table laughed and pretty damn hard. I know that many of these people are what I would consider overt racists. The rest just aren't that bright.

The excuse of "just joking," then, was really a cop out. Jokes were a useful vehicle for shoring up intergroup boundaries. They perpetuated racist ideas in a disarming way. If challenged, they were easily dismissed as well-meaning, good fun.

Justification

Justifications are the opposite of excuses. Scott and Lyman (1968) argue that a justification acknowledges responsibility for the talk, but denies that the talk was problematic or wrong. Indeed, the talker *justifies the content* of the talk itself as right. In this study, racetalkers did this as well. They referred to norms and experiences rather than "facts" in arguing that their talk was correct. As Jürgen Habermas (1984, 15) says, "The agent makes the claim that his behavior is right in relation to a normative context recognized as legitimate, or that the first-person utterance of an experience to which he has privileged access is truthful or sincere." By referring to norms or experiences rather than "facts," the talker makes a claim that is not easily critiqued. It is more straightforward to interrogate an assertion framed as a fact—as in the statement "all blacks are poor"—than it is to interrogate an experience—as in "my black roommate's family act that way."[1] Habermas argues that such arguments are irrational. However, as we see in the data, these norm/experience justifications were often persuasive, despite their illogical bases.

In this study, racetalkers primarily referred to experiences rather than norms in their justifications, as in this incident (also discussed in the chapter on brownness), in which Hedwig (white) and her friend Matt (white) talked about work:

> Matt said, "I swear there are so many Mexican people that work around here. None of 'em speak even a word of English. No green card, no nothing. And they're making good money. It pisses me off." I asked, "Now how do you know they don't have green cards or anything?" He said, "I just know, okay? I've talked to enough of them to know. That's how they all are."

When challenged, Matt justified his characterization of Mexicans because of his personal experience with them: "I've talked to them. . . . That's how they are." Cher (white) recorded a similar conversation:

> Cher: You know who's cute? Tiger Woods.
> Billy (white): You like niggers?
> Cher: What?
> Billy: You like niggers?
> Cher: I don't like that word.
> Billy: Oh. I know, I'm not a racist. I have been called a nigger and I am not one. I'm just around them all of the time.

Billy justified his talk by saying that he hung around with black people a lot. As a quasi insider, Billy claimed the right to use the term "nigger." Using the term did not make him a racist in his eyes. Rachel (white) challenged a joke, pointing out the problematic content to its participants:

> At a wedding reception, a white guy named Shane told another white guy, Jim, a joke. The joke is as follows: there was this black dude on *Who Wants to Be a Millionaire?*, who used all of his lifelines on the one hundred dollar question. First he polled the audience, but they had no idea, so the results of the poll didn't help him. Then he used the fifty/fifty option, but he still couldn't figure it out. He chose to call his mother for the phone-a-friend option, but she was unable to come up with the answer given only two choices. What was the one hundred dollar question? "Who is your father?" Jim and Shane laughed hysterically. I said, "You guys are such assholes. Do you understand how stereotypical that joke is?" Shane replied, "Oh, it's all in good fun. I have more minority friends than white friends."

Shane justified the joke by saying that he had a lot of minority friends. Like Billy, he saw himself as an insider, and therefore the content of the joke should not be taken in a damning way.

This is a fascinating justification: I have lots of black or brown friends, so my talk is not harmful. If these people were truly insiders in the black/brown communities, one might expect them to (a) avoid this sort of racetalk altogether, or at least to (b) confine this insider talk to occasions when they are with members of the black/brown communities. I would not expect black/brown allies to share this sort of racetalk with dominants. When "insider" racetalk is uncritically shared with dominants, they might easily misconstrue it as a racist attack, and—worse—they might repeat the talk to other dominants on other occasions. Thus, as with excuses, the justifications were hollow and unconvincing.

Some people saw through the thin justifications, and they challenged them, as in this incident recorded by Cheyenne (white):

> My young son, Lou, was talking to my mother about how he couldn't wait to get home because "his homie" was going to spend the night. My mom said "You're the wrong color to have one of those." Before I had a chance to say anything, my other son, Rico (his twin) blurted out, "Well that was a stupid thing to say!" I just started laughing out of surprise at Rico's comment. Then Lou said, "Yeah, I can't believe that my Nana's a racist!" She said, "I'm not a racist! I had a black roommate in college and I liked her a lot." My sister joined in the conversation and said, "Oh, you had a black roommate in college and that makes you not a racist?" Mom replied, "Well at that time very few, if any, people roomed with blacks, especially in the South where I was. We were the only people on campus who had mixed roommates." Then Rico again commented, "Wow, I can't believe that my Nana's a racist."

Cheyenne's family—even the kids—challenged the salience of Nana's justification. They dismissed her initial racetalk as well as her justification as racist fodder.

Counterattack

An interesting way of handling a challenge was for the person who was challenged to levy a counterattack. In so doing, the racetalker became defensive, as in this incident recorded by Cher (white):

> Justine: Remember back during all the race problems on campus?
> Cher: No, I wasn't here yet.
> Justine: Well, we wrote in to the campus paper complaining about the black caucus. We wanted to know why there was no white caucus. That is discrimination against us.
> Cher: Why?
> Justine: Because we don't have one.
> Cher: What do you call society?
> Justine: Don't give me your inequality bullshit. Everyone is equal now from what happened in the Civil Rights of the '60s.
> Cher: A little bit. But you cannot tell me everything is equal now. Why are there more blacks in poverty and in low income areas?
> Justine: I am not a racist. Don't think that. I just don't think they are smart enough to get out of it. I grew up in the city [Chicago]. I know how it is.

Justine defensively counterattacked Cher—"don't give me your inequality bullshit"—in an attempt to silence her. But Cher persisted, and Justine acquiesced with a justification—"I grew up in Chicago; I know how it is."

Some counterattacks were strengthened by the prevailing doxa. Hedwig (white) challenged Don and Marie's (both white) ideas about Middle Easterners, and they got angry at her for it:

> Marie commented on how they found out that there are thousands of Muslim men living here legally, attending our schools. I said, "So what? They can't have an education too?" Don said, "Yeah. They should go back to their own country to get their education there. We need to get them out of here." Marie agreed: "We can't trust any of them. Any of them could be terrorists." I said, "Yeah, but most probably aren't. You think we should send them all out because of their skin color?" Don said, "Yeah, and you know what? If you don't like it, then why don't you go with them? We're just informed about things. You don't even watch the news. You don't even know what's going on. Something bad is going to happen and we need to be prepared."

Charles Lemert (2002) discussed 9/11 as a "dark day" that engendered "dark thoughts." As seen in these data, that is an apt characterization. In the months following 9/11, anyone who critiqued the United States's actions at home or abroad was roundly silenced as anti-American. Old Vietnam-era slogans like, "America: Love it or leave it," were resurrected and used to quell any opposition. Here Don and Marie told Hedwig to leave the United States if she did not like the way that Middle Easterners were being treated.

Rachel (white) recorded a similar interaction that indicated the effectiveness of counterattacks on silencing a challenge to racetalk:

> I talked with Ron (white) while we were out one night about the war. He said, "those fucking sandniggers; just bomb the hell out of 'em. Why don't we just take Afghanistan out anyway? We don't need them for anything anyway." I asked Ron how he could feel that ways about an entire group of people based on one set of events. He retaliated with, "I'm just being honest, Rachel. You are always trying to defend somebody." I said, "I'm not trying to defend what the terrorists did. I just think that it's ridiculous and ignorant to say 'sandniggers' and that we should get rid of all Middle Easterners just because we got bombed. Frankly, I'm not surprised that we got bombed. It is naïve of this country to think that we can stick our noses in everything and not get fucked with." Ron was getting really agitated as he could see that he was not going to get away with what he had said. There were six other people who came into the conversation through the course of it. No one backed what either of us was saying, but Pat did say that we definitely should take out as many Taliban supporters as we could and that "Osama Bin Laden does not deserve to keep on living with his long-bearded ass." I walked away with two of the girls from the group. I knew that I wasn't getting anywhere with those guys. Mandy said, "Just forget it. Those two are ignorant and don't want to hear your education right now."

Even though Mandy seemed to agree with Rachel, she was not willing to support her in the face of a silencing counterattack. Rachel's "education" was no match for this pro-American rhetoric. Thus, the sociopolitical context of a challenge affected its success.

Counterattacks resembled excuses and justifications in that the retaliators sought to avoid responsibility for the problematic content of the talk. In many incidents, the retaliator turned the tables, arguing that the *challenger* was the one with a problem. The challenger—by disrupting the hegemony of the talk—had made the error, not the racetalker. Here is an example from Jaime's (white) field notes:

> I was doing laundry with Michael (my white boyfriend) and he asked me where my whites were. I said, "over there." He said, "I'm not your black Sambo boy." I said that sounded a little racist. He said that I was the bad one because slavery was wrong and he's not my slave.

Michael set up a joke that did not work. He associated white laundry with white people, and doing laundry with black slavery. When the joke flopped, he tried to save face by turning the tables on a confused Jaime, protesting that she was ordering him around like a slave. His counterattack sought to rectify an awkward situation and externalize blame for it altogether. Rachel (white) recorded a similar incident:

> A group of (white) friends and I were sitting at a local bar discussing various rappers. We talked about how good looking Ice Cube and LL Cool J were. Steve sat down and asked what we were talking about. Amy said, "Fine black rappers." Steve said, "Oh, you like that whole jungle fever thing, huh?" I couldn't believe that people still said, "jungle fever," and so commented: "Steve, what are you talking about? Do you have something against white girls thinking that black guys look good? What's your problem?" Steve said, "I didn't mean to piss you off. I'm getting out of here. Damn! I was just making a comment." He got up and left and didn't talk to any of us for the rest of the night. He shot me a dirty look when I left as if I was the one who said something offensive.

Steve—embarrassed as a result of Rachel's challenge—reframed the situation so that Rachel was the one at fault. In his counterattack, Steve blamed Rachel for disrupting the taken-for-granted peace of the conversation. Therefore, Rachel was the one with whom everyone should be angry, not Steve. He punished her for pointing out the underlying racism of his comment, and he marginalized her in the process. Observers of this incident were warned as well: you challenge the talk, you pay the price.[2] It was easier to go along with the racetalk than it is to be the scapegoat.

Mix-n-Match

The categories of accounts discussed in this chapter are not mutually exclusive. People mixed and matched accounts when responding to challenges. Consider this incident recorded by Estella (white):

> My friends and I were watching TV and I made a comment about how hot Taye Diggs is. Bob (white) said, "You think he's hot? He's black." I said, "I don't care if he is purple. He is hot. I don't give a damn about that shit." Bob said, "Shit girl, I was just joking. I am Mexican remember." I said, "I know. I am just giving you a hard time."

When challenged, Bob used a mild counterattack: "Shit girl." An excuse: "I was just joking." And a justification: "I am Mexican, remember." Bob's account was a triple threat. It effectively disarmed the situation and Estella relaxed.

DO CHALLENGES WORK?

The data indicate that making a challenge was a social risk for the challenger, as s/he threatened the discursive capital associated with racetalk. An important question to ask at this point was whether or not the risk was worth it. Were various challenges effective in altering the racetalk in a particular context?

Basically, it is hard to know. As each incident was a cross-sectional peek into the power of language in a given situation, we cannot be sure if all of the challenged racetalkers altered their talk in future scenarios. If we followed each racetalker around over a period of months, introduced several challenges along the way, and then subsequently investigated whether or not there was a change in the content and/or frequency of the racetalk, then we could be more certain. However, that was not part of the research design. In most cases, contact with racetalkers was episodic rather than ongoing.

Luckily, several challengers did have ongoing relationships with people whom they regularly challenged. By looking to their field notes, we can gauge the effectiveness of different challenges. They reveal that the results of challenges were mixed. Some people continued their racetalk with impunity, even pride, while others altered their behavior in noticeable ways.

Impunity and Pride

In some cases, regardless of the frequency and urgency of the challenge, racetalkers continued with their talk with impunity, if not pride. Rachel (white) recorded an incident with a casual acquaintance:

> At a party on a Saturday night, I met a guy who usually doesn't hang around with my crowd, Carl. We started talking and he told me about the church he goes to and how much he hates drinking and the guys in the group. I agreed that they are sometimes assholes, but think that for the most part they are OK. I told him that I am a sociology major. He asked what I was taking and I told him that I'm in an African American history and leadership class. Carl blurted out, "Oh I don't like black people." I go, "What the hell are you talking about?" He said it again and then proceeded with, "I hate the way they dress. I hate the way they sit in the car all tipped back. I hate the cars they drive. I hate the odors they give off. And I could never date a black woman. I hate those lips. They are way too big. And their asses are way too big. And their hair always smells gross to me." I asked him, "Do you know how shitty that is? Are you OK with being a racist asshole?" We argued about whether he was being judgmental or not. Carl said that judgment always has an element of right and wrong to it, and he was not saying that anyone is right or wrong, he "just doesn't want to hang out with 'em." He later told me that his dad is the biggest racist I could ever meet and that he was raised in a "strict Chris-

tian family." I told him that maybe he should take his little attitude to church and read the Bible to see what his faith says about his bad attitude.

Rachel did not have an ongoing relationship with Carl. However, this incident shows that, despite her challenge, Carl adhered to his racist perspective. He even seemed energized by it, proud of it. Thus, Rachel's immediate challenge did not alter Carl's behavior. We do not know if it had any longer-term effects.

In Hedwig's (white) field notes, we are given a more longitudinal look into the effectiveness of challenges. In particular, we see that Hedwig challenged her friend Lanie (white) repeatedly to no avail. In one incident, Hedwig told Lanie about a party that she went to, and how she danced with a coworker, Chuck (black):

> Lanie asked, "Who is Chuck?" I told her he was the black guy from work. She said, "Oh yeah, the nigger." Then she told me about her night at a bar. "Yeah—you woulda liked it there. We were the only white people there. It was all niggers. And all they played was nigger music." I said, "I wish I could understand your ignorance sometimes. I just don't get it. Sometimes I wonder if you just say it because you know it will piss me off. Or do you really feel that way?" Lanie said, "No. I really feel that way. They're niggers."

On another night, Hedwig went to a bar with Lanie and her brother, Drew. Drew told them about a call-in radio show he listened to in the morning:

> "Some fucking black guy called in and was talking about the war. He said he would rather go to jail than fight for our country because all we do is repress black people. That's bullshit, man." I asked him, "Are you a prejudiced jackass like your sister?" He responded, "Fuck yeah! I hate fucking niggers. We should send them all back to Africa. Here this guy is complaining about our country . . . then he should go back to where he came from. Our country gives them so much and all they do is complain." I said, "That's bullshit. We don't give them anything. We push them into the city, make it practically impossible for them to move up in society, and then we complain that they're dirtying our streets." He said, "Bullshit! Half of our tax money goes to them so they can live in Cabrini Green [a Chicago project]. We give them everything and they just keep complaining. We just need to send them back to Africa where they came from." I said, "I can't believe you two. You are the two biggest ignorant assholes I have ever met in my life."

Yet Hedwig kept hanging out with Lanie, maybe in the hopes of changing her. But as Lanie's own comments showed, she fully embraced racism:

> Lanie told me that she was thinking of moving to an apartment with a girl from school. She's concerned that it's in a bad neighborhood. I asked her if the girl was

black. She said that she was Mexican. Then she said, "Oh yeah, that reminds me. That's how I know that my mom is prejudiced. I was talking to her about moving out and she asked me, 'What color is this girl that you want to move in with?' That's so awesome! I knew that she was racist too."

In coding her own data, Hedwig noted Lanie's pride in her racism. Did Hedwig's challenges help to interrupt Lanie's racetalk? Probably not. If anything, they seemed to provide Lanie with the opportunity to expound upon—if not celebrate and proselytize—her racist principles. Thus, for people like Lanie and Carl who have fundamentally embraced racism as part of their identities, challenges may not be effective. This does not mean that one should not undertake them. They provide the challenger a voice that disrupts the discursive capital of the racetalk, even if the racetalker is unaffected.

Effective Challenges

In some cases, racetalkers seemed to understand the concerns of their challengers, and they altered their behavior accordingly. For example, Sophia (white) wrote this:

My cousin married a Puertoriquena. They have two kids now. They are great kids. My father is the godfather to the younger one. When my cousin and his wife were first married and they had their first kid, my dad used to crack jokes about their kid stealing hubcaps when he got older. He even did it in front of my cousin a couple of times! My dad thought it was funny, because apparently Puerto Ricans steal hubcaps. He doesn't make these jokes any more because my mother reamed him out about it.

Sophia provided a longitudinal description of her father's behavior before and after her mother "reamed him out." Sophia's language implied that her mother's challenge of her father was serious and perhaps severe, but it was effective. He stopped the offensive behavior after the confrontation. Rori (white) recorded this incident:

Earlier today on my residence hall, I noticed a drawing on Chris's (white) dry erase board on his door. It was Osama Bin Laden with a missile pointed at the character's butt. I erased his image. I later noticed on the same board a drawing of Bin Laden hanging from a tree. I erased it again. He re-drew it later. I confronted Chris in part because it is part of my job [as residence assistant] to discourage discrimination of any kind. I asked him to keep these kinds of images off of his board because it may offend some people. I told him that I could understand his outrage towards the person, but I still disagreed with it. Chris also posts the temperature in Afghanistan. I'm not sure why he does it except that he is a meteorology major. But the temperature in Afghanistan seems to suggest further hostile feeling toward the country and the Taliban.

Rori recognized the potential effect on Middle Easterners and maybe even blacks with the lynching photo. After much negotiation with Chris, she got him to alter his behavior. Rori may not have changed Chris's mind, but she may have prevented him from further marginalizing people. She might have even averted future incidents: if people became incited by such drawings and they could not find the real Bin Laden, perhaps a surrogate would do.

In other challenges, people altered their behavior immediately and with little conflict. For example, Cheyenne (white) wrote:

> One day I was talking with my friend Louise (white) and her husband, Don (white). I was contemplating moving to a new town. Don said, "You should move out by us because there's no niggers out there." Of course, my children were in the same room so I told him, "Please don't use that word in front of my children." He said, "Oh, OK."

Don did not excuse, justify, or counterattack. He seemed to see Cheyenne's point and acquiesced immediately. Even if he was embarrassed by her challenge, he did not try to save face by externalizing the talk. Her challenge was effective. In a similar incident, Blueangel (black) wrote:

> I was studying with Jeff, a white classmate, for a midterm. We went to study in the lounge in the basement. I was studying and not really paying attention to what people around us were saying, so when Jeff commented, "Would they speak English?" I did not know what the heck he was referring to. Then I realized that there was a group of Asian students next to us speaking their native tongue. I looked at him, and he apologized, but I think he wanted me to agree with his opinion.

Blueangel merely gave Jeff a look, and he apologized for his racetalk. Others were silenced by silence, as in this incident recorded by John (white):

> I went tailgating with my girlfriend, Jen, her brother, Nate, and his girlfriend, Jane. We passed an Indian male by a truck. Nate said, "Look at that drunk chink!" I think he thought we would laugh at him, but we didn't.

Nate was embarrassed at his failed joke, so he simply stopped using racetalk.

In the scenarios documented by Blueangel and John, participants did not have strong preexisting bonds. Blueangel and Jeff were just classmates studying together. John had a close relationship with Jen, and she was close with her brother, Nate. But the double-date aspect of the scenario made it more uncertain, more formal. Both incidents indicated the fragile, contradictory nature of racetalk. If it was uttered among people who had a strong bond and a long history—as with Hedwig and Lanie—racetalk might have been more caustic and less challengeable. However, if racetalk was introduced into a new group with tenuous relationships, a challenge was more likely to be effective in the moment. In such situations, the racetalker was sensitized to indicators of whether or not s/he addressed a group that would welcome such comments (Habermas 1984). Racetalkers tested various social situations to see what would be accepted and what would not. These data tell us that even subtle cues might signal that the racetalk is unacceptable.

Taken together, then, it is hard to know when a challenge will be effective. People with strong identities who use racetalk in "safe spaces" may not be moveable. People who use racetalk in order to fit into a social setting rather than truly subscribe to racism may be more affected by a challenge. It is also important to ask, What is an "effective" challenge? Is a challenge effective if the racetalker merely closets her/his racetalk, saving it for more friendly turf? Or is effectiveness measured by whether or not a person eradicates racetalk from her/his lexicon and worldview? I suppose you have to pick your battles. For some, like Cheyenne who simply did not want her children to be exposed to the word "nigger," temporarily silencing a racetalker was the goal. Likewise, it did not matter to Rori whether or not Chris changed his views about Bin Laden. She merely wanted him to desist from propagating violence on his message board. On the other hand, in the case of Sophia's family, it was important for her father to see his Puerto Rican daughter-in-law and grandchildren as full members of the family rather than as criminal stereotypes. There are so many factors at work in each context that challengers themselves have an exigent task indeed. These data show that challenging racetalk is effective in some cases, and therefore is an important endeavor in interrupting the dialectical reproduction of racism.

Consistency

One important issue in the effectiveness of a challenge was the consistency of the challenger. If a person always interrupted racetalk under any circumstance, like Cheyenne and Rachel, then their peers learned to anticipate and maybe even respect that critique. However, if a person was a racetalker herself, then a challenge from her may not be taken seriously at all. Take Katie (white) for example. Katie herself expressed traditional racism in her field notes and focus groups, asserting that the use of "Canadians" by restaurant servers was a justifiable means of economic resistance.[3] Members of Katie's focus group often argued with her, accusing her of being hopelessly and unreflectively racist. Yet, in her field notes, it was clear that Katie began to actively challenge other racetalkers, particularly her friend Nick (white). Katie observed that Nick often made fun of people "who are different from him," and she told him that "the only reason he degrades them is to make himself feel he is on a higher level than he is." On another occasion, Katie wrote:

> While we were driving, a man merged into the left lane, and Nick shouted that the man was "a stupid fucking Muhammad." I told him that was rude and he began to talk the way that some Indians talk. I slapped him and told him to stop.

In another incident, she wrote:

> We were at a restaurant and there was diversity [it wasn't all white]. He told me that there were too many spics in the world and niggers need to go back to Africa. I told him that he needs to go back home because I was sick of hearing his nonsense.

Nick must have been confused. Was this the same girl who derided black people for "showing off" through their music? Who defended her use of "Canadians" to justify the poor service she provided to black and brown people? Who laughed at the term "nigger lip?" What was going on? Katie persisted in interrupting Nick's racetalk, and he finally offered an account:

> Nick tried to justify his racism by saying that not only does he have many friends that are "like him," but also blacks, Mexicans and others. He told me that he even has friends that are "white trash." I told him that the only reason he has those friends is to make himself feel more justified about himself. I believe that Nick feels that he is better than anyone else, especially a minority, but also me. I have concluded that Nick is a racist bastard without many morals and too ignorant to notice so.

As Katie correctly pointed out, Nick justified his racetalk by claiming personal knowledge of "them," thereby entitling him to critique "them." It took Katie many attempts to even get Nick to offer a justification, however. She was not consistent in her behavior. I am still unclear whether Katie actually changed her views on racetalk throughout the project, which others did (see chapter 10), or if she had been so thoroughly sanctioned by her focus group that she wanted to appease them. In the margins of her field notes, she wrote, "Why am I friends with this guy?" "Stupid white boy." "Hostile." If you want to effectively challenge racetalk, you must follow the "golden rule" and be consistent. Otherwise, your efforts will be easily dismissed.

NO ACCOUNT REQUESTED

Strikingly, as mentioned at the beginning of this chapter, the typical response to racetalk was *not* to challenge it. Instead, the modal response was to go along with the racetalk. When researchers recorded racetalk, they often challenged it rhetorically in their field notes. But they tended not to do so in the moment. This inaction is partly explained by their methodological mandate: researchers were charged with (a) not inciting racetalk and (b) acting as they usually would in observing it. I urged them to recognize that even the lightest flinch might send racetalkers underground if they thought they were being judged. Nevertheless, I encouraged researchers to challenge racetalk if they normally would, as did Rachel and Cheyenne. "Normal" interaction helped to insure natural data. Based on the paucity of challenges, therefore, it is safe to guess that most researchers would not normally challenge racetalk.

Fitting In

Many researchers went along with the racetalk in order to fit in. As Joe Feagin et al. (2001, 196) argue, "many whites recognize and condemn virulent racism, even while continuing to practice racism themselves, if only to get along with other whites." Here, Roger (white) recorded in his field notes the mental aerobics that he went through in order to fit into an uncomfortable situation:

> I sat watching these cop reality shows on TV, and my girlfriend's roommate, Lili, asked me why they seem to always get black people. She said this after they had just caught a young black man after a high speed pursuit in a stolen car. Her voice had a slight seriousness to it, but it was also tainted with animosity toward African Americans. I could tell that she wanted me to say something that confirmed her meager observation, so I restated a crude statement that my grandfather used to say about how some of "them" are just born wild and that it can't be changed. OK—a definite faux pas on my behalf and I wouldn't have said it if I hadn't been slightly (actually more than slightly) inebriated. But she chuckled and went back to watching the show. Had I been of clear head, I would have simply answered her question on a factual basis about racism in our system, and also social inequalities that produce and perpetuate it. However, our conversation was not in any way hate filled, although we did make crude stereotypes that made "us" different from "them."

Interestingly, Roger pointed out that he felt pressured by Lili to agree with her. More likely, he felt that he would hurt her feelings or embarrass her if he disagreed with her. So he went along with the talk in order to make *her* feel socially acceptable, despite the unacceptability of her talk. Roger blamed his complicity on alcohol, promising that he would have taken the less traveled path if he had been sober. Lili genuinely turned to Roger for information, and he missed his "teaching moment" (see Feagin and Vera 2001; and hooks 1994a). The road less traveled is harder and lonelier. It is much easier to validate someone's racetalk and go with the flow.

The absence of a challenge did not mean that everyone agreed with the content of the racetalk. A couple of people expressed concern about the talk after the fact, even though they did not interrupt the incident as it occurred. Lavinia (white) recorded the following incident:

> Josh (white), a friend of mine, came up to visit me and told me he had a bad day at work. He said he had been stuck working in a room he usually didn't [work in], alone with only the company of a [white] maintenance man. The problem was the maintenance man kept making derogatory racial comments to him about other employees and about people on *Jerry Springer* and other talk shows. This was making Josh uncomfortable because he was friends with some of the black guys who worked there. Occasionally, one of them walked through the room, and the maintenance man would shut up. We discussed how the maintenance man should be able to voice his racist opinions to all if he really did feel that strongly, instead of quieting down whenever a black employee approached. He seemed vocal enough to Josh.

The talker was sensitized enough to censor his comments around a person of color, but he used Josh's white skin as a cue that he would (a) want to hear, and (b) agree with his race talk. Indeed, although offended, Josh did not protest. Although other research shows that whites do not see race as central to their identity (Omi 1999), subjects in this study used white skin as a "ticket" to participation in certain conversations, even among strangers. Simply being perceived as white conferred insider status. Whites in this study regularly operated under this basic assumption, and few "insiders" challenged the racetalk.

Savvy Surveyors

Perhaps there were so few challenges because racetalkers were savvy in their selection of audiences. Both Habermas (1984) and Bourdieu (1977) argue that people anticipate whether or not their talk will be welcome, and they self-censor. The data show that racetalkers were aware of the larger, evolving political context, and they consciously monitored their behavior accordingly. Consider this example recorded by Rori (white):

> I was at a Halloween party. One girl came as Fidel Castro. Someone said he'd considered coming as Bin Laden, but he wasn't sure that it was socially

acceptable yet. He said, "All I would need is a turban to look like one of those towel heads."

This racetalker was perceptive. He tested the mood of the crowd in order to maximize his discursive capital and minimize the potential for challenges. Racetalkers were adept at reading and working the sociopolitical climate.

Futility

Still other people seemed to avoid making challenges because they predicted that they would be futile. Some implied that challenging the racetalk would cause more harm than good, as in this incident recorded by Cher (white). She had been warned by Joey (white) not to react to racetalk when she came to visit his family:

> Now I know your opinions towards other races. I feel the same way, equality and understanding, the unfair injustices. But to forewarn you, my dad is racist and makes some comments. Please don't say anything to him. He will look down on you if you do.

During the evening, Joey's father did indeed make a remark (about working at a grain plant, discussed in a previous chapter). Later, Joey said, "I told you he was racist. I tried to talk to him about it, and he got mad and wouldn't listen. So I don't know what to do." Joey chose his battles carefully, and he did not want to incur his father's counterattack. He did not want Cher to stir the waters. Similarly, Sophia (white) wrote:

> Today I was at my brother's house. His girlfriend and her family were there for dinner. Her father is totally old. He was saying all these racist things. He was using words like, "colored." Then her sister got into it, and she was using more current racist words. They were talking about "how colored people are everywhere now." I was just sitting there trying not to say anything about it. My brother kept a watchful eye on me, too. He knows how I feel about all that. He was waiting to see if I would say anything to them. I didn't. I don't know them well enough to give them a piece of my mind yet, so I just had to leave the room.

Sophia and her brother communicated without words. He appealed to her discretion, hoping she would not embarrass him by attacking his girlfriend's family. Despite her resistance, Sophia acquiesced in order to smooth the waters.

These incidents highlight the social nature of racetalk. Sometimes, people's desire to fit in without disrupting the flow of the conversation was greater than their need for accountability. Even Scott and Lyman (1968, 55) concede that "under certain situations behavior that would ordinarily require an account is normalized without interruption of any call for an account." Although "sociability" does seem to be an important factor, it is not, however, sufficient for explaining the pervasiveness and coarseness of uninterrupted private race talk. Power is omitted from Scott and Lyman's analysis.

RACETALK AS THE EXPRESSION OF LEGITIMATE IDEAS?

The fact that so few accounts were requested or provided tells us a great deal about the strength of racist ideology. Racetalk concerns the exercise and protection of power. Because racist ideology is deeply embedded in our social structures and practices, a racetalker possessed the authority of our history and culture, which is conferred by the habitus (Bourdieu 1977). That is, the racetalker was the privileged voice, protected by a legacy of racism. Accounts were not necessary because they were already implicitly supplied by our extant racial ideologies. Indeed, the racetalker often earned discursive capital as a result of her/his comments, underscoring the social value associated with the content of the talk. The *challenger* was one who took a risk and went against the grain. In this study, few people took that risk. Instead, their silence and/or participation helped to perpetuate racism, even when some participants were silent.

Again, racetalk is paradoxical. The same racetalk documented here might be roundly denounced if it were made in public. If the above comments were made in open classrooms, workplaces, churches, courtrooms, or legislatures, the speaker would have had to account for the talk. Recently, for example, white fraternity members at an Alabama university dressed in blackface and Klan garb for a Halloween party. They enacted mock lynchings. Photos of the party made it onto the Internet, eliciting public outrage. Had these photos not been made public, however, I doubt that many people would have loudly problematized this behavior.

We seem to be a society of schizophrenic racists. The official American face is antiracist and colorblind.[4] Bell (1992) argues that this colorblind façade actually liberates whites to practice racism. Thus, the real-life practices of everyday people undermine the few antiracist inroads that have been made into American institutions and ideologies. This paradox indicates that, although identity politics have tempered the way that we handle race as a structure (Collins 1998), it has not yet affected the way we think and feel about race. Private talk provides a locus of resistance to an ostensibly multicultural society.

Racetalk is context-specific, arising and developing according to the social pressures of the situation. Racetalkers recognize that their perspective is not endorsed by the lifeworld, and they choose their audience carefully. Within the cloistered confines of their conversations, racetalkers tend to assume that their talk will be welcomed. As Habermas (1984, 19) argues, "in everyday life, however, no one would enter into moral argumentation if he did not start from the strong presupposition that a grounded consensus could in principle be achieved among those involved."[5] It appears that racetalkers often did not intend to argue their case at all. Rather, they presupposed consensus before making their initial remarks.[6]

The meager number of challenges may be used as evidence that (a) racetalk reflects a shared understanding of race embedded in our habitus; and/or (b) racetalk is hegemonic, so that few are able or willing to challenge it at all. Thus, the answer to my initial question—Is racetalk the expression of legitimate ideas?—seems to be a qualified "yes." The fact that racetalk was not opened to debate in public conversations reinforced the power of the racialized myths constructed through racetalk. If we are not able to and/or interested in openly interrogating myths, then they persist and fester. The myths themselves become taken as rational, at least within the confines of the private conversation in which they are expressed.

CONCLUSION

My conclusion, following Bonilla-Silva (2003), is that racism is not in fact dead. Antiracism has not become a new doxa. As Charles Mills (2003, 36–37) argues, "The merely formal rejection of white-supremacist principles will not suffice to transform the United States into a genuinely racially egalitarian society, since the actual social values and enduring politico-economic structures will continue to reflect the history of white domination." Instead, the doxa has shifted slightly. The official voice of the doxa declares that public expressions of racism will be frowned upon and sanctioned. This rhetoric conveys a message of unity to the otherwise disenfranchised: we welcome you as a necessary, integral part of the whole. Yet, this is a superficial message at best. It is a slogan with the veneer of justice. It does not have the backing of everyday actors who must enforce it on a daily basis in order for threats of sanction to have real teeth. It is useful in quelling serious criticism of the relations of ruling, but it is a mere bone tossed to the masses, assuaging them.[7] This bone distracts everyday people from the hierarchical underlayment of the doxa, in which racism is a useful tool in maintaining power and privilege among elites. The elites—uninterrogated—are then free to manipulate the racial regime in their own favor (Bell 1992; Collins 2000; Fine and Weis 1998).

Beneath the superficial colorblindness of the doxa lies a more careful racism that is markedly similar to the previously overt racism of the old doxa. People selectively choose their audience, transferring old ideas in new ways. People creatively locate and/or construct pockets of respite from what they might conceptualize as "thought police," censors who seek to quash racetalk altogether. In these refuges, old racist ideas are renewed and accepted as largely legitimate, thereby insulating the doxa from challenge.

NOTES

1. Of course, the challenger could argue that generalizing from a small sample of one or two people is scientifically impossible, but the essence of the norm/experience argument is more slippery than a fact-based argument.

2. Although Rachel continued to make challenges throughout data collection.

3. Katie argued that, because servers depended on tips for a significant proportion of their income, it behooved them to profile different categories of customers according to the amount of work required and the potential payoff for that work.

4. Feagin (2000) provides evidence that right-wing factions come close to openly condemning people of color, but they do so by using highly coded language. One needs to read between the lines to find the slurs, but they are just below the surface. Although this sort of public discourse is marginalized, the impact of the ideology is great due to the power of the speakers.

5. As discussed in a previous chapter and as evidenced in this chapter, racetalk does not fit Habermas's (1984) criteria as rational, largely because it is not open to interrogation.

6. For many generations, racetalk was a central part of the fiber of the lifeworld in this society. It informed formal as well as informal practices. However, through civil rights and other antiracist endeavors, racetalk has been opened to critique and recast as problematic and politically incorrect. In Habermas's (1984) terms, racetalk has been cast out of the *lifeworld* and marginalized. Nevertheless, many people still maintain racetalk within their *worldviews*. Racetalkers choose the context of their talk so as to minimize the need to justify their position (Bourdieu 1977). Like Habermas's "mythical worldviews," racetalkers remove their talk from the public view, making it harder to interrogate in a rational manner. The paradoxes of racetalk allow it to persist and fester.

7. It is akin to what Seymour Martin Lipset (1981) calls the leveling of the masses, tactics like the Electoral College that are designed to make the masses feel included and powerful, even though their input is minimal, contained, and largely symbolic.

THE ACTORS

9

BRIDGING BOUNDARIES

Counterhegemonic Practices

Sister! Your foot's smaller but it's still on my neck!

—Pat Parker (1978)

Racetalk actively reinforced the structure of domination by marking and policing racial/ethnic boundaries. People who challenged racetalk were often silenced, if anyone challenged it at all. Thus, there are many obstacles to crossing racial boundaries. People who challenged racial boundaries were sanctioned in many ways. However, actors are not helplessly constrained by the structure of domination. Actors can act. They can take counterhegemonic action by crossing boundaries, although crossing may be costly to some.

In this chapter, I examine the various ways that people intentionally crossed boundaries and at what cost. Talk was used to challenge old tropes, reframing them in a more enlightened, accurate way. Other times, the tropes were reified. Some attempts at crossing were successful while others failed. If "successful," the boundary was crossed in such a way that the power of old, divisive stereotypes was diminished and new, counterhegemonic possibilities emerged. If it "failed," then at the end of the encounter, the boundaries were once again valorized and justified. In analyzing these strategies and outcomes, I provide insight into ways that individual actors can work together to challenge the structure of domination in their everyday lives.

NOT SO CLEAR-CUT: THE BLURRINESS OF BOUNDARIES

How do we know that boundaries are not fixed and impenetrable? Why do people attempt to cross at all, given the power of policing orthodoxy? One reason that people attempt to cross is that their everyday realities provide social opportunities to do so. People recognize the tractability of the boundaries themselves. For example, Harley (white) eavesdropped on two black men while waiting in line in the cafeteria:

> At lunch today, two black guys were standing with me in the lunch line—one in front, and one behind. They were talking over me about how they only care about the history of their people, and that's all that should be taught. I didn't flinch or say anything; I just listened. Then, when the guy ahead of me picked up a plate, he handed it to me before he took one for himself. I was confused.

Harley had assumed—due to the politics of this conversation and the pervasive trope of blackness in society—that these men were black militants who hated whites. She was, therefore, confused when one of the men treated her like a peer and passed her a plate. He did so even before taking one for himself. In this instance, the previously stark outlines of the habitus blurred. The boundaries blurred as well.

Elizabeth (black) observed the boundaries melt away in a most unusual way. She went to a casino. She left her ID at home, so she could not get in. She was waiting around for her friends in the lobby area:

> This white lady came up to me and asked if I wanted to join her family for dinner. Well I was shocked—me eat dinner with these white strangers? She said the casino gave them four buffet tickets and there were only three of them. So I went. I can truly say that as I walked with them to our table, I felt all eyes on us. So I just smiled and walked like we were family—me being adopted of course—ha ha. Well to make a long story short, we ate and conversed and it was like being with my own family.

Elizabeth was amazed by this experience. She shared it with a black friend, who disabused her of her boundary-free vision:

> Whoa did he make a big deal of it. He said, "I can't believe you ate with them, I could never do that." I said, "Why not? Them people [are] like me and you, and the food was free." He said I was crazy and he just couldn't see himself eating with white folks. I said that I used to feel that way, but I've had several occasions that changed my mind. I remember when I had dinner with the faculty in the sociology department. I was so nervous, not just because they were white but they

were all educated. I was afraid I would do something silly. But they all were great and ate dinner just like black folks, somewhat (smile).

For Elizabeth, the boundaries were not clear-cut. She saw wiggle room that empowered her to take boundary-crossing risks. Real life does not always conform with racist orthodoxy. There are seeds of heterodoxy laying around. The willing and able collect them and use them in order to breach boundaries. In this study, people's ability to sow the seeds varied quite a bit.

NAMING THE ELEPHANT IN THE ROOM

In interracial social situations, difference loomed large like an elephant in the room that everyone pretended not to notice, even while they maneuvered around it awkwardly. Occasionally, people used racetalk to name the elephant—call race for what it was—in order to move on. Take, for example, this incident recorded by Jonathan (white):

> I was delivering with another co-worker, Tyrone. He is black and he was listening to the stereotypical "black" music. He asked me if I like this kind of music. I said it was alright to listen to. He then asked if I would fuck a black girl. I laughed in shock, but Tyrone said, "Seriously, it's all the same on the inside." I didn't say anything. He then said he just likes to fuck with all the white boys. I didn't feel threatened; it was funny.

Tyrone sensed racial tension and sought to diffuse it. He did so (a) by naming the elephant: race. And (b) he invoked their commonalities as straight men: having sex with women. He seemed to be testing Jonathan, shocking him to see how he would react. Could Jonathan handle this relationship? Apparently so. Although this moment was strained, it seemed to relax their future interactions. Lavinia (white) recorded a similar incident:

> Mel (white) said that during his first semester as a freshman, he went to his first class and sat in the back of the room. Then this black guy sat down next to him, turned and said, "So it looks like we're the only two black guys in this class." The black guy cracked up, since Mel is obviously not African American. They've been friends ever since.

Black students often face the experience of being in the numerical minority in college classrooms, which is a source of discomfort. However, this student turned the situation on its ear and brought Mel into the joke, even though he was ostensibly an outsider. Mel breached the racial boundary in a lasting way.

Other people dealt with the elephant by minimizing it. For example, Joan's (white) friends trivialized their racial/ethnic differences:

> My Indian boyfriend told me about the names that he and his friends call each other. For instance, he is the "brown boy," because he is Indian. They call another guy "black boy," and another, "yellow boy." They also refer to each other as kinds of chocolate: milk, dark, and white. Ever since he told me that, I call him "brown boy" and he calls me "his little white girl."

While this strategy worked within the group—in which they agreed upon their use of terms—it often looked strange to outsiders:

> My boyfriend was playing video games with his friends and the characters on the screen were colors. As they played, they yelled out things like "Kill the black boy!", referring to the character on the screen, as opposed to the green one and the purple one. People walked past their room and stared at them because they were screaming this out. They stopped yelling after that.

Joan's friends minimized the power of racial and ethnic differences within their group by decontextualizing them from their historical legacies. This strategy sufficed for them, even though it did not work in mixed company. They moved beyond the elephant in the room in order to build more complex relationships.

SHARING STORIES: EDUCATING ONE ANOTHER

Once people no longer viewed racial difference as an obstacle, they often began to share personal stories and standpoints. These were the kinds of conversations people have when they get to know each other—they shared their backgrounds in the hopes of strengthening their blossoming relationships. For example, Blueangel (black) talked to a Greek friend of hers: "He told me how his grandma came off the boat so she did not know much English. They just spoke Greek at him." This was a simple, nonjudgmental conversation about language. In another conversation, Blueangel (black) talked to a white guy on her hall about tanning:

> He explained to me that he was Swedish and that in the sun he does not tan; he burns. I said that I understood, because I got extremely dark in the summer time. He said that when the Vikings came over, they saw the sun and turned back around to their homeland of snow and little sun.

Here Blueangel and her friends merely shared information about the differences they experienced due to their race.

Other conversations were more pointed, geared toward clearing up misinformation that one group might have learned about the other. For example, Anastasia's (black) brother Wendal (black) talked with a friend, Mark (white):

> Mark said the only reason white women want black men was because of sex and money. He said that black men have always wanted white women. Wendal said, "No, that is a myth. Blacks were afraid to go with white women because they would be lynched. Also, white women were seen as tarnished. Rather, it was white men who have always wanted black women, because they raped them during slavery."

Wendal used the trust of their friendship to correct Mark's misinformation, and because of their trust, Mark was able to hear the information and not react defensively. Building trusting relationships was therefore an important element in challenging the structure of domination.

FINDING THE CONNECTION

Merely sharing background information was not enough to forge a bond between people across color lines, although it was a useful tool in getting to that point. To connect on a deeper level, people sought commonalities between them despite their obvious racial/ethnic differences. For example, Joan (white) recorded this incident:

> My friend Carol (white) told me about her job. She is the only woman and the only white person. When the guys at work found out that she spoke Spanish, they became more accepting of her.

Carol's coworkers saw her language skills as a point of connection, despite her gender and racial difference from them. Carter (black) and Mitch (white) made a similar connection in this conversation about a band they liked:

> Mitch: I've seen them play, man. They get down!
> Carter: Really? Are they a funk band?
> Mitch: Yeah, they're diverse too.
> Carter: Is the drummer black or white?
> Mitch: He's black. I've never seen a white drummer that could blast a funky groove.

Carter: You know, come to think of it, I haven't either. At least, I can't think of any right now.

Mitch and Carter did not shy away from race as a topic—indeed it strengthened their musical connection.

A connection did not have to be grounded in reality in order for it to work. For example, Maggie (Latina) joked with Cary (white) over dinner:

Maggie: Are you going to eat that? It's so gross.
Cary: I felt like spicy Mexican food today. You know to fulfill my Mexican blood.
Maggie: What are you talking about? You have no Mexican blood. You are related to your cousins that are half Mexican, but not your half. That does not make you Mexican.
Cary: Yeah, well, the blond hair and white skin doesn't mean anything. I know there is some Mexican in me, so I'm going to feed it. Hahahah.

Cary fabricated a connection to Maggie—and she knew it—but it was successful. Precious (black) recorded an incident also grounded in myth:

I overheard Johnson (black) and Luke (white) talking about how Luke was up all night getting it on with his wife. While Luke walked away, Johnson said, "He's a black man trapped in a white man's body.'"

To connect with Luke, Johnson invoked the trope of the black buck. However, he used it as a term of endearment rather than as a means to reify this racist image. Underscoring this connection, Precious hand-wrote in her field notes, "This is how we identify with them." In another incident, Precious wrote:

I told Penelope and Johnson that I saw an Asian with an afro earlier that day. Penelope said, "Japanese get their hair permed to be kinky like ours. They love hip hop in their culture."

Whether or not this is true, Penelope appreciated what she saw as an attempt to bridge boundaries.

In some racetalk, finding a connection led to warm interchanges that boded well for future boundary spanning, as in this conversation between good friends Carter (black) and Jerry (white). They discussed Carter's girlfriend (white):

Jerry: I can tell you like her.
Carter: Why do you say that?
Jerry: Just look at yourself! You get all googly whenever you see her! I can see you blush even!

Carter: No, you can't!
Jerry: Yeah! I mean, you're not even white and your face gets red!

Jerry thought that it was sweet that Carter blushed—just as a white guy like Jerry might do. The good will in this interchange itself was noteworthy given that they discussed an interracial relationship, which would typically be sanctioned by policing orthodoxy. Instead, Jerry and Carter's connection helped them overcome "typical" orthodoxy, and they celebrated the breaching of racist boundaries.

Once a connection was formed, an alliance could be formed, as in this incident recorded by Rachel (white):

> I was walking out of African American history class the other day and this black guy from class, Bertrand, stopped me. He said, "Hey, does this class bother you? You know, being one of the only white people? Definitely the only white girl that says anything, you know?" I said it only bothered me when I have to hear black people in the class or the black teacher talking about "I know none of you wanna deal with white folks, but you better learn how cuz you're gonna have to deal with 'em the rest of your life whether you like it or not." Bertrand agreed that he didn't think that was fair, and he was offended by those kinds of comments too. He told me that if I want to comment on anything he would support me. He said, "Now you know if you gonna say anything defendin' anything, you better get an intelligent brother like me to get your back. Don't go around saying nothing and then look around for somebody because they not gonna be there for you [without my help]." It was a relief that Bertrand talked to me when he did. I was feeling pretty uncomfortable.

Rachel was a getting a minor in Black Studies, and she was one of the few whites who routinely took such courses. She had slowly earned the trust of Bertrand, who recognized her to be an ally.

Sometimes the commonality was not mutually agreed upon. One person might assume a stronger bond than the other. In such instances, it could be used to take dominants down a peg or two, as in this incident recorded by Missy (white):

> My friend's Mexican husband, Jesus, asked what nationality I am. I told him that one of my nationality is Polish. He asked me how and when my family came here [to the United States] I told him that my great grandparents took a boat over here. He said, "So you're a wetback?"

Jesus used racetalk to point out a connection between her life and his—they both were members of devalued immigrant groups. However, he did so sardonically. Jesus went on to deride Polish as "Polacks, poor, dirty people who don't shower every day and wear the same shirt every day." Instead of using their connection as a means to strengthen their relationship, he seemed to be putting her in her place, using irony to imply, "You are not better than Mexicans just because you are white: our ethnic stereotypes are the same." Perhaps after some reflection Missy could see this racetalk as a tool to strengthen her interracial friendships. But when she recorded the incident, she was offended.

BONDING THROUGH CONTRAST

In the racetalk, people tended to focus on differences rather than commonalities. They contrasted their group to the others. However, contrast could be a tool to bring the groups together. As such, people made jokes about the difference. They connected as people *in spite* of their differences. For example, Jaime (white) wrote:

> I was sitting at breakfast with Roy (black) and we observed the windy, cold-looking weather outside. We observed that crazy people only wore sweatshirts when it looked like it was freezing outside. Roy joked that when it's cold out you see white folks with shorts and a T-shirt when black folks are wearing winter coats. And when black folks are wearing scarves, white folks think it's nothing. All of us just laughed.

Similarly, Roger (white) eavesdropped on a conversation between two white and one black men:

> The African American said, "I don't know how you do it. Brothers hate the cold. And you all be skiing and playing hockey. It's crazy!" The white guys chuckled and they all began talking about how they were going out drinking this weekend.

Understanding and bridging boundaries meant dealing with perceptions of how "we" do things versus how "they" do things. Precious (black) listened to a conversation between Johnson (black), Luke (white), and Murray (black) while they all smoked pot. Johnson said of Luke, "He's a white boy used to smoking two hits per joint and then passin' it."

Carter (black) recorded another conversation contrasting white and black styles of worship. He was talking with his white friend Bev:

> Carter: So how's church going for you?
> Bev: Really good! Hey, I'm not trying to be racist or anything, but I'm going to a black people's church this Sunday.

Carter: Oh, cool!

Bev: Yeah, I wanna check it out. I'm interested in how their service may be different from the ones I usually go to.

Carter and Bev already had something in common: she dated a black man, and he dated a white woman. Yet even though they had a trusting bond—he knew where she was coming from—Bev still felt the need to assure Carter that she was not being racist. Indeed, he was very supportive of her plans. In many circumstances, then, contrasting the racialized experiences of different groups was a way of breaching boundaries in a successful manner.

Contrast with an Edge

In much of the racetalk, when people contrasted their group with another, there was an edgy subtext. In these circumstances, racetalk critiqued the underlying racism in society, even while attempting to overcome it through an interracial/ethnic connection. For example, John (white) recorded this incident:

My roommate (white) and I had people over for dinner: two African American women, one Mexican woman, and my roommate's white boyfriend. All of these people were my friends. In a conversation about movies, the Mexican woman referred to me as a "cool white boy."

This women contrasted John with other "white boys," implying that he was better than the rest of them. In other words, John was an exceptional white boy. This remark made him feel good. He felt accepted in spite of his whiteness, which might ordinarily be a handicap in an interracial friendship. Cheyenne's (white) friend Mary (black) was less subtle:

We were out at a bar. After being hit on several times, Mary said, "Man, white boys are some stupid mother fuckers." I said, "Hey, I'm white!" Mary said, "Yeah, but you're not white to me. You're different."

As in the incident with John above, Mary contrasted blacks with whites but made an exception for Cheyenne.

Other messages lurked in the contrasts as well. For example, Cheyenne had a conversation with Lena (Latina), her sister-in-law, and Wade (white) her brother. Lena and Wade worked together:

Wade told a crazy story about him and another guy from work. Lena said, "What a bunch of crazy white boys." My brother replied, "yeah, well if it ain't white, it ain't right."

Lena implicitly contrasted whites (crazy) with Latinos (sane). In response, Wade invoked an old rhyme that was historically used to glorify whiteness. He used it as a tongue-in-cheek critique of whiteness.

Guido (Latino) recorded another edgy critique: "I called my roommate Skippy a 'dumb honky' today because he microwaved his salad and then didn't like how it tasted." Skippy and his friends constantly called Guido a "spic." Guido played on that here in this racetalk. The subtext here was that only a dumb white guy would think that a salad could or should be microwaved—and it took a "spic" to point that out. In another incident, Cheyenne went to a party with Mexican Americans:

> Someone told a sexual joke and someone didn't "get it." My friend Virginia said, "Why don't you go ask Cheyenne—she's one of them crazy white girls!" Of course I laughed and responded, "Yeah that's why everybody wants a white girl!"

Quick-witted Cheyenne recognized that Virginia was lumping her into the stereotype that white girls are oversexed, and she quickly rebounded with some oppositional identity work—"yeah, that's why everybody wants me."

In all of these incidents, racetalk contrasted racial/ethnic groups, but with a critical edge. This talk reinforced interracial connections, but—because of the edge—the interactions could have gone another way. People could have been offended and challenged the racetalker, thereby damaging the bond. In order for the edgy contrast to be successful, the participants required a bond of trust based on a shared background: the bonds of family members, old friends, and roommates. This talk builds a bond because there is already a trusting connection. It is not for the fledgling relationship. As we shall see below, without a foundation of trust, the positive effect of an antiracist critique could easily be lost in translation, and sardonic racial critiques could backfire.

The Double Edge of Contrast: Reifying Tropes

In some racetalk, contrasting differences had a *double edge* to it. The first edge was embedded in the content of the talk, as in the racetalk just discussed. The second edge was in the way that the talk was used and received. If used successfully, then people walked away feeling closer, as if they stood on a level playing field. Yet, the contrast could exacerbate and legitimate differences instead of operating as a unifying critique. In this case, the participants did not feel closer. Instead they felt offended or violated. The contrast backfired. This was especially likely when the talk contained an old trope or slur. For example, Katie (white) wrote:

> When I went to a party at my roommate Tim's (Latino) fraternity house, he warned me that I was a white girl in a brown house and I was going to get hit on a lot because browns and blacks have a thing for white girls. This was true too.

Tim's warning reified the buck image, and Katie bought into it. As such, she and Tim were further divided rather than unified.

In another example, Lavinia (white) worked as a night security officer in the dorms. Her main job was to check IDs before letting people in. One night a white male and an Asian male approached the window. They appeared to be friends. As the Asian produced his ID, the white man joked, "Look at that. Asians have such stubby fingers, he can't even get his ID out. Come on you stupid chink!" Then he asked, "Are minorities allowed in the dorms tonight?" This white guy humiliated his "friend" in front of a complete stranger. Guido (Latino) recorded numerous such incidents, uncovering a theme in his relationship with his white fraternity brothers. In one incident, Guido recorded this: "My white roommate Skippy said that I did a 'spic-tacular' job on the dishes. I told him that he was really 'honk-tacular.'" In another incident, Guido's white fraternity brothers talked about where to go out one night. Guido was joking around, saying "yes" to every suggestion:

> Skippy said that I was once again spic-tacular, and Burt said that the minority vote didn't count, referring to me because I was Mexican. Later, Skippy's girlfriend asked if she could throw out the beans on the table. She then said, "Don't worry, Guido. I'm not talking about you."

Until logging field notes for this project, Guido did not even recognize how often his ethnicity was invoked in a pejorative manner by his closest friends. His feelings were hurt, and he began to realize that these men rarely interacted with him without centralizing his ethnicity. The elephant was always in the room, and his friends used it as a weapon rather than moving beyond it once and for all. As I discuss in a later chapter, Guido slowly problematized his friendships as demeaning and eventually confronted them.

Carter (black) had similar interactions with various white people. In this incident, he talked about his hometown with a floormate, Brent (white):

> Carter: Where are you from again?
> Brent: Cooperstown.
> Carter: Man, I swear I know someone from there. Name some people that go here from Cooperstown.
> Brent: Do you know Letecia Williams?
> Carter: I'm not sure. How does she look?
> Brent: Kinky curly hair. She's real ghetto!

Carter: Nah, I don't think I know her.
Brent: I can't stand her. She just bothers me.
Carter: Anyone else?
Brent: I can't really think of anyone right now.

Carter inferred by Letecia's ethnic name that she was black. But, to underscore this information, Brent continued to racially code her rather than constructively describe her: "Kinky, curly hair," "real ghetto." In his field notes, Carter said that he was put off by this racetalk, which was presumptuous and inappropriate. Brent implied that Leticia's race explained his distaste for her, even as he talked to a black man. Perhaps he thought they could bond by trashing this woman. He was wrong.

In another incident, Carter talked to his friend Selena (Latina). She said, "Why is it that black guys always hit on me?" He answered: "I couldn't tell you. Why do you ask?" Selena explained: "Well, I was in the student center today and this black guy came up to me and was asking for my name and number." "Oh yeah?" Carter replied. He then changed the subject. Carter did not know what to say when Selena asked him to speak for black men. He also sensed that she was insulted by the black man's come-on, and he did not know how to respond. In both cases, the attempt to bond backfired, distancing Carter from the racetalker rather than drawing him in. Others recorded failed contrasts as well. Barbara (white) wrote:

> I was attending a dinner in the company of a group of friends. One of the invited guests was Hispanic. My friend, Milt (white)—Vice President of his church—made a comment about the Hispanic man (an employee of his). He said, "Someone get him a taco."

In spotlighting this man's ethnicity—"get him a taco!"—Milt's comment backfired. Barbara made a point in her field notes of underscoring Milt's affiliation with a church. Religious herself, Barbara expected more out of a man who called himself a Christian. Instead, Milt blundered, caricaturing his guest rather than making him feel welcome.

In a similar incident, Anastasia (black) watched *Jaws* with some white friends, Matt and Joseph. She observed that the woman swimming in the ocean swam gracefully. Matt said, "Yeah because she isn't black. Black people don't have any swimming pool in the ghetto." Anastasia told him to shut up. As with Guido and his white friends, this was not an isolated comment. On another occasion, she was talking with Matt and Joseph:

> We were talking about my roommate, Becky (white), from freshman year. Matt told me that she was getting married. We continued to talk about her because we

don't like her. Then he said, "She asked about you. She asked, 'How is that black bitch Anastasia doing?'" I asked him if she really said that and he said, no, he was just joking.

Matt thought—based on their friendship—that it would be acceptable to joke with Anastasia in this manner. He was wrong. He abused their trust and used their racial difference in an entitled, unreflective manner to hurt Anastasia, even though he meant to be funny.

It appears, based on the racetalk in this study, that people of color run emotional risks when they befriend whites. Whites use double-edged contrasts in ways that are funny to them, but that inadvertently[1] harm their "friends." In these cases, whites thought that they could invoke racetalk with impunity under the auspices of friendship. But in so doing, they undermined the core of the friendship itself.

Some people successfully breached racial boundaries, but they made blunders and used racetalk. Racetalk can damage the trust that allowed them to cross the boundary in the first place. Such racetalk reified the racial boundary in the end. Jay (Asian) recorded a particularly poignant example of this violation of trust:

Michael (white) has a very compulsive personality I think stemming from his ADD. I don't think he's racist, he makes racist jokes sometimes but I personally think he makes them for the shock value more than actual beliefs. He came from Russia being singled out as a Jew. He never knew his father and was raised entirely by his mother who spoiled him. His confidence is built on believing that he has to be better then everyone else and he is very competitive. He constantly argues with another one of my friends over the most trivial things. Michael was a childhood friend and we grew up in a very diverse neighborhood with a large Jewish population and a larger then average Asian population. It was a Saturday night, I was bored out of my mind and so was he. We decided to go for a ride and cruise to find things to do. He picked me up and when I got into the car he "showed me" (played the song) "Brian's Freestyle" by CKY2K. The song is very racist, a white guy impersonates an Asian with a thick accent commenting on Asian culture and Asians in America. Now, I am an Asian American so I felt personally attacked by this song. I told him, "this song is pretty racist," and he replied by "yeah, that's why it's funny." I told him that it wasn't funny to me even though I did laugh at some points in the song.

Jay worked hard to legitimate Michael's actions—"he has ADD"—even though it offended him. Michael abused their friendship, which Jay valued:

He was playing the song loud and people in the street could hear it and it felt really awkward to me. Because he was my friend he thought it would be OK for him to play the song and take enjoyment out of it. Truthfully I really didn't mind too much. He said that I could make racist jokes about Russians or Jewish people. I really didn't want to make a big deal about this because it was all in the name of fun and he didn't expect me to take offense to the song which I didn't. I think if I heard it from somebody that I didn't know I would have been more offended.

Jay explained away the behavior in order to maintain the friendship. But Jay's excuses were weak. Indeed, he seemed to doubt them even as he wrote them.

EMPATHY

Joe Feagin, Hernan Vera, and Pinar Batur (2001) assert that a lack of empathy is one of the most compelling reasons that racism endures. Empathy is different from sympathy, which means to feel sorry for someone. In contrast, "empathy involves identifying strongly with the circumstances and pain of another human being" (229). According to Vera (2003), human society is impossible without empathy. At the same time, we must temper our empathy. We cannot be moved by every injustice, or we will never stop weeping. Total empathy would be disastrous. However, in steeling ourselves against the anguish of routine injustice, we have gone too far. We have shut out other people's suffering so effectively that we have lost the ability to take the role of the other, to feel and to see the world as others do. Vera and his colleagues argue that racism—through overt and symbolic violence—quashes empathy by desensitizing us to others' suffering. As discussed in this book, the various structures of racism actually *legitimate* people's suffering. Thus, a key to ending racism is to nurture empathy. We should attempt to truly hear and feel the world as others do. As Feagin, Vera, and Batur (2001, 229–30) argue, "an act of daring and the courage to cross often forbidden social borders are necessary to exercise human empathy of this character."

Interracial/ethnic empathy can be fostered by crossing social borders. For example, in this incident, Hedwig (white) and Chuck (black) attended a party for a Mexican coworker, Carla. A lot of the guests were Mexican. Hedwig and Chuck talked about him being the only black man at work.[2] He said,

Yeah, I really feel comfortable now at work. I didn't always feel that way though, being a brother in the suburbs. Sometimes people look at you funny. But yeah, I can really say I feel comfortable with everyone now and I'm glad of it.

Later, the guests encouraged Hedwig and Chuck to dance. He resisted so Carla dragged Hedwig onto the floor:

She took me out and I commented on how I felt stupid that I was the only white person dancing. A couple of times I said, "I feel so white!" Later, I tried to get Chuck to dance again. I said, "Come on it's fun! You don't think I feel silly dancing out there? I'm the only white girl here!" He said, "Well look at me. I'm the only brother. You think I don't stand out?"

Hedwig had a slight glimpse into the experiences that Chuck faced every day, and she empathized with him.

For others, the journey to empathy was longer and more painful, as in this incident recorded by Jean (white):

This summer I was a camp counselor. I started orientation later than everyone else because I was hired to fill a spot that a girl had backed out on. I arrived at camp nervous to join this already formed group and worried about the summer to come (7 weeks). Four of the counselors were Hispanic. I became really good friends with two of them. We hung out and had very open, honest conversations. They told me that I was racist, which I vehemently denied. They argued that if I had been walking down the street, I wouldn't have given them a second look. I replied that that may be true, but it would be because I didn't know them. They then said that if a group of my friends and I were at a party and they approached me, I wouldn't take the chance to get to know them. I was baffled. How could they say these things about me?

Jean was slowly affected by her new friends' assertions:

I then realized that I was in a unique situation. I was forced during one week of staff orientation to get to know everyone on a deep personal level or else the summer wouldn't go well. We weren't in a normal society where people were judged on the basis of skin color. We sang songs and played games all day in our sweet little community. I realized that what my new friends were saying about the real world might be true. Maybe if I had met them on the street, I wouldn't have been as accepting. This camp experience opened my eyes. I learned a lot about myself and society as a whole.

Jean came to empathize with their feelings as outsiders, transforming their relationship from being antagonistic to being mutually beneficial and rewarding. They became allies.

Sophia (white) recorded another moving epiphany:

One of my oldest and closest friends is Hispanic. She is second generation to this country. We have been friends since fourth grade. I remember being in her house and marveling at the cultural differences between the two of us. I learned how to make homemade tortillas, enchiladas, and stuff. I also remember my friend being very embarrassed of her own culture. She never wanted to talk about it in front of other people, besides me. She used to be teased by her other relatives. They would tell her that she was a "white girl." The part that I don't want to admit . . . but for the sake of this project. . . I remember us teasing each other. She used to call me things like Polack and Polish princess. And I used to call her things like bean and even spic. We never seemed to mind when it was each other calling ourselves that. But once one of our other friends said something like that to her, and she really cried hard! I think that is when I stopped saying things like that to her.

When Sophia recognized the power of slurs to inflict pain, she empathized and reformed. Blueangel (black) had a conversation with her friend Andy (white) that blew her mind:

I asked Andy why he listened to hip hop music, especially music targeted towards the black community. I did not see anything wrong with it. It just puzzled me that he listened to traditional jazz, hip hop, and on the flip side listened to classical music and heavy metal bands. Most white boys [who listen to black music] only listen to Dr. Dre or Snoop Dogg, neither of whom have much to say that's positive about the black community. Andy's first response was that he listens to hip hop because he can learn from it. He learns about the problems plaguing the black community, and how artists like Mos Def are the Jesse Jacksons of their time: "Mos Def is saying some powerful shit in his lyrics and most of the black community doesn't see what a prophet this man is. Mos Def is able to send messages out through his music." I listened to everything he was saying and was like, "This is not the shit I'm used to hearing from a white person."

Andy elaborated with a critique of the racial regime:

He said, "I don't see myself as a white American. I know I'm white and that can't be denied, but I was raised differently from my other counterparts. I was home schooled, so I did not have that much interaction with a lot of people. I did not witness or be a part of the prejudiced school system in my community. Also, because I started college when I was 16, I was exposed early to the other cultures you wouldn't see in my hick hometown. I don't have the arrogance that most white Americans have about themselves. They want everyone to know that they are not just white, but Americans. After the September 11 incident, I see so many people with this 'United We Stand' shit and flags on their cars, homes, and backs. These are the same people easily willing to kick the shit out of a Middle Easterner because 'they could all be terrorists and we need to protect our country.' Throughout history, white Americans are ready and willing to kill or fuck up a person's reputation because that person was not white. I don't want to be a part of that, and I am not a part of that, so I don't consider myself white American."

As Andy argued, when you truly empathize with someone, you become their ally. You fight for them as you would for yourself, as in this incident recorded by Jaime (white):

> My (black) friend Roy was telling me that he and his white friend applied to Burger King when they were younger. They both had no experience. They hired his friend and not him. So his friend's dad went and asked why they didn't hire Roy too. They then hired Roy right on the spot saying that they didn't want a lawsuit.

Empathy engenders advocacy.

Achieving empathy was not a simple matter. In order to truly hear another person's perspective, people had to suspend their own self-interest. They had to take the other person's stories as real to her/him, even if they did not jive with their own experiences.

Failed Empathy

Empathy can, of course, fail. People might listen to others and try to identify. But if they cannot go beyond their own experiences as the reference point for judging another's suffering, then true empathy cannot occur. I have seen many dialogues between white, brown, and black women fall apart when empathy fails. For example, I belonged to an interracial group of women that met monthly to discuss racism. One of the goals of the group was to form interracial bonds and alliances on campus. In these meetings, black and brown women shared their experiences of discrimination, pain, and isolation with white women, who genuinely wanted to listen and connect. In their efforts at empathy, however, white women encountered a pitfall. In attempting to bond through commonalities, many white women made the analytical leap between racial oppression and gender oppression. They offered counterexamples of their suffering as [white] women in a sexist society. These women meant well. The pitfall occurred because they did not recognize the differences in gender versus racial regimes. Yes, these white women had experienced myriad obstacles due to gender. But they still maintained white privilege, which the black and brown women did not possess. As African American poet Pat Parker (1978) once wrote of her white peers in the women's movement, "Sister! Your foot's smaller but it's still on my neck!" The white women in my group—in their effort to place themselves in the black and brown women's shoes—did so without being able to abandon their white privilege. Indeed, when women of color pointed this out to them, white women often became defensive, and many even cried. In crying, the white women had fully succeeded in silencing the black and brown women's issues, recentering their own victim status. Empathy failed.

In the racetalk in this study, there were several such attempts at empathy that failed. Some people were unable to go beyond their own experiences, no matter how often they tried. For example, Katie (white) tried on several occasions to understand Tim, her Mexican roommate. She was not able to do so. She wrote:

> Tim pronounces Latinos as Lat-in-os with an emphasis on "Lat" because he says that nobody knows how to pronounce it correctly. I told him that I had never heard of that pronunciation. He has me saying this now as a joke.

Tim wanted Katie to understand his language, but she had no connection to it nor any desire to acquire new knowledge—"I had never heard that pronunciation." Instead of empathizing, she dismissed his endeavors. She pronounced it as he asked, but "as a joke." Similarly, Jaime (white) recorded this incident:

> Roy and I talked about who we looked like in our families. I look like my dad because of my nose, but also like my mom. Roy said he looked like his dad, not his mom. He said his dad is lighter, though, and he used to be lighter when he was younger until he got burnt. So he is darker brown but not totally black. He said his mom looks like an Indian. His grandma actually has some Indian in her, but he didn't know the tribe. He doesn't look like his mom at all. He said his grandma is yellow. So his grandma shows that Indian trait. I said that I didn't think his mom looked Native American, but oh well.

Like Katie and Tim, Roy and Jaime had an ongoing relationship in which Roy repeatedly tried to bridge boundaries. Here, he trusted Jaime to understand the nuances of color that are familiar to African Americans—but he was mistaken. They were lost on her. In coding her field notes, Jaime wrote that Roy was "stereotyping Native Americans." Like Katie, Jaime was unable to forge empathy due to her facile notions of race and ethnicity and the primacy that she placed on whiteness.

Reflexivity and Renewed Efforts

I end this section with a caveat: even though these attempts failed, they were genuine attempts. Without making such efforts, the walls and borders remain unbreached. We must make these challenges, learn from them when we fail, and attempt again with this new information. As we will see in a later chapter, there is ample evidence that by approaching racial boundaries reflexively, learning from our mistakes, and reapproaching them, we can indeed breach them in meaningful ways. Vera (2003) argues that racism is a skill that must be learned. As such, racism can be undermined by nurturing the lost skills of empathy. Mastery of these new skills requires time and effort, trial and error. So, following Vera, we must be patient and resilient, because empathy engenders justice.

TRULY CROSSING OVER: DECONSTRUCTING THE BOUNDARY

Truly crossing over from one side to the other of a racial/ethnic barrier was rare and difficult for subjects in this study, despite various attempts. Some strategies—like empathy and finding commonalities—were more effective than others—like using double-edged racetalk. Barrie Thorne (1993) studied crossing of gender boundaries among school kids[3] in her book, *Gender Play*. Like racial boundaries, gender boundaries are entrenched, reified, and policed in serious ways. Thorne's site of inquiry was elementary school playgrounds and classrooms. She found that most kids do not try to cross the gender boundaries. Even the teachers themselves use boundaries to control the children. For example, teachers encourage kids to sit boy-girl, or they pit boys against the girls in spelling bees. These strategies highlight a boundary, and they discourage the kids from intentionally breaching them.

Nevertheless, crossing did occur. Thorne proposed three criteria for successful crossing: (1) The child must be sincere in her/his desire to cross. (2) The child must be willing to try repeatedly to cross, until s/he is finally accepted. (3) The child must possess skills that are appropriate for activities on the "other side." The status of the crosser mattered too: popular kids could cross back and forth with no penalty to their identity, while "average" kids had to struggle according to these rules.

Crossing completely over *racial* boundaries required similar criteria. As shown above, many people failed to meet one or more of the criteria. Perhaps they were insincere or they gave up after one failed attempt. Yet, some people persevered and completely crossed. For example, Rachel (white) crossed as a Black Studies minor, becoming accepted as a peer by black students like Bertrand. Rachel earned acceptance across the boundary by (1) showing authentic, sincere respect to her black peers and the course material; (2) making repeated efforts at crossing; and (3) demonstrating in class discussion that she had the skills required to truly belong as a Black Studies student. When actors were insincere, it showed. For example, Precious (black) wrote, "Penelope (black) told me that she said hi to a white girl at school, and the girl said,

"What's up, player?" Penelope thought the girl was "trying to be black" and it struck her as odd and inauthentic. Penelope was unsure if the girl was caricaturing blackness. In contrast, Rachel did not co-opt slang and try to pass as "black"—instead she tried to succeed as a *white* Black Studies minor.

On rare occasions, a person became so fully involved in crossing that s/he attempted to alter her/his identity in order to fully fit. This incident was recorded by Blueangel (black):

> I met a resident [in the dorm] who introduced himself as Keshaun, accent on the "a." He is Asian American and his real name is Ted, an Anglo-Saxon name. But he called himself Keshaun because he hung out with black people and the residents on his floor call him black.

Ted/Keshaun crossed successfully. Perhaps, like Rachel, he did not need to so radically alter his identity in order to do so.

CONCLUSION

The structures in the racial regime are powerful forces maintaining age-old divisions among people of color. These divisions serve the larger purpose of reinforcing the hierarchical system of racism. Yet, as shown here, the structures are not omnipotent and deterministic. People can and do cross the boundaries. Crossing costs, though. Some cross more successfully than others, weakening and/or reifying racial boundaries as they scale the walls. This chapter provides insight into the usefulness of different crossing techniques. In order to break down the system of racism, people must attempt to cross boundaries. They should do so reflexively, taking note of the effect they are having on people as they cross. People should cross sincerely, being as authentic as they can be so as to avoid reproducing damaging tropes. By successfully crossing, we nurture empathy. Only by crossing these boundaries can we dismantle the power of policing orthodoxy, which keeps people "in their place."

NOTES

1. I am giving whites the benefit of the doubt here. There is little evidence in the data that these whites wanted to cause harm. They were simply unreflective and overentitled.

2. Most of their other coworkers were white, and they were not at the party.

3. Thorne calls her subjects "kids" rather than "children" in an attempt to use their own language for defining themselves.

10

THE ACCIDENTAL ANTIRACIST

Research as a Tool for Raising Consciousness

Sciences and their societies, it turned out, co-constructed each other.

—Sandra Harding (1998, 2)

Can a research methodology form the basis of social transformation? Can it foster empathy, help debunk myths, and reeducate people about inequalities? Yes, under certain circumstances. For decades, methodologists have examined qualitative research strategies as to the impact that they have on both subjects (Burawoy, Gamson, and Burton 1991; Hertz 1997; Horowitz 1986; Kreiger 1985; Naples 1996; Peshkin 1986) and researchers (Berg 2004; Creswell 1997; Denzin and Lincoln 2000; Lofland and Lofland 1994; Miller and Tewksbury 2001). The verdict has been mixed. Qualitative research has been cast at its worst as an instrument of oppression, co-opting and silencing marginalized people (Collins 1998; Romero and Stewart 1999). At its best, it has been used as a tool for empowerment, giving voice to the less powerful (Burawoy, Gamson, and Burton 1991; Harding 1991; Naples 2003; Reason and Bradbury 2001). This body of scholarship effectively exposes and critiques the power of the researcher over the researched, admonishing researchers to use their power cautiously and reflexively (McCorkel and Myers 2003).

This chapter takes a slightly different tack, examining the ways that *researchers* rather than *subjects* can be transformed and empowered through the process of collecting and analyzing data. Specifically, I analyze the transformations among the team of researchers who collected these data on racetalk. As discussed earlier, the purpose of using a research team was to be able to cull as broad an array of data as possible. The goal was not to create antiracists. However, as the data collection culminated, the team reported experiencing profound intellectual and social changes—sometimes troubling and other times inspiring. The project accidentally produced a group of people with emerging antiracist perspectives. Changes in their perspectives initiated ripple effects in their social lives. After debriefing the research team and analyzing their feedback, I see the potential in this project to form a basic blueprint for action research projects geared toward engendering antiracist consciousness and action.

THE IMPACT OF THE PROCESS OF INQUIRY: SUBJECTS AND RESEARCHERS

In epistemological discussions regarding qualitative projects, it is increasingly recognized that the researcher's values and identities are brought to the site in ways that can inform the process of data collection and analysis. A researcher's "lens" (Lofland and Lofland 1994) or "standpoint" (Collins 2000; Harding 1991; Hartsock 1983; Smith 1987) can lead a researcher to become interested in a topic; it can provide (or hinder) access to a site; it can affect her ability to be an accurate listener/recorder of data; it can make her more (or less) trustworthy and credible in the eyes of the subjects; and it can affect rapport (for more, see Burawoy, Gamson, and Burton 1991; Horowitz 1986; Kreiger 1985; Naples 1996; and Peshkin 1986). Thus, acknowledging and interrogating one's lens or standpoint is not only relevant for understanding the production of data, but also promotes a more nuanced, sociologically meaningful analysis of data. As standpoint theorists have long asserted, all research—even the most scientifically rigorous—is socially situated.[1]

Being a researcher means occupying a position of power: the researcher can affect subjects, both intentionally and unintentionally (Burawoy, Gamson, and Burton 1991). Being a reflexive researcher means constantly monitoring and trying to control the various, inevitable changes in the field (Hertz 1997). Simply by their presence, researchers disrupt the natural setting, potentially altering future outcomes (Roethlisberger and Dickenson 1939).[2] Barrie Thorne (1993) for example, recognized that her visibility as an adult in a classroom of adolescents affected the kids' interactions with each other, the classroom material, and the teachers. Adult status connoted power in this context. She had to carefully navigate allegiances between herself and the kids (who were the source of data) and between herself and teachers (who gave her access to the classroom, which could be revoked at any time).

Following Thorne, Debra Van Ausdale (Van Ausdale and Feagin 2002) strove to achieve the status of "non-sanctioning adult," so as to gain access to preschoolers' intimate relationships. She was so successful, in fact, that she accessed startling data. Her poignant data exposed racism among preschoolers, thus creating another dilemma. As a researcher, she was officially accountable to the parents and administration of the daycare. Van Ausdale was able to use her power as a researcher, as well as her powerful data, to create dialogues between parents and teachers in an effort to understand the ways that racism was being learned and reproduced.

Epistemologists concerned with the potentially exploitative nature of the researcher-researched relationship have sought strategies for engendering positive change on behalf of the subjects. Feminist research (DeVault 1999; Harding 1991; Naples 2003; Reinharz 1992), ethnomethodology (Burawoy, Gamson, and Burton 1991), and participatory action research (Bray et al 2000; Patai 1991; Reason and Bradbury 2001; Stringer 1999) are all geared toward transforming and empowering subjects—with the considered cooperation and input from subjects. This type of research intentionally seeks to undermine the power relationship between the researcher and the researched, striving to create a partnership between the two. There is much debate about how successful a researcher can be in fully eliminating the power differential.[3] Nevertheless, these efforts indicate a critical understanding of the politics of research and are important attempts to maximize the benefits of research for the subjects in the context of an unequal relationship. These egalitarian methods demonstrate the opportunity for research to be used as a strategic tool for fostering social change.

True to the goals of egalitarian research, however, we should expect that changes will be fostered in researchers as well as subjects. Indeed, my chief concern in this chapter is to extract the wisdom gleaned from action research and use it to analyze the changes that occurred among my team of researchers. Other scholars have focused on the ways that the qualitative researcher—as a social being—is changed through the research process, even when using less egalitarian methods. Because the data are filtered through the researcher, s/he cannot help but be affected by the data collection endeavor as well as by the actual data (Berg 2004; Lofland and Lofland 1994). For example, researchers may form enduring relationships with subjects (see Carpenter et al. 1988; Letkemann 1980). Indeed, leaving the field at the end of the project may be very difficult. Researchers will likely become sympathetic to the subjects, even if their analysis is critical of them.[4] Researchers may become so personally involved with subjects that it is challenging to decipher where the researcher role ends and the personal relationship begins.[5] Qualitative methods primers advise fledgling researchers to manage their feelings, reactions, and behaviors while conducting research (Berg 2004; Creswell 1997; Denzin and Lincoln 2000; Lofland and Lofland 1994). The underlying message of this advice is that changes in the researcher are inevitable, but they should be controlled so as to minimize stress and accusations of bias. Such warnings are sage advice in the context of positivism that continues to shape the reception of qualitative research in the discipline.[6]

In this chapter, however, I suggest that we reexamine the message, allowing ourselves to conceptualize a research project that might intentionally manipulate the relationship between the researcher and the data so as to increase the potential for social action. Rather than minimize the impact of the research process on the researchers, I explore the benefits of maximizing its impact. In this view, research has the potential to build a grassroots community that challenges the hegemony of racism in the United States. In particular, as my team of researchers recorded the data and discussed them together in focus groups, they began to confront previously hegemonic ideas and practices about race in their inner networks. This raised the team's awareness of a practice that had been hiding in plain sight. Their new lens altered their standpoints on many issues.

ACCIDENTAL ANTIRACISTS: HOW INQUIRY CONFRONTED IDENTITY FOR THE TEAM

The act of inquiry, through participant observation coupled with focus groups, affected myriad transformations among the team. Once I began to take note of the changes, I asked researchers to write personal testimonials regarding the effects of collecting data over the intensive two-month period. I asked them to think about the various ways that they thought about race, themselves, and their social networks now that they had completed copious field notes and emotional focus groups. From these testimonials, the field notes, and the videotapes of the focus groups, several patterns emerged.

Stress of Collecting Data

Team members reported that the very act of collecting data produced stress. Immediately after being trained in data collection, many of them scoffed, saying, "No one in my social network talks like that." But within days—sometimes even minutes—of beginning the data collection process, researchers were often stunned at the prevalence and frequency of racetalk that they encountered. Initially, researchers did not know what to do when an incident occurred. As Janet (black) said, "When my friend started saying shit, I was like, oh my god, what do I do?!" It took some time for researchers to learn to play off routine racetalk as they normally would. Focus groups were used to share tactics for "acting normal"—which was critical for collecting data in a natural setting.

Other researchers were stressed by the level of secrecy involved in writing field notes and keeping them unobtrusive. Rocker (white), as we have seen, fancied himself a quasi skinhead. Due to his like-minded peer group from whom most of his data were collected, Rocker's field notes were filled with invective. Not heeding the warnings about keeping notes hidden from plain view, Rocker had scrawled his field notes on small pieces of paper that littered his room. One night after much drinking, Rocker's roommate, Todd (white), walked out of his room carrying the scraps of paper. He confronted Rocker, pointing out direct quotes from Todd and Rocker's private conversations. Rocker explained, "It's something for class." This apparently smoothed the waters. However, Rocker's carelessness with his data could have damaged relationships in his intimate circle. The whole team dealt with the stress of being discovered throughout the data collection period.

The stress was heightened for the researchers in Phase 1. Because their focus groups were scheduled at night rather than as part of a class period, these researchers had to be cunning. Jonathan (white) wrote about the stress of collecting data under these circumstances in his field notes:

> I just reread the guidelines for this project and found out that I'm supposed to record data every night! This is very hard for me to do. All of my roommates and I stay up really late. I usually end up passing out downstairs. I can't retreat upstairs early to do it [field notes] because it would be noticed. Especially when I have to go to focus groups. I try to sneak out, but I am always asked where I am going. If I don't say, my roommates are offended and become suspicious. This is near impossible to keep up with.

All in all, then, the mere process of collecting data imposed stress upon the researchers that they had not anticipated. They dealt with this stress by writing in their field notes and connecting with me and their teammates in focus groups.

Undermining the Hegemony of Racetalk

As they collected data, the team observed everyday interactions in a new light. Initially, they were shocked by what they observed. They could not believe that they had never noticed the prevalence and content of racetalk before now. On paper, their data read like Jim Crow–era obloquy. But they had not been magically transported back in time. The team was overwhelmed by the fact that the racetalk in their field notes was commonplace, normal, and heretofore uninterrogated. Researchers reported being rattled by their new lens, often wondering if they were reading things accurately. Sophia (white) wrote,

> I am frustrated because I find that I notice the race of people more than I feel like I did before. I also feel that sometimes I read too much into things that are going on or being said. I am glad that I am doing this because I think it's important, but it is sometimes hard.

Similarly, Rori (white) wrote that the project "made me hyper-sensitive to racetalk in my everyday life. I had to [make myself] notice it in the beginning, then I could not discontinue noticing its occurrence afterward, even after data collection ended." She saw this change as a good thing: "I appreciate its value as a mechanism towards helping me to better understand racism."

Elizabeth (black) began to notice that a professor was treating her differently from the white students in class. She wrote in her field notes: "Today I sat in class and found myself analyzing everything he said and how he said it." She observed that when she answered a question, he would tell her that she was wrong. When a white student said the same idea in different terms, he said that the answer was correct. Others in her class [Cocoa (Latina) and Jonathan (white) from her focus group] confirmed her concerns. In her field notes, she debated how to handle this:

> I have, in the past, noticed how professors tend to show favoritism among white and male students. Though I have gotten upset about these things in the past, I never acted on them or questioned my professors.

After thinking about their interactions for some time, Elizabeth approached the professor. He dismissed her concerns, explaining that her answers were just wrong. Elizabeth wrote:

> This made me so uneasy, and I started to question this project and myself. Was I being paranoid? [It took me a while to ask], "Was he just trying to reverse the situation to make me feel like I was overreacting?"

The focus groups helped her to reframe the issue—one that she only problematized at all because of her role in the data collection.

All of the researchers reported a heightened sensitivity to racetalk that they had previously overlooked, and their awareness did not disappear once the data collection period ended. Through the process of inquiry, the team achieved a consciousness that, eventually, undermined the hegemony of racetalk as a practice.

Effects on Relationships

The team reported that data collection affected how they thought and felt about the people in their inner circles. Recording racetalk in field notes made the talk concrete and gave it a life of its own. When the talk came from a close friend or relative, researchers became uneasy with how to continue relationships in the future. Throughout the project Hedwig (white) had numerous confrontations with her friends. Recall the comments of her friend Lanie (white), as a self-avowed racist, and Don and Marie (both white), who urged her not to date a black man and supported violence against Middle Easterners. Hedwig reflected on her challenges in her field notes:

> I must say that since this project started, I have been really shocked by the way my friends are. I guess I always knew they were kind of like this, but it never bothered me to the extent that it does now. I mean, these are some of my closest friends and when I write their words down here, they just sound so ignorant. It really bothers me.

In another example, Eliza (white) called me on the phone to recount her first incident. She had been talking with an old family friend, Tom (white), about a lawsuit at the restaurant where her son worked. A woman had been fired, and she threatened to sue the restaurant for racism. Eliza never mentioned the race of the woman (whose mother was white and father was black). Tom began a long "lecture" on the matter, explaining that "it's typical for blacks to sue employers for racism just to get out of doing work. That's what they always do." Eliza was stunned. Tom's comments did not fit with her image of this man. Eliza didn't know how to proceed. She neither wanted to make him look bad nor to hurt his feelings.

After reminding Eliza of the layers of confidentiality embedded in the project, I also assured her that Tom's talk was "normal" if not mainstream. Racetalk is spoken by all people; it did not mean that they were "bad." At this point, Eliza offered evidence that Tom was indeed a good man—he had been to divinity school, he was a family counselor, and he was a published author. Eliza then began to recollect other incidents from her own past where blacks seemed to be claiming racism without cause. At first, I didn't follow her train of thought; but then I realized that Eliza had so successfully framed Tom as "good" that she began to wonder if he weren't also correct. At the end of the conversation, I urged her to write down all of this information so as to accurately represent the incident and its context.

This conversation provided insight into the mental machinations one might use to make sense of racetalk. It is one thing to hear racetalk from a stranger or from someone easily dismissed as "bad" for various reasons. It is quite another to hear racetalk from someone who is valued. Eliza was jarred by the "bad" talk coming from this "good" person, and she needed to make a choice: (1) Dismiss Tom's talk as irrelevant and move on. Her new training as a race-talk researcher would not allow her to do this, but she may have been doing so for years without noticing. (2) Decide that she had been wrong about Tom for all of those years and recast him as "bad." His legacy of "good works" would not allow her to do this. (3) Reject the good-bad dichotomy, and treat the incident as an opportunity to create a dialogue about race. Assume that Tom is not a static entity, but one who is shaped by the larger society—meaning that he can also change. Eliza was not yet comfortable enough to take this option. I asked Eliza if she had challenged Tom, and she said, "No! I just wanted the conversation to end." She hoped that her silence would help to preserve their relationship, even though she had been intellectually changed by the incident. Or (4) reframe the talk as "good" or correct, thereby justifying Tom's talk. In so doing, she absolved him of being labeled racist. Eliza's comments suggested that she had chosen this option: Tom *is* a good man, and now that I think about it, I *have* known blacks to act that way. Like others in this project, Eliza justified the racetalk and its speaker. By the end of the project, Eliza's field notes indicated a nuanced analysis of racetalk that evolved beyond "good" versus "bad." Thus, this one conversation was only a snapshot of her thought processes. However, by talking through her quandary aloud on the phone, Eliza offered a glimpse into the personal conflict elicited by interrogating racetalk.

Some researchers on the team handled this conflict more proactively. For example, Guido (Latino) was a researcher with Hispanic first and last names. Before this project, he nevertheless identified with his mother's Irish ethnicity. He had a large shamrock tattoo with the word "Irish" on his shoulder. He was a member of a white fraternity. His data were rife with derogatory remarks that his "brothers" made toward him. Recall that a fraternity brother told him that he did a "spic-tacular" job washing the dishes. Menial jobs in the house were routinely left to Guido, because they were deemed "appropriate" due to his ethnicity. Although Guido actively buried his Mexican identity in favor of his Irish identity, collecting data made it clear to him that his best friends saw him as Mexican first—and this was an identity to be mocked rather than celebrated. Two years after he finished collecting data, Guido approached me on campus and said that he had finally begun to accept the fact that his brothers weren't really his allies. He had begun to challenge the talk, explaining to them that what they said was hurtful. His brothers apologized, assuring Guido that they never meant to hurt his feelings—they were just "playing around." The brothers still were friendly, and they no longer made Mexican jokes about him—at least to his face.

Other researchers challenged their intimates as well. Rori (white) reported this:

> I shared my information with my boyfriend after we were done [collecting data]. [He] would get incredibly mad at me during these discussions and tell me that is was not his fault that he was a white male. I would tell him that I was not accusing him of personal wrongdoing but telling him about the general situation. This was important for me to tell him. . . . This project had a few immediate negative effects upon my relationships, but overall the outcome has been positive.

Other challenges did not end so positively. Lavinia (white) had a heated argument with her friend Jeremy (white). She was angry at him for saying, "I don't care too much about inequalities on a societal level; I look out for my interests in the **real** world" [emphasis in original]. Incensed, Lavinia began "lecturing" him about the complexities of inequality, explaining that,

> complacent people like him are part of the problem, whether or not each of those people singularly has been racist or caused any unequal opportunities. I realize he's not in the best employment situation and he deals with a lot of crap, but I try to explain that he needs to just realize the advantages he automatically gains through his skin color and gender/sex.

This conversation ended in a stalemate. Jeremy said that he was glad that Lavinia cared, but "he didn't want to concern himself with these problems because he had enough of his own." Lavinia's final, unsuccessful retort was that "it was nice that he could choose to ignore these problems. I was angry that I, once again, did not change his view."

Once the hegemony of racetalk had been exposed, the team interpreted and reacted to their friends' ordinary racetalk in new ways. The fact that several researchers refused to acquiesce as usual and, instead, took the risk of challenging this racetalk indicates the possibility for an antiracist consciousness—developed through the research process—to affect behavior.

Critique of Self

In addition to affecting how they saw their peers, collecting data also led the team to start to think of themselves in a more critical light. Initially, researchers expressed amusement as they began to recognize their own use of racetalk. For example, Elizabeth (black) recorded the following incident:

> Me and my friend walked past the tanning booth. I laughed and stated, "They a trip! Don't like black people but always frying their skin to try to look like us!" Then I noticed what I said and was like, "Damn!"

Others were sardonic and resigned, like Jonathan (white), who wrote:

> All of us skipped our classes today. We were sitting around watching TV. There
> was the typical conversation while watching; all niggers are criminals, funny little
> gooks. This all has become commonplace in our conversations. It goes back and
> forth until all of the stereotypes are out. Then it stops until something else hap-
> pens. If this is considered racist, I guess we all are.

Alice (white) said this:

> After the "Race Talk" project was over I had a new respect for what I said and for
> what I heard. Whenever I make a racial slur now, I always seem to be apologiz-
> ing to myself. Like "I shouldn't have said that," or "gosh that was really mean."
> Before I never did that because I never really noticed how bad it sounded. I re-
> ally feel this project helped me to open up and really hear all the race talk that
> goes on around me that I never really noticed before.

Alice did not really alter her behavior, she just noticed it more. She went on to
say that she has since encountered many rich sites of data and wishes she had
had access to them while collecting data. Rather than being turned off to racetalk altogether, Alice has become more intrigued. Similarly, Barbara (white)
remarked upon her own racial vocabulary, which she began to notice as a result of the research process:

> We were discussing our data collection in our focus group. I related my first in-
> cident to the group and used the word, "Nigger." The only members of the group
> present were whites. When the only black member of the group arrived, I was
> still discussing my entry, and instead of saying, "nigger," I started to say, "the N
> word." The group mentioned that to me. I wondered why I was doing that. Was
> I afraid of offending her [the only black member]?

Barbara reflected on this insight in her field notes as well as in discussion with
her group.

Once the team began to recognize the pervasiveness of racetalk, even in
their own vocabularies, many became analytical. After the data collection period ended, for example, Elizabeth (black) wrote, "I never knew how I myself
have said things and continue to say things that are discriminating against others. These are the things you are unaware of until you are trained to notice the
private realm of racism." Rori (white) wrote this:

> I immediately began to question my own thoughts about other races. I started to
> feel bad about my thoughts and tried to rationalize them. I concluded that I
> needed to redefine who I was, not only as a white person, but as a female living
> in a male-dominated society.

Harley (white) had no background in critical or sociological thought. Indeed, she was a staunch believer in the existence of a colorblind society, and she often became agitated in focus groups. Once the project ended, however, her way of thinking about race began to shift. She wrote:

> Since this project, I am constantly observing; becoming more of a sociologist. I have also watched myself more, listening to myself to evaluate my own speech and attitudes. Upon reflection, I believe that I can stereotype with the best of them. . . . I have not yet decided whether that makes me part of the problem or if it is just the fact that I know the stereotypes and am pointing them out.

While Harley had not radically changed her position, even she was becoming more critical of her own role in perpetuating racism. Although she had never taken a sociology course, she recognized and valued her analytical (*qua* sociological) skills culled through the process of inquiry.

Roger (white) critiqued his own field notes. He wrote an incident about playing a game in which he pretended to step out in front of a passing car. When a car full of black people stopped, he ran away in fear. In describing this incident, Roger used many code words to refer to race. Roger reflected on his word choice in his field notes:

> My description was laced with stereotypes and racism. True as it may be that I was avoiding harm by fleeing the scene, the dramatization was emphasized by my use of loaded terms. I made the African American men in my story seem as if they were gangsters or people of such a devious nature that my life was at genuine risk of being terminated. And even if it was, I didn't need to single out the African American race as I did to convey my message.

Roger could have simply edited his word choice when writing his original field notes, so as to make himself look better on paper. No one would have known what he actually said except for him. Roger had more integrity than that. Instead, he recognized his own loaded language and faced it head on. The process of writing and analyzing field notes helped to reframe an everyday event in a critical way.

Critique of the Structure

Through the research process, some members of the research team began to recognize that racism is a structural phenomenon that affects all people rather than an individual idiosyncrasy. This was an important realization for all researchers, but it hit home especially for researchers of color. In a racial regime that has been legitimized over generations, subordinates often internalize racist messages like "if you fail, it is your own fault" (MacLeod 1995). By learning to see the forest (racism) through the trees (individual shortcomings), researchers of color began to externalize blame for their immobility.

Elizabeth (black) provides an excellent example of a researcher of color coming to evaluate the racial regime. She took the GRE[7] while collecting data. While preparing, she began to listen more closely to arguments that the tests are biased: "This young lady said that the GRE is biased and made for white people, because they know that minorities are not trained to take those tests." Elizabeth doubted this woman's perspective, thinking she was using racism as a crutch. Then she took the GRE herself. Afterward, Elizabeth wrote in her field notes: "I went to take the GRE which was crazy as hell. This test was so hard, I mean there were words I have never heard, less seen." Elizabeth was able to see her lack of knowledge as a systemic issue rather than blaming herself. Her plans for the future have a new frame:

> I have been very frustrated lately, trying to get into grad school, find a job, finish up the semester. It's funny—when you're younger, you're told to go to school and you can be whatever you want to be. But what happens when your GPA isn't high enough to permit you into that program, or your ACTs aren't high enough to get you into college? The system is not with me; it's against me. They're setting me up for failure. Then they put the tokens in to say, "See you can do it too." But really we can't.

Elizabeth was somewhat fatalistic in that last note. But she felt relieved at her recognition of the structural constraints that limited her. She was able to try to forgive herself for what society considered failure.

Later in the data collection period, Elizabeth began to examine her own neighborhood in Chicago. Again, she employed a structural analysis to explain their poverty rather than "blaming the victim" as she might normally do:

> I was sitting on my porch. I was watching the children who have no support and probably never will get out of this neighborhood. Then I think, I've gotten to get out for school. But I'll be right back here [after college]. Then if I do leave, it will be just to another [similar] neighborhood. Will I ever have a house in the suburbs with a fence and a yard with grass? Well, it's kind of sad, but it all has to do with inequality. Things are set up to keep drug dealers on my corner, and gang bangers on my block. I don't see any recreational centers in my neighborhood, but I see a liquor store on every corner, not to mention a fast food restaurant.

Elizabeth's neighborhood may sound like an Elijah Anderson (1999) cliché, but in Chicago, such neighborhoods are plentiful. Through her participation in this project, in addition to her other courses in sociology, Elizabeth began to reframe racial problems structurally rather than individually.

Validation, Solidarity, and Empowerment

The interaction and dialogue that team members created in the focus groups were perhaps the most important aspect of this research process in altering the team. When the team came together, they had a safe place to share stories and receive sympathy, feedback, and support. Here, they could explore their uncertainty, ask each other questions about race that they could not in other social settings, and voice their concerns about the research process, themselves, and their social networks. They developed connections across race and gender lines that empowered them and validated their concerns. Sherry (black), for example, said that the project made her feel better equipped to handle racetalk as it emerged in her everyday life. Before the project, racetalk often took her off guard and made her feel uncomfortable. But after writing about it and hearing other people's data, she no longer took it so seriously. She said, "I now laugh in their faces and tell them they're going to racist hell." Rather than shrinking away from the talk and feeling helpless and victimized, Sherry felt emboldened to shut the talk down, albeit in a nonthreatening manner.

Cocoa (Latina) reflected on the ways that the process of inquiry built connections between racially and ethnically diverse teammates. She wrote this after the data collection ended:

> I think the project helped those who didn't know the many faces of racism [to understand] how it affects us as people of color. It helped them realize that racism isn't just what happened to James Byrd in Texas, who was dragged to death. But [it happened] to me, the Latina sitting next to you whose first encounter with racism was when her high school classmate called her people, "dogs." And whose bank account was illegally frozen for three weeks by her bank because they were suspicious of her college loan check—"She, a Hispanic, can't be getting a college education. This check must be a fraud." After meeting with the focus group the first time I felt good. These are people I can trust. I did not feel alone.

Even Harley—who was often at odds with the majority of the team during focus group discussions—said this about the project:

> I should reiterate my appreciation to the group for letting me be able to express my feelings and ask questions. I feel that the openness of the group helped me to have the courage to ask other people questions too. The group was a safehouse to build strength and courage to be able to candidly talk to people of other races [in our everyday lives] about the same types of issues.

The project created an interracial/interethnic community for the team that was otherwise lacking in many of their lives.

The consequences of this new, empowering network were great. Through the research process, many researchers grew to become engaged antiracists. Cocoa (Latina) wrote this:

> This project helped many of us deal with our anger with this world. By learning how to identify racism we learn how to speak up against it. People will deny it, saying "That's not racist!" and we can fire back "Oh yes it is and I can tell you why!". . . After this project, I found myself listening to people more and questioning or theorizing how they came to their thoughts and conclusions. I can honestly say that in every one of my classes and personal conversations, if someone said anything racist or discriminatory, I challenged them. I'm not afraid to speak up and tell them that what they said or did is racist. I don't think anyone from my focus group will ever be afraid again. To me, this is one of the greatest skills I attained from this group. But knowing that there will be others out there to back me up and support me gives me a stronger will and voice against racism.

Cocoa was the exception rather than the rule: few of the other researchers vowed to vigilantly attack racism whenever it occurred. However, as fledgling antiracists, many took risks that they might not have taken otherwise without having been part of the research project. Guido challenged his fraternity brothers. Elizabeth challenged one of her professors. This was a risky act that potentially jeopardized her grade for that course as well as her reputation within her department. She also recorded another act of resistance in her field notes:

> Today in class my professor asked me, "Why do blacks call each other nigger but don't like it when it comes from a white person?" I proudly stated that I'm just one person and I do not represent the black race, nor do I speak for them. He looked so stupid. I think this project taught me well.

Lavinia and Rori challenged their close friends. These small acts interrupt the hegemony of racism, and they break the silence that perpetuates the racetalk.

INSTRUMENTAL METHODOLOGIES

The researchers in this project were forced through the process of inquiry to confront their everyday realities in ways that engendered antiracist sentiments and actions. The method itself was instrumental in bringing about these changes. The strength of the method was that the focus-group dialogues were ongoing in a context of academic legitimacy and grounded in sociological literature. These were not like the weekend retreats sponsored on many campuses, which are geared toward building multicultural unity. While those endeavors are useful and interesting, they have drawbacks: they do not occur in the participants' natural setting; they are short in duration; and it is challenging to sustain the progress that comes out of them once people go back to their "real" lives. The weekend retreats help to address the self and one's individual role in reproducing racism. The racetalk project expands that critical lens to one's entire social world. As one researcher, Adelle (Asian), wrote:

> What [this project shows] me is that it is one thing to teach students from the lectern about race relations, and it is another to send them out into the field, their own field, to assess what is going on around race, in their very own environments. What people get from the lectern and what they get with their own engagement is vastly different—even if it doesn't necessarily lead to the same political conclusions. From the lectern, they get the "supposed to." From the fieldwork, they get to assess for themselves. They get an opportunity to think, to see, to analyze, instead of just learn what the rules are for a particular class, professor, or topic.

Through collecting data, racism came alive in personal and concrete ways. Researchers grappled with their relationships with talkers and the content of their talk. They stood back and considered: "This is not some skinhead or deviant—this is my mom, whom I love, whom I will continue to love. How can that be?" They learned empathy for other people's positionalities. Data collection precipitated an interaction with everyday racism that was powerful in its effects on the team members and, ultimately, their social networks.

I have been cautious in this chapter to talk about the ways that the research process can foster *antiracism* rather than *activism*. I distinguish between the two as such: the concept "antiracism" comes out of the critical white studies literature that asserts that structural racism will remain intact until whites themselves—those who benefit the most from racism—begin to recognize and actively challenge its supremacy (see Bonilla-Silva 2001; Doane and Bonilla-Silva 2003; Feagin 2000; Frankenberg 1993; Rasmussen et al. 2001). Rather than framing racism as a problem for people of color to fix—which has a blame-the-victim effect when racism persists—antiracism recognizes that the dominant group needs to begin to disrupt the structure of racism from the top down. Antiracism is a way to raise the consciousness of the dominants, make them uncomfortable with privileges, and start getting them mobilized. Activism is the extension and amplification of antiracism, requiring a concerted effort to dismantle the existing structure of racism on multiple fronts. The team in this project were not activists. They were fledgling antiracists.[8] Their consciousness was raised; privileges and allegiances were problematized in new and painful ways; and, at the end of the project, they began to seek ways to subvert the structure of racism.

I have argued that the research methodology used in this project helped to engender an antiracist outlook. But will there be lasting effects on the team? Will they go on to become activists? On a small scale, many of them already acted as activists while part of the team. Some took personal risks and challenged their intimate circles. Breaking the silence on racism is a form of activism. Karyn McKinney and Joe Feagin (2003, 249) employ a useful metaphor to analyze the many actions and inactions (see also Feagin and Vera 1995) that whites can take when encountering interpersonal racism:

> White officiants are usually the most active in perpetuating antiblack discrimination, as they make the key decisions and articulate the important racist attitudes. Other white actors act the part of the acolytes, for they discriminate against African-Americans or other people of color partly or mainly because they are told to do so by their employers. Yet other whites stand by and observe while the officiants and/or acolytes carry out overt discrimination against people of color. Passivity is a very important buttress of contemporary racism.

In this metaphor, *most* people fit into this passive congregation of observers. The researchers in the racetalk project were no longer passive congregants. This change in the team represents an important antiracist transformation that may have positive ripple effects in their social networks. It certainly is a necessary step toward becoming an antiracist activist.

CONCLUSION

As Sandra Harding (1998) asserts, science emerges from the social world and it can affect the social world. Examining the impact of data collection on the researchers points to strategies for social change ideas. This chapter focuses on ways that the research act can help to make the personal into the political. Interrogating everyday, hegemonic reality, in concert with an interracial team of researchers, not only can help to break down racial barriers, but can create an antiracist consciousness. This intellectual change is important in that it may form the impetus for future activism. As Harley (white) said, "people keep talking about [the ideas] later, and that's a good start." Even if their activism is played out in the microcosms of their private worlds, the silence is broken, and the hegemony of racism is disrupted. By emulating this research model, others might foster such transformations as well. In so doing, we help give voice to antiracist heterodoxy. We build bridges across the racial chasm based on empathy, knowledge, and political alliances. And we help to reform the racial regime which has persisted for so long.

NOTES

1. Despite the benefits of acknowledging and interrogating your lens, doing so also makes the researcher more vulnerable to attacks of bias by critics from more traditional, positivist camps. However, reflexive researchers handle this attack with the following counterargument: acknowledging your lens ensures a better, more accurate research product. Because you have acknowledged your values, you know that you have to work harder to assure critics of the rigor and validity of your research (see Kreiger 1985 and Thorne 1993).

2. Decades ago, in their project in the Hawthorne Works of the Eastern Electric Company in Chicago, Fritz Roethlisberger and William Dickenson showed us that the research process itself can change the ways that subjects work together and conceptualize their productivity. Much subsequent reflexive scholarship has elaborated on the ways that the research endeavor affects subjects, both positively and negatively.

3. For more on this debate, see Rosanna Hertz (1997) and Shulamit Reinhartz (1992). They argue that even researchers who are committed to sharing data with subjects and working together to develop conceptual and analytical frameworks—those who deliberately share ownership and control of the project—reclaim and exercise their power in one way or another: through writing, presentation, and/or publication, the researcher becomes the authority at the end of the day.

4. See Michael Schwalbe's (1996) study of the mythopoetic men's movement, for example.

5. See Patricia and Peter Adler's (1998) discussion of their use of the "parent-as-researcher" method.

6. For more on positivism, see Popper 1965, 1968; Kuhn 1996; and Lakatos 1989. To read about its impact on knowledge, see Harding 1991, 1998; and Smith 1990.

7. GRE stands for Graduate Record Exam—the test required for admission into many graduate programs.

8. Even though they were not all white, they were all fledgling antiracists. The people of color on the team were not new to racism when they joined the project. But they had learned to cope with it effectively, rationalizing that most whites were not racist, or that its occurrence was rare. Collecting data with an interracial team impeded their coping strategies and brought racism to the forefront of their daily encounters in new ways. In the focus groups, people of color learned that many whites actually did wish them ill, when previously they had only suspected the pervasiveness of such sentiments. Indeed, because the data came from such a broad array of subjects—teachers, police, students, servers, salespeople—it became less viable to rationalize that only a few radical whites perpetuated racism. Researchers of color connected to their white teammates as allies in the quest to understand and interrupt white racism. Thus, I consider them antiracists as well.

THE CONSEQUENCES

⬤⬤ DIALECTICS REVISITED

Racetalk and the Racial Regime

The truth of the interaction is never entirely contained in the interaction.

—Pierre Bourdieu (1977, 1981)

I began this book with a promise to provide a dialectical analysis of the importance of everyday interactions for reproducing racism. At this point, I recap the heart of dialectics. Structures constrain individuals, both limiting and enhancing their choices (Giddens 1984). Structure and action are inseparable. Opportunities vary according to one's structural location or positionality (Collins 2000), so that race, gender, class, and sexuality simultaneously affect individuals' options. However, people are not helplessly determined by the structures: they act, make choices, innovate, and challenge structures. Often, the choices that people make help to reinforce rather than alter the structures (West and Zimmerman 1987). Everyday people go along with the status quo for many reasons. There are costs for acting against structures (Bourdieu 1977). People often do not even recognize that they are unreflexively following the rules, because structures are hegemonic (Gramsci 1932/1975; 1971). Yet, by recognizing the structures and their effects, and by working together, people can change structures (Bourdieu 1977; Habermas 1984; Giddens 1984; Marx 1867/1967; Weber 1921).

This chapter is designed to underscore the major dialectical mechanisms of racism. As such, I concentrate on the ways that racetalk reinforces structure and the ways that it provides opportunities for agency. Critical race theory is the most useful tool in making this connection clear.

THE DIALECTICS OF RACETALK

My goal is to show that racetalk is a private practice that shapes social structure and vice versa. That is, racetalk is part of the dialectical process that reproduces racism. To attain this goal, I must first establish that racetalk is more than mere words: it is action. Next, I must show that action impacts structure. And last, I must show that structure shapes action. Critical Race Theory (CRT) ties individual acts of racism to structural racism, primarily by examining the law. These theorists argue that epithets and acts are cut from the same cloth—one would not happen without the other. Our structures promulgate speech and action. In particular, analyzing the institutions of segregation and law illustrate the way that speech, action, and structure are all interconnected. Through these analyses, we see that racism is truly part of the doxa. Racetalk is protected and legitimated by law: our codified ideologies.

Is Speech Action?

Yes. Evidence for this claim can be found in analyses of the law.

Brown v. the Board of Education. Like other CRT scholars, Charles Lawrence (1993) analyzes the politics of the *Brown v. the Board of Education* Supreme Court decision (1954), focusing on the logic of the case and its ramifications. When the Supreme Court decided that separate was not equal, a major element of its logic was that the separation of the races created a stigma for black people. In effect, segregation produced a caste system that was antithetical to American principles of equal citizenship. Thus, Lawrence emphasizes, *Brown* held that segregation was unconstitutional because it sent a message that black children were untouchables:

> It stamps a badge of inferiority upon blacks, and this badge communicates a message to others in the community, as well as to blacks themselves. Therefore, *Brown* may be read as regulating the content of racist speech. (59)

To Lawrence, *Brown* embodied the regulation of white supremacy. His reading of *Brown* is important for arguing that a precedent has been set by the high court of the land: speech and action are intertwined.

Lawrence nods to civil libertarians who see him as conflating speech with action. He argues that racist speech has the unique quality of being inextricably linked to action: "My suggestion that racist conduct amounts to speech is premised upon the defamatory message of white supremacy to achieve its injurious purpose" (60). Racist conduct is informed and legitimated by racist speech and vice versa. One would not persist without the other.

Lawrence underscores this point with a concrete example: outlawing "white only" and "colored only" signs. The Court declared these signs unconstitutional. They had to be removed from public spaces. Ostensibly, these signs were merely *messages* of segregation. They were not literal structures constraining people's behavior. Indeed, not everyone even complied with the signs. Many black people entered through "white only" doors without meaning to and often without punishment. Likewise, whites could drink from "colored" water fountains with impunity. These signs did not necessarily alter action. Yet the Court ruled the signs illegal anyway because the *message* was illegal. The signs were part of the larger practice of segregation—a system of oppression.

Thus, Lawrence argues that race as a social construction only has meaning because we mold our actions to fit with ideology: "The cultural meaning of race is promulgated through millions of ongoing contemporaneous speech/ acts" (61). He argues that these meanings are so ubiquitous as to seem natural:

> It is difficult to recognize the institutional significance of white supremacy or how it acts to harm, partially because of its ubiquity. We simply do not see most racist conduct because we experience a world in which whites are supreme as simply "the world." (62)

Lawrence writes, "Racism is both 100 percent speech and 100 percent conduct. Discriminatory conduct is not racist unless it also conveys the message of white supremacy" (62).

The First Amendment and Fighting Words.   The First Amendment to the U.S. Constitution guarantees the right to free speech. Freedom of expression is one of the most fundamental rights protected by the Constitution (Matsuda 1993). The framers of the Constitution recognized the potential for the powerful to ignore the voices of the powerless, or worse, to sanction those voices. As Mari Matsuda explains, "Power is jealous, and the temptation to stifle legitimate opposition is too great" (32). Thus, speech is recognized by our governing bodies as powerful in affecting action and structure. However, speech in the United States is so wholly protected because it is categorically separated from action. According to this logic, speech must be protected because it generates ideas and allows for dissension. The assumption is that most speech in itself cannot cause harm: sticks and stones can break my bones, but words will never hurt me.

However, as Matsuda points out, "There is much speech that comes close to action" (32). The law recognizes this potential. As such, there are several exceptions to the protections of speech. Speech that incites irrational mob behavior is outlawed. Thus, it is illegal to yell "Fire!" in a crowded theater. Seditious speech is illegal: you cannot incite people to overthrow the government or commit treason. Most relevant to this study is the "fighting words" exception, which outlaws words that incite interpersonal violence. In order to fit this exception, these words must "bring men to blows." Thus, although our Constitution protects speech—largely because it is seen as separate from action—the law also recognizes that speech and action can be interconnected.

Limits to the First Amendment.   If speech is related to action, and if fighting words are outlawed, then wouldn't racetalk be outlawed as well? No. There are key assumptions in the law that leave racetalk unregulated. Much CRT scholarship is geared toward critiquing this gap in the law, showing that the law fails to protect an entire segment of the U.S. population. These scholars offer suggestions as to how to rectify the gap by making the law's assumptions more congruent with reality.

Matsuda (1993) argues that racist speech comes close to fitting the fighting words exception, but it does not quite fit. Most people do not "come to blows" in response to racist speech: "The problem is that racist speech is so common that it is seen as part of the ordinary jostling and conflict people are expected to tolerate, rather than as fighting words" (35). People pride themselves on walking away from racetalk rather than physically defending their honor. This is ironic as well: "Lack of a fight and admirable self-restraint then defines the words as nonactionable" (35).

If enough people came to blows, would racetalk become outlawed speech? The answer to this question varies according to one's position in the racial regime. If the fighting was done by blacks and browns who are stereotyped as violent criminals, I doubt it. Based on past evidence, I surmise that blacks and browns who fought back would be arrested for giving into their "criminal nature" rather than exercising their constitutionally protected rights. If, however, the fighting was done by outraged whites on a large, well-publicized scale, then perhaps the doxa might shift. But there is already orthodoxy in place for dismissing antiracist actions by whites: they are bleeding-heart, guilt-ridden race traitors. Yet, Matsuda's argument is potent nonetheless: when victims rise above racism they effectively buy into its future.

Lawrence (1993) critiques the inaccurate assumptions built into the law. He says that, regardless of whether the insult is face-to-face, the comment is immediately injurious, like a slap in the face. Thus, racist speech should be treated like action. The law should prohibit racist speech even if it does not lead to physical blows. Racist talk itself should be conceptualized as a "blow." Lawrence writes,

Assaultive racist speech functions as a preemptive strike. The racial invective is experienced as a blow, not a proferred idea, and once the blow is struck it is unlikely that dialogue will follow. (68)

Expecting people to fight back after a racist assault is foolhardy. First, the victim's immediate response is often to emotionally recoil. Lawrence says that this reaction "temporarily disables the victim" (68). Second, once the epithet has been hurled, it is hard to redress it. The damage is done. He likens racist hate speech to homophobic speech. If a man is called a "faggot," for example, he may deny being gay. But the accusation is out there, and it is impossible to "un-ring the bell." Being called a "liar" or a "nigger" has the same effect.

Another reason that victims may not react violently is that the message simply echoes larger cultural ideals that are well ingrained in our consciousnesses. Hate speech is doxa, made normal by our habitus. Lawrence says, "The racist name caller is accompanied by a cultural chorus of equally demeaning speech and symbols" (68). How can you fight that? Because of the barriers to fighting back, our current system is an "inadequate paradigm" for regulating this speech.

Matsuda offers a more comprehensive approach to racism, arguing that it "comprises the ideology of racial supremacy and the mechanisms for keeping selected victim groups in subordinated positions" (23). Racism consists of several implements:

1. violence and genocide
2. racial hate messages, disparagement, and threats
3. overt disparate treatment
4. covert disparate treatment and sanitized racist comments

She argues that speech and acts are not separable—the "violence of the word" links the two.

Matsuda argues for a definition of racist speech that protects the victims. She recognizes that the definition must be narrow in order to fit within the parameters of the First Amendment. She takes an historical, sociological approach to amending the law. Her proposed definition is this:

I believe racist speech is best treated as a sui generis category, presenting an idea so historically untenable, so dangerous, and so tied to perpetuation of violence and degradation of the very classes of human beings who are least equipped to respond that it is properly treated as outside the realm of protected discourse. (35)

What would be included in this definition? She delineates the following criteria for evaluating speech:

1. The message is of racial inferiority.
2. The message is directed against an historically oppressed group.
3. The message is persecutory, hateful, and degrading. (36)

Racetalk fits all of these criteria.

How can we tell if the talk causes harm in ways similar to actions? CRT urges us to look to the victim group to tell us. Dominants may find the speech funny. One of the privileges of being in a dominant group is defining the terms of the situation. The dominant perspective is unlikely to problematize racist speech. It is, therefore, important to prioritize the effects of the talk as defined by those on the receiving end of it.

Does Action Make Structure?

Yes. As Derrick Bell (1992) writes, "Racial policy is the culmination of thousands of individual practices" (7). The everyday actions by common people coalesce to construct patterns of behavior, institutions, official policies, and ultimately structures. Thus, structure does not exist without actors.

As I have argued, racetalk is a tool used by individual agents to reinforce three different intertwining structures of racism: signification, domination, and legitimation (Giddens 1984). These structures are not mutually exclusive. They overlap, reinforcing one another. Racetalk signifies whiteness as valuable, while signifying blackness as a source of pollution and contagion. Whiteness is signified as the polar opposite of blackness (Warren and Twine 1997). Brownness is signified somewhere in the middle—neither black nor white, but certainly more black (devalued) than white (valued). As such, brownness signifies pollution as well, but it is more variable, more open to negotiation than is blackness. Based on these ranked significations, racetalk reinforces racial domination of whites over other groups. This structural arrangement is legitimated through racetalk. Taken together, individual speech/acts help to form and fortify the racial regime.

In addition to the everyday people who act, structures are run by powerful individual actors, working in concert to maintain social order. Those in power shape policies so as to benefit themselves (Reskin 1988). Structures may change, but they do so only at the will of the elites and with interests of the elites in mind. For example, Bell argues that any racial advancements that have been made in the United States in the past century (1) cost whites very little—like the MLK holiday in which everyone gets a day off, and (2) are largely symbolic. They do not eliminate racism or even atone for past injuries from the racial regime. The changes are bones thrown to pacify the dogs. Whites only grant concessions to blacks when it will do the whites the most good or the least damage.

Bell refers to *Brown v. Board of Education* (1954) to underscore his argument. Of course, this landmark antidiscrimination case argued that separate was not equal. This decision changed the school system, as well as every other public space shared by blacks and whites. Many civil libertarians herald this case as breaking down trenchant racial barriers. Bell disagrees. He sees it as an attempt to pacify antiracists rather than seriously alter the racial regime. He argues that, in fact, *Brown* has bolstered racism over time. Bell argues that if we carefully examine the documents surrounding *Brown*, we see the calculative manipulations to insulate the elites and their lay white allies. *Brown II* was decided a year later, and it argued for a delay in the application of the law. This delay was intended to give schools time to reorganize and to allow white people time to adjust psychologically to having to share with degraded blacks. During this time, many school districts implemented policies to circumvent the *Brown* decision. For example, Durham, North Carolina, created county and city districts. It then desegregated the schools within each district. As it turned out, the city schools were in black neighborhoods and the county schools were in white neighborhoods: problem averted. Other communities used the time to institute a bevy of private educational opportunities, siphoning fearful whites out of the soon-to-be-integrated schools (Myers 1999). As such, the law was not radical, and it did not solve the problem of disparate resources in black and white schools (Bell 1992). It gave a veneer of justice to the old structure, which persisted due to individuals' collective actions.

Does Structure Impact Action?

Yes. Talk derives much of its meaning from the structure. The structures help to form the habitus that informs people's everyday interactions (Bourdieu 1977). Matsuda (1993) discusses this interconnection between structure and speech in her analysis of the law. She cites several cases where hate speech was used in public settings against members of a marginalized racial/ethnic group. She explains that the mainstream press ignores the frequency of racist speech, making it seem that such incidents are random, isolated, and inconsequential. Society fails to recognize the structure of racism as a context in which these acts occur. We erroneously approach racist speech as the work of a few bad apples rather than a fruit of a poisoned tree. In fact, racist speech is patterned and persistent, and it has a huge impact on the tenacity of white supremacy.

Lawrence (1993), like Bourdieu, argues that the ubiquity of racism in modern U.S. society affects the marketplace of ideas in an unequal way—privileging the racist over the victim. He writes,

> I fear that by framing the [First Amendment] debate as we have—as one in which the liberty of free speech is in conflict with the elimination of racism—we have advanced the cause of racial oppression and placed the bigot on the moral high ground, fanning the flames of racism. (57)

Lawrence argues that, instead of privileging the bigot, we should listen to the voices of the victims. Then, we can begin to understand the human impact of our racist institutions.

The Law and the State.   Racism is, in fact, built into all of our major social institutions. Most relevant to the above discussions are the institutions of the law and the state. The law seeks to limit discrimination, but it protects it as well (Bell 1992). Bell admits—to be fair—that there are limits to what the law can do, because racism is so deeply embedded in our culture and ideologies. The law makes incorrect assumptions:

> Racism is more than a group of bad white folks whose discriminatory predilections can be controlled by well-formed laws, vigorously enforced. Traditional civil rights laws tend to be ineffective because they are built on a law enforcement model. They assume that most citizens will obey the law; and when law breakers are held liable, a strong warning goes out that will discourage violators and encourage compliance. But the law enforcement model for civil rights breaks down when a great number of whites are willing—because of inconvenience, habit, distaste, fear, or simple preference—to violate the law. It then becomes almost impossible to enforce, because so many whites, though not discriminating themselves, identify more easily with those who do than with their victims. (55–56)

The doxa is racist. Why punish individuals who carry out our larger cultural ideals in practice? Similarly, Matsuda (1993) examines the paradoxical nature of hate speech law. Some speech is outlawed, while other speech is protected. Because laws are made by elites in society, speech is only outlawed if the elites can be harmed by it in some way. If the speech benefits the elites, it will be allowed.

Structures impact individuals. Matsuda argues that in protecting certain hate speech, we send powerful messages to the victims of that speech: "As much as one may try to resist a piece of hate propaganda, the effect on one's self-esteem and sense of personal security is devastating" (25). This creates a profound sense of "aloneness." She points to multiple recent legal cases that failed to punish racist acts, and she writes,

> When hundreds of police officers are called out to protect racist marchers, when the courts refuse redress for racial insult, and when racial attacks are officially

dismissed as pranks, the victim becomes a stateless person. Target-group members must either identify with a community that promotes racist speech or admit that the community does not include them. (26)

When hate speech is officially tolerated, there are lifelong consequences for the victims.

The law's refusal to acknowledge the pain of hate speech adds injury to insult: "The second injury is the pain of knowing that the government provides no remedy and offers no recognition of the dehumanizing experience that victims of hate propaganda are subjected to" (Matsuda 1993, 49). The state, then, is an agent of racism. It protects individuals' speech even when that speech is degrading and dehumanizing. As Matsuda states, "One can dismiss the hate group as an organization of marginalized people, but the state is the official embodiment of the society we live in" (49).

CRT scholars argue that the First Amendment is actually a tool of the elite to maintain discrimination, even while claiming to oppose it. Matsuda (1993) says that the law takes an extreme, absolutist approach to the First Amendment, often at the expense of antidiscrimination goals. Historically, the United States has taken a hard-line position on speech in order to curtail the elites' discretion in airing some speech while silencing other speech. In a democratic nation, the elites should not be allowed to decide who is heard. Most people would agree with this. But is this how it works? Whose speech is most likely to be heard?

Free speech is intended to encourage an open marketplace of ideas in which the best ideas rise to the top. Lawrence (1993, 77) says that black and brown people have found the opposite to be true: "The American marketplace of ideas was founded with the idea of the racial inferiority of nonwhites as one of its chief commodities, and ever since the market opened, racism has remained its most active item in trade." This market devalues or silences black and brown voices: "Their words are less salable" (78). In this marketplace, black and brown people bear the burden of justification, of substantiating claims of racism. This system punishes those most likely to suffer under it. Like Matsuda, then, Lawrence sees the First Amendment as a mask for a laissez-faire approach to the perpetuation of racism. As such, the state endorses racism through its complicity. We must begin to hold elites accountable for this bias in the system. Lawrence writes, "When we valorize bigotry, we must assume responsibility for the assaultive acts of those emboldened by a newfound status as defenders of the faith" (86).

The elites use the First Amendment to create the official façade of an egalitarian doxa. Yet, the doxa is not, in fact, egalitarian. It protects speech that silences the less powerful. Despite its intentions to the contrary, the voices of the powerful are still amplified above the subordinates'.

Other nations take a more wholistic approach. The reasoning is that free speech is meant to protect free citizens. A nation should ensure that its citizens are free in order for free speech to have any teeth. The UK, for example, is committed to free speech, yet it has criminalized speech that incites discrimination and racial hatred (Matsuda 1993). Almost all racetalk would fall under this category. This does not mean that the UK is racism-free. It means that the state at least rhetorically protects the target-group members.

Matsuda recognizes that racism is a structural problem with no one cause or effect. As she writes, "Part of the special problem of racist speech is that it works in concert with other racist tools to keep victim groups in an inferior position" (39). Like Lawrence, she believes that individuals should be held accountable for their role in its perpetuation. Law is one of the most respected and influential institutions in our structure. Although the law is not colorblind, Matsuda does not advocate ripping up our case law and starting over. She advises that we *transform* the law from within with a more educated, critical perspective. Her proposal adheres to the following principles: "the need to fight racism at all levels, the value of explicit formal rules, and a fear of tyranny" (38).

Lawrence, too, calls for a reformation of the law, eradicating inaccurate assumptions. For example, the law allows for the regulation of speech that is "offensive" according to community standards. Lawrence asks, Whose community's standards are considered? Clearly, communities of color find racist speech offensive. The fact that their perspective is not considered valid in regulating such speech indicates the racial politics embedded in the law. Lawrence argues that "offensiveness" is too subjective to be a useful legal category. The law does, however, provide recourse for people who have been *injured* by others. Lawrence argues that racist speech causes injury, not offense. As such, it should be regulated and punished. Brown provided the framework to help this argument hold up in court.

The equal protection clause that operated under *Brown* regulated government action. The First Amendment regulated private speech. Some might argue that Lawrence is conflating the two in his analysis of *Brown*. He anticipates this critique, arguing that the state sets the context for private interaction. If certain relationships are legally discouraged, then private freedoms are not really free. Individual interactions must therefore be considered within the context of the state—an institution inbued with racism (Bonilla-Silva 1999).

Housing, Neighborhoods, Communities. While it may not be intuitive, our patterns of housing and neighborhood communities are institutions as well. Like the law and the state, racism is built into these patterns in historically marked, lasting ways. Douglas Massey and Nancy Denton (1993) show that segregation cripples communities of color by cutting them off from resources, jobs, transportation, and education. Thomas Sugrue (1996) has shown that segregation in Detroit was perpetuated by realtors, who used racism as a way to make profit. They taunted whites with potential black neighbors, playing on their fear of the possibility of "invading blacks" who would "lower property values." Whites sold their homes at lower prices. The realtors then sold them at a substantial markup to middle-class blacks or browns.

Bell (1992) argues that desegregation has not improved the lot of blacks. He says that inner cities are the result of desegregation policies, where official Jim Crow laws were removed but no real attempts were made to redistribute life chances across the races. Inner cities are alienated communities, and people are suffering: "What we now call the 'inner city' is, in fact, the American equivalent of the South African homelands" (4). Ghettos "breed despair," which is compounded when residents compare themselves to images on TV: "images confirming that theirs is the disgraceful form of living. . ." (4; see also Anderson 1999). Bell recognizes that segregation was "hateful" as well, but, he writes, "if I knew that its return would restore our black communities to what they were before desegregation, I would think such a trade entitled to serious thought" (60). When desegregation erased the official laws enforcing segregation, it left minorities with no one to blame for their emiseration but themselves (MacLeod 1995): no one is forcing you to live here. If you don't like it, move! Of course, moving is not a viable option for people with no assets and few savings.

Religion. Racism is also embedded in the institution of religion. Everyday people look to religion to guide their actions. If churches teach religion, then people feel justified in acting upon this morally authorized lesson (Lawrence 1993). The church taught that slavery was acceptable (Feagin and McKinney 2003). The Klan recruited members from white churches. Recall from a previous chapter the incident observed at the Sunday school class: the teacher literally taught the children that white is good and black is sin by using black and white pieces of paper. White churches have long justified racism.

Education. Racism is, of course, part of the education system, as shown by *Brown* and other cases, including *McLaurin v. Oklahoma State Regents*. McLaurin, a black student, was allowed access to a white school as long as he sat in an area roped off from the rest of the class. The Court determined that this was unconstitutional, yet schools continue to be centers for racism. Lawrence (1993) refers to a 1988 incident at the University of Wisconsin, in which members of the Zeta Beta Tau fraternity held a mock slave auction, complete with blackfaced pledges. More recently, in 2001, members of Auburn University's Delta Sigma Phi and Beta Theta Pi fraternities dressed in blackface for a Halloween party. Other members dressed as Klansmen and militia types enacted mock lynchings of the "black" men (photos can be viewed at http://www.alabamacenterforjustice.com/FratBias.html). Partygoers were suspended for "potentially offensive and racist conduct." Their acts were not defined as inherently, obviously offensive, but *potentially* offensive. The implication is that only some people—subordinate people—are sensitized to hate speech. Despite punishing the students, the school still operated as a site where like-minded students could congregate and act out their racist scenarios. The structure enabled the actors.

THE TRANSFORMATIVE POWER OF LANGUAGE

Racism and racetalk are two sides of the same coin. They affect one another, reproducing the racial regime on a day-to-day basis. When we recognize this process, it is easy to become overwhelmed by the persistence of racism over time and the creative ways that people themselves participate in its endurance. However, the major insight of dialecticians is that the structures are not omnipotent. People can and do act. Although they tend to act in ways that reproduce the racial regime, they do not have to. People made the regime—they simply forgot that they did so (Weber 1921/1979).[1] Weber says that this collective amnesia leads people to feel powerless in the face of social structures. He uses the metaphor of an iron cage to describe people's sense of helplessness. However, there is an antidote to this amnesia. Weber argues that a charismatic leader can come roust people out of their catatonic state of helplessness and inspire them to make change. Other theorists argue that *language itself* holds the seeds of structural reformation.

Pierre Bourdieu (1991) and Jürgen Habermas (1984) both argue for the progressive, liberative, revolutionary power of language. Bourdieu asserts that people can connect in a common cause once they give voice to their concerns. What Bourdieu calls "heretical resistance" to the doxa—language that challenges racist orthodoxy—does occur. By giving voice to heretical heterodoxy we are able to undermine the salience of the doxa. Bourdieu (1991, 127–28) has great faith in the power of language to transform society:

> Politics begins, strictly speaking, with the denunciation of this tacit contract of adherence to the established order which defines this original doxa; in other words, political subversion presupposes cognitive subversion, a conversion of the vision of the world.

We cannot engage in counterhegemonic practices until we envision an alternative to the existing regime. Language helps us to explore alternatives. We have to stand outside of our everyday lives and imagine a new world order, one in which racism is not a structuring principle. In the next and last chapter of this book, I explore strategies for interrupting the racist cycle of talk, action, and structure.

NOTE

1. Weber uses the term "rationalization" to refer to the process through which people forget that they made social structures and that they, therefore, can change them.

⑫

PRAXIS

In Search of a Balm

> Myths unexamined do not become truths; and those who order their lives
> on myth are doomed. Still, a great number of Americans seek out and cher-
> ish myths. They lament the good old days, and call for a return to values and
> patterns that had the appearance of utility in the past. They refuse to look
> at reality; they embrace the soothing balm of the political and religious
> soothsayer who reinforces their parochial beliefs. Authoritarian societies
> have many "thou shalt nots" in their lexicon, the most dangerous of which
> is "thou shalt not think."
>
> —Gerald Unks (1995, 11)

The major argument in this book is this: although American people publicly
claim to be colorblind and antiracist, examining their private talk reveals a different reality. Indeed, this research indicates that "old" racism has not died out.
It has simply gone underground and become more nuanced. People now keep
such talk private. Although cautious about saying racist things in "mixed company," people in this study talked freely among themselves. Racetalkers assumed that the content was acceptable to the participants in conversations. Indeed, based on the paucity of challenges to the racetalk, this appears to be an
accurate assumption. Having the right skin color served as a "ticket" to racetalk.

Whites' racetalk indicated a fear of an impending takeover. Through their
racetalk, whites sought to safely contain people of color by dehumanizing
them and keeping them under surveillance. Whites' overall approach to people of color was bifurcated: on the one hand, whites disdained them for failing

to meet the white standard. On the other hand, whites resented and feared any advancements made by people of color. In either case, people of color bore the brunt of the attacks. As Warren and Twine (1997) argue, the racial polemic in the United States consistently values and protects whites over "others." The significations of blackness and brownness as degraded outsiders helped to legitimate the continued domination of whites above other people of color. Through racetalk, everyday people helped to reinforce the larger racial regime.

Racetalk is a form of symbolic violence (Bourdieu 1977) in which old hierarchies are legitimated and reinforced. Racetalk keeps people "in their place" without requiring the use of force. It is especially successful when people of color themselves buy into and police the very racial/ethnic boundaries that help to keep them oppressed. Ignoring racetalk means to be complicit with racism *writ large*.

REIFICATION: THE CONSEQUENCES OF RACETALK

Giddens (1984, 180) argues that when a system is legitimized, people take it for granted and uncritically act according to its tenets. When they do, they "reify" the existing system:

> [Reification] should be seen as referring to forms of discourse which treat [structural] properties as "objectively given" in the same way as are natural phenomena. That is to say, reified discourse refers to the "facticity" with which social phenomena confront individual actors in such a way as to ignore how they are produced and reproduced through human agency. . . . It concerns the consequences of thinking in this kind of fashion, whether such thinking is done by those who call themselves social scientists or by lay members of society.

When reification occurs, people are more likely to support the system than to challenge it (see also Lukacs 1922/1968). Thus, the system of inequality persists.

Do the data in this study indicate that the system of racism has been reified? Yes. Racism turns people into things, separating them from their humanity. People come to be seen as disposable. Consider this incident recorded by Sena (Latina):

> At Christmas this year, I was in line at a store when this man (white) in his 50s was saying to his wife that he was driving down the street and some "spooks" (black boys) were beating up this "spic" (Mexican). He said, "Why should I have called the police? I don't care about those people."

Or this incident recorded by Ashley (white):

> My boyfriend (white), my friend Stef (white), and I went out to dinner. After din-
> ner we went to Wal-Mart. When we were leaving Wal-Mart, two Mexicans
> walked out in front of our car. Stef yelled, "Stop! Don't hit those Mexicans, it will
> take weeks to get the grease off the car."

Roger (white) observed this racetalk:

> On the news, there was a headline about how some 400 people were burned alive
> in Borneo, and how they had had their hearts cut out. Upon hearing this, I said,
> "Holy shit!" My roommate (white) said, "Ah, it's probably just a bunch of black
> people." I looked at him hoping he would expand on his thoughts. He said, "Well
> it is!" I shook my head a little and went back to reading.

In these incidents, real and potential violence that was inflicted upon people
of color was seen as an inconvenience or—worse—a form of entertainment. It
was not a cause for alarm. Indeed, in the process of reification the next step is
to advocate overt violence against people of color as a means of social control.
Jean (white) logged this incident:

> I was at a restaurant with a bunch of old high school friends. We sat down, and
> Jo (white) mentioned the recent attack on New York. Leroy (black) remarked,
> "We should just kill all those towel heads and get it over with." Some people
> around the table laughed. Others said nothing.

By "saying nothing," people went along with racism, and helped to perpetuate
it. As they acquiesced to pejorative tropes of different races and ethnicities,
people—both white and nonwhite—helped to reify racism, seeing it as natural, unavoidable, and inevitable. Some even saw violence as desirable.

Negotiated meanings affect power relations that affect abstract ideologies,
and round and round, in and out of time. The racial regime works to perpetuate racism in spite of modern antiracist inroads. Resistance does occur, but it
is easily quashed by the orthodoxy of the regime. Indeed, much resistance
takes shape within the existing regime, using the extant framework as the basis of a counterstance (Anzaldua 1999). Take, for example, oppositional identity work, in which a marginalized group reclaim a devalued status and reinvest it with their own meanings. They take the newly transformed identity and
use it as a progressive tool for empowerment. Oppositional identity work has
limited success in reforming structures due to its reliance on the dominant
regime. By reclaiming a devalued status—like "ghetto"—marginalized people
often unintentionally reinforce their own subordination in the eyes of the
dominants (see MacLeod 1995; Schwalbe and Mason-Schrock 1996).

The bottom line, then, is that racetalk matters, even though it is casual, often humorous talk not intended for public consumption. Racetalk matters because it is part of a larger racial regime in which meanings are constructed in concert over time in such a way as to perpetuate unequal power relations. As Pierre Bourdieu (1977, 170) writes,

> "Private" experiences undergo nothing less than a change of state when they recognize themselves in the public objectivity of an already constituted discourse, the objective sign of recognition of their right to be spoken and to be spoken publicly: "Words wreak havoc," says Sartre (1971), "when they find a name for what had been up to then lived namelessly."

Racetalk names villains and victors. The havoc of racism persists. In later writings, Bourdieu (1991, 127) states:

> We know that the social order owes some measure of its permanence to the fact that it imposes schemes of classification which, being adjusted to objective classifications, produce a form of recognition of this order, the kind implied by the misrecognition of the arbitrariness of its foundations: the correspondence between object divisions and classificatory schemes, between objective structures and mental structures, underlies a kind of original adherence to the established order.

Contemporary racetalk builds upon the system of meanings constructed in previous generations. But it does so carefully. Racetalk exemplifies a classification system that is misrecognized for what it is—racism—even as it reproduces the racist regime of old. The regime is hegemonic, and we tend not to problematize it, lest we be attacked as heretics.

DEALING WITH THE IMPLICATIONS OF THESE DATA

When I talk about this project, people react in interesting ways. Many are shocked and dismayed at the content of the racetalk. Yet, they often try to find ways to dismiss the significance of the data, or to distance themselves from it. People search for ways to separate these data from their everyday lives. For example, I recently had a conversation with a small group of graduate students, in which I read them several pages of raw data and asked them to try to analyze it. Instead of constructing analytical categories, however, they began to ask questions about the sample of subjects. One person stated, "Well, it's pretty rural around here." He implied that only "hicks" or "hillbillies" used racetalk. I clarified that a lot of the data were collected in and around Chicago, as well as from other parts of the country—rural and urban. Another person countered, "Well, Chicago is one of the most segregated cities in the country. Of course entrenched segregation would spawn racetalk." Someone else added, "I grew up in a segregated (white) neighborhood in Chicago, and we never talked that way. There must be something else going on with those subjects. They must be angry." I found this conversation interesting. I had a hard time rerouting the discussion to data analysis at all. These graduate students were determined to dismiss the content.

I ended the dilemma with these assurances: the casual talk captured in this study was everyday banter among friends, family, lovers, students, and teachers. This talk was Americana. It is precisely the mundane nature of this talk that makes it so compelling. One need not wear a white sheet and whistle Dixie to celebrate the structure of racism. Everyday people help to reproduce white supremacy through their casual talk. That is, racetalk is not simply the individual expression of prejudice. It is political in that it expresses an agreed-upon racist ideology, or doxa. This ideology embodies a folk knowledge that makes sense of the world—a habitus (Bourdieu 1977)—and it is used to assess right and wrong on a larger scale (Bonilla-Silva 2001).

Bonilla-Silva (2001, 63) argues that ideologies are meanings that express "relations of domination." Dominant ideologies become "master frameworks" used to measure all other races/ethnicities. Bonilla-Silva maintains that white ideology reproduces white supremacy in that it accounts for (justifies) racial inequality, it normalizes whiteness, and it provides the basic scripts and rules of engagement for all actors. Dominant ideologies help whites to maintain power by manufacturing consent (Burawoy 1982)—both among whites and among people of color, who internalize white supremacy as well. As van Dijk (1993) asserts, the white dominant group is able to reproduce its abuse of power only through an integrated system of discriminatory practices and sustaining ideologies. Everyday conversation helps these ideologies take root, and these in turn justify discrimination. Structure and action are dialectically interconnected, and racetalk helps link white supremacist ideology with practice. Therefore, as stated above, racetalk is a tool for continued oppression of people of color. Racetalk is part of a larger racial regime, and it works together with other discriminatory practices. As Feagin et al.(2001, 222–23) write,

> The varied manifestations of wasteful racist action have led many observers to think of them as distinctly different or isolated events rather than as interrelated parts of the same social phenomenon. The white employer who passes over a black person for a job and the white contractor who excludes black construction workers do not consider themselves in the same category as whites burning

crosses. Yet their covert and subtle discriminatory actions differ only in the weapons being used.

Racetalk, then, is another discriminatory weapon that ensures the continuation of the racial regime.

IS RACISM PERMANENT?

Derrick Bell (1992) poignantly argues that racism is a permanent part of American society. He cites Frantz Fanon (1967), who saw racism as embedded in our psychology, society, economy, and culture. Bell, like Fanon, doubts that "modern structure, deeply poisoned with racism, would be overthrown" (x). From this perspective, there is nothing that we can do to end racism. We can only try to adjust to the system and cope with it as best we can. He writes, "African Americans must confront and conquer the otherwise deadening reality of our permanent subordinate status. Only then can we prevent ourselves from being dragged down by society's hostility" (12).

Bell's book *Faces at the Bottom of the Well* is a series of fictional thought pieces that approach racism counterhegemonically.[2] In one of his pieces, Bell fantasizes about legalized racial preferencing. He envisions a system of "racial realism," whereby racism is recognized as an inescapable part of society. In such a system, whites who want to discriminate could—as long as they had a license to do so. Whites would have to post their licenses in their places of business so that people of color would be duly warned. The licenses would outline what they could and could not do. Discrimination licenses would have to be renewed regularly, and they would be expensive (he proposes that they cost 3 percent of the white's income). People caught discriminating without a license would be severely punished. In Bell's vision, this system would erase uncertainty for people of color who constantly wonder if they're being discriminated against. This new system would perhaps alleviate the rage of constantly second-guessing. If we accept racism as permanent, new possibilities like this open up. This policy would diminish the power of private, secret collusion against people of color by making discrimination a matter of public record: "Paradoxically, gaining the right to practice openly what people now enthusiastically practice covertly, will take a lot of joy our of discrimination and replace that joy with some costly pain" (61–62). It is quite fascinating. We need not be depressed by the permanence of racism. But we do need to be motivated to find new policies in order to deal with it.

The data in this book echo Bell's outlook on the status of race relations in the United States. It is disheartening to note that, over time, racetalk has become rationalized (Weber 1921/1979). People have come to take it for granted, and we have forgotten that we can challenge the talk instead of going along with it. Because it is rationalized, it is less open to challenge. As Jürgen Habermas (1984, 70) might describe it, racetalk entails "normatively ascribed agreement versus communicatively achieved understanding." Racetalk is paradoxical. On the one hand, it has been culturally decentered, so that—as part of colorblind rhetoric (Collins 1998)—it is disallowed and sanctioned in many social settings. Yet, at the same time, it flourishes in private settings. There, racetalk is part of a racial worldview that is so central to our lexicon that it needs little introduction or shared background meanings in order for it to be understood. In these settings, racetalk embodies a lifeworld, which Habermas (1984, 70) defines as "the correlated processes of reaching understanding. . . . This lifeworld background serves as a source of situation definitions that are presupposed by participants as unproblematic." The lifeworld adapts, keeping racism alive even while disguising our society as a colorblind social order.

PRAXIS

Marx's concept of "praxis"—or practical activity—reminds us that theory and research are only relevant in their capacity to help transform society for the better. As he said, "The philosophers have only interpreted the world, in various ways; the point, however, is to change it" (Tucker 1970, 109). As Weber (1921/1979) argued, we must imagine an alternative arrangement and get to work making it a reality. Bell (1992) does this beautifully and we can too.

Using Habermas's (1984) communicative action as an analytical framework, let us take this imagination mandate to heart. Habermas argues that if people communicate rationally and openly, then they can work together to build consensus. A system based on consensus would treat everyone as peers with equal voices, and everyone's interests would be fairly represented. Habermas envisions a system that builds empathy, which Feagin et al. (2001) and Hernan Vera (2003) have argued is necessary for eradicating empathy. Through such an approach, we might foster what bell hooks (1995) calls "beloved communities," in which everyone would be valued. Thus, communicative action is an attractive model to examine.

First, we must ask, What does rational communication look like? According to Habermas, people communicate rationally (a) when they speak their minds as accurately as possible without holding back; (b) when they speak truthfully, to the best of their knowledge; and (c) when they are prepared to defend their assertions with facts. Rational communication is not dogmatic, nor wedded to a particular belief system. It is oriented toward the empowerment of all people. Thus, Habermas imagines a world in which people speak truthfully from their hearts with no fear of reprisal. They speak with the intentions of building strong community bonds in which everyone is valued and protected.

Can racetalk be transformed into a tool for communicative action? Maybe. It would certainly require an extreme makeover first. Most importantly, racetalk is not rational by Habermas's definition. People do not use racetalk openly, and they often use it even when they believe it is inaccurate. They avoid situations where they will have to defend it. If they do defend racetalk, they rely on norms and experiences rather than facts. It would be hard to transform racetalk as it is now into Habermasian rational communication.

Yet, we *can* use the private realm as a locus to begin making racetalk available for discussion, if not debate. Rather than ignore it or closet it when it occurs, we could use racetalk as an opportunity to help each other unlearn misinformation about various racial/ethnic groups. Open dialogues could be nurtured so that *racetalk*—talk that demeans and degrades people of color— could be transformed into *conversations about race and racism*. Such conversations could integrate information from history and social science rather than myth and stereotype. By being honest about our curiosity and misconceptions about race—in a respectful and genuine manner—we might air out and eventually cleanse our imaginations, which have for so long been tainted by racism. This is not exactly Habermas's vision of communicative action, but it is a step in that direction. It moves us toward a state of being that is prerequisite in order for communicative action to be effective: a state in which we are more pure of heart and mind. It also would move us toward empathy, which is key to undermining entrenched racism (Feagin et al. 2001; Vera 2003).

MAKING CHANGE

Realistically, making change will be difficult. Yet, as I have argued throughout this book, we *can* make change. We can strive for beloved communities (hooks 1995). That is the liberating potential of the dialectic. Here, I offer several suggestions for working toward a new regime in which race is not used as a central structuring factor. This is not an exhaustive list of possibilities. Indeed, I hope that, as you read this book, you fantasized about some strategies of your own. To paraphrase Hillary Clinton (1996), it takes a village to make a better world for everyone.

- **Scrutinize your own racetalk.**
  One of the reasons that racetalk is so important is that it is so widespread. Many people across race, class, gender, age, and sexuality lines

use racetalk in their everyday lives. A first step toward making change involves identifying and examining your own racetalk. Under what circumstances do you use it? What kinds of racetalk do you use? Recognize the sociohistorical context of the racetalk that you use. Educate yourself about the roots and implications of your racetalk. If you do not wish to give up racetalk altogether, then at least be an informed user. Understand that your racetalk helps to signify racism on a larger societal level. Be as responsible in that construction of meanings as you can be.

- **Make the invisible visible.**

Talk about racism with people. Use existing research findings from antiracist scholarship as evidence in making the racial regime visible and problematic. Only by recognizing its existence and interrogating the mechanisms of its reproduction can we begin to confront it.

- **Encourage educated counterstances.**

Take a stand against racism and racist practices. Use data rather than emotion as ammunition in finding holes in the doxa. Launch formidable heterodoxy. As Bourdieu (1991) argues, once a challenge is vocalized, it may be a catalyst around which other relevant challenges coalesce. Similarly, hooks (1989) argues that we should "talk back," speaking out against unjust practices. Otherwise, our silence marks our complicity.

- **Fight back?**

We should *talk* back, but should we also *fight* back? A genuine temptation may be to fight fire with fire, to strike back at oppressors by degrading them through racetalk. This may certainly assuage negative feelings and provide a sense of vindication. Charles Lawrence [III] (1993) and Mari Matsuda (1993) assert that fighting back immediately, in the heat of the moment, might help redefine racetalk as actionable speech. Patricia Hill Collins (1998) argues that in many cases we should fight back, but we should pick our battles carefully. If we fight all of the time—due to the pervasiveness of racetalk—we could burn out and/or lose any credibility that we have. Strategies for fighting back should be considered before enacted. Society often constructs our options as binaries or dichotomies, like powerful/powerless, good/bad, white/black, reason/emotion. If we buy into these oversimplified dichotomies in evaluating and reacting to social problems, then we often fall into a trap of reifying the existing binary. Instead, our strategies should be creative and varied. They should recognize the diversity of possibilities in both assessing and reacting to a given situation.

- **Nurture empathy.**

Seek conversations about race and racism even though they may be painful. Be willing to listen undefensively. Recognize that you have learned misinformation about your own group and others, and be willing to unlearn that misinformation by incorporating new information into your worldview. Try to see the world from another position, and respect that position even if it is different from your own. We cannot build a non-racist society if we do not empathize with people who suffer under racism (Feagin et al. 2001; Vera 2003).

- **Revisit political correctness?**

You may be wondering if I am essentially calling for a reinvigoration of political correctness, or if I am calling for something altogether different. I would like to pull out the best insights of political correctness and weave in other insights from the research process as well. What is wrong with political correctness? It cannot be understood without placing it into a larger politicoracial context.

Collins (1998) examines a brief history of race and rhetoric. She begins with desegregation, during which time blacks and whites came into closer proximity to one another and the official lines demarcating space were blurred, but not obliterated. She says that as whites and blacks lived and worked closer together, "theories of black inferiority became increasingly attributed to cultural differences" (82). Blacks who did not fit into the pejorative tropes were dubbed "exceptional." Collins argues that exceptional blacks are still so rare that they are "collected and owned" like trophies by whites. The exceptional ones eventually changed the rules of racial etiquette, so that overt racetalk was no longer socially acceptable. They helped to foster political correctness. As Marilyn Frye (1992) argues, this movement was designed to educate dominants about the power of language to oppress. It encouraged dominants to be respectful of people's differences rather than reify and commodify them. Yet, policing of racetalk rubbed many whites the wrong way:

> Whites now felt themselves to be the targets of surveillance. Whites who spoke openly of their belief in black inferiority found themselves censured and evaluated as "racist" and backward. A rhetoric of colorblindness was instituted, so that to talk of race at all meant that one was racist. (Collins 1998, 82)

Although rhetoric shifted through political correctness, the underlying belief in blacks' inferiority persisted. Collins points to coded language, like welfare queen and drug dealer, which conveys racial information without naming it as such. The data in this book support Collins's assertion—indeed, the racetalk in this book indicates a highly elaborate system of meanings geared toward reproducing racial hierarchies.

Thus political correctness in its current incarnation did not succeed in reforming the structure of signification. It merely masked it. In so doing, political correctness may have done more harm than good. By masking the pejorative significations of blackness and brownness under the guise of colorblindness, we have created a new rhetoric that allows dominants to look the other way as major segments of the population continue to suffer under the racial regime (Bonilla-Silva 2001). Colorblindness blames people of color for problematizing racism: *they* are the ones who see color, therefore *they* are the racists. Dominants are absolved from culpability in the racial regime (Bonilla-Silva 2003).

What is good about political correctness? Its push for respect and empathy remains valuable and important. It recognized that language is a powerful tool that can be used for symbolic violence or for liberation (Bourdieu 1977, 1991; Habermas 1984). Political correctness was effective heterodoxy. It helped to shift the doxa slightly even though it did not entirely dislodge it from the habitus of racism. Political correctness provides a place to start; it is not an end in and of itself.

- **Do not underestimate the possibilities of insider status.**

Much racetalk is uttered to a select audience of people who are presupposed to agree with it. As such, when you hear racetalk, it is often because you have been granted insider status. This provides you access to a process through which meanings are negotiated. Insider status is a powerful resource that you can use in interrupting racetalk. As Habermas (1984, 112) argues:

> Understanding [verstehen] a symbolic expression fundamentally requires participation in a process of reaching understanding. Meanings—whether embodied in actions, institutions, products of labor, words, networks of cooperation, or documents—can be made accessible only from the inside. Symbolically restructured reality forms a universe that is hermetically sealed to the view of observers incapable of communicating; that is, it would remain incomprehensible to them. The lifeworld is open only to subjects who make use of their competence to speak and act. They gain access to it by participating, at least virtually, in the communications of members and thus becoming at least potential members themselves.

In this study, we have seen that social pressures associated with insider status often lead people to avoid rocking the boat or jeopardizing their insiderness. That is, people maintained silence rather than challenging problematic racetalk. As Habermas (1984, 71) might say, people often treat racetalk as a "mythical worldview," in which "the linguistic worldview is reified as the world order and cannot be seen as an interpretive system open to criticism." But this assumption is incorrect. Racetalk—though powerfully intertwined with action—is still *talk*. It can be critiqued.

When you hear racetalk, you hear evidence that you have broken the "hermetic seal" and accessed the private realm of racism. Rather than go along with it in order to remain part of the group, take advantage of your insider status. Recognize yourself as an agent in the production of knowledge. You too have a role in the signification of meanings and symbols. Instead of being a passive observer, you can choose to interrupt racetalk.

- **Use the extant bond of intimacy as a resource rather than a hindrance.**

A common thread throughout much of the racetalk is that it tends to occur in an intimate setting among people who have an ongoing, trusting relationship. That trusting relationship itself may form the basis of positive, constructive interventions. As Collins (1998) said, dichotomies like good/bad and right/wrong oversimplify the social world. Racetalk is not always clearly good or bad, and racetalkers almost never are clearly demarcated by this binary measure of value. Rather than be constrained by the binary, it might be more productive to focus on your common bond with the racetalker. Your bond provides you the benefit of the doubt. Just as people use racetalk because they assume it will be accepted, assume that your counterstance will be heard and valued as well. If you do not make this assumption, it is harder to take the risk of interrupting the talk at all.

- **Interrupt racetalk in a constructive, consistent manner.**

Recognize and anticipate that there is often a backlash effect: the challenger is construed as the offending party for having disrupted the tenor of the conversation. When the racetalker becomes defensive—most people do not want to be thought of as racist (Feagin et al. 2001)—s/he is likely to employ some face-saving strategy that denies responsibility and/or the importance of the talk. Brainstorm about ways to interrupt racetalk without condemning the speaker. Recall that Cheyenne (white) asked her friend not to use racetalk around her children. Her comment was reasonable and nonthreatening. He readily complied. Often, effective challenges will take time, persistence, and consistency.

This is not to say that racetalkers should be coddled. They already occupy a position of privilege in a conversation, and the content of their talk is supported by the weight of the racial regime. Racetalkers, therefore, are not victims of their challengers. However, with their privilege comes powerful racist orthodoxy geared toward silencing and marginalizing challengers. My advice here is geared toward breaking through the orthodoxy, so that the challenge can be heard and behavior can be altered.

One cannot do this by being ejected from the conversation, by being silenced or shunned. Therefore, walk a fine line of heterodoxic tact.

Few challenges to racetalk produce consensus. However, interrupting the racetalk is a step toward negotiating alternative definitions of the situation. We do racism through our overt acts and our complicit silence. We can undo racism through counterhegemonic practices. We may help change the construction of symbolic meanings of race, so that future racialized conversations are more open, and further negotiations might occur.

CONCLUSION

To finally conclude, then, we are constrained by the power of our racial history, but we are not powerless to change it. Racetalk is an everyday occurrence that most every person has access to in some form or another. As such, it is an equal-opportunity locus in which to generate change. The racial regime was constructed through collective action. It can be dismantled through collective action, as well.

NOTES

1. Feagin, Vera, and Batur (2001) argue that racism is a huge waste of moral and material resources that hurts all people.

2. Paul Beatty's (2001) novel, *The White Boy Shuffle*, argues that black people should commit suicide, publicly, when they have had enough of the daily episodes of racism. One black woman slashed her wrists when a white cashier refused to put her change in her hand. Beatty, like Bell, asserts that racism is permanent and must be met with shocking new approaches that rupture the hegemony that protects it.

REFERENCES

Acker, Joan. 1990. "Hierarchies, Jobs, Bodies: A Theory of Gendered Organizations." *Gender & Society* 4: 139–58.

Adler, Patricia, and Peter Adler. 1998. *Peer Power*. New Brunswick, NJ: Rutgers University Press.

Andersen, Margaret. 2003. "Whitewashing Race: A Critical Review Essay on 'Whiteness.'" In *White Out: The Continuing Significance of Racism*, edited by Ashley W. Doane and Eduardo Bonilla-Silva. New York: Routledge.

Anderson, Elijah. 1999. *Code of the Street*. New York: Norton.

Anzaldua, Gloria. 1999. *Borderlands/La Frontera: The New Mestiza*. San Francisco: Aunt Lute Books.

Armour, Jody David. 1997. *Negrophobia and Reasonable Racism: The Hidden Costs of Being Black in America*. New York: New York University Press.

Austin, J. L. 1971. *How to Do Things with Words*. Cambridge, MA: Harvard University Press.

Bagdikian, Ben H. 2000. *The Media Monopoly*. Boston: Beacon Press.

Bauman, Zygmunt. 1976. *Towards a Critical Sociology: An Essay on Commonsense and Emancipation*. London: Routledge.

Beatty, Paul. 2001. *The White Boy Shuffle*. New York: Picador.

Bell, Derrick. 1992. *Faces at the Bottom of the Well*. New York: Basic.

Bem, Sandra. 1993. *The Lenses of Gender: Transforming the Debate on Sexual Inequality*. New Haven, CT: Yale University Press.

Berg, Bruce Lawrence. 2004. *Qualitative Research Methods for the Social Sciences*. Boston: Allyn & Bacon.

Bergen, Doris L. 2002. *War and Genocide: A Concise History of the Holocaust*. Lanham, MD: Rowman & Littlefield.

Biddle, Bruce J. 1979. *Role Theory*. New York: Academic Press.

Bobo, Lawrence, James R. Kluegel, and Ryan A. Smith. 1997. "Laissez-faire Racism: The Crystallization of a Kinder, Gentler, Antiblack Ideology." In *Racial Attitudes in the 1990s*, edited by Steven A. Tuch and Jack K. Martin. Westport, CT: Praeger.

Bonilla-Silva, Eduardo. 2003. *Racism without Racists: Color-Blind Racism and the Persistence of Racial Inequality in the United States*. Lanham, MD: Rowman & Littlefield.

——. 2001. *White Supremacy & Racism in the Post–Civil Rights Era*. Boulder, CO: Lynne Rienner Press.

——. 1999. "The New Racism: Racial Structure in the United States, 1960s–1990s." In *Race, Ethnicity and Nationality in the United States*, edited by Paul Wong. Boulder, CO: Westview.

——. 1997. "Rethinking Racism: Toward a Structural Interpretation." *American Sociological Review* 62: 465–80.

Bonilla-Silva, Eduardo, Tyrone Forma, Amanda Lewis, and D. Embrick. 2003. "It Wasn't Me: How Race and Racism Will Work in the 21st Century." *Research in Political Sociology* 12: 111–34.

Bonilla-Silva, Eduardo, and Tyrone A. Forman. 2000. "'I Am Not a Racist But . . .': Mapping White College Students' Racial Ideology in the USA." *Discourse and Society* 11, no. 1: 50–85.

Bourdieu, Pierre. 1991. *Language and Symbolic Power*. Cambridge, MA: Harvard University Press.

——. 1977. *Outline of a Theory of Practice*. Cambridge: Cambridge University Press.

Braverman, Harry. 1976. *Labor and Monopoly Capital: The Degradation of Work in the Twentieth Century*. New York: Monthly Review Press.

Bray, John N., Linda L. Smith, Joyce Lee, and Lyle Yorks. 2000. *Collaborative Inquiry in Practice: Action, Reflection, and Making Meaning*. Thousand Oaks, CA: Sage.

Brown, Elaine. 1992. *A Taste of Power: A Black Woman's Story*. New York: Doubleday.

Bulmer, M. 1982. "When Is Disguise Justified?" *Qualitative Sociology* 5: 251–64.

Burawoy, Michael. 1982. *Manufacturing Consent*. Chicago: University of Chicago Press.

Burawoy, Michael, Joshua Gamson, and Alice Burton. 1991. *Ethnography Unbound*. Berkeley: University of California Press.

Carpenter, Cheryl, Barry Glassner, Bruce D. Johnson, and Julia Loughlin. 1988. *Kids, Drugs, and Crime*. Lexington, MA: Lexington Books.

Chin, Frank. 1991. *Donald Duk*. New York: Coffee House Press.

Choi, Susan. 1993. *American Woman*. New York: HarperCollins.

Chomsky, Noam. 1965. *Aspects of the Theory of Syntax*. Cambridge, MA: MIT Press.

Churchill, Ward. 2002. *Struggle for the Land: Native North American Resistance to Genocide, Ecocide, and Colonization*. New York: City Lights Books.

——. 1998. *A Little Matter of Genocide: Holocaust and Denial in the Americas, 1492 to the Present*. New York: City Lights Books.

Clarke, Richard A. 2004. *Against All Enemies: Inside America's War on Terror*. New York: Free Press.

Clinton, Hillary Rodham. 1996. *It Takes a Village*. New York: Simon & Schuster.

Collins, Patricia Hill. 2004. *Black Sexual Politics: African Americans, Gender, and the New Racism*. New York: Routledge.

———. 2000. *Black Feminist Thought*. New York: Routledge.

———. 1998. *Fighting Words: Black Women and the Search for Justice*. Minneapolis: University of Minnesota Press.

———. 1986. "Learning from the Outsider Within: The Sociological Significance of Black Feminist Thought." *Social Problems* 33, no. 6: 14–32.

Connell, R. W. 2001. *The Men and the Boys*. Berkeley: University of California Press.

———. 1987. *Gender and Power*. Stanford, CA: Stanford University Press.

Creswell, John W. 1997. *Qualitative Inquiry and Research Design*. Thousand Oaks, CA: Sage.

D'Orso, Michael. 1996. *Like Judgment Day: The Ruin and Redemption of a Town Called Rosewood*. New York: Boulevard Books.

Davies, Kevin. 2001. *Cracking the Genome: Inside the Race to Unlock Human DNA*. New York: Free Press.

Davis, Angela Y. 1983. *Women, Race, and Class*. New York: Vintage.

Delgado, Richard, and Jean Stefancic. 2004. *Understanding Words That Wound*. Boulder, CO: Westview.

———. 2001. *Critical Race Theory: An Introduction*. New York: New York University Press.

Della Fave, Richard L. 1980. "The Meek Shall Not Inherit the Earth: Self-Evaluation and the Legitimacy of Stratification." *American Sociological Review* 45, no. 6: 955–71.

Dennis, Rutledge M. 1993. "Participant Observations." In *Race and Ethnicity in Research Methods*, edited by John H. Stanfield and Rutledge M. Dennis. Newbury Park, CA: Sage.

Denzin, Norman, and Yvonna Lincoln, eds. 2000. *Handbook of Qualitative Research*. Thousand Oaks, CA: Sage.

DeVault, Marjorie L. 1999. *Liberating Method: Feminism and Social Research*. Philadelphia: Temple University Press.

Diamond, Jared. 1992. *The Third Chimpanzee*. New York: Perennial.

DiMaggio, Paul, John Evans, and Bethany Bryson. 1996. "Have Americans' Social Attitudes Become More Polarized?" *American Journal of Sociology* 102: 690–755.

Doane, Ashley W., Jr. 1996. "Contested Terrain: Negotiating Racial Understandings in Public Discourse." *Humanity and Society* 20, no. 4: 32–51.

———. 1997. "Dominant Group Identity in the United States: The Role of 'Hidden' Ethnicity in Intergroup Relations." *Sociological Quarterly* 38: 375–97.

———. 2003. "Whiteness Studies: A Critical Appraisal." In *White Out: The Continuing Significance of Racism*, edited by Ashley W. Doane and Eduardo Bonilla-Silva. New York: Routledge.

Doane, Ashley W., and Eduardo Bonilla-Silva, eds. 2003. *White Out: The Continuing Significance of Racism*. New York: Routledge.

Doob, Christopher Bates. 1999. *Racism: An American Cauldron*. New York: Longman.

Dray, Philip. 2003. *At the Hands of Persons Unknown: The Lynching of Black America*. New York: Modern Library.

Du Bois, W. E. B. 1996. *The Souls of Black Folk*. New York: Penguin.

Durkheim, Emile. 1893/1997. *The Division of Labor in Society*. New York: Free Press.

———. 1895/1964. The *Rules of Sociological Method*. New York: Free Press.

Duster, Troy. 2001. "The 'Morphing' Properties of Whiteness." In *The Making and Unmaking of Whiteness*, edited by Birget Brander Rasmussen, Eric Klinenberg, Irene J. Nexica, and Matt Wray. Durham, NC: Duke University Press.

Edwards, Richard. 1980. *Contested Terrain*. New York: Basic.

Ehrenreich, Barbara. 2002. *Nickel and Dimed: On Not Getting By in America*. New York: Owl Books.

Eitzen, Stanley, and Maxine Baca Zinn. 2004. *Social Problems*. Boston: Allyn & Bacon.

Ellsworth, Scott, and John Hope Franklin. 1992. *Death in a Promised Land: The Tulsa Race Riot of 1921*. Baton Rouge: Louisiana State University Press.

Espiritu, Yen Le. 1997. *Asian American Women and Men*. Thousand Oaks, CA: Sage.

Essed, Philomena. 1991. *Understanding Everyday Racism*. Newbury Park, CA: Sage.

Fanon, Frantz. 1967. *Black Skin, White Masks*. New York: Grove Press.

Fausto-Sterling, Anne. 1992. *Myths of Gender: Biological Theories about Men and Women*. New York: Basic.

Feagin, Joe R. 2000. *Racist America: Roots, Current Realities, and Future Reparations*. New York: Routledge.

———. 1991. "The Continuing Significance of Race: Antiblack Discrimination in Public Places." *American Sociological Review* 56: 101–16.

Feagin, Joe R., and Karyn D. McKinney. 2003. *The Many Costs of Racism*. Lanham, MD: Rowman & Littlefield.

Feagin, Joe R., and M. P. Sikes. 1994. *Living with Racism: The Black Middle Class Experience*. Boston: Beacon.

Feagin, Joe R., and Hernan Vera. 2001. *Liberation Sociology*. Boulder, CO: Westview.

Feagin, Joe R., Hernan Vera, and Pinar Batur. 2001. *White Racism: The Basics*. New York: Routledge.

Fields, Mamie Garvin, and Karen Fields. 1985. *Lemon Swamp and Other Places: A Carolina Memoir*. New York: Free Press.

Fine, Michelle. 1997. "Witnessing Whiteness." In *Off White: Readings on Race, Power, and Society*, edited by Michelle Fine, Lois Weis, Linda C. Powell, and L. Mun Wong. New York: Routledge.

Fine, Michelle, and Lois Weis. 1999. *The Unknown City: Lives of Poor and Working-Class Young Adults*. Boston: Beacon.

Fine, Michelle, Lois Weis, Linda C. Powell, and L. Mun Wong, eds. 1997. *Off White: Readings on Race, Power, and Society*. New York: Routledge.

Forman, Tyrone, Carla Goar, and Amanda Lewis. 2002. "Neither Black Nor White? An Empirical Test of the Latin Americanization Thesis." *Race and Society* 5: 67–86.

Frankenburg, Ruth. 1993. *White Women, Race Matters: The Social Construction of Whiteness*. Minneapolis: University of Minnesota Press.

———. 2001. "The Mirage of an Unmarked Whiteness." In *The Making and Unmaking of Whiteness*, edited by Birget Brander Rasmussen, Eric Klinenberg, Irene J. Nexica, and Matt Wray. Durham, NC: Duke University Press.

Franklin, Donna. 2001. *What's Love Got to Do with It?* New York: Simon & Schuster.

Fraser, Steven, ed. 1995. *The Bell Curve Wars: Race, Intelligence, and the Future of America.* New York: Basic.

Frye, Marilyn. 1992. "Getting It Right." *Signs* 17: 781–93.

Gallagher, Chip. Forthcoming A. "Color-Blind Privilege: The Social and Political Functions of Erasing the Color Line in Post Race America." *Race, Gender, and Class* 10, no. 4.

———. Forthcoming B. "Transforming Racial Identity Through Affirmative Action." In *Race and Ethnicity: Across Time, Space and Discipline*, edited by Rodney Coates. New York: Brill Publishers.

———. 2003. "Miscounting Race: Explaining Whites' Misperceptions of Racial Group Size." *Sociological Perspectives* 46: 381–96.

Gerard, Philip. 1994. *Cape Fear Rising.* Winston-Salem, NC: John Blair Publishers.

Gibson, Timothy A. 1998. "I Don't Want Them Living Around Here: Ideologies of Race and Neighborhood Decay." *Rethinking Marxism* 10: 141–54.

Giddens, Anthony. 1984. *The Constitution of Society.* Berkeley: University of California Press.

Giddings, Paula. 1996. *When and Where I Enter: The Impact of Black Women on Race and Sex in America.* New York: Bantham.

Ginsberg, Elaine, ed. 1996. *Passing and the Fictions of Identity.* Durham, NC: Duke University Press.

Glaser, Barney, and Anselm Strauss. 1967. *The Discovery of Grounded Theory.* Chicago: Aldine.

Goffman, Erving. 1956. *Presentation of Self in Everyday Life.* Edinburgh: University of Edinburgh.

———. 1981. *Forms of Talk.* Oxford: Blackwell.

Golden, Daniel. 2003. "At Many Colleges, the Rich Kids Get Affirmative Action." *Wall Street Journal* (Eastern Edition), February 20.

Gonzalez, Roseann Duenas, and Ildeko Melis. 2000. *Language Ideologies: Critical Perspectives on the Official English Movement.* New York: Lea.

Gramsci, Antonio. 1932 (1975). *Letters from Prison: Antonio Gramsci*, edited by Lynne Lawner. New York: Harper Colophon.

———. 1971. *Selections from the Prison Notebook.* New York: International.

Greisman, Harvey C. 1986. "The Paradigm That Failed." In *Structures of Knowledge*, edited by Richard C. Monk. Lanham, MD: University Press of America.

Guglielmo, Thomas A. 2003. Rethinking Whiteness Historiography: The Case of Italians in Chicago, 1890–1945." In *White Out: The Continuing Significance of Racism*, edited by Ashely W. Doane and Eduardo Bonilla-Silva. New York: Routledge.

Habermas, Jürgen. 1984. *The Theory of Communicative Action, Volume One: Reason and the Rationalization of Society.* Boston: Beacon Press.

Hacker, Andrew. 2003. *Two Nations: Black and White, Separate, Hostile, Unequal.* New York: Scribner.

Harding, Sandra. 1991. *Whose Science? Whose Knowledge?* Ithaca, NY: Cornell University Press.

———. 1998. *Is Science Multicultural?* Bloomington: Indiana University Press.

Hartsock, Nancy. 1983. *Money, Sex, and Power.* Boston: Northeastern University Press.

Hawley, Scott, and Catherine Mori. 1999. *The Human Genome: A User's Guide.* San Diego, CA: Academic Press.

Hekman, S. 1997. "Truth and Method: Feminist Standpoint Revisited." *Signs* 22: 341–65.

Herrnstein, Richard J., and Charles Murray. 1999. *The Bell Curve: Intelligence and Class Structure in American Life.* New York: Free Press.

Hertz, Rosanna, ed. 1997. *Reflexivity and Voice.* Thousand Oaks, CA: Sage.

Hochschild, Arlie. 1985. *The Managed Heart: Commercialization of Human Feeling.* Berkeley: University of California Press.

hooks, bell. 1996. *Reel to Real: Race, Sex, and Class at the Movies.* New York: Routledge.

———. 1995. *Killing Rage: Ending Racism.* New York: Henry Holt.

———. 1994a. *Teaching to Transgress.* New York: Routledge.

———. 1994b. *Outlaw Culture: Resisting Representations.* New York: Routledge.

———. 1992. *Black Looks: Race and Representation.* Boston: South End Press.

———. 1984. *Feminist Theory: From Margin to Center.* Boston: South End Press.

———. 1981. *Ain't I a Woman?: Black Women and Feminism.* Boston: South End Press.

Horowitz, Ruth. 1986. "Remaining an Outsider: Membership as a Threat to Research Rapport." *Urban Life* 14: 409–30.

Hunter, Margaret. 2002a. "'If You're Light You're Alright:' Light Skin Color as Social Capital for Women of Color." *Gender & Society* 16: 175–93.

———. 2002b. "Rethinking Epistemology, Methodology, and Racism: Or Is White Sociology Really Dead?" *Race & Society* 5: 119–38.

Huxley, Aldous. 1998. *Brave New World.* New York: Perennial.

Johnson, Charles S. 1943. *Patterns of Negro Segregation.* New York: Harper & Brothers.

Johnson, Kevin R., ed. 2003. *Mixed Race America and the Law.* New York: New York University Press.

Jorgenson, David E., and Cristabel B. Jorgenson. 1992. "Age and White Racial Attitudes: National Surveys, 1972–1989." *Sociological Spectrum* 12: 21–34.

Kennedy, Randall. 2003. *Nigger: The Strange Career of a Troublesome Word.* New York: Vintage.

Kilson, Martin, and Clement Cottingham. 1991. "Thinking about Race Relations: How Far Are We Still from Integration?" *Dissent* (fall): 520–30.

Kincheloe, Joe L., Shirley R. Steinberg, and Aaron D. Gresson III, eds. 1997. *Measured Lies: The Bell Curve Examined.* New York: St. Martin's.

Kivel, Paul. 1996. *Uprooting Racism: How White People Can Work for Racial Justice.* Gabriola Island, BC: New Society.

Kreiger, Susan. 1985. "Beyond 'Subjectivity:' The Use of Self in Social Science." *Qualitative Sociology* 8: 309–24.

Kuhn, Thomas. 1996. *The Structure of Scientific Revolutions.* Chicago: University of Chicago Press.

Lakatos, Imre. 1978. The *Methodology of Scientific Research Programmes*. New York: Cambridge University Press.

Lawrence, Charles R. III. 1993. "If He Hollers Let Him Go: Regulating Racist Speech on Campus." In *Words That Wound: Critical Race Theory, Assaultive Speech, and the First Amendment*, edited by Mari J. Matsuda, Charles R. Lawrence III, Richard Delgado, and Kimberle Williams Crenshaw. Boulder, CO: Westview.

Lemert, Charles. 2002. *Dark Thoughts: Race and the Eclipse of Society*. New York: Routledge.

Letkemann, P. 1980. "Crime as Work: Leaving the Field." In *Field Work Experience*, edited by W. Shaffir, R. Stebbins, and A. Turowetz. New York: St. Martin's.

Lispet, Seymour Martin. 1981. *Political Man: The Social Bases of Politics*. Baltimore, MD: Johns Hopkins University Press.

Loewen, James W. 2000. *Lies Across America: What Our Historic Sites Get Wrong*. New York: Touchstone.

———. 1996. *Lies My Teacher Told Me: Everything Your American History Textbook Got Wrong*. New York: Touchstone.

Lofland, John, and Lyn H. Lofland. 1994. *Analyzing Social Settings: A Guide to Qualitative Observation and Analysis*. Belmont, CA: Wadsworth.

Lorde, Audre. 1984. *Sister Outsider*. New York: Crossing Press.

Lukacs, Georg. 1922 (1968). *History and Class Consciousness*. Cambridge, MA: MIT Press.

Luttrell, Wendy. 1997. *School-Smart and Mother-Wise: Working-Class Women's Identity and Schooling*. New York: Routledge.

MacLeod, Jay. 1995. *Ain't No Makin' It: Aspirations and Attainment in a Low-Income Neighborhood*. Boulder, CO: Westview.

Marable, Manning. 1997. *Black Liberation in Conservative America*. Boston: South End Press.

Marcuse, Herbert. 1964. *One-Dimensional Man*. Boston: Beacon.

Marks, Jonathan. 2002. *What It Means to Be 98 Percent Chimpanzee: Apes, People, and Their Genes*. Berkeley: University of California Press.

Martinez, Ruben. 2002. *Crossing Over: A Mexican Family on the Migrant Trail*. London: Picador.

Marx, Karl. 1867/1967. *Capital: A Critique of Political Economy, Volume 1*. New York: International.

Massey, Douglas, and Nancy Denton. 1993. *American Apartheid: Segregation and the Making of the Underclass*. Cambridge, MA: Harvard University Press.

Matsuda, Mari J. 1993. "Public Response to Racist Speech: Considering the Victim's Story." In *Words That Wound: Critical Race Theory, Assaultive Speech, and the First Amendment*, edited by Mari J. Matsuda, Charles R. Lawrence III, Richard Delgado, and Kimberle Williams Crenshaw. Boulder, CO: Westview.

Matsuda, Mari J., and Charles R. Lawrence III. 1993. "Epilogue: Burning Crosses and the R.A.V. Case." In *Words That Wound: Critical Race Theory, Assaultive Speech, and the First Amendment*, edited by Mari J. Matsuda, Charles R. Lawrence III, Richard Delgado, and Kimberle Williams Crenshaw. Boulder, CO: Westview.

Matsuda, Mari J., Charles R. Lawrence III, Richard Delgado, and Kimberle Williams Crenshaw. 1993. *Words That Wound: Critical Race Theory, Assaultive Speech, and the First Amendment*. Boulder, CO: Westview.

McCorkel, Jill A., and Kristen A. Myers. 2003. "What Difference Does Difference Make? Position and Privilege in the Field." *Qualitative Sociology* 26, no. 2: 199–231.

McIntosh, Peggy. 2001 (1988). "White Privilege and Male Privilege: A Personal Account of Coming to See Correspondence through Work in Women's Studies." In *Race, Class, and Gender*, edited by Margaret L. Andersen and Patricia Hill Collins. Belmont, CA: Wadsworth.

McKinney, Karyn D., and Joe R. Feagin. 2003. "Diverse Perspectives on Doing Antiracism." In *White Out: The Continuing Significance of Racism*, edited by Ashley W. Doane and Eduardo Bonilla-Silva. New York: Routledge.

Miller, J. Mitchell, and Richard Tewksbury. 2001. *Extreme Methods: Innovative Approaches to Social Science Research*. Boston: Allyn & Bacon.

Mills, C. Wright. 2000 (reprinted). *The Power Elite*. New York: Oxford University Press.

Mills, Charles W. 2003. "White Supremacy as Sociopolitical System." In *White Out: The Continuing Significance of Racism*, edited by Ashley W. Doane and Eduardo Bonilla-Silva. New York: Routledge.

Moraga, Cherrie. 1995. "Art in America con Accento." In *Latina: Women's Voices From the Borderlands*, edited by Lillian Castillo-Speed. New York: Simon & Schuster.

Morrison, Toni. 1993. "On the Backs of Blacks." *Time* (fall), p. 57.

Myers, Kristen. 2004. "Ladies First: Race, Class, and the Contradictions of a Powerful Femininity." *Sociological Spectrum* 24, no. 1: 11–41.

———. 2003. "White Fright: Reproducing White Supremacy through Casual Discourse." In *White Out: The Continuing Significance of Racism*, edited by Ashley W. Doane and Eduardo Bonilla-Silva. New York: Routledge.

———. 2001. "The Paradoxes of Anti-Racist Work: The Impact of Standpoint on Strategy." *Humanity and Society* 25, no. 2: 131–52.

———. 1999. "Racial Unity in the Grass Roots? A Case Study of a Women's Social Service Organization." In *Still Lifting, Still Climbing: African American Women's Contemporary Activism*, edited by Kimberly Springer. New York: New York University Press.

———. 1998. "Allegiances, Coups, and Color Wars: A Strategy for Breaking the Silence on Race Issues in the Classroom." *Transformations* 9: 183–95.

Myers, Kristen A., and Passion Williamson. 2001. "Race Talk: The Perpetuation of Racism through Private Discourse." *Race & Society* 4: 3–26.

Naples, Nancy A. 2003. *Feminism and Method: Ethnography, Discourse, and Activist Research*. New York: Routledge.

———. 1996. "A Feminist Revisiting of the Insider/Outsider Debate: The 'Outsider Phenomenon' in Rural Iowa." *Qualitative Sociology* 19: 83–106.

Okada, John. 2003. *Feminism and Method: Ethnography, Discourse, and Activist Research*. New York: Routledge.

———. 1978. *No-No Boy*. Seattle: University of Washington Press.

Omi, Michael. 1999. "Racial Identity and the State: Contesting the Federal Standards of Classification." In *Race, Ethnicity, and Nationality in the United States*, edited by Paul Wong. Boulder, CO: Westview.

Omi, Michael, and Howard Winant. 1994. *Racial Formation in the United States: From the 1960s to the 1990s*. New York: Routledge.

Padavic, Irene, and Barbara Reskin. 2002. *Women and Men at Work*. Thousand Oaks, CA: Pine Forge.

Parker, Pat. 1978. *Movement in Black: Collected Poetry of Pat Parker*. Oakland, CA: Diana Press

Parkin, Frank. 1979. *The Marxist Theory of Class: A Bourgeois Critique*. London: Tavistock.

Patai, D. 1991. "Testimony, Action Research, and Empowerment: Puerto Rican Women and Popular Education." In *Women's Words: The Feminist Practice of Oral History*, edited by S. B. Gluck and D. Patai. New York: Routledge.

Perel, Shlomo. 1997. *Europa Europa*. New York: John Wiley & Sons.

Peshkin, A. 1986. *God's Choice: The Total World of a Fundamentalist Christian School*. Chicago: University of Chicago Press.

Popper, Karl. 1968. *The Logic of Scientific Discovery*. New York: Harper and Row.

——— . 1965. *Conjectures and Refutations*. New York: Harper and Row.

Ramirez, Deborah A. 2000. *A Resource Guide on Racial Profiling Data Collection System: Promising Practices and Lessons Learned*. Washington, DC: U.S. Department of Justice.

Rasmussen, Brigid Brander, Irene J. Nexica, and Matt Wray, eds. 2001. *The Making and Unmaking of Whiteness*. Durham, NC: Duke University Press.

Reason, Peter, and Hilary Bradbury. 2001. *Handbook of Action Research: Participative Inquiry and Practice*. Thousand Oaks, CA: Sage.

Reinharz, Shulamit. 1997. "Who Am I?" The Need for a Variety of Selves in the Field." In *Reflexivity and Voice*, edited by R. Hertz. Thousand Oaks, CA: Sage.

——— . 1992. *Feminist Methods in Social Research*. London: Oxford University Press.

Reskin, Barbara. 1988. "Bringing the Men Back In: Sex Differentiation and the Devaluation of Women's Work." *Gender & Society* 2: 58–81.

Rich, Adrienne Cecile. 1974. "The Burning of Paper Instead of Children." In *Poems: Selected and New 1950–1974*. New York: Norton.

Riggs, Marlon. 1986. *Ethnic Notions*. San Francisco: California Newsreel.

Risman, Barbara J. 1999. *Gender Vertigo: American Families in Transition*. New Haven, CT: Yale University Press.

Roberts, John M. 1997. *A Short History of the World*. New York: Oxford University Press.

Rockquemore, Kerry Ann, and David L. Brunsma. 2001. *Beyond Black*. Thousand Oaks, CA: Sage.

Roethlisberger, Fritz Jules, and William J. Dickenson. 1939. *Management and the Worker*. Cambridge, MA: Harvard University Press.

Romero, Mary, and Abigail Stewart, eds. 1999. *Women's Untold Stories*. New York: Routledge.

Ronais, Carolyn Rambo, and Carolyn Ellis. 1989. "Turn-ons for Money." *Journal of Contemporary Ethnography* 18, no. 3: 271–98.

Russell, Kathy, and Midge Wilson. 1997. *Divided Sisters*. New York: Anchor.

St. Jean, Yannick, and Joe R. Feagin. 1998. *Double Burden: Black Women and Everyday Racism*. Amonk, NY: M. E. Sharpe Press.

de Saussure, Ferdinand. 1974. *Course in General Linguistics*. Glasgow: Collins.

Schmidt, Ronald. 2000. *Language Policy and Identity Politics in the United States*. Philadelphia: Temple University Press.

Schwalbe, Michael. 1996. *Unlocking the Iron Cage*. New York: Oxford University Press.

Schwalbe, Michael L., and Douglas Mason-Schrock. 1996. "Identity Work as Group Process." In *Advances in Group Processes*, vol. 13, edited by Barry Markovsky, Michael J. Lovaglia, and Robin Simon. Greenwich, CT: JAI Press.

Scott, Marvin B., and Stanford M. Lyman. 1968. "Accounts." *American Sociological Review* 33: 46–61.

Shakespeare, William. 2003. *Hamlet*. New York: Washington Square Press.

Shakur, Assata. 1988. *Assata: An Autobiography*. New York: Lawrence Hill.

Shaw, Stephanie J. 1996. *What a Woman Ought to Be and Do: Black Professional Women Workers during the Jim Crow Era*. Chicago: University of Chicago Press.

Sherrer, Christian. 2001. *Genocide and Crisis in Central Africa: Conflict Roots, Mass Violence, and Regional War*. New York: Praeger.

Shultz, Amy, Faye Knoki, and Ursula Knoki-Wilson. 1999. "'How Would You Write about That?' Identity, Language, and Knowledge in the Narratives of Two Navajo Women." In *Women's Untold Stories*, edited by Mary Romero and Abigail Stewart. New York: Routledge.

Smith, Dorothy. 1990. *The Conceptual Practices of Power*. Boston: Northeastern University Press.

——— . 1987. *The Everyday World as Problematic*. Boston: Northeastern University Press.

Sollors, Werner. 1999. *Neither Black Nor White but Both: Thematic Explorations of Interracial Literature*. Cambridge, MA: Harvard University Press.

——— , ed. 2000. *Interracialism: Black-White Intermarriage in American History, Literature, and Law*. New York: Oxford University Press.

Staples, Brent. 1986. "Just Walk on By: A Black Man Ponders His Power to Alter Public Space." *Ms* (September).

Steeh, C., and H. Schuman. 1992. "Young White Adults: Did Racial Attitudes Change in the 1980s?" *American Journal of Sociology* 98: 340–67.

Steinbeck, John. 1939/2002. *The Grapes of Wrath*. New York: Penguin.

Stowe, Harriet Beecher. 1852/1982. *Uncle Tom's Cabin*. New York: Bantam.

Strauss, Anselm, and Juliet Corbin. 1990. *Basics of Qualitative Research*. London: Sage.

Stringer, Ernest T. 1999. *Action Research*. Thousand Oaks, CA: Sage.

Sugrue, Thomas. 1996. *The Origins of the Urban Crisis*. Princeton, NJ: Princeton University Press.

Takaki, Ronald. 1994. *A Different Mirror*. Boston: Little, Brown.

Tamale, Sylvia R. 1996. "The Outsider Looks In: Constructing Knowledge about American Collegiate Racism." *Qualitative Sociology* 19: 471–95.

Tan, Amy. 1996. *The Hundred Secret Senses*. New York: Ivy Books.

——. 1992. *The Kitchen God's Wife*. New York: Ivy Books.

——. 1990. *The Joy Luck Club*. New York: Ivy Books.

Tate, Greg. 2003. *Everything but the Burden: What White People Are Taking from Black Culture*. New York: Broadway Books.

Thompson, John B. 1991. "Editor's Introduction." In *Language and Symbolic Power*, by Pierre Bourdieu. Cambridge, MA: Harvard University Press.

Thorne, Barrie. 1983. "Political Activist as Participant Observer." In *Contemporary Field Research*, edited by R. Emerson. Prospect Heights, IL: Waveland.

——. 1993. *Gender Play*. New Brunswick, NJ: Rutgers University Press.

Timmer, Doug A., and D. Stanley Eitzen. 1998. *Crime in the Streets and Crime in the Suites: Perspectives on Crime and Criminal Justice*. Boston: Allyn & Bacon.

Tucker, Robert C. 1970. *The Marx-Engels Reader*. New York: Norton.

Turner, Patricia A. 1993. *I Heard It through the Grapevine: Rumor in African-American Culture*. Berkeley: University of California Press.

Unks, Gerald, ed. 1995. *The Gay Teen*. New York: Routledge.

Van Ausdale, Debra, and Joe R. Feagin. 2002. *The First R*. Lanham, MD: Rowman & Littlefield.

Van Dijk, Teun. 1993. "Analyzing Racism through Discourse Analysis: Some Methodological Reflections." In *Race and Ethnicity in Research Methods*, edited by John H. Stanfield and Rutledge M. Dennis. Newbury Park, CA: Sage.

Vera, Hernan. 2003. "Racism and the Aim of Society." Paper presented in the session, *Social Theory: Race and Equality*, American Sociological Association. August 2003, Chicago, IL.

Wald, Gayle Freda. 2000. *Crossing the Line: Racial Passing in Twentieth-Century U.S. Literature and Culture*. Durham, NC: Duke University Press.

Walker, Alice. 1983. *In Search of Our Mother's Gardens*. New York: Harcourt Brace Jovanovich.

Wallace, Michele. 1994. *Black Macho and the Myth of the Superwoman*. London: Verso.

Warren, Jonathan W., and France Widdance Twine. 1997. "White Americans, the New Minority? Non-Blacks and the Ever-Expanding Boundaries of Whiteness." *Journal of Black Studies* 28: 200–18.

Waters, Mary. 1996. "Optional Ethnicities: For Whites Only?" In *Origins and Destinies: Immigration, Race and Ethnicity in America*. Belmont, CA: Wadsworth.

Weber, Max. 1921/1979. *Economy and Society*. Berkeley: University of California Press.

West, Candace, and Don H. Zimmerman. 1987. "Doing Gender." *Gender & Society* 1: 125–51.

Williams, Patricia J. 1991. *The Alchemy of Race and Rights*. Cambridge, MA: Harvard University Press.

Wilson, Midge, Ronald Hall, and Kathy Russell. 1993. *The Color Complex*. New York: Anchor.

Wilson, Terry P. 1994. *Lakota: Seeking the Great Spirit*. New York: Dimensions.

Wilson, William Julius. 1999. *The Declining Significance of Race: Blacks and Changing American Institutions*. Chicago: University of Chicago Press.

———. 1997. *When Work Disappears*. New York: Vintage.

———. 1990. *The Truly Disadvantaged: The Inner City, the Underclass, and Public Policy*. Chicago: University of Chicago Press.

Winant, Howard. 1999. "Racism Today: Continuity and Change in the Post–Civil Rights Era." In *Race, Ethnicity and Nationality in the United States*, edited by Paul Wong. Boulder, CO: Westview.

———. 1997. "Beyond Blue Eyes: Whiteness and Contemporary U.S. Racial Politics." In *Off White: Readings on Race, Power, and Society*, edited by Michelle Fine, Lois Weis, Linda C. Powell, and L. Mun Wong. New York: Routledge.

Winch, Peter. 1970. "Understanding a Primitive Society." In *Rationality*, edited by Bryan Wilson. London: Oxford University Press.

Woo, Deborah. 1989. "The Gap between Striving and Achieving: The Case of Asian American Women." In *Making Waves: An Anthology of Writings by and about Asian American Women*, edited by Asian Women United of California. Boston: Beacon.

Wright, Lawrence. 1994. "One Drop of Blood." *The New Yorker*, July 25, 1994, 46–55.

Wu, Frank H. 2003. *Yellow: Race in American Beyond Black and White*. New York: Basic.

Wyatt, Gail. 1997. *Stolen Women: Reclaiming Our Sexuality, Taking Back Our Lives*. New York: John Wiley & Sons.

Xiong, ThaoMee, and Beverly Daniel Tatum. 1999. "'In My Heart I Will Always Be Hmong:' One Hmong American Woman's Pioneering Journey toward Activism." In *Women's Untold Stories*, edited by Mary Romero and Abigail Stewart. New York: Routledge.

Yamato, Gloria. 1988. "Something about the Subject Makes It Hard to Name." In *Changing Our Power: An Introduction to Women's Studies*, edited by Jo Whitehorse Cochran, Donna Langston, and Carolyn Woodward. Dubuque, IA: Kendall-Hunt.

Zweigenhaft, Richard L., and G. William Domhoff. 1999. *Diversity in the Power Elite: Have Women and Minorities Reached the Top?* New Haven, CT: Yale University Press.

INDEX

accordion effect, 43
action, 42–44; and accordion or butterfly
  effect, 43; communicative, and
  rational communication, 270–71; and
  duality of order, 43–44; on impact of
  language games, 43. *See also* speech
  as action
action and structure, 256–62; arguments
  on tendency to privilege bigots, 258;
  frequency of public hate speech, 257;
  racism reflected in *Brown v. Board of
  Education*, 256–57; religion, 261. *See
  also* housing, neighborhoods, and
  communities; law and state; schools
  and racism
activism, 245–46
adult status, as power, 232
Afghanistan, war in, 87–88
aggression and policing, 177–80
America's racist history, 18–19. *See also*
  history of blackness in America
amnesia, collective, 262
antiracism. *See* research and antiracism
anti-Semitism, 74–75

Anzaldua, Gloria: on brownness as
  ambiguous counterstance, 134–35; on
  identity and language, 133–34; on loss
  of culture, 133. *See also la facultad*
Asians. *See* brownness
assaultive racist speech, 254–55
Auburn University and racism, 261–62
avoidance, 187

Batur: desensitivity to suffering and
  empathy, 224; on racist speech as
  weapon of discrimination, 268–69;
  white and black racism, 20–22
Bell, Derrick: on creation of inner cities
  due to desegregation, 261;
  exceptional status of blacks and
  discriminate discrimination, 122–23;
  Faces at the Bottom of the Well and
  permanence of, 269; lack of racial
  neutrality according to, 25; on limits
  of law in limiting discrimination, 258;
  on racism reflected in *Brown v.
  Board of Education*, 256–57
bigots, privileging of, 258

ABOUT THE AUTHOR

Kristen Myers is associate professor of sociology at Northern Illinois University. She has published articles on diverse topics including antiracist work, ladyhood, gay and lesbian police officers, and racetalk. She enjoys integrating her research and teaching endeavors. Myers is developing plans for two new projects: first, a study of women soldiers returning home from war in Afghanistan and Iraq; and second, a study of hypersexualization of young girls.